SPENSER'S RUINS AND THE ART OF RECOLLECTION

REBECA HELFER

Spenser's Ruins and the Art of Recollection

UNIVERSITY OF TORONTO PRESS
Toronto Buffalo London

ISBN 978-0-8020-9067-6

Printed on acid-free, 100% post-consumer recycled paper with vegetable-based inks.

Library and Archives Canada Cataloguing in Publication

Helfer, Rebeca, 1969–
Spenser's ruins and the art of recollection / Rebeca Helfer.

Includes bibliographical references and index.
ISBN 978-0-8020-9067-6

1. Spenser, Edmund, 1552?-1599 – Criticism and interpretation.
2. Memory in literature.   3. Ruins in literature.   4. History in
literature.   5. Mnemonics in literature.   I. Title.   II. Title: Ruins and the
art of recollection.

PR2367.M434H45 2012   821.3   C2012-901079-0

University of Toronto Press acknowledges the financial assistance to its publishing program of the Canada Council for the Arts and the Ontario Arts Council.

 Canada Council   Conseil des Arts
for the Arts   du Canada

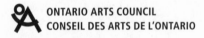 ONTARIO ARTS COUNCIL
CONSEIL DES ARTS DE L'ONTARIO

University of Toronto Press acknowledges the financial support of the Government of Canada through the Canada Book Fund for its publishing activities.

For
I.A.M.
Set me as a seal upon your heart

Contents

Acknowledgments

Throughout my edification, so to speak, I have had wonderful teachers who have inspired me and guided me – especially my once and future advisor, Anne Lake Prescott, whom I admire just a little bit idolatrously, and to whom I will always be grateful. I am also grateful for my superb and supportive colleagues in the English Department at U.C. Irvine, particularly my extraordinary fellow early modernists, Julia Lupton and Victoria Silver, who continually amaze me with their brilliance and generosity. This book has benefited enormously from the help of generous and insightful readers: Sheila Cavanagh, Patrick Cheney, William Engel, David Galbraith, Theresa Krier, as well as anonymous readers, and especially Graham Hammill, who has been an astonishing source of guidance and friendship. I am grateful to my editor at University of Toronto Press, Suzanne Rancourt, for her unwavering support throughout the very long process of publication. I am also fortunate to have received two generous grants from U.C. Irvine, from the International Center for Writing and Translation and from the Humanities Center, which have enabled me to complete this project. The love and support of friends and family has sustained me through this (again) very long process, for which I am grateful beyond words; their names are written in my book of memory and on my heart. My greatest debt of gratitude belongs to my husband, and collaborator in every sense. I dedicate this labour to my love, Ian Munro, who has made this book – and so much more – possible.

Preface: Preamble to Ruin

This book explores Edmund Spenser's profound engagement with locational memory, colloquially known as the art of memory. My approach to this topic is grounded in two distinct yet related critical interventions. First, I argue that the tradition surrounding the art of memory has generally been framed in too limited a fashion. Renaissance applications of the art of memory's "places" and "images" are typically understood in three relatively narrow ways: in rhetorical terms, as a means of creative invention; in hermetic terms, as a means of accessing esoteric wisdom; and in literary terms, as a means of making poetry more memorable. Yet in a discourse that extends from Plato through Cicero to Augustine (and, I argue, continues through Chaucer, Castiglione, and Sidney to Spenser), the art of memory would be better understood as a story about history, a means of participating in a broad conversation about how the ruins of the past survive in the memory of later minds. Throughout this discourse, the art of memory is understood as *foundational* to poetry, not *applied* to it, although each writer explored here appropriates the method of the poets in order to criticize the political uses of poetry, challenging historical fictions of permanence with fictional histories about perpetual recollection.

Secondly, because the extent and significance of the art of memory has been underestimated, the extent and significance of Spenser's engagement with it has been underappreciated. I see the art of memory as fundamental to the entire Spenserian project, from his earliest work on Jan Van der Noot's *Theatre for Worldlings* to the posthumously published *Mutabilitie Cantos* and *Viewe of the Present State of Ireland*. As well as being a guiding principle of Spenser's poetics, the art of memory holds a central place in his politics, allowing him to express profound scepticism about the cultural and imperial fictions that have long been thought to define his work and beliefs. Spenser's principal vehicle for engaging with the art of memory is the *topos* of ruin, a master metaphor for the Renaissance as well as the longer tradition that he explores. Scholars have traditionally understood the early modern fascination with ruin in relation to Virgil, as the ideal literary model for early modern attempts to repair history's ruins. When seen through a romantic lens, the impossible longing to rebuild the past in Virgil's image produces pathos and ambivalence. Yet rather than nostalgically yearning to reconstruct the past, Spenser locates cultural renewal in ruin itself. As a figure for poetry throughout his poetry, ruin represents both a place in which to remember the past and a space of innovation. Though long seen as Virgil's heir for England, Spenser uses the *topos* of ruin to interrogate all aspects of this alleged inheritance: the political value of Troy's ruins; the framing of conquest as *translatio*; the promise of poetic immortality; the ideal of heroic authorship; and, most pointedly, the model of epic as handmaiden to empire and fictions of imperial permanence. Through these interrogations, ruin emerges as the location for an ongoing art of recollection. Readers are Spenser's true memorial architects, I will suggest, perpetually rebuilding the ruins of fiction, history, empire, and learning through their dialogue with writing.

Chapter 1 divides roughly into two parts. The first part places Spenser's poetic art of memory in a critical context, exploring how the art's origin story – the apocryphal tale of the poet Simonides, who discovered the art by recollecting a fallen house and the dead buried inside, according to their places – relates to tales of Troy's ruin as recalled in epic underworlds. The second part explores the art of memory in dialogue with Plato's, Cicero's, and Augustine's writing, as well as the classical epics they rewrite and the writers they influence. Chapter 2 considers Spenser's *Shepheardes Calender* in the context of Cicero's, Plato's, and Chaucer's uses of the art of memory. Chapter 3 explores *The Ruines of Time* in the *Complaints* volume as a memorial for Philip Sidney that engages with the art of memory in his *Apology for Poetry*, and that recalls the art's place in Spenser's *Calender*. Chapter 4 examines stories about history in the first three books of *The Faerie Queene*, specifically the role of Augustine's art of memory in Spenser's treatment of allegory, and in the context of Trojan (and pre-Trojan) origin tales. Chapter 5 turns to reminders of the art of memory in the last three books of *The*

Faerie Queene, *The Viewe of the Present State of Ireland*, and *The Mutabilitie Cantos*, where I suggest that Spenser stages his ambivalent relationship to England and empire through ironized memorials. And moving beyond the death of the author into Spenser's own reception history, the Conclusion reflects upon the destruction of the Bower of Bliss and the uses Milton makes of Spenser's ruins.

SPENSER'S RUINS AND THE ART OF RECOLLECTION

Spenser's Complaints: The Fall of Troy, the Ruin of Rome, and the Art of Recollection

This study begins with a new reading of an old story: the tale of Simonides, the ancient Greek poet who according to legend discovered the art of memory. The Roman orator Antonius recounts this tale in Cicero's dialogue *On the Orator*, winking to indicate its apocryphal status:

> I am grateful to the famous Simonides of Ceos, who, as people say, first invented an art of memory. For they relate, that when Simonides was at Crannon in Thessaly, at an entertainment given by Scopas, a man of rank and fortune, and had recited a poem which he had composed in his praise, in which, for the sake of embellishment, after the manner of the poets, there were many particulars introduced concerning Castor and Pollux, Scopas told Simonides, with extraordinary meanness, that he would pay him half the sum which he had agreed to give for the poem, and that he might ask the remainder, if he thought proper, from his Tyndaridae, to whom he had given an equal share of praise. A short time after, they say that a message was brought in to Simonides, to desire him to go out, as two youths were waiting at the gate who earnestly wished him to come forth to them; when he arose, went forth, and found nobody. In the mean time the apartment in which Scopas was feasting fell down, and he himself, and his company, were overwhelmed and *buried in the ruins*; and when their friends were desirous to inter their remains, but could not possibly distinguish one from another, so much crushed were the bodies, Simonides is said, from his *recollection of the place* in which each had sat, to have given satisfactory directions for their interment.[1]

"Simonides, or whoever else invented the art," Antonius adds, "wisely saw, that those things are the most strongly fixed in our minds, which are communicated to them, and imprinted on them, by the senses" and "that of all the senses that of seeing is the most acute" (187). Although he demurs from being "prolix and impertinent upon so well-known and common a subject," Antonius still reviews the apparently commonplace "rules" of artificial memory. Simonides "is reported to have discovered that it is chiefly order that gives distinctness to memory," he explains, that "certain places must be fixed upon, and that of the things which they desire to keep in memory, symbols must be conceived in the mind, and ranged, as it were, in those places" (186, 187). This describes the art of memory, less colloquially called locational memory, as it is best known: by mentally constructing a place, usually a building or a book, filled with memorable images or symbols, orators could remember long speeches by figuratively "walking through" or "reading from" an imagined memorial location. Paradoxically, Antonius makes these techniques memorable by evoking the legendary tale that he had so lightly dismissed: "we may be enabled to impress on ourselves by the creation of imaginary figures, aptly arranged, to represent particular heads, so that we may recollect thoughts by images, and their order by place" (188). He thus treats the tale of Simonides as a heuristic device, a story that edifies its audience about the process of memorial edification.[2] The topics or "heads" of Antonius' discourse can be pictured as the heads of people in a certain order around a table, a lesson which in effect re-enacts the tale of Simonides' discovery. This tall tale thereby allows Antonius to demonstrate *how* the art of memory works, even if he presents it merely as a useful fiction.

Yet the importance of this old story – old even in republican Rome – to *On the Orator* (and to this study) lies in Cicero's creative reformation of it. Following Antonius' discussion of memory, Cicero interrupts his narrative to suggest how this seemingly trivial myth of memorial ruin bears upon his own story of Rome's ruinous fall. At the beginning of Book 3 Cicero announces the deaths of Crassus and Antonius and the decline of the other interlocutors, making it clear that Rome's collapsing political structure forms the unseen frame for this ostensibly pastoral dialogue about rhetoric. Cicero depicts Rome as a crumbling cultural edifice, which, by analogy with the tale of Simonides, leaves the interlocutors "buried in ruins" (186). "Such misfortunes afterward fell upon the commonwealth," he writes, "that life does not appear to me to have been taken away from Lucius Crassus by the immortal gods as a privation, but death to have been bestowed on him as a blessing . . . If any fortune had rescued you from so barbarous a death, the same fortune would have compelled you to be a spectator of the ruins of your country" (194–5). Calling *On the Orator* a "bitter remembrance" to these interlocutors, Cicero then casts himself in the role of a new Simonides, reconstructing Rome's ruin in order to fashion his dialogue as a mnemonic edifice. "Let us deliver as a memorial to posterity the remaining and almost last discourse of Lucius Crassus," he exhorts, clarifying the central ambition of *On the Orator* (196). With this segue, Cicero rewrites the tale of Simonides as a frame tale for his story of Rome's history, radically expanding Antonius' limited view of the art of memory as a method of recollecting long speeches, connecting the art of memory as a method of individual recollection with the collective matter of memory: history.[3] In so doing, Cicero constructs his dialogue as a location for locational memory, a textual edifice that dramatizes its own process of edification.

Yet lest his audience view *On the Orator* as the complete recovery of the past, Cicero punctures fantasies of rebirth by disclosing the precarious status of his own reconstruction. Reviving the subtext of the tale of Simonides disregarded by Antonius – namely, that a poet discovered the art of memory – Cicero underscores that his dialogue is not simply the "light of truth" but also a fiction (92). Indeed, he reveals how story and history are inextricably entwined in this narrative. Recalling the events that "ruined the commonwealth," Cicero admits that "I, who was not present at this dialogue, and to whom Caius Cotta communicated only the topics and heads of the dissertation, have endeavored to shadow forth in the conversation of the speakers those peculiar styles of oratory, in which I knew that each of them was conspicuous" (192, 196). His narrative comes second-hand, Cicero confesses, confronting the fiction of total recall with the necessity of imagination to any historical reconstruction. This revelation reshapes his memorial. As in the tale of Simonides, Cicero's recollection takes place from within the symbolic space of a ruined edifice – and remains there, inverting the usual assumption that mnemonic places are complete and unchanging structures. That he portrays this dialogue not as an immortal monument but as vulnerable to time's scythe in turn reframes the tale of Simonides: the process by which Simonides discovers the art of memory ultimately matters more in this work than the end result. With its ruined edifice representing Rome itself, *On the Orator*'s immortality derives from the space it creates for dialogue, both among the speakers and for readers. Cicero thus uses an old method for new matter, not to remember ancient history but the recent past, in the process teaching readers how to continue making Simonides' discovery anew.

This study also seeks to cast an old story – Edmund Spenser's complex, career-long engagement with the art of memory – in a new light. The art of memory has often been viewed in terms of the rules Antonius relates: the use of imaginary places and vivid images to impress meaning upon memory. To be sure, Spenser makes abundant use of mnemonics in this capacity, though he also uses the now-arcane art in more complex and compelling ways than have been fully recognized. Just as Cicero expands our view of what mnemonics can represent, from a technique for individual recollection to a story about how we remember collectively, so Spenser renovates the art of memory in Ciceronian fashion, treating it as a way to explore how to recollect the ruins of the past. In the broadest terms, this study explores Spenser's uses of the art of memory throughout his career as a theory and practice of poetry, through which he examines the relationship between story and history, and between poetry and power. As I will argue, Spenser embeds within his poetic structures a history of dialogue and debate about the art of memory from ancient Greece to Renaissance England. This art is foundational to Spenser's work because it allows him to articulate complaints about the seminal story of history as it was retold and re-enacted from antiquity through the Renaissance: tales of Troy's ruin and re-edification. Throughout his writing, Spenser represents the art of memory both as a fiction-making device and as a means of re-forming collective memory: specifically, he criticizes the use of Trojan tales for political, religious, and historical ends – including the imperial ideology often associated with Spenser himself. Although sometimes viewed as a minor part of Spenser's work, I suggest that the art of memory holds a central place in his writing, as a set of aesthetic principles and as a strategy for representing his profoundly complex views about how poetry can speak to power.

What is the art of memory? To understand Spenser's multifaceted use of the art of memory involves something of a sea change in our thinking. Historically, this art has been constructed in dichotomous ways: as hermetic esoterica or humanist craft, as a method for remembering or for inventing, as a science of knowledge or something like science fiction. Describing the art's historical transformation in *The Art of Memory*, Frances Yates writes, "The orator's memory, rigidly trained for his practical purposes, has become the Platonic philosopher's memory in which he finds his evidence of the divinity and immortality of the soul," and therefore "the transition from Cicero, the trained rhetorician and religious Platonist, to Augustine, the trained rhetorician and Christian

Platonist, was smoothly made."[4] As this brief genealogy suggests, Yates views the art of memory as a distant cousin of *anamnesis*, and her primary interest lies in the mystery of how a simple rhetorical technique emerged utterly transformed in the early modern period as a hermetic philosophy and practice: a new art of memory that encompassed Neoplatonic and cabalistic wisdom, expressed itself through various forms of poetry, prose, and political tracts, and embraced philosophical, pedagogical, political, and religious reform.[5] By contrast, Mary Carruthers' *The Book of Memory* overturns an idea that Yates' work helped to popularize: the notion that the art of memory radically changed in the movement from so-called oral to literate cultures. Carruthers argues that traditional strategies of art of memory found continual use from the earliest antiquity to the highest Middle Ages within a metaphoric place largely ignored by Yates: the "book of memory," a symbolic edifice or container (e.g., library, treasure chest) that formed a location for recollection. Unlike Yates, who focuses primarily on illuminating the spaces of the architectural mnemonic, from ordinary buildings to the more elaborate structures of memory theatres, Carruthers demonstrates how writing on, and reading from, such a "book of memory" is central to the art of memory from its inception and throughout its history. Just as significantly, she further clarifies both how and why "the 'art of memory' is actually the 'art of recollection' " – not only a "retrieval system" for memory but also a method of invention, the creative uses of knowledge now called originality.[6] Carruthers thereby illustrates how such edification extends far beyond memorial edifices per se.

My work builds upon that of Yates and Carruthers (literally, metaphorically speaking), though with key differences. Although Yates and Carruthers write histories of the art of memory, both view it as fundamentally atemporal, a rhetorical technique unrelated to historical narrative. The best example of this may be the tale of Simonides itself, which they both regard as an important historical source yet treat much as Antonius does: as simply a heuristic tale. In short, Carruthers and Yates both make the tale of Simonides foundational to their historiography but do not treat the story itself as though it matters, beyond what it has to teach about a once common rhetorical technique. For Yates, "the art belonged to rhetoric" originally and later migrated to other fields, where fact and fiction would ultimately mingle in new and unexpected ways. Carruthers emphasizes the creative uses of the art, yet she also thinks of it more in terms of historical fact than historical fiction. "Two traditions are frequently confused," she argues in *The Craft of Thought*:

"the model of memory as inherently locational, and having a particular cognitive role to play" and the tradition "that defines memory temporally, as being 'of the past.'"[7] Yet what they regard as two separate traditions, I will argue, should not be separated. The distinctions that Yates and Carruthers draw between space and time, story and history, rhetoric and related fields, come together in the art of memory tradition recollected by Spenser.

In this study I treat the art of memory first and foremost as a *poetic* method. Building on the work of Eric Havelock and others who have demonstrated the mnemonic origins of epic, in both its composition and its transmission, I consider this art as a form of storytelling, across a range of fields.[8] Carruthers' insight that the "activity of recollection" is "actually closer in meaning to the modern 'cognition,' the creative process of thinking," also represents a crucial starting point for this study. I similarly frame the art of recollection not as narrowly limited to memory but rather as engaging all of the faculties of human psychology – imagination, reason, remembrance – in order to create something new from something old: in metaphorical terms, in order to re-collect, re-form, re-member the raw materials of memory and knowledge. Even before Yates' groundbreaking work, scholars such as Beryl Rowland, Walter Ong, and Paolo Rossi recognized the important place of the art of memory in poetry and in poetics; since then, the art's applications and implications have been broadened extensively in the work of Judith Anderson, Lina Balzoni, and William Engel, among others. As Engel explains, "the legendary beginning of the arts of memory developed out of the artistic practices of a man who saw poetry, painting and mnemonics in terms of intense visualization," and "the same Simonides who, according to Plutarch, first equated poetry's methods with those of painting."[9] Nevertheless, scholars have usually portrayed the art of memory as a technique *applied* to poetry, which borrows the rhetorical strategy of using places and images to make its matter memorable; in so doing, they tend to separate the techniques of locational memory from the narratives in which they are embedded. But the stories themselves matter as much as the method of their construction. Heuristic tales about recollection can be understood as part of an interdisciplinary debate about poetry's place in culture, particularly by incorporating critical responses to Trojan stories of history. In this study, I explore three representatives of the art of memory tradition gestured to by Yates – Plato, Cicero, and Augustine – as key intertextual figures in Spenser's writing. As these writers demonstrate, the art of memory found use as a method of fiction-making, and as a means of exploring the political implications of fiction-making, in the context of rhetoric, philosophy, theology, as well as poetry. As Spenser remembers this tradition throughout his writing, he reflects upon how poetry represents power; how political fictions find re-enactment within history; and how stories about history might edify readers and royalty alike.

I situate Spenser's varied use of the art of memory specifically in relation to figures and thematics of ruin, a *topos* that represents the common place of both Trojan tales and their counter-narratives. My use of the term "ruin" is necessarily broad, referring to both books and buildings, and often (as in *On the Orator*) a book *as* a building. For the most part, I use the word "ruin" figuratively, to describe language and poetry. Such ruins nevertheless encompass both memorial and material fragments – not only of stone, though physical ruins are frequently the subject of the poetry explored here, but also writing itself, conceived of (as Petrarch called his poetry) as *ruinae*.[10] Spenser's literary ruins, I argue, represent the art of memory as both method and matter. To be sure, Spenser has long been understood as a "poet of mutability." Willy Maley describes Spenser as "a poet of ruins," arguing that "salvaging and ruining are the two main processes in which Spenser is engaged"; along similar lines, Jennifer Summit proposes that "Spenser creates what we might call a poetics of wreckage, an extended meditation on the project of cultural recovery that accompanied England's long Reformation."[11] In this study, I explore a related process of ruining and recollecting in the context of Trojan tales, paradoxically to suggest that where poetic ruins are concerned, not all roads lead to Virgil's (or Ovid's) Rome. Indeed, in many respects I am attempting to widen our picture of Spenser as *either* England's new Virgil or a new Ovid, by exploring a longer tradition of writing about ruin in a variety of forms.

Ruin represents a master metaphor of sorts in the Renaissance for the activity of disinterring the past for the present, and in this regard it connects in important ways to the Greek meaning of "metaphor," to carry across or over, and to its Latin equivalent, "translation." As a figure of transport, ruin relates to the transmission of culture, *translatio imperii et studii*, imagined from antiquity through early modernity as the westward translation of empire and learning. As more than just metaphor, the ruins of writing share common ground with the ruins of history. The wars of republican Rome provide the central context for Cicero's rewriting of the tale of Simonides in *On the Orator*; so too in Plato's dialogues, where the Peloponnesian wars frame his recollections-as-*anamnesis*; so too in Augustine's writing, in which the sack of Rome (not once, but as repeated throughout history) provides the impetus for his investigations of time and memory. Spenser's poetry recalls these earlier locations of ruin from Greece to Rome (and beyond), but a more local context – that is, his place and position as a colonial administrator in an Ireland continually at war – also profoundly shapes his vision of recollection. The cycles of ruin and re-edification that mark history are part of the pattern of poetry's continued life, for Spenser as for the writers he emulates. The ancient pun in "edification," building and learning, is central here: heuristic tales like that of Simonides, though tales told out of school, aim to edify.[12]

Spenser's most famous use of the art of memory illustrates my discussion to this point. When critics consider Spenser's use of mnemonics, they inevitably think of England: the allegory of English history in Book 2 of *The Faerie Queene*, the Castle of Alma. In this memorable space of the soul, readers discover at once the human body and England's body politic, the processes of individual recollection as well as the formation of England's collective memory. Spenser constructs Alma's Castle as a memory theatre, one that exemplifies the art of memory as a method of composition: the use of places and vivid images – here rooms and allegorical personifications – make the Castle of Alma memorable. But this mnemonic space represents both an edifice and a process of edification, emblematized by the activity of the allegorical historiographer "aged *Mnemon*" in the brain-turret of the castle.[13] Readers advance through three rooms portraying faculty psychology: imagination, reason, and finally memory. In this back room, the aged Eumnestes (good memory) and his helper Anamnestes (recollection) gather together decaying history texts that represent a mingling of matter and memory (2.9.55). Ruin figures centrally in Spenser's portrait of this space – a "chamber all . . . hangd about with rolles, / And old records from auncient times deriu'd / . . . That were all worme-eaten, and full of canker holes" (2.9.57) – and in the process of recollection illustrated within it:

> That chamber seemed ruinous and old,
> And therefore was remoued farre behind . . .
> And therein sate an old oldman, halfe blind,
> And all decrepit in his feeble corse,
> Yet lively vigour rested in his mind . . .

This man of infinite remembrance was,
And things foregone through many ages held,
Which he recorded still, as they did pas,
Ne suffred them to perish through long eld,
As all things else, the which this world doth weld,
But laid them vp in his immortall scrine,
Where they for euer incorrupted dweld . . .

Amidst them all he in a chaire was set,
Tossing and turning them withouten end;
But for he was vnhable them to fet,
A litle boy did on him still attend,
To reach, when euer he for ought did send;
And oft when things were lost, or laid amis,
That boy them sought, and vnto him did lend. (2.9.55–8)

Within the space of this ruinous edifice, readers are edified about the activity of memory: the recollection of history from the remains of other texts, a process described as "withouten end." On the one hand, this portrait of the human psyche demonstrates how individual memory works: the mind continually gathers or finds, recollects, what it needs in its symbolic library. On the other hand, this allegory of the soul illustrates the activity of fashioning collective memory as stories of history. In effect, the Castle of Alma stands as a heuristic, one that teaches the art of memory as a method of recollecting the ruins of the past, demonstrated by Eumnestes' and Anamnestes' continual activity of gathering the matter of England and shaping it into memorial structures: historiography written on the page and in the brain. As a mnemonic space, Alma's Castle joins buildings and books as locations for recollection continually falling to ruin and being recollected from ruin. Eumnestes builds his library from the fragments of broken ones, an activity reflected in the title of the history that the future King Arthur reads there, *Briton moniments*. As with Cicero's revised tale of Simonides, Spenser's story of England's history suggests how individual and collective memory are shaped by analogous methods of edification.

The dependence of "good memory" (Eumnestes), upon "recollection" (Anamnestes), highlights the interrelation between two forms of memory that scholars typically divide: mnemonics as a rhetorical technique, and *anamnesis* as a philosophical and religious tradition.

Anamnesis is often associated with divine, even magical memory: the recollection of things past that were never experienced and yet, because of the immortality of the soul, can nevertheless be found there. In the context of Plato, Janet Coleman argues that "*anamnesis* is not a mnemonic technique for recalling instances, places, and things experienced," adding that "Plato expresses a horror of those techniques like writing which will cause men to lose true knowledge."[14] To be sure, Plato rejects mnemonic techniques as tools of a trade, but this is only part of the picture. As I argue later in this chapter, Plato treats the art of memory in a far more expansive way than Coleman and others suggest, appropriating this poetic-rhetorical method for philosophical matters and framing *anamnesis* as a rewriting of commonplace fictions. In some dialogues (the *Phaedrus* in particular), *anamnesis* helps to demystify origin stories, especially allegories of the soul that sacralize tales of Troy; in these contexts, the idea of prior knowledge is less an attempt to establish absolute categories of "true knowledge" than a way to demonstrate the complex interdependencies of history and mythic stories. Even later allegorical interpretations of Plato's writing that explore *anamnesis* as a means of synthesizing philosophy and theology – most notably Augustine's, which similarly aligns mnemonics with divine *anamnesis* – criticize interpreting epic (especially Virgils' *Aeneid*) as an allegory of the souls' journey through time, and offer new allegories of the soul in its place.[15] As Spenser's Neoplatonic Castle of the Soul suggests, he recalls this allegorical tradition precisely in order to reform it: specifically, by equating *anamnesis* with the recollection of origin stories about, and throughout, history.

Aristotle defines recollection in ways that illuminate Plato's provocative term of art. In *On the Soul* and its appendix *On Memory and Recollection*, Aristotle provides an account of faculty psychology that persists from antiquity through the early modern period. Describing the "method of recollection" common to all human souls, mind and body, Aristotle writes that "images are naturally fitted to occur in a certain order," drawing upon artificial memory (such as the orator's movement through a memorial edifice) to describe the mind's natural practices. "Sometimes one takes a short cut, and chooses a starting-point which . . . will lead one straight to the thing one wishes to recollect," Aristotle explains, "but for the most part, one has to pass through other images first, before one reaches the image of the penultimate item in the series"; but "even so," he adds, "the method of recollecting is the same as when one takes a short cut, if one considers how each item in the series is related to its successor."[16] Aristotle grounds this method of recollection, indeed most activities of the soul, in mnemonic theory: the idea that people need images (as well as places for them) in order to think, beyond the basic processes of sensing, imagining, reasoning, and even remembering. Though not a creative writer himself, Aristotle portrays this as a fundamentally creative activity: put metaphorically, as a process of recollecting and reforming the matter of memory already stored in the mind's own treasury. Where this matter comes from, and where it leads, he never says explicitly, instead leaving this question to the Platonists. But though Aristotle's division of memory and remembrance from recollection represents a sober reworking of metaphysical *anamnesis*, it also fundamentally builds upon Plato's ideas. Aristotle's decision to retain the term *anamnesis* for what might just as easily (or more simply) have been called "dialectical thinking," or "imaginative reasoning," or "philosophical discourse," helps to explain Plato's thinking: recollection entails dismantling and reforming preconceived ideas, relocating the source of knowledge internally, rather than in external authorities.[17] Aristotle's account of recollection allows the premise of Platonic recollection to stand, with its implied challenge to edification as conventional wisdom.

Writing on Aristotle, Richard Sorabji reminds readers that the word *anamnesis* derives from the verb *anamimneskein*, "to remind," and that it translates properly as "to be reminded."[18] For Spenser as for his implied interlocutors, "being reminded" by writing prompts a dialogue with texts figured not as monuments but as edifices *in* ruins, as remains of writing that make up the matter of memory and form the building blocks for new literary edifices. As I argue throughout this study, writing is a crucial *reminder* for Plato, Cicero, and Augustine, central to how they imagine recollecting the past. For all three writers, the matter of recollection is inextricable from the issue of how story relates to history, both on the page and, in Yates' phrase, in the "theatre of the world." All three writers are concerned with how human narratives of history – specifically, tales of Troy – relate to fictions of divinity both *in* and *as* history. This tradition suggests another way of thinking about *anamnesis*. By being reminded, we come to know – imagine, reason, and remember – what we have never experienced personally: history. Given the intermingling of story and history, each of these writers explores the issue of how to "tell the truth" about past in both senses, how to discern and articulate it, through recollection.

This provides a context in which to understand the Castle of Alma's somewhat puzzling suggestion that the prior knowledge found in the back chamber of the human psyche is historiography, writing about the remains of the past that the soul recollects. To be sure, in the early modern world *all* of history was divine and thus all recollection was, in one sense, the memory of divinity; just as the secular and the sacred mingle in Alma's allegory of the soul – "O worke diuine," as Spenser calls it, at once "imperfect" and "perfect," "mortall" and "immortal" – so history itself connects humanity with divinity (2.9.22). But the *writing* of history, historiography, represents an entirely human construct, with the complex exception of scripture – and, of course, interpreting the word of God in the age of mechanical reproduction was no simple matter. This forms but one context for a complaint central to Spenser's writing: that stories of history are retold and re-enacted by self-fashioned gods of state to justify the end of "empire without end."

England's New Virgil?

The Castle of Alma joins a method of memory to matters of memory – and the story itself matters. The history that Arthur reads (and the Author writes), *Briton moniments*, redacts Geoffrey of Monmouth's twelfth-century *History of the Kings of Britain*, which adopts a Trojan genealogy for England and connects the Matter of Troy, and the Matter of Rome, to the Matter of Britain. Geoffrey's story begins with the fall of Troy and the Trojan Brutus' founding of Britain, and ends with a prophecy of the repair of Arthur's once and future kingdom, a prophecy ostensibly fulfilled in the sixteenth century with the providential rise of the House of Tudor. As a rewriting of the Trojan legend for England, this episode has often been taken as evidence that Spenser modelled his career on Virgil and his celebration of Roman Empire in the *Eclogues* and the *Aeneid*. Calling "Spenser 'the Virgil of the Elizabethan golden age,'" Yates writes that "the concept of Elizabeth as the imperial virgin is the lynch-pin of his poem."[19] Exploring the mythology inspired by Elizabeth, Yates calls her "Astraea-Virgo, the just and pious virgin, whose return in [Virgil's] Fourth Eclogue heralds the golden age of empire," and who in England "becomes an imperial virgin."[20] This renewed Golden Age joins "the complex tissue of Elizabethan imperialism," she argues, "through which Astraea-Virgo becomes the perfect symbol for the British Virgo" and for "the Tudor claim to Trojan descent."[21] It is the place of this Virgilian legacy in Spenser's poetry – particularly, the use of Trojan tales to legitimize empire – that I hope to complicate in this study, building upon the scholarship of the past few decades.

To be sure, there is not *one* Trojan legend, but there can be no doubt about the persistence of Trojan tales throughout history; indeed, the frequent visions and revisions of Trojan tales characterize the history of historiography. From antiquity through early modernity, versions and perversions of the Trojan myth provided useful fictions by which poets and princes could portray the transmission of empire and learning from a fallen Troy to Greece, Rome, Northern Europe, and even the New World, continuing on Troynovant's westering path until time's end (and beyond). The *Aeneid* is central here, for in rewriting Homeric epic Virgil adapts the mytho-historical Trojan war in order to create an epic fiction of Rome's imperial origin and destiny: the flight from ruined Troy to found eternal "Troynovant." The *Aeneid* opens with Jove comforting Venus by confirming the destiny of her son Aeneas: "Thou shalt see Lavinium's city and its promised walls; and thou shalt raise on high to the starry heaven great-souled Aeneas . . . [who] shall wage a great war in Italy, shall crush proud nations, and for his people shall set up laws and city walls . . . from this noble line shall be born the Trojan Caesar, who shall limit his empire with ocean, his glory with the stars," fulfilling Jove prophecy for Rome's *imperium sine fine*, "empire without end."[22] Throughout Virgil's epic, this prophecy is repeated in variation as Aeneas gradually learns about his destined role in founding Italy, a role that he continually forgets and must be reminded of. In the catabasis of Book 6, Aeneas journeys to the underworld where he confronts the human remains of Troy, the symbolic ruins of Troy's former empire, yet takes comfort in the prophecies of his father, Anchises, who declares that Augustus, "a son of a god" who will be descended from Aeneas, "shall again set up the Golden Age amid the fields where Saturn once reigned" (6.777–808). As Yates explains, the *Aeneid's* vision of Rome's imperial immortality, when read in conjunction with Virgil's prophetic *Fourth Eclogue*, was later interpreted as Christian allegory: "Now the Virgin returns, the reign of Saturn returns . . . and a golden race springs up throughout the world."[23] The birth of Christianity during the Roman Empire helped Virgil's poetry to attain the status of divine prophecy, if never uncontroversially.

Just as Renaissance historians sounded the death knell for the legitimacy of Trojan narratives, European rulers, including the Tudors, revived Trojan ancestries, along with claims to inheriting old and new worlds. These contradictions played hard against each other, particularly in England, where, from a Protestant perspective, it was clear that Rome's fabled "eternal" empire had fallen to ruin. With this view, motivated at least in part by England's religious and political separation from the Catholic church, came the concomitant desire to separate English and Roman history, to make England and Rome distant cousins within a shared Trojan family. Renewing the Trojan legend allowed the Tudors, in a sense, to rewrite history. On the one hand, direct Trojan ancestry diminished Rome's imperial importance in England's national identity; on the other hand, tracing Tudor lineage to Trojan origins allowed England to perform on the world stage along with Europe's other, more powerful, new "Troys." Converting Virgilian epic into Christian allegory thus afforded a religious means to a political end, a divine rationale for power and empire-building. This was true for Protestants, who continued to assert Rome's destined role in the drama of Christian end-time by casting it as the "Anti-Christ" rather than (as the Catholic church and Holy Roman Empire saw it) as the earthly City of God.[24] The drama of Gloriana's rule thus formed but one scene in a European pageant of imperial self-fashioning.

Viewed in this context, Spenser has long been seen as a champion of Elizabethan imperialism. Conveying Virgil's literary ruins for England's edification, making pagan antiquity safe for Protestant empire, traditionally has been the symbolic foundation upon which critics have constructed Spenser as England's new Virgil – for better and for worse. Consider the following two roughly contemporaneous examples. Praising Spenser's Virgilianism, Lawrence Manley writes that "Spenser, in assuming the Vergilian mantle, prepares for the rebirth of Orpheus in himself and . . . for his time."[25] Describing "Spenser's struggle to recover the Orphic power" as "an effort to reverse the historical corruption of civic culture, to restore the dead to life," Manley compares "this situation by analogy with that of Vergil, a poet who built one city from the ashes of another."[26] As a counterpoint, Stephen Greenblatt famously criticized Spenser for his participation in and representation of Elizabethan imperialism, arguing in *Renaissance Self-Fashioning* that "Spenser worships power" and, further, that his art "does not lead us to perceive ideology critically" because it is "yoked to the service of a reality forever outside itself, dedicated to 'the Most High, Mightie, and Magnificent Empresse . . . Elizabeth by the Grace of God Queene of England Fraunce and Ireland and of Virginia, Defendour of the Faith.'"[27] In Greenblatt's account, Spenser registers the cost of empire-building even while endorsing and contributing to its ruinous effects: he argues that Spenser's work, "like Freud's, bears witness to the deep complicity of our moral imagination even in its noblest and most hauntingly beautiful manifestations in the great Western celebration of power . . . Alongside Freud, we may invoke Virgil, whose profound adoration of Augustus is tempered but never broken by a bitter sense of all that empire forces man to renounce, to flee from, to destroy."[28] Whereas Manley portrays Spenser as repairing the ruins of history and thus renovating English culture, Greenblatt sees this idealized history as masking the brutal truth of English empire, built partly upon the ruin of Ireland. However, in effect Manley's and Greenblatt's arguments are based on the same premise: that Spenser was an ideologue of the Elizabethan state – a role modelled on Virgil.

Renaissance Self-Fashioning, which takes both its title and central conceit from Spenser's work, frames self-fashioning partly through tropes of ruin and recollection. As Greenblatt writes in his introduction, "When in 1589 Spenser writes that the general intention and meaning that he has 'fashioned' in *The Faerie Queene* is "to fashion a gentlemen . . . he is drawing upon the special connotations for his period of the verb *fashion* . . . [which] seems to come into wide currency as a way of designating the forming of a self."[29] For Greenblatt, Spenser exemplifies a tension between interiority and exteriority, between self-control and state control, between a new freedom to invent one's self and the forces that prevent one from doing so, that marks the Renaissance as novel. "If we say that there is a heightened awareness of the existence of alternative modes of social, theological, and psychological organization," he argues, "we must say that there is a new dedication to the imposition of control upon those modes and ultimately to the destruction of alternatives."[30] The episode in *The Faerie Queene* epitomizing this dynamic, Greenblatt argues, is the destruction of the Bower of Bliss (to which I turn in the conclusion), which he interprets as Spenser's ruination of the Irish "other" for the purpose of fashioning an English "self." When Greenblatt evokes Freud's *Civilization and its Discontents* – with its famous analogy of the human psyche to the city of Rome and the layers of ruin that symbolize the unconsciously repressed truth of the past – he argues that Spenserian self-fashioning amounts to *conscious* repression, an intentional forgetting or erasure of the violent foundations of both self and society. "If all of civilization rests, as Freud argues, upon repression," Greenblatt argues, then remembering amounts to regarding the self "as temporary, time-conditioned, and contingent as those vast European empires form whose power Freud drew his image of repression."[31] As he suggests, such an awareness of ruin is the mark not only of early modernity – when "not only in Italy, but in France and England as well, the old feudal models gradually crumbled and fell into ruins, [and] men created new models" of identity – but also of post-modernity: "the places in which our social and psychological world seems to be cracking apart are those structural joints visible when it was first constructed."[32] Understanding such structures, Greenblatt further argues, means recognizing that "the chief intellectual and linguistic tool in this creation was rhetoric . . . Rhetoric was the common ground of poetry, history, and oratory; it could mediate both between the past and the present and between the imagination and the realm of public affairs. Encouraging men to think of all forms of human discourse as argument, it conceived of poetry as a performing art, literature as a storehouse of models . . . Rhetoric served to theatricalize culture, or rather it was the instrument of a society which was already deeply theatrical."[33]

For the past generation, scholars have been responding to Greenblatt's sharp critique of Spenser's poetry and its relationship to power. In the chapters to follow, my debt to the scholarship of the past few decades will become clear; for now I will simply say that this response has been wide and varied, and has produced a substantially more complex vision of Spenser's poetics and politics, especially his views of empire and Ireland. Thanks to the work of more recent historicist critics we now understand far more about Spenser's experience and actions in Ireland, about his complicated relationship to this place, and about the significance of the Irish location to all his later work, especially *The Faerie Queene*. From another angle, the work of the past few decades on Spenser's humanism has revealed profound complexities in his literary treatment of the Tudors and Trojan fictions of empire, and his emulation of Virgil's legacy. Nonetheless, as scholars have argued, Greenblatt's crucial link between humanism and colonialism has ironically resulted in a divided Spenser, Spenser the Humanist and Spenser the Colonist.[34] These two Spensers often seem to have little in common, yet a common assumption of Virgilian imitation unites them. If seeing Spenser in terms of an older Virgilian model of heroic settlement has been replaced by a newer Virgilian model of brutal colonial fiction-making, the idea of Virgil's centrality is nevertheless retained. As a result, Spenser scholars have tended to stress the very quality that Greenblatt denied: Spenser's ambivalence about his cultural and political roles, particularly as a Virgilian poet. "Ambivalence" became a keyword in Spenser studies to describe a Spenser divided against himself, caught between imitation and repudiation.

This emphasis on ambivalence resulted not only from Greenblatt's challenge but also from Thomas Greene's influential study of early modern imitation, *The Light in Troy*. Greene explores the Renaissance problem of recollecting the past within a psychological matrix, in terms related to Greenblatt's (perhaps coincidentally, given their close publication dates). *The Light in Troy* examines Renaissance responses to ruin, focusing on both the ambivalence ruin provoked and creative attempts to surmount this ambivalence. As Greene's title suggests, Virgil stands as the hallmark by which to judge early modern imitative success or failure. Arguing that "the humanist poet is not a neurotic son crippled by a Freudian family romance, which is to say he is not in Harold Bloom's terms Romantic, [but] is rather like the son in a classical comedy who displaces his father at the moment of reconciliation," Greene's work nevertheless seems to reproduce the very anxiety of influence that it purports to reject. A sense of the tragic dimension of early modern imitation, the pathos of ruin, pervades his study: "The ruined edifice becomes a symbol of a larger entity, an entire civilization, and the double act of gathering stones and then repiecing a design stands for the doomed modern effort of imitative revival."[35] In this light, ruin represents not only a desire for "a reincarnation or a rebirth" but also the failure to realize this desire;[36] after all, what poet could truly hope to rebuild the past in Virgil's image or repeat his claim to endless empire? Arguing that Petrarch "first understood how radically classical antiquity differed from the Christian era," Greene describes Petrarch's "struggle to discern a self or compose a self which could stand as a fixed and knowable substance" as a failure to imitate Virgil's example: "the poet's historical isolation prevented him from resurrecting Virgil."[37] To differing degrees, poets (including Spenser) have been judged by their ability to imitate Virgil.

Yet the attempt to imagine imitation in creative terms, to see ruins as building blocks for invention and innovation, represents the part of Greene's legacy that I explore in this study. In some respects, this is a matter of how we see the part in relation to the whole. Did Renaissance writers truly hope to rebuild the past, or was the ruin itself the object of fascination and potential? Reflecting upon similar issues, Margaret McGowan asks whether the early modern poet "really believe[d] that his poems could resurrect and keep alive the splendid shapes of ancient Rome by delving for its fragments and reassembling the ruins that remained," or really attempted "to effect the magical transfer from past to present, from broken pieces to visions of whole monuments."[38] Mc-Gowan's reply, that "critical opinion is divided," serves as a segue to her own less divided opinion: "however much [early modern poets] had relied on the absent spirits of classical Rome, on the beckoning ambivalence of the ruins, and upon the visible renewal of Rome," they also succeeded in "creat[ing] something new."[39] Ambivalence about imitation never prevented it; indeed, such dividedness inspired and even structured the reception of the past – most evidently, for Petrarch and his imitators. So even though early modern writers clearly grappled with Virgil's legacy, we need to continue entertaining the counter-intuitive notion that ruin itself created a space of possibility for fashioning new cultural edifices.[40]

In this study, I explore the art of memory as a way to reimagine how ruin relates to recollection in Spenser's writing and beyond. What distinguishes my argument from that of Greene and Greenblatt, and even more recent Spenser criticism that has tackled these issues, is an insistence on alternatives to Trojan models of poetry and power. Rather than caught between imitating Virgil and refusing to do so, or between wishing to imitate Virgil and being unable to do so well, my reading of Spenser shows him as outlining a model of cultural formation directly opposed to imperial fictions of permanence. To be sure, the context of Ireland and Spenser's colonial experience presents a radical challenge to this model; in my final chapter, which focuses on the second half of *The Faerie Queene* and *A Viewe of the Present State of Ireland*, I will return to the idea of Spenserian ambivalence, although in terms less anxious than rhetorical. Even in the *Viewe*, I will argue, we find an elaboration of exactly the sort of "alternative modes of social, theological, and psychological organization" which Greenblatt insists that Spenser attempts to erase and forget.[41] As I hope to make clear throughout this study, Spenserian "self-fashioning" in fact depends upon remembering ruin, rhetorically, historically, and poetically. The space of ruin allows Spenser to criticize the fact that (as Greenblatt observes) "Elizabeth's exercise of power was closely bound up with her use of fictions," and to address the fiction of her as "a living representation of the immutable within time, a fiction of permanence."[42] Such complaints are not limited to Elizabeth or England but rather reflect the larger issue of how stories become history, and how poetic fictions find a place on the political stage as well as on the page. To pursue the conjunction of individual and collective memory, psychology and history, throughout Spenser's writing and emblematized in the Castle of Alma, I consider how Spenser looks beyond Virgil's example see a longer history of recollecting the self and society from the ruins of the past: specifically, to earlier and later authors who articulate complaints about fashioning rulers or states as divine. Spenserian self-fashioning addresses the problem of representing stories as history, fictions as truth, given their place in the real world of power and politics. Indirectly, Spenser's complaints complicate the notion that Trojan fictions were uncritically accepted until the Renaissance, when a new vision of history that made writers aware of Rome's ruin produced a sharp break with the past. As Spenser's writing suggests, ruin was always a *topos* in which writers criticized Trojan tales and their political uses. Throughout his career, Spenser continually undercuts the fiction of the "Renaissance" as a grand historical shift.

Spenser's *Complaints* volume, which contains his only poetry about ruins per se, provides an important introduction to many of these issues. Published between the two halves of *The Faerie Queene*, this volume interrupts Spenser's presumed Virgilian career path in order to remember the road not taken.[43] The *Complaints* features Spenser's original ruins poetry and poetry that he retranslated for the volume, producing a multifaceted dialogue about ruin and memory, Virgil's legacy and Trojan tales. Yet what makes the *Complaints* particularly illustrative of Spenser's matter and method as a poet lies in its complex relationship to Jan Van der Noot's *Theatre for Worldlings*, a formative location for Spenser's edification about the art of memory. Containing Spenser's earliest work as a poet – his anonymous translations of ruins poetry by Petrarch and Du Bellay – the *Theatre* likely showed Spenser the possibility, and even pleasure, of ruin. Yet when Spenser retranslates much of this same ruins poetry for the *Complaints* volume, recalling both the matter and the method of the *Theatre*, he does so partly as a challenge to the Virgilian fictions represented there. As writing that spans nearly two decades of Spenser's career, the *Complaints* suggests how ruin informs his vision of edification and empire, and how it speaks to his "complaints" writ large.

Van der Noot's *Theatre for Worldlings* itself offers important insights into early modern uses of the art of memory. This structure could be seen as a typical Renaissance memory theatre, a place where the mind, in Yates' words, "grasps the highest reality through a magically activated imagination"; alternatively, the *Theatre* could be viewed as a typical medieval "theatre of the world," a form of complaint that illustrates "the insubstantial nature of the phenomenal world," as Carl Rasmussen argues.[44] Read either way, the *Theatre* is a mnemonic space, and an edifice intended to edify. Upon entering the *Theatre*, readers are greeted with Van der Noot's baroque introductory epistle to Queen Elizabeth, followed by three sets of "emblems" which combine poems about ruin – Petrarch's, Du Bellay's, and possibly Van der Noot's original poems based on the book of Revelation – with pictures to illustrate them. Taken together, these emblems dramatize the work's central message about "the vanitie and inconstancie of worldly and transitorie thyngs," elaborated in a none too "Briefe Declaration" about the fall of the City of Man and the rise of the City of God.[45] Sometimes characterized as England's first emblem book, the *Theatre* combines visual and verbal elements in ways that relate specifically to the memory arts. Describing the "relationship between emblem books and the *ars memorativa*," Michael Bath writes that the "invocation of the Horatian *ut pictura poesis* formula becomes almost a reflexive response in emblem books, as do references to . . . Simonides' proverb that painting is mute poetry and poetry a speaking picture."[46] As scholars have argued, emblem books illuminate how locational memory (as poetry or painting) speaks to the human psyche: even in print, we learn and remember best when given vivid pictures and place markers for them. A still more complex understanding of the art of memory relates to another tale of Simonides, frequently cited in emblem books: the analogy between poetry and painting. In the context of comparing different ways of representing history, Plutarch writes that "Simonides calls painting silent poetry, and poetry voiced painting, because whereas painting presents us with events as if they were actually happening, words describe and relate the same events of the past. It is true that the presentation in the one case depends on colours and shapes, and in the other on words and phrases, so that they differ in the material and means they employ to imitate reality; nevertheless, they both basically have the same purpose: the best historian is the one who uses emotions and characters to make his narrative a reflection of events, as a painting is."[47] Plutarch suggests, as Cicero does with his rewriting of the tale of Simonides in *On the Orator*, the art of memory describes both a method of memory associated with "speaking pictures" and a matter of memory associated with narrative – specifically, stories about history. What unites poetry with painting in both tales of Simonides relates to the representation and recollection of the past. This helps to explain Van der Noot's and Spenser's similar use of the art of memory as a strategy for constructing historical fictions.

But on the issue of which stories can best represent history and how, Van der Noot and Spenser part company. Van der Noot's lengthy Protestant polemic rewrites the book of Revelation for early modern England, heralding the destruction of Rome's unholy church and the rise of the New Jerusalem. In the introductory epistle, Van der Noot denies. "vsing flatterie or glosing, as they" – courtiers, that is – "do most comonly" when "ambitiously seeking after prefermentes and honoure" (sig. A4v), though his praise of England and Elizabeth often sounds just like that: "[That] the good kings & princes which feare the Lord, shal haue peace and comfort bothe in this worlde, and in the worlde to come . . . is also to be seene at this day most euidently in the realmes and countreyes under your Maiesties dominion, whiche God hath blessed in suche sort, that it may truly be sayd, that the kingdome of *Saturne*, and the Golden worlde is come againe, and the Virgin *Astraea* is descended from heauen to build hir a seate in this your most happie countrey of *England*" (sig. A6). In the manner described by Yates and so often ascribed to Spenser, Van der Noot renders Virgil's *Fourth Eclogue* as a Protestant prophecy with which to exalt Elizabethan England's Golden Age. If not uncommon for Protestant polemics, as noted above, this vision of history nevertheless, ironically, makes Rome central to the drama of salvation: as a path, so to speak, to the City of God. Van der Noot's positioning of England as a New Jerusalem writ small could be explained in the context of his personal history, as a Dutch poet who found refuge in England from religious persecution.[48] Readers might also understand the *Theatre* as celebrating Protestant ideals while politely skirting the issue of whether or not England truly held a special place in the path to eternity. Nevertheless, Van der Noot's courtly praise of Elizabeth represents epic fictions as sacred truths, using poetry to fashion power in ways that Spenser ultimately rejects. Though it may be tempting to equate Van der Noot's politics (or theology) with Spenser's, as scholars sometimes do, I will suggest that this confuses issues of method with other matters. To be sure, the *Complaints* emulates the mnemonic devices found in the *Theatre*, which clearly influence Spenser's work throughout his career. But as I will discuss later in the chapter, Spenser retranslates the ruins poetry of the *Theatre* for the *Complaints* in order to tell a different story, one that implicitly criticizes Van der Noot's glorification of Gloriana and that reframes poetry's truths as only human, concerned as much with the here and now as with the hereafter. Such complaints ultimately relate less to Spenser's religious beliefs than to how he imagines poetry's relation to power. Nor are they simply his own. Rather, Spenser's complaints find a fuller context in the art of memory tradition, which I will discuss in the next section before returning to the *Complaints*.

Writ small, the Castle of Alma also emblematizes Spenser's engagement with the issues I have been discussing. As noted above, the Trojan history that Arthur reads in the chamber of memory implicitly represents cultural and imperial transmission as a Virgilian fantasy of repairing the ruins of the past. Yet the actual story that *Briton moniments* tells, a chronicle of unending ruination in which ruler after ruler lays waste to the nation he is supposed to edify, directly undermines this fantasy. Such ruins may well connect the symbolic space of Alma's Castle of the Soul with Spenser's ruined castle in Ireland, Kilcolman, and perhaps with Spenser's own psyche. In this regard the Castle of Alma may stage his ambivalence, being of two minds about empire and its effects, by representing both Trojan tales and the ongoing ruin of history. But there is a yet another aspect to this history: against the fact of the endless ruination of the world, and against the imperial fictions that authorize this ruination, is the *action* of Eumnestes and Anamnestes: specifically, the endless project of recollecting the ruins of the past. These overlapping frames capture the critical debate about Spenser's project sketched above in miniature. Viewed from one perspective, Spenser writes a Trojan history for England and thus plays the heroic role of Virgil. From a second perspective, Spenser criticizes Trojan stories of ruin and repair by portraying something like the true history of England's empire and the ruins upon which it continues to rise. And from a third perspective, the tension between Trojan tales and the reality of ruin is reframed by the method of recollection, the process that for Spenser defines the work of self-fashioning, both in writing and in the world. Though hardly his only representation of the art of memory, the Castle of Alma epitomizes the art's complex role within, and significance to, Spenser's entire body of work.

In what follows, I explore how and why Spenser's writing recollects dialogue and debate about the art of memory, and the uses – literary, political, theological, historical – to which the art has been put. The importance of dialogue – among writers, with and within writing – frames this study.[49] In the works of Plato, Cicero, and Augustine, the continuities of the art of memory help create a self-reflexive discourse, novel responses to the past that Greene calls "heuristic" imitation. The "modern voice distinguishes itself from the older voice," he writes, such that "each imitation . . . dramatizes a passage of history, builds it into the poetic experience."[50] The dialogue examined here works through a series of interrelated narratives that not only exemplify a method but also illustrate its relation to matters of memory. My method mirrors Spenser's, in this regard. In order to uncover and track the complexities of Spenser's ongoing conversations with the past, I employ a style of argumentation that might best be described as recursive, in that patterns and motifs re-appear throughout the different chapters of the book. My approach is fundamentally intertextual, implicitly arguing for a more intimate relationship between primary text and background source than is sometimes assumed. The non-Spenserian works I examine are thus intertexts in a precise sense, as Spenser incorporates them into his corpus through recollection.

Theatres of Memory

The next portion of the chapter explores Spenser's art of memory within its broader context, providing an overview of the dialogue into which he inserts himself. I position the three main authors I will be examining throughout Spenser's poetry – Plato, Cicero, and Augustine – in relation to one another and to the literary tradition that they in turn profoundly influence. Since I take these authors "out of order" in the remainder of the book, here I will attempt to place them in a kind of order both chronological and topical, around a central question: how is poetry related to the art of memory? I consider the art's origin as a method of storytelling grounded in an understanding of human psychology (how people imagine, think, remember, and learn) which a variety of fields – rhetoric, philosophy, theology, and history – both appropriate and transform, and which shapes literary theory and practice. I do so by placing heuristic tales of the art of memory, such as the tale of Simonides, in the context of debates about poetry's place in culture.

Writing about how such tales relate to the art of memory, Carruthers describes them as "inventory fables," as "stories devised to help make an inventory of elementary learning," and explains that this "genre of mnemonic storytelling" served as "basic training in *memoria* and was cultivated in Hellenistic schools."[51] As Carruthers argues, the principal example of such a story, the tale of Simonides, is heuristic in a limited sense: "I am not interested in considering such questions as 'Did Simonides actually invent the art of memory that is memorialized in this story?'; . . . or 'What does it say about human (or ancient Greek) psychology. . .?,' or 'What does it signify that the gods, Castor and Pollux, called Simonides out of the hall in the nick of time?' . . .The Simonides story is . . . not about origins or about poets or about feasts, but about learning some principles of a craft."[52] The questions irrelevant for Carruthers' purposes are the very ones that I pursue here. As I argue, these stories matter not only for *how* they teach a method of creative memory but also for *what* they teach about the complex relation between truth and fiction, story and history, humanity and divinity, psyche and society. Understanding such tales in this way necessitates a shift in perspective: it means reading them as literature – poetry lessons, so to speak. This shift allows for a greater appreciation of the poetic basis of mnemonic theory and its complex reception in the fields of rhetoric, philosophy, theology, and, in all of them, history. Such a shift in perspective also highlights issues of how poetry speaks to power, writ small in the tale of Simonides. After all, the anger of Simonides' wealthy patron at having to share his praise with the twin gods sets the stage for the story. To be sure, the tale of Simonides teaches a rhetorical method, but it also tells a story about poetry's place in the republic.

I will explore how the tale of Simonides is precisely concerned with "origins" and "poets" and "feasts," initially by attempting to answer Carruthers' rejected question about Castor and Pollux. The presence of Castor and Pollux in the tale of Simonides, as well as the fact that it takes place at a banquet, connects it strongly to what could be called the ur-tale of mnemonic recollection: Odysseus' recounting of his journey to the underworld during a banquet in Book 11 of the *Odyssey*. Homer's underworld formed the commonplace for remembering the past as tales of Troy's ruin. The story begins with the threat of forgetfulness represented by Circe, whose magic makes men forget themselves and their humanity, yet she directs Odysseus to the land of the dead, where memory is symbolically restored. The underworld is where Odysseus encounters history, where he meets the dead and engages in mutual storytelling. As scholars have suggested, epic underworlds function as important locations for memory, and the journey through the underworld demonstrates the basic techniques of the art of memory: the hero traverses a series of places in which he remembers the past and divines the future.[53] The twin gods Castor and Pollux play a central symbolic role in Odysseus' description of his experience:

And I saw Leda, who had been the wife of Tyndareos,
and she had borne to Tyndareos two sons with strong hearts,

Kastor, breaker of horses, and the stronger boxer, Polydeukes.
The life-giving earth holds both of them, yet they are still living,
and, even underneath the earth, enjoying the honor
of Zeus, they live still every other day; on the next day
they are dead, but they are given honor even as gods are.[54]

These demigods allow for an exchange between death and life, mortality and immortality, that mirrors their own liminal, go-between status.
This resembles the role Odysseus fashions for himself, as a figure who
having emerged from the underworld speaks with (and for) the dead.
This description of the twin gods thus suggests the significance of their
symbolic role in the tale of Simonides. In both cases, Castor and Pollux
teach how to translate between the living and the dead; to remember a
ruined past; to create immortality through poetry, symbolically returning the dead to life, if only temporarily. In a sense, the tale of Simonides conflates the location of Odysseus' story with the location of its
telling, overlaying the space of the feast with that of the underworld,
turning the banquet hall itself into both a place of death and a place of
recollection.

As scholars such as Milman Parry demonstrated long ago, mnemonic
methods were the foundation of epic, playing a central role in both
their composition and transmission; epic tales were fashioned through
the memorial manipulation of places and images, as well as repeated
phrases, representing the moving parts of poetry and performance over
time and space. Homer reminds readers of this mnemonic tradition
when a rapt listener interrupts Odysseus' tale:

Odysseus, we as we look upon you do not imagine
that you are a deceptive or thievish man, the sort that the black earth
breeds in great numbers, people who wander widely, making up
lying stories, from which no one could learn anything. You have
a grace upon your words, and there is sound sense within them,
and expertly, as a singer would do, you have told the story
of the dismal sorrows befallen yourself and all of the Argives.[55]

At face value, this interruption attributes truth to poetry; the "grace" of
Odysseus' words that so enthrals his listeners convinces them that he
must be telling the truth. Yet the implicit characterization of wily Odysseus as one of those "who wander widely" and make up lying stories
builds into the written narrative a remembrance of the oral origins of

Trojan tales, recalling a bardic tradition of performing stories about history that seemingly could teach little to anyone. As the *Odyssey* thus draws attention to its own complex negotiation of story and history, the problem of how the past is remembered and re-enacted emerges as an clear point of tension.

Homer's underworld relates to Plato's objections to poetry, which have less to do with the stories themselves than with the role of stories in society: the representation of fictions as divine truth, the manipulation of memory in the service of power. As Eric Havelock argues, Plato presumably exiles poetry from both his ideal Republic and his real Academy because, as the collective memory that edified Hellas, its power exceeded that of either the page or the stage.[56] The power of performance that Plato rejects relates to the re-enactment of Trojan tales in the world of the living and in the realms of pedagogy and politics, which whether framed as new tales or variations on old ones attempts to evoke similar beliefs in enraptured audiences. Such rote and repeated recollection, Plato implies throughout his dialogues, in fact reveals a form of forgetting. Against such forgetfulness, Plato radically reforms the method and matter of memory.

Rather than simply exiling poetry, Plato appropriates its power to engage the human psyche for philosophical aims.[57] Although later allegorical interpretations of Plato's writing work to align philosophy and theology with epic, I explore how Plato's own fictions respond to and rewrite the tendency to interpret Homeric epic as an allegory of the soul – a journey through history, figured emblematically in Odysseus' journey to the underworld.[58] Plato's dialogues are memorable for poetic stories like the "Myth of Er" and the "Allegory of the Cave," but I will focus here on Plato's method as a storyteller, particularly as it dovetails with his critique of Trojan tales. As discussed above, Platonic recollection has usually been seen as a separate tradition from the art of memory, and this division parallels a distinction often made between the Plato of "forms" and the Plato of "fictions." Put as a question, does Plato position forms as ideal, prior knowledge of divinity, or is this a useful fiction for locating knowledge within the self rather than in external authorities? Both are correct in that Plato's reception history offers both answers. Platonic *anamnesis*, which depends upon the immortality of the soul, has repeatedly been interpreted allegorically, as well as non-allegorically and even anti-allegorically. My own interest here lies with Plato the poet, who interrogates the uses of fiction by creating his own.

The complex role of mnemonics within epic traditions forms the background to Plato's engagement with, and rewriting of, the art of memory. Placing heuristic tales about the art of memory, like that of Simonides, in the context of the epic reveals how this method of recollection relates to matters of poetry in a variety of ways: as story and history, past and present, performance and power. Plato's dialogues repeatedly suggest that the art of memory was derived from – and derivative of – epic, and was used to tell the same kinds of stories about love and war, gods and humans, drawn from tales of Troy's ruin; indeed, Plato intimates, the tale of Simonides itself represents a rewriting of Trojan tales. Plato, and later Cicero and Augustine, each adopt the art of memory as a method of fiction-making to criticize old stories of history about Troy's ruin and to construct new counter-narratives that disclose fictions of power and ideological uses of poetry. In so doing, I argue, each writer redefines poetry's place in culture.

Plato and the Poets: Philosophy's Art of Recollection

When at the start of *On the Orator* the interlocutor Scaevola suggests, "Why should [we] not imitate Socrates in the *Phaedrus* of Plato?" performing this dialogue in a reminiscent location – an ideal place in the country, beneath the shade of a "plane tree" – begins as a game (12). Yet this playful opening belies the serious role that Plato's dialogue plays in Cicero's own. As I suggest, *On the Orator* reveals the art of memory at play in Plato's dialogue, just as the *Phaedrus* illuminates the seriousness of Cicero's re-enactment of the past. These dialogues address the rivalry between rhetoric and philosophy as forms of education, but they also clarify what these fields of knowledge hold in common: storytelling, as a method of edification that shapes the matter of memory, both individual and collective. The question of memory's place in culture implicitly frames the *Phaedrus* from its beginning – when Socrates asks, "Where do you come from, Phaedrus my friend, and where are you going?" – to its end, when they consecrate the place of their dialogue as a commonplace of common wealth: the place where "friends have all things in common."[59] Moving the location for memory from the artificial locations of mnemonics to the naturally seductive sweet spot of dialogue, Plato thereby positions philosophy (here as throughout his dialogues) as the ideal space for recollection, for dialogue that truly edifies.

By re-enacting the *Phaedrus* (and in more ways than one), Cicero's *On the Orator* remembers the art of memory's long and complex reception history in philosophy's domain. As I argue, the *Phaedrus* collapses distinctions between rhetoric and poetry, implying that orators have simply appropriated the mnemonic methods and epic matters of poets, performing old love stories about history – origin tales of Hellas' gods and heroes – in new guises. Less criticizing poetry per se than the use of poetry as a form of political theatre, Plato's dialogues focus on the illegitimate power that fiction acquires when it is presented as truth – even as Plato himself appropriates poetry's power for philosophical aims. When Cicero in turn appropriates the art of memory in order to tell a new story about Rome's history, recollecting the wars of a past generation as a prologue to his own fin-de-siècle republic, he indicates his debt to the *Phaedrus* beyond mere performance – that is, Cicero imitates Plato's mode of imitation, borrowing the method of poets, pedagogues, and politicians for new matters of memory, ruin, and re-edification.

Performance plays a key part in the *Phaedrus*, first by connecting the dialogue's location with locational memory. Because Plato sets all but this dialogue in Athens proper, the chance encounter of Socrates and Phaedrus outside the city leads, appropriately enough, to their initial discussion about place and memory. Socrates surmises that Phaedrus came to this secluded spot in order to practise delivering a speech (477). Teasing Phaedrus about his acting ambitions, Socrates says, "I believe he had learned the whole speech by heart, unless it was a very long one, and he was going into the country to practice declaiming it [when] he fell in with one . . . to share his frenzied enthusiasm" (476). Phaedrus confesses to being caught: having been entranced by Lysias' sophistic argument that true love leads only to destructive deception and thus should be avoided in favour of honest friendship, Phaedrus had wanted to make Socrates an unwitting audience for a repeat performance of Lysias' speech. "It really is perfectly true," Phaedrus explains, "that I have not got the words by heart, but I will sketch the general purport of several points . . . taking them in order one by one, and beginning at the beginning" (477). Exactly *how* Phaedrus describes remembering this speech, by recalling the topics (rather than the words per se) "in [the] order" of their delivery, suggests a casual familiarity with the art of memory. Crucially, though, Socrates guesses that Phaedrus has a written copy of this speech and, because he asks to read it rather than watch its re-enactment, this same writing structures their dialogue.

This introductory exchange hints at the dialogue's complex treatment of the art of memory. Although best known for Socrates' rejection of the written word as impermanent, the *Phaedrus* condemns the art of memory only to redeem it in reconceptualized forms, both written and spoken. To be sure, Socrates scorns mnemonics as merely a method of memorization. Mocking the "inventor" of "the indirect censure in mnemonic verse" and what such memory aids can teach, he asks Phaedrus a rhetorical question of his own: "What are we to say of his *Muses' Treasury of Phrases* with its reduplications and maxims and similes?" (512, 513). Naturally, Socrates' question also provides an implicit answer: such books of memory offer only the appearance of wisdom. Although Socrates never tells *the* tale of Simonides, his complaint about writing nevertheless seems designed specifically to refute the truth of Simonides' other discovery: that poetry is a speaking picture, and painting is silent poetry. "The strange thing about writing, which makes it truly analogous to painting," Socrates instead contends, is that "the painter's products stand before us as though they were alive, but if you question them . . . from a desire to be instructed, they go on telling you just the same thing forever" (521). As though revising Simonides' famous phrase, Socrates reframes writing as both dumbshow and silent picture. Writing only seems to preserve memory when in truth, he argues, it destroys memory because it never changes, an argument which he claims speaks to all forms of artificial memory.

Yet Socrates' infamous tale of Theuth illustrates the dialogue's complex appropriation of the art of memory.[60] When recounting why the Egyptian king Thamus wisely rejected the god Theuth's new invention, writing, Socrates tells an origin story of artificial memory that, I would argue, implicitly replaces the tale of Simonides. To Theuth's offer of "a recipe for memory and wisdom," Thamus responds that writing instead "will implant forgetfulness in [the] souls" of his subjects, who "will cease to exercise memory because they rely on that which is written, calling things to remembrance no longer from within themselves, but by means of external marks"; he thereby concludes that writing "is not a recipe for memory" but merely a "reminder" (520). Thamus' view that writing would cripple memory echoes Socrates' own, but the *Phaedrus* as a whole suggests just the opposite: writing serves as a necessary "reminder" that, when engaged in dialogue, aids in recollection in the broadest possible sense.[61] Despite Socrates' admonitions against writing, Lysias' written oration continually prompts the dialogue about love and learning. Writing allows Socrates and Phaedrus to ask questions, even demand answers, for by probing Lysias' amorous paradoxes they come to agree that love leads not to ruin but to re-edification. Implying that "telling the truth" means discernment rather than dogma,

Socrates ironically teaches Phaedrus how to use writing: as an implied interlocutor, and as a tool of self-fashioning in philosophical education. The dialogue's central issue relates less to writing than the use of discourse writ large. After all, writing is ancient history, Socrates implies with his tale of Egyptian hieroglyphics, as the artificial memory and pictorial language that predates Simonides.

Socrates also locates an earlier origin point for the art of memory when, albeit indirectly, he criticizes its use in oral as well as written forms. He implies that Greece's collective sense of both the past and present has been shaped by dramatic re-enactments of Trojan origin stories. The commonplace method and matter of poets and orators finds its origin in the misty prehistory of epic performance, Socrates reminds his audience, facetiously asking whether Phaedrus is "acquainted only with the 'Arts' or manuals of oratory by Nestor and Odysseus, which they composed in their leisure hours at Troy" (506). He makes similar connections between mnemonics and Trojan tales in other dialogues. In *Hippias Major*, Socrates feigns forgetfulness about the eponymous orator's art of storytelling. "I quite forgot about your mnemonic art," he says coyly, used "to tell . . . stories"; Hippias happily reminds Socrates that he has "composed a discourse" set "after the fall of Troy" (1539). In *Hippias Minor*, he once again apologizes for having "forgotten to mention your art of memory, which you regard as your special glory," and then reminds Hippias to resume storytelling: "Were you not saying that Achilles was a true man, and Odysseus false and wily?" (206). Socrates also repeatedly associates poetic uses of locational memory with Simonides specifically, suggesting parallels between tales of Simonides and tales of Troy as similar stories about recollecting the dead from the ruins of history's underworld. When in the *Protagoras*, Socrates asks the eponymous orator "to justify Simonides" with his rhetorical art, "lest our Simonides be sacked by Protagoras like another Troy," he links these legends as twin tales of ruin, remembered in like fashion (334). The storied debate about poetry's place in the *Republic* also turns on a tale of Simonides. Here, Socrates ridicules the "riddling definition of justice . . . that Simonides gave after the manner of poets," redefining such poetic justice – what "you and Homer and Simonides [call] stealing . . . for the benefit of friends and the harm of enemies" – as a fiction misrepresented as truth (581–4). He then encourages his interlocutors to "take up arms against . . . Simonides" (586) by redefining justice, as well as the proper uses of poetry, and defines the terms under which poetry would be readmitted to their republic: "we must not take such poetry seriously as a serious thing that lays hold on truth" (833).

When responding to Lysias' written speech in the *Phaedrus*, Socrates self-consciously performs the part of a poet, one who uses mnemonic devices to recollect tales of Troy. By styling himself a performer, he exposes how divisions between rhetoric and poetry, orality and literacy, story and history, collapse in fiction, crossing disciplinary boundaries paradoxically in order to claim poetry as philosophy's common property. To Lysias' argument about the dangers of love – that it leads to madness, ruin, despair – Socrates offers two replies, both of which imply that Lysias has intoxicated Phaedrus with old wine (love stories of Troy's history) in a new bottle, delivering stale tales as novel truths. He first reiterates Lysias' views on love, but then rejects his own argument as blasphemous, asking how love can be evil if truly divine. This introduces Socrates' second response, represented as a recollection of a palinode by the poet Stesichorus:

> Now for such as offend in speaking of gods and heroes there is an ancient mode of purification, which was known to Stesichorus, though not to Homer. When Stesichorus lost the sight of his eyes because of his defamation of Helen, he was not, like Homer, at a loss to know why. As a true artist he understood the reason, and promptly wrote the lines:
>> False, false the tale.
>> Thou never didst sail in the well-decked ships
>> Nor come to the towers of Troy. (490)

"After finishing the composition of his so-called palinode," concludes Socrates, Stesichorus "straightway recovered his sight." What Homer's blindness prevented him from seeing, and what Stesichorus learned the hard way, Socrates suggests, was the cause of their punishment: telling "lies about the gods," in this case the semi-divine Helen. But Socrates seems less invested in criticizing poets than in putting Hellas' seminal fiction in its proper place. This ambiguous apology speaks doubly, at once absolving Helen of blame for igniting the Trojan War while also intimating that Helen is no more than an allegorical myth of Hellenic origins. In effect, Socrates challenges the Trojan War as *the* commonplace of Greek memory at its very source: without Helen, no dangerous beauty or forbidden love would have launched a thousand ships or toppled the legendary "towers of Troy," the symbolic ruins that were the foundation of Greek edification.

The pretence of mnemonic performance – as Socrates says, the palinode "I shall now pronounce is by Stesichorus" (490) – becomes the pretext for a new story about philosophy's art of recollection.[62] When presumably recollecting Stesichorus' palinode, Socrates creates his own originary tale about love-as-recollection, a story of history that tacitly replaces a love of Helen with a love of wisdom. "Now it's here that I shall show greater wisdom than these poets," he confesses, for "I shall attempt to make my due palinode to Love before any harm comes to me for my defamation of him" (490). Claiming the tale is not his own, Socrates performs the part of a poet as he argues, against Lysias' sophistry, that love leads not to ruin but to recollection, to heaven rather than to hell. "False is the tale," he begins, echoing Stesichorus' phrase, "that when a lover is at hand favor ought rather to be accorded to one who does not love, on the ground that the former is mad, and the latter sound of mind" (491). Rather, "the greatest blessings come by way of madness, indeed of madness that is heaven sent" (491). Reforming his allegedly blasphemous remarks about the relationship between humanity and divinity, Socrates asserts that love acts as a reminder of the time when "we beheld with our eyes that blessed vision, ourselves in the train of Zeus" (497). "The soul is immortal," he declares, a winged chariot that travels the highways of the gods, but when "burdened with a load of forgetfulness" it falls to earth (493–5). The remainder of the tale that follows, discussed more fully in the next chapter, describes how love allows fallen, forgetful souls to regrow wings and ascend anew to the heavens. In what may well be a revisionary version of the Cupid and Psyche myth, Socrates poetically describes how the god of love conquers all – that is, unless people learn how to master their own souls. Underscoring the human tendency toward idolatry, fashioning one's self and others as though love gods, he uses allegory to unveil allegory, lies to tell truths, heuristic tales to teach an art of philosophy: "only the soul that has beheld truth may enter into this our human form – seeing that man must need understand the language of forms, passing from a plurality of perceptions to a unity gathered together by reasoning – and such understanding is a recollection of those things which our souls beheld aforetime as they journeyed with their god" (496). As Socrates concludes, "Therefore is it meet and right that the soul of the philosopher alone should recover her wings, for she . . . is ever near in memory to those things in a god's nearness whereunto makes him truly god" (496).

By creating a new story of love opposed to Trojan love stories, by replacing Troy's ruins with those of the self, the *Phaedrus* illustrates how philosophy offers another way to remember the past, and an alternative form of edification. With his tale of Stesichorus, Socrates relates an origin story of natural memory that complements and contradicts his origin story of artificial memory, the tale of Theuth. Against Theuth's judgment that writing would lead to forgetfulness, Socrates' supernatural prehistory posits that people are born forgetful; and against Lysias' clichéd argument that love leads to ruin both personally and politically, Socrates' reframes love as the path to re-edification. In so doing, he dramatically reforms what recollection can mean both individually and collectively.

In place of Troy's ruins, the *Phaedrus* thereby tells a new story of history that illustrates another means of speaking with the dead: in dialogue with writing.When Phaedrus responds to this tale and the tale of Theuth by labelling them fictions – "it is easy for you, Socrates, to make up tales from Egypt or wherever else you fancy" (520) – for once he is right, if for the wrong reasons. As Socrates clarifies, his literary method matters far less than what his stories mean, and he emphasizes the need to interpret tales allegorically since, in writing as in the world, fictions can both be given and taken as the truth itself. "When an orator, or a king, succeeds in acquiring the power of a Lycurgus, a Solon, or a Darius, and so winning immortality among his people as a speech writer," Socrates asks Phaedrus, "doesn't he deem himself a peer of the gods while still living, and do not people in later ages hold the same opinion of him when they contemplate his writings?" (503). Albeit indirectly, Socrates suggests what truly matters about his tales – what they reveal about the the relationship between poetry and power – and he thus can claim to have "told the truth" here, despite veiling it in fiction (520). Given that stories are not always circumscribed by the page or the stage, the ability to recognize fiction in all its forms marks the end of Socrates' lesson for Phaedrus and readers alike: "We may regard our literary pastime as having reached a satisfactory conclusion," he says (523–4).

Socrates' tale of Stesichorus – a tale that might be easily dismissed as a trivial fiction, as Antonius treats the tale of Simonides in *On the Orator* – suggests how Plato remakes poetry's art of memory in philosophy's image. He repeatedly rewrites the underworld places of epic, which function as mnemonic spaces in multiple regards: as clearly demarcated locations, filled with vivid images and personifications, which allow both characters and readers to recollect the ruins of the past.[63] Describing the soul's cycles of birth and rebirth, and what happens when a soul has finished its first earthly life and is "brought to judgment," Socrates relates: "some are taken to be punished in the places of chastisement beneath the earth, while others are borne aloft by Justice to a certain region of the heavens, there to live in such manner as is merited by their past life in the flesh. And after a thousand years these and those alike come to the allotment and choice of their second life, each choosing according to her will" (495–6). In contrast to the static, eternal judgments of Homer's underworlds, where the past exists perpetually fixed outside time, Socrates fashions his underworld as a place of change and choice. Even as he reminds readers of epic places of memory, Socrates also demarcates and describes another space of his own design: "that place beyond the heavens" about which "none of our earthly poets has yet sung, and none shall sing worthily" and which may only be reached through philosophy (494).

Plato remakes the places of memory – poetry's underworld and heavens – throughout his dialogues, fashioning allegorical spaces that dramatize a method of sceptical interpretation. The "Myth of Er" ends the *Republic* with a story of a warrior who "after coming to life related what, he said, he had seen in the world beyond" (839). "No divinity shall cast lots for you" in this place where "you . . . choose your own deity" and human choice reigns supreme (841). But before returning to the world, Er had explained, each must forget the underworld: the souls "all journeyed to the Plain of Oblivion . . . [where] they camped . . . by the River of Forgetfulness, whose waters . . . they were all required to drink" (844). Er was not allowed to drink the water in order that he might bring this story back, Socrates tells Glaucon in the final paragraph of the dialogue, "and so . . . the tale was saved . . . and it will save us if we believe it, and we shall safely cross the River of Lethe, and keep our soul unspotted from the world" – an ironic end that reflects upon Socrates' own end, his trial and condemnation for disbelief (844). When Socrates describes philosophical education as recollection in the *Phaedo*, arguing that "learning is [the] recollection" of prior knowledge from a prior existence, his revisionary tale of the underworld similarly reflects ironically upon Socrates' life and death (59). Relating how "those who are judged to have a life of surpassing holiness . . . are released and set free from confinement in these [underworld] regions of the earth," he concludes with a defence of poetry: "Of course, no reasonable man ought to insist that the facts are exactly as I have described them," he confesses, but then adds that "we should use such accounts to inspire ourselves with confidence, and that is why I have already drawn out my tale so long" (94–5). This apology for poetry recalls the *Apology*, where Socrates stands trial for lies about the gods: "guilty of corrupting the minds of the young, and of believing in deities of his own invention instead of the gods recognized by the state" (10). Because the charges against Socrates are based partly on fictions – his own as well as others' – this dialogue broaches the problem of judging fiction *as* truth.[64] Through his use of allegory, Plato exposes the perils of speaking truth to power and the necessity of "speaking other." As Socrates in his own defence remembers his service during the Peloponnesian wars, the ruin of Athens (rather than Troy) provides the trial's historical context. Symbolically recollecting a house in ruins, the decline of Athens and death of Socrates, is foundational to Plato's project.

How and why Plato appropriates an old method of poets for new philosophical matter is nowhere more clearly illustrated than in the *Symposium*. Framed as "a gigantic exercise in oral recall," as Michael Murrin puts it, the *Symposium* remembers Socrates' life and legacy in ways reminiscent of the tale of Simonides.[65] The *Phaedrus* and the *Symposium* have a Castor and Pollux – like relationship, sharing a common topic, love, and though set in different places – the pleasant place outside Athens in the *Phaedrus*, a banquet hall in Athens in the *Symposium* – both dialogues explore locational memory as a tool of philosophy as well as poetry. The *Symposium* ostensibly concerns Phaedrus' complaints about love poetry, which echo those of Socrates in the *Phaedrus* – and are similarly presented as a palinode.[66] "The tale is not my own . . . that I am going to tell," Eryximachus claims when introducing their subject, insisting that it "properly belongs to my friend Phaedrus": why "not one single poet has ever sung a song in praise of so ancient and so powerful a god as Love?" (531). The implied subject is whom poetry "properly belongs to" in Greek culture, and Socrates positions poetry as the common property of all. Here as in the *Phaedrus*, he portrays philosophers (among other lovers) as poets in their own right, and for a similar reason. Socrates performs the part of a poet for an ironic purpose: in order to reveal how self-fashioned gods of both stage and state are built upon epic fictions of love and power.

The *Symposium*'s frame tale, with its multiple layers of recollection, announces that this dialogue inextricably mingles truth and fiction: the speakers who remember the symposium were infants when it took place (though one of them initially forgets this, as though to indicate its continued life in the collective memory of Athens); moreover, the speakers' second-hand source remembers the event only partially at best, given that it was long ago and he slept through part of the party.[67] Apollodorus, the principal speaker, admits that his tale can tell only partial truths, for his source "did not pretend to reproduce the various speeches verbatim, any more than I could repeat them word for word as I had them from him"; instead, as he clarifies, "I shall simply recount such passages as the speaker or the thought itself made, so far as I could judge, especially memorable" (532). As Apollodorus' confession suggests, he remembers this story according to methods of artificial memory, using places and images to maintain the order of topics (rather than the exact words) which he then elaborates upon: these are the heads of dialogue that also represent the heads of the speakers, as in the tale of Simonides. Throughout the dialogue, moreover, Apollodorus draws attention to his use of mnemonics, and in ways that mirror the narrative methods of the speakers he remembers: from the start, they agree that "the best way would be for each in turn from left to right to address the company and speak to the best of his ability in praise of Love."[68] They also agree that Phaedrus "should open the debate, for besides being head of the table he is the real author of our discussion" (532). That "the real author" of this dialogue cannot be named with certainty points to an important irony: namely, that to stay alive in memory, this dialogue necessarily must change with its continued dissemination. As in *On the Orator*, the architectural mnemonic never fully reconstructs the past, but the *Symposium*'s imperfection enacts its own ideal: immortality as a living art of memory.

To dramatize the uses and abuses of love stories about history, Socrates plays the part of poet, responding to the tales of the *Symposium*'s two poets, Aristophanes and Agathon, in what amounts to a poetry competition. Reversing their usual roles, the comic poet Aristophanes delivers a thinly veiled tragedy about Athens, while the tragic poet Agathon offers a divine comedy with himself cast as the god of love. Aristophanes' well-known story of how Zeus divided the sexes invokes the Peloponnesian wars as evidence that love leads to ruin without due obedience, or fear, of the gods: "For there was a time, I repeat, when we were one, but now, for our sins, God has scattered us abroad, as the Spartans scattered the Arcadians," warning that "there is every reason to fear that, if we neglect the worship of the gods, they will split us up again" (545). Agathon in turn promises to correct lies about the gods, as in "those old stories of the gods we have read in Hesiod," which he rejects as "the work not of Love but of Necessity – if, indeed, such tales are credible at all" (547). Fashioning love as Cupid, the youngest and most beautiful god, the force that conquers all, and the source of all poetry, Agathon thereby also fashions the god of love in his own image – as a poet: "so divine a poet that he can kindle in the souls of others the poetic fire, for . . . we are every one of us a poet when we are in love" (549).

Socrates answers Agathon's and Aristophanes' commonplace tales with a new love story about history, recollecting his own edification in the philosophy of love as taught to him by Diotima. Although promising to tell the "truth about love" (551), he nevertheless imitates Agathon's view that every lover becomes a poet, fashioning love in his own decidedly less flattering image. With a Hesiodic origin tale, Socrates ironically confirms Agathon's charge that tales of divine love are indeed born of human necessity: "Need came begging at the door," having heard the "gods making merry" when celebrating Aphrodite's birth, and "thinking that to get a child by Resource would mitigate her penury," conceives Love in the "garden of Zeus" (555). Born among the gods but not divine himself, this god of love is not "delicate and lovely as most of us believe, but harsh and arid, barefoot and home- less," living in poverty, "at once desirous and full of wisdom, a lifelong seeker after truth," and forever in "need" (555–6). By fashioning him- self idolatrously, Socrates redefines Love in human terms: as "a lover of wisdom" (556).

Socrates' tale tacitly refutes the party's premise, praising love but not as a god. Unlike those who swear that Love is "a great god" and those who "deny that he's a god at all," Diotima (as Socrates relates) defines love as "halfway between mortal and immortal" but still a "very pow- erful spirit," locating it somewhere in the middle, where the truth lies: "it is only through the mediation of the spirit world that man can have any intercourse . . . with the gods" (554–5). If not a god per se, Love is nevertheless divine and, like poetry, is "common to all" (557). Just as "there is more than one kind of poetry in the true sense of the word – that is to say, calling something into existence that was not there be- fore, so that every kind of artistic creation is poetry, and every artist is a poet," Diotima explains, so "that's how it is with Love": the shared "longing for happiness" connects "the various fields of business, ath- letics, philosophy, and so on," yet only the poets are "given the name that should apply to all the rest as well" (557). By analogy with lov- ers of all kinds, she implies that lovers of wisdom are poets too. Be- cause "in love with the eternal," Diotima claims, "every one of us . . . is longing for the endless fame" – the desire for "immortality" that connects everyone from parents to poets (560). She thus redraws the lines between poetry and philosophy by virtue of their common place in love: "those whose procreancy is of the spirit" bring forth "Wisdom and all her sister virtues," and "it is the office of every poet to beget them, and of every artist whom we may call creative" (560). This idea of philosophy *as* poetry is emblematized through the famous vision of the ladder of love. "Mounting the heavenly ladder, stepping from rung to rung," the lover of wisdom moves "from bodily beauty to the beauty of institutions, from institutions to learning, and from learning in general to the special lore that pertains to nothing but the beautiful itself – until at last he comes to know what beauty is," a place she calls the "sanctuary of Love": "an eternal oneness, while every lovely thing partakes of it in such sort that, however much the parts may wax and wane, it will be neither more nor less, but still the same inviolable whole" (563). Socrates concludes his performance by admitting it can be taken as allegorically – "So you may call this my eulogy of Love, Phaedrus, if you choose; if not, well, call it what you like" – but a fiction which also reveals important truths about how the "Love [of wisdom] will help our mortal nature" (563).

Alcibiades' drunken eulogy for Socrates suggests as much, creating important parallels between the tale of Simonides and the *Symposium* as symbolic edifices about the process of edification, and as memorials to the dead. A late arrival to the banquet, Alcibiades can remind readers of Castor and Pollux, the gods who miraculously save Simonides from ruin. However, no gods from the machine rescue Socrates, an irony that might allude to Athens' defeat in the Peloponnesian wars and Alcibiades' part in "the ruin of the state," as Thucydides' history attests.[69] Plato ironically casts Alcibiades, whom Socrates must answer for at his trial, as the principle character witness for the defence. As if testifying, Alcibiades swears, "I'm bound to tell you the whole truth and nothing but the truth," adding that "Socrates must pull me up if I begin telling lies" (568). His allusions to Socrates as a Pan-like poet recalls, or portends, the prayer to Pan at the end of the *Phaedrus*, where (as here) poetry and philosophy must occupy a common place. "He reminds me of Marsyas the satyr," Alcibiades quips, in a foreboding allusion to the piping satyr of Dionysian poetry who foolishly and fatally challenged Apollo to a singing contest: "the only difference, Socrates, between you and Marsyas is that you can get just the same effect without any instrument at all – with nothing but a few simple words, not even poetry" (566–7). Alcibiades similarly compares Socrates to "those little sileni . . . modeled with pipes or flutes in their hands, and when you open them down the middle there are little figures of the gods inside," as a metaphor for Socrates' search for truth within the self (567). In the process of revealing Socrates' "little game of irony," Alcibiades offers a heuristic for reading Plato's dialogues: to open them up is to read Socrates allegorically, as a philosopher-poet and friend of the state (567).

For drama lovers, Plato puts on a morality play in which Socrates' life story replaces old tales of love and war about Greece's mythic origin with a new tale about Athens' current state. Plato also clarifies that poetry and philosophy, in theory and practice, occupy a common place. The party ends with Socrates still conversing with the poets "Agathon and Aristophanes and . . . the gist of it was that Socrates was forcing them to admit that the same man might be capable of writing both comedy and tragedy – that the tragic poet might be a comedian as well" (574). As Plato suggests, Socrates represents a unique third kind of poet, the lover of wisdom who falls between these two extremes in the *satura*-like mixture of satire: storytelling and truth-telling. In and as dialogue, Plato's writing recalls poetry's important place in the house that Socrates built.

*   *   *

Plato's use of tales to tell truths may be best explained by Aristotle – ironically enough, given his rejection of such myths. On the one hand, he clearly denies the metaphysical underpinning of Platonic recollection, *anamnesis*, and nowhere more clearly than in the *Metaphysics*. Here, Aristotle refutes ideas such as the ecstatic "Form" of beauty and goodness that Socrates describes in the *Symposium*: "The claim, for instance, that the Forms are paradigms and that the other entities participate in them accordingly is quite empty of content, amounting to no more than poetic metaphors."[70] Addressing "adherents of the Theory of Forms who hold that the Forms are numbers," he reaches similar and still more suggestive conclusions: "What a mess! Internal inconsistency spiced with contempt for common sense; Simonides' 'long story' springs to mind" (442). On the other hand, Aristotle clearly embraces the larger truths that such fictions can tell. "To be fair," he writes, "we should take their account of nature seriously enough to question it," and in the process Aristotle helps to make explicit what Plato's dialogues merely imply (443).

Aristotle's search for metaphysical meaning begins with a tale about "the early history of philosophy," in which "wonder" connects the "lover of stories" with the "lover of wisdom" (9):

The man who is puzzled and amazed is thought to be ignorant (hence the lover of stories is, in a way, a lover of wisdom, since a story is composed of wonders). And so, if men indeed began to philosophize to escape ignorance, it is clear that they pursued science for the sake of knowledge and not for any utility . . . So it is clear that we seek it for no other use but rather, as we say, as a free man is for himself and not for another, so is this science the only one of the sciences that is free . . . for this reason it is with justice that its acquisition would not be thought to be human. For in many ways the nature of men is enslaved. Thus, according to Simonides: "Only a god might have this boon . . .," and a man might not be thought worthy to seek out knowledge itself. (9)

Recalling another tale of Simonides, Aristotle counters the myth that the gods will be envious of those who seek philosophical knowledge. "Such a science" as philosophy "would be that which a god would most choose," he writes, adding "if indeed any [science] is divine"; as he concludes, "So all sciences are more necessary than this one, and none is better" (9–10). Even as Aristotle disputes the idea that freedom of knowledge belongs to "only a god," and generally dismisses "the lies of seers" (9), he also praises the "lovers of stories" as "lovers of wisdom," precisely because both share a sense of wonder. As Aristotle implies, love indeed forms a common place for poets and philosophers – the desire for what rarely can be verified and yet still must be imagined. What Plato calls "recollection" involves all the soul's faculties (imagination, reason, and memory) in the service of creating self-knowledge, a form of education that depends upon wonder, and whose method amounts to a dialectical process of breaking down and reassembling prior knowledge, ruining and reforming sacred truths. In a sense, Aristotle may affirm Socrates' metaphysical assertion in the *Phaedrus*: "I am a lover of these divisions and collections, that I may gain the power to speak and to think, and whenever I deem another man able to discern an objective unity and plurality, I follow 'in his footsteps where he leadeth as a god'" (511–12).

Tales of Simonides in Cicero's *On the Orator*

In *On the Orator*, Crassus cannot resist stating the irony that Socrates' memory depends upon writing: "Socrates . . . whose great genius and varied conversation Plato has in his Dialogues consigned to immortality . . . himself . . . left us nothing in writing" (209). But the irony runs deeper than Crassus realizes, for he cannot know that Cicero will similarly consign him and the other speakers to immortality in writing. In both dialogues, the interlocutors cannot see what lies beyond the boundaries of their pastoral discourse, an irony that both Plato and Cicero explore from the perspective of memory. Yet both dialogues ultimately represent their own written memorials less as an immortal monument than as an unfinished edifice, even one in ruins, awaiting future renovation by future readers. Socrates' view of writing in the *Phaedrus* – that someone "must be really ignorant . . . if he imagines that the written words can do anything more than remind" (521) – fundamentally shapes Cicero's transformation of the art of memory in *On the Orator*.[71] As I argue here, Cicero reframes the speakers' playful re-enactment of the *Phaedrus* with a more elaborate performance as a new Simonides. When he interrupts the dialogue to memorialize the death and decline of these speakers (especially his role model, Crassus), he creates a *Symposium*-like narrative of ruin and recollection that re-forms the sweet spot of philosophical dialogue for rhetoric. Like Plato, Cicero borrows an old method of poets – the art of memory – for new matters, replacing old tales of Troy with a new story of history; like Plato, he positions poetry as the common place of lovers of wisdom in all fields of study; and like Plato, he presents his fiction not as *the* truth but as a means of challenging conventional wisdom, as a method by which speakers and readers can ask questions and demand answers.

An ongoing subtext in the debate about rhetorical education, a debate in which Crassus assumes the posture of an idealist and Antonius takes the position of a realist, the art of memory speaks to the work's broader dialogue about how to remember the past for the present. Before Antonius tells the tale of Simonides and explains mnemonics, he introduces them with another tale, that of Themistocles – a story that makes his disdain for impractical philosophical learning evident. Antonius offers a mock performance of the *Phaedrus* that, in effect, reverses Socrates' tale of Theuth, his story of King Thamus' rejection of the god's gift of writing. Antonius' tale of Themistocles (a story ostensibly true but clearly apocryphal), coyly reverses Socrates' implicit rejection of artificial memory-as-writing. The storied Greek figure of Themistocles ultimately rejects the art of memory, according to Antonius, as an unnecessary aid to his already remarkable natural memory: "Among the Greeks, Themistocles the Athenian is reported to have possessed an incredible compass of understanding and genius; and a certain person of learning and singular accomplishments is said to have gone to him, and offered to teach him the art of memory, an art then first made public. When he inquired what that art could do for him, the professor replied that it would enable him to remember every thing; when Themistocles rejoined, that he would oblige him much more if he could instruct him how to forget, rather than to remember, what he chose" (171–2). The reason Themistocles rejects the art of memory is the very reason Antonius welcomes it. Themistocles may have had a memory so powerful that "nothing which had once entered his mind could ever slip out of it," but this makes him the exception that proves the rule: because all people forget, Antonius argues, we must "cultivate our memory" (172). Whether fact or fiction, he suggests that this tale tells an important truth about the human condition. "I am not possessed of such intellectual power as Themistocles had, that I had rather know the art of forgetfulness than that of memory," he remarks, and so gives thanks "to the famous Simonides of Ceos" for inventing the art of memory (186). When Antonius then describes the techniques of artificial memory as an answer to inevitable forgetfulness, he recuperates another tale of Simonides implicitly rejected by Socrates in the *Phaedrus*: the idea that painting is silent poetry, and poetry a speaking picture. As Antonius explains, "this faculty of artificial memory practice will afford" the creation of "speaking pictures" that can answer the human psyche's need for images, whether as verbal or visual pictures: "the derivation of similar words converted and altered in cases, or transferred from particulars to generals, and the idea of an entire sentence from the symbol of a single word, after the manner and method of a skillful painter, who distinguishes spaces by the variety of what he depicts" (188). Reversing Socrates' refusal of poetry and painting as equally dumb, incapable of speaking or teaching, Antonius embraces the art of memory, partly in order to emphasize that philosophy holds no place in his *real* republic.

Despite (or because of) his love of all things Greek, Crassus poses similar challenges to Plato's Academy, also defending the art of memory's role in rhetoric and education. Charging that the Greek philosophers "despised the exercise of oratory" and thus divided a once united house of knowledge by separating philosophy from rhetoric, Crassus argues that "at the head of [the] party was Socrates," who "separated in his discussions the ability of thinking wisely and speaking gracefully, though they are naturally united" (208–9). Lamenting the "destruction" caused by these "separations," Crassus vows to restore their union in the "complete orator," symbolically repairing the ruins of the past (212–13). Though famously committed to history as "the light of truth" (92),

Crassus argues that art – including the art of memory – plays a necessary role in this endeavour. "In every thing, without doubt, truth has
the advantage over imitation," he asserts, "and if truth were efficient
enough in delivery of itself, we should certainly have no need for the
aid of art" (256). But since this has never been the case, Crassus reclaims
the power of performance for oratory: "orators, who are the deliverers
of truth itself, have neglected this whole department," while "players,
who are only the imitators of truth, have taken possession of it" (256).
To describe what makes a performance artful, Crassus echoes Antonius' description of the art of memory as a "speaking picture." Listing
the disparate "tones" the orator may employ, Crassus describes them
as "presented to the orator, as colors to the painter, to produce variety"
(257). Indirectly, he compares the delivery of a memorable performance
to "the faculty of artificial memory" by virtue of their shared methods:
"the manner and method of a skillful painter," in Antonius' words, who
"distinguishes spaces by the variety of what he depicts" (188).

Crassus obliquely reminds his audience that the art of memory's use
in rhetoric as in poetry was always for the purpose of performance –
delivery, that is – and that without such art, truth itself dies, producing
only what he calls "miscarriages with regard to the commonwealth"
(260). To illustrate this, Crassus reminds his audience about the origins
of mnemonics in epic performance, and thus the connection between
rhetoric and poetry. Recollecting powerful dramatic re-enactments of
the fall of Troy – "O father, O my country, House of Priam! / . . . All
these did I behold enwrapt in flames, / And life from Priam torn by
violence" – Crassus concludes his discussion of delivery with a delivery itself, representing birth and cultural rebirth:

'Twas at the time when Paris wedded Helen
In lawless nuptials, and when I was pregnant,
My months being nearly ended for delivery
Then, at that very time, did Hecuba
Bring forth her latest offspring, Polydore. (257–8)

Yet, Crassus clarifies, an orator's "emphatic delivery" should "not [be]
imitated from the theatre and the players, but rather from the camp
and the palaestra" (258). Demonstrating how to adapt the method as
well as the matter of the poets, Crassus re-enacts a half-remembered
oration from his youth about the ruin of Rome. His partial recollection of this oration – "Whither shall I turn? To the Capitol? But that is

drenched with the blood of my brother! Or to my home, that I may see my distressed and afflicted mother in all the agony of lamentation?" (256) – also proves ironically prophetic, reframing Rome's civil strife in *On the Orator* as a repeat performance.

When Cicero interrupts the dialogue to remember a Rome "buried in ruins," he performs the role of a new Simonides, recollecting the past within the mnemonic space of writing figured as a ruined edifice, and as a mingling of fact and fiction. In so doing, Cicero expands upon his speakers' views on the art of memory from the perspective of hindsight: poetry's art of recollection allows him to negotiate the boundaries of story and history, as well as philosophy and rhetoric. Because this dramatic re-enactment cannot reconstruct the past or return the dead to life, the written dialogue itself provides a natural antidote to forgetfulness as a "reminder." The impossible fantasy of "remembering everything" (as Themistocles could) comes to the fore: Cicero longs to "retain a lively remembrance" of his heroes and to "render their fame, if I could, imperishable," but the story comes to him second hand, making his history only partly true (85). Rather than a structural problem, his confession reframes immortality as both a poetic and perpetual art of recollection. Explaining how he "shadow[s] forth" rather than reconstructs the past, he writes that "there is not any of us, when he reads the admirably written dialogues of Plato, in . . . which Socrates is represented, who does not conceive of something still greater of him about whom is written" (196). In part, this means imagining Antonius and Crassus as more complex than Cicero's representation of them. It also means recognizing Antonius' and Crassus' own self-fashioning as part of a larger aesthetic of using art to conceal art: whereas "Antonius thought that his oratory would be better received by the Roman people if he were believed to have no learning at all," Cicero explains, "Crassus desired not so much to be thought unlearned as to . . . prefer, on every subject, the understanding of our countrymen to that of the Greeks" (83). In life as in art, in other words, the impossibility of total recall or complete truth speaks to the necessity of imaginative reconstruction, a fiction-making method that allows Cicero, like Plato, to remember the past not exactly as "the light of truth" but as true nonetheless.

Like Plato, Cicero reimagines the art of memory as an art of dialogue, a show that must go on and keep changing in order to stay alive. Describing his art of making appropriate what has been appropriated from the past, he writes: "Here the recollection of an old tradition must be revived in my mind . . . a recollection not indeed sufficiently distinct, but adapted" for new times and places (7). By rewriting and re-enacting the tale of Simonides, Cicero juxtaposes the flawlessness of the architectural mnemonic with a story of that mnemonic's origin in a ruined edifice. Because he places realities of destruction and deterioration against dreams of perfection and permanence, an atemporal and abstract art of memory becomes historical and concrete – unending by virtue of its imperfection – and recollection itself the ongoing task of future readers.

*   *   *

The overlap in Virgil's and Cicero's lives and careers can make for too neat a contrast between their visions of Rome's history: whereas Virgil envisions an endless imperial Rome that symbolically repairs the ruins of Troy, Cicero portrays a republican Rome falling into ruin and continually being recollected from it. This opposition between permanent repair and perpetual recollection stands somewhere near the heart of my project, which, as I discuss above, mostly frames Virgil through his poetry's long, complex reception. Like Ovid, Virgil subjects Trojan tales to all manner of sceptical treatment and, far from portraying endless empire, instead depicts ruinous violence that ends in fragmentation. However, the tradition that established a Virgil as a Golden Age prophet and symbol of empire matters a great deal to later writers – not least of all Augustine, who by moving from his youthful passion for the *Aeneid* to the work of Cicero, as I will discuss shortly, begins his journey toward Plato and finally God. In other words, Augustine takes Virgil much as Plato takes Homer: as a common place of collective memory. But before turning to Augustine, I will briefly explore how the *Aeneid* remembers Plato's implicit complaints about poetry's underworld, even as Virgil rewrites Homeric epic. The *Aeneid* returns to the underworld as a place of memory, a mnemonic space in which to recall the past. Yet Virgil recalls not only tales of Troy for ruin and repair but also a Platonic narrative of the soul's ruin and re-edification, drawn from the *Phaedrus* and the *Republic*, thus raising issues of how story relates to history.[72]

When Aeneas encounters his father Anchises in the Elysian Fields of the underworld, he also sees a large group of souls at the shore of the "stream of Lethe," and asks who they are. Anchises replies that they are souls who will return to the world in a second body:

> When they have turned Time's wheel a thousand years,
> The god calls [them] in a crowd to Lethe stream,
> That there unmemoried they may see again
> The heavens and wish re-entry into bodies.[73]

He invites Aeneas to meet them and "take / The roster of my children's children here, / So you may feel with me more happiness / At finding Italy" (6.961–4). By "my children's children," Anchises means the entire genealogy of Roman leaders, down to the present day: all are waiting to come into the world and act out the history of Rome. A clear source for this vision of rebirth is Plato's "Myth of Er" in the *Republic*, although with crucial differences. Plato's vision of an underworld where "God is blameless" depends upon human choice, in sharp contrast to the stories of divine punishment that fill Homer's underworld, which Plato tacitly represents as lies about the gods.[74] Virgil rewrites Plato's myth so that souls are reincarnated at the command of the god who "calls in a crowd to Lethe stream" – from one perspective, correcting the blasphemy committed by Socrates. By connecting this process to Rome's great leaders, waiting for their call to duty, Virgil places the entire span of Roman history under the sign of a divine, fated plan.

Yet like Plato, Virgil also represents the underworld as a place of forgetting, challenging the truth of his own history at key points and offering a Socratic perspective on political fictions. Significantly, Virgil never has Aeneas recount his experience in the underworld, unlike Homer's representation of Odysseus-as-storyteller. And although Aeneas compares himself with Orpheus as he contemplates his descent (6.175), Virgil himself actually plays this Orphic role: as a poet able to speak with the dead, to remember the past and make it memorable, but also as an untrustworthy bard like Odysseus, telling tales of questionable value. Virgil's counter-narrative to his own fictions emerges most clearly when Aeneas departs the underworld through what appears to be the wrong door: not the Gate of Horn, "whereby the true shades pass with ease," but the Gate of Ivory, through which "false dreams are sent / . . . by the ghosts to the upper world" (6.1212, 1214–15). Virgil ironically implies that the *Aeneid's* vision of the past and future represents a fiction – a fact that will be forgotten. Like Er in the *Republic*, Virgil remembers what Aeneas (and his ancestors) may forget. Fashioning the underworld as a place of forgetting thereby serves as an indirect reminder for readers. Even as the *Aeneid* sings Caesar's praises, Virgil recalls Plato's complaints about political fictions, in the world as in history's underworld.

Augustine's *Confessions*: Recollecting History's Gold

With his *Confessions*, Augustine reforms Cicero's and Plato's arts of memory, entering into a dialogue about poetry's place in culture and extending it to the field of theology.[75] If Augustine's debt to the art of memory seems clear, precisely how it figures in his narrative remains a matter of debate. Frances Yates writes that "Augustine is not discussing or recommending the artificial memory" per se in the *Confessions*, though "it is . . . almost unconsciously implied in his explorations" and thus "raise[s] speculations as to what a Christianized artificial memory might have been like."[76] By contrast, Mary Carruthers argues that Augustine's "description of how invention occurs as an activity of *memoria* clearly belongs to the ordinary pedagogy of rhetoric" that he taught; "God is indeed beyond memory" for Augustine but also "the only way there is through and by means of it," Carruthers further suggests, and so he ultimately "gives [memory] a metaphysical twist."[77] Yet how we read Augustine depends, in part, on how we read his relationship to Cicero and Plato, or more broadly, how we read the relationship of theology to rhetoric and philosophy. Although Augustine neither believes Socrates' tall tales nor cares about the continued life of Cicero's city, his allegorical method suggests what he holds in common with these writers: a desire to replace old ideological fictions with new ways of remembering the self and society. As I argue here, Augustine seeks to supplant epic with scripture as his culture's "book of memory" and authorizes himself to play the part of a poet to do so, using stories to tell history, creating veils that unveil, appropriating the art of memory and making it appropriate to his allegory of sin and salvation, fashioning a memoir at once individual and collective. The *Confessions* represents Augustine's art of recollection as both a method and matter of memory, at once temporal and timeless, fictional as well as truthful.

On the one hand, Augustine borrows the method of poets and pedagogues alike in order to expose political fictions of divine self-fashioning, and, on the other, to reimagine the soul's edification in ways that revise common tales of collective memory.[78] But rather than transforming Virgilian epic into Christian allegory, as scholars sometimes suggest, Augustine instead produces an allegory of his soul's journey, remembering the past through pagan and Christian writing. Like Plato and Cicero, he explores the art of memory as a means of storytelling both in writing and in the world, criticizing the Trojan tales of ruin and repair – for Augustine, epitomized in Virgil's *Aeneid* as the prophecy of Rome's "empire without end" – which shaped collective memory and beliefs in late imperial Rome. Through his investigation of locational memory, Augustine returns to debates about the ideal location for memory in culture.

Augustine portrays his soul's reformation as an art of recollecting the ruins of the past. "My soul is like a house," he confesses to God at the start of his autobiography: "It is in ruins, but I ask you to remake it."[79] Like Aeneas searching for Italy, Augustine begins by searching for home – that is, the divine within. "What place is there in me to which my God can come," he asks himself, "what place that can receive the God who made heaven and earth?" (22). Yet the question of "place" extends beyond Augustine to issues of cultural edification that his allusions to epic signal. From the start, he recalls the effect of Virgil's epic on his early education: "I was obliged to memorize the wanderings of a hero named Aeneas, while in the meantime I failed to remember my own erratic ways. I learned to lament the death of Dido, who killed herself for love, while ... I was dying, separated from you, my God and my Life, and I shed no tears for my own plight" (33). A tacit competition between epic and scripture as "books of memory" frames the *Confessions*. Having misspent his youth memorizing the *Aeneid* rather than scripture, Augustine recognizes the error of his ways: he confesses that his love of poetry symbolically turned him into a ruined Troy or Carthage, causing him to forget himself without knowing it. As Augustine suggests, however, such regrets and recriminations are less personal than they might first appear.

City of God, written in the wake of the sack of Rome in AD 410, provides the clearest answer to the question of why Augustine gives the *Aeneid* such a prominent place in the *Confessions*. Explaining that Virgil "is read by boys, in order that this great poet, this most famous and approved of all poets ... may not readily be forgotten by them," Augustine suggests that his education mirrors the collective edification of imperial Rome.[80] Framed at least partly as historiography, *City of God* implicitly repudiates the *Aeneid* as an allegory of Rome's history. Here, Augustine argues that Aeneas' journey from Troy's ruins to Rome's so-called "empire without end" cannot provide a path from the City of Man to the City of God, even allegorically. Throughout *City of God*, he works to distinguish Rome's foundational fictions – the symbolic repair of Troy's ruins, the divine genealogy that authorizes this vision, the providential place of Rome in history – from its true history of ruin and conquest. Charging that Rome's real history has been concealed most perniciously by its historians, Augustine laments being "forced to bring forward these facts because their authors have not scrupled to say and write that the Roman republic had already been ruined" long before AD 410 (68–9). Exploring Rome's history as both fact and fiction, he writes: "The city of Rome . . . was first built and inhabited, as I have heard, by the Trojans, who, flying their country, under the conduct of Aeneas, wandered about without making any settlement," until arriving at Italy's shores (76). Though Augustine accepts this as ancient history, he nevertheless reminds readers of the divine fictions that pervade its reiterations, both past and present.[81] "Caesar in modern times believed no less that he was descended from Venus" – that is, through her son, Aeneas – "than the ancient Romulus believed himself to be the son of Mars," Augustine complains (76). He concludes that such divine fictions have attempted to mask Rome's true imperial history, its lust for conquest and the spoils of war. By swearing that "empire is the gift of Jove," Augustine asserts, Romans simply renamed their desire for dominion (123). After all, he asks, "What are kingdoms, but great robberies?" (112).

To define the relation between the cities of Man and God, Augustine argues against those who claim that Rome's ruin signals the end of the world, rejecting interpretations of scripture that would confirm Rome's imperial myth.[82] As Augustine implies, so-called Christian allegories of epic depend upon fictions of Rome's endless empire and its gods: Jove, Aeneas, Caesar. Because the two cities intermingle within history, he reasons that the spiritual journey cannot be understood as a movement from place to place or even from time to timelessness; in other words, souls do not move from the City of Man to the City of God like Aeneas going from Troy to Italy.[83] Rather, the journey between cities (and from ruin to re-edification) takes place not only at time's end, when the cities divide, but also *in* time. Exploring this in *On Christian Doctrine*, Augustine writes that souls "do not come to Him who is everywhere present by moving from place to place, but by good endeavor" and, in effect, edification.[84] Replacing the epic journey with a scriptural one, he describes the Israelites' exodus from Egypt, which provides his model of reading scripture (rather than epic) allegorically. "Just as the Egyptians had not only idols" detested by the Israelites, Augustine writes, "so also they had . . . gold and silver [that] the Israelites took with them" on their journey in order "to put to better use": "In the same way all the teachings of the pagans contain not only simulated and superstitious imaginings and grave burdens of unnecessary labor, which each one of us leaving the society of pagans . . . ought to abominate and avoid, but also liberal disciplines more suited to the uses of truth, and some most useful precepts concerning morals . . . [and] these are, as it were, their gold and silver" (75). Rather than rewriting the *Aeneid* as a Christian allegory, as critics often argue, Augustine invests pagan "spoils" – and implicitly, history's ruins – with a new meaning: as one basis of spiritual reformation. Still, the value of such spoils depends upon their use, as matter that can lead to either ruin or re-edification. When fashioned as idols of poetry or power, as divine rather than human, this "gold and silver" is "injuriously abused in the worship of demons" (75). He instead exhorts readers to "take this treasure . . . for the just use of teaching the gospel . . . to be converted to Christian uses" (75). Against those who insist that Athens has nothing to do with Jerusalem, Augustine affirms that all of history is divine – and so to find God means to remember the past.

Augustine's *Confessions* dramatizes the process of conversion presented in *On Christian Doctrine*, borrowing the method of the poets, the art of memory, to tell a new story of history: an allegory of his soul's journey from ruin to reformation that extends to all souls. "It was from the Gentiles that I had come to you," Augustine writes, "and I set my mind upon the gold which you willed your people to carry away from Egypt for, wherever it was, it was yours" (146). In his symbolic exodus, Augustine transports the "gold" of virtuous pagans, while remaining aware that this same gold can be used to fashion idols. Describing a spiritual alchemy by which he "converts" spoils into gold and thereby reforms his soul, Augustine recalls the path paved for him by Cicero and Plato. "The prescribed course of study brought me to a work by an author named Cicero," he writes, remembering how "it changed my prayers to you . . . All my empty dreams suddenly lost their charm and my heart began to throb with a bewildering passion for the wisdom of eternal truth" (58–9). This passion for wisdom leads Augustine to the "books of the Platonists," which teaches him to "look for truth as something incorporeal"; through these books, he writes, "I caught sight of your invisible nature, as it is known through your creatures."[85] For Augustine as for Plato, writing functions as a crucial "reminder," a spur to recollection. Taking Plato figuratively rather than literally, Augustine approves of his central spiritual insight: that divine revelation can be found through self-discovery and self-knowledge, as a process of finding God within. But to tell the truth, Augustine also lies – or rather, uses storytelling for his own ends. Answering those who might call his *Confessions* merely fictional, Augustine replies: "Although I cannot prove to them that my confessions are true, at least I shall be believed by those whose ears are opened to me by charity" (208). This confession of his Platonic method also relates to the matter of Augustine's memory, which he represents as the recollection of divine love.

Following the examples of Plato and Cicero, Augustine converts the art of memory into the method and matter of his edification, by which he builds the City of God both from and within the City of Man. Declaring that his soul stands a house "in ruins" and asking God "to remake it" (24), Augustine uses tropes of architectural mnemonics to describe his spiritual renovation:

> I rise by stages towards the God who made me. The next stage is memory, which is like a great field or spacious palace, a storehouse of countless images of all kinds which are conveyed to it by the senses . . . When I use my memory, I ask it to produce whatever it is I wish to remember . . . Some memories present themselves easily and in the correct order just as I require them . . . and as their place is taken they return to their place of storage, ready to emerge again . . . This is what happens when I recite something by heart. (214)

His search for divinity takes place within metaphors – "a great field or spacious palace, a storehouse of countless images" – that are commonplaces of the art of memory. "Whatever it is I wish to remember" can be retrieved from his memory, Augustine asserts, even as he thoroughly complicates what recollection means in this memoir: "All this goes on inside me, in the vast cloisters of my memory . . . the sky, the earth, and the sea, ready at my summons . . . everything," he adds, "except the things which I have forgotten" (215). Writing (both pagan and Christian) serves as Augustine's reminder, allowing him to recollect what he has "forgotten" yet paradoxically never experienced: the prior knowledge that is collectively remembered as history.

Augustine remembers God not simply by applying rhetorical methods to theology. Rather, like Plato and Cicero before him, he explores the limits of mnemonic techniques before radically altering the art of memory for a new place, time, and purpose.[86] Wondering whether God can "be found in the memory in the same way as Carthage, which I have seen, is present in my memory," Augustine concludes that "this cannot be the case" (227). Then asking "why do I ask what place is set aside in my memory as your dwelling, as if there were distinctions of place in the memory?", he provides an answer at once old and new: "Truly you do dwell in it," Augustine says of the divinity within his soul, "because I remember you ever since I first came to learn of you, and it is there that I find you when I am reminded of you" (231). These paradoxes point to his transformation of an art of memory in which writing – Cicero's and Plato's, as well as scripture – serves as a reminder, prompting Augustine's dialogue with divinity. In essence, Augustine's conversion turns the art of memory into an art of salvation. Indeed, his conversion experience is a reminder to read scripture. Augustine recalls hearing a voice: "Whether it was the voice of a boy or a girl I cannot say, but again and again it repeated the refrain, 'Take it and read, take it and read' . . . I stemmed the flood of tears and stood up, telling myself that this could only be a divine command to open my book of Scripture and read the first passage on which my eyes should fall" (177). In what amounts to a Christian allegory of Virgilian lots, scripture supersedes epic as Augustine's book of memory: writing by which he remembers the past and glimpses the future. Yet this moment of divine revelation also serves as a complex reminder of the art of memory's use in the art of storytelling, for Augustine's conversion experience recalls and rewrites "the story of Antony['s]" conversion: "I remembered how he had happened to go into a church while the Gospel was being read and had taken it as counsel" (177). Augustine's remembrance of Antony's turn toward scriptural study takes on a larger and more evidently literary significance in the context of *On Christian Doctrine*, where he writes that ordinary people should not "feel themselves injured by Antony, the holy and perfect Egyptian monk, who is said to have memorized the Sacred Scriptures simply by hearing them, without any training in reading, and to have understood them through prudent thinking" (4). These tales about Antony, a monk famous for his extraordinary memory, echo the tale of Themistocles in *On the Orator* and, by association, the tale of Theuth in the *Phaedrus*. Like Themistocles, Antony is an exception to the rule that people need writing as a reminder, a spur to recollection, ironically exemplifying the need to cultivate memory in all forms – written and oral, natural and artificial. In this sense, the Egyptian Antony himself represents an example of Augustine despoiling "Egyptian gold." In another sense, Antony serves as a reminder of the tale of King Thamus, whose scepticism about the truth of writing speaks to the *Confessions* as writing that should not be read as gospel truth.

Augustine offers a model for reading his *Confessions* allegorically when describing his art of recollecting scriptural poetry, for he remembers the Psalms as history writ small and large:

Suppose that I am going to recite a psalm that I know . . . my faculty of attention is present all the while, and through it passes what was the future in the process of becoming the past. As the process continues, the province of memory is extended in proportion as that expectation is reduced, until the whole of my expectation is absorbed . . . What is true of the whole psalm is also true of all its parts and of each syllable. It is true of any longer action in which I may be engaged and of which the recitation of the psalm may only be a small part. It is true of a man's whole life, of which all his actions are parts. It is true of the whole history of mankind, of which each man's life is a part. (278)

In the movement from syllable to psalm to scripture, Augustine draws an analogy between an individual's life and "the whole history of mankind, of which each man's life is a part."; The same "process" by which Augustine remembers the Psalms, and the significance of his allegorical interpretation, provides a method for reading his *Confessions* and understanding their meaning. Augustine is not just Augustine: he is Cicero's ruined Rome, Virgil's ruined Troy, Dido's ruined Carthage, Simonides' ruined banquet hall, and the ruined soul of Plato's antiquity. He is, above all, the embodiment of the soul that remembers divinity. This does not negate the temporal element of Augustine's recollection but rather reinforces it, for his spiritual reformation depends upon recollecting history. Augustine's memory "is prodigious . . . a vast, immeasurable sanctuary" ultimately because it represents not only himself but also collective memory (216).

In Augustine's poetics, the *Aeneid* marks a path he refuses to follow. Against Virgilian fictions of Rome's permanence, against Christian allegories of Virgil that make time's end contingent upon Rome's end, Augustine represents his story of history as an ongoing art of recollection and reformation. Appropriately, *Confessions* ends at the beginning, with his allegorical interpretation of the book of Genesis. Starting a journey that makes dialogue with writing both a means and an end to spiritual edification, Augustine writes that "this longing of mine does not come from a desire for earthly things, for gold and silver, precious stones and fine garments, worldly honours and power, sensual pleasures or the things which are needed for my body and for my pilgrimage through life"; rather, "The whole treasury of wisdom and knowledge . . . I seek in your books" (255). The *Confessions* continually dramatizes Augustine's process of edification, recollecting himself from ruin, a lesson gleaned from the past and held up for future imitation. Plato's story of the fallen soul and Cicero's history of a ruined Rome are remembered within Augustine's allegory of spiritual reformation. Just as Plato redefines philosophy as the appropriate place for memory, and just as Cicero recuperates the art of memory for rhetoric, so Augustine translates the art of memory into theological terms. These three writers suggest that poetry will always hold a place in the Republic because of, as well as in spite of, its critics. Like those he remembers, Augustine writes himself as a book of memory, but a work still in progress.

Dante and Petrarch: *amor summus roma*

Augustine's authority loomed large for later writers, who faced the choice of either accepting his anti-epic position or attempting to reconcile epic with scripture. Both Dante and Petrarch, albeit in very different ways, adopt and adapt the method and matter of Augustine's *Confessions* for new literary edifices, fashioning allegories of love that also represent stories of history. The palindrome *amor summus roma*, which makes remembering love equivalent with remembering Rome, is central to Dante's and Petrarch's poetry. The key differences between them lie in ruins.

Dante's poetry represents the most overt attempt to answer Augustine's critique of epic fictions within the epic itself. In a sense, Dante's entire career rewrites the *Confessions*: from his poetic conversion narrative in the *Vita Nuova*, which he calls his "Book of Memory," to *Paradise*, where Dante envisions himself as gathered into God's own book of memory.[87] *The Divine Comedy* attempts to reconcile Virgil and Augustine, human and divine love, secular and sacred writing, in part by returning the art of memory to its traditional place in poetry: to history's underworld. Refashioning the *Aeneid*, Dante returns to the Matter of Troy even as he rejects its gods, with Virgil serving as Dante the Pilgrim's guide through underworld "burial places of memory," in Ronald R. MacDonald's phrase.[88] Within this space of recollection, Dante extends Virgil's teleological vision of history from here to eternity, imagining (or reaffirming) a line from Rome's "empire without end" to time's end, to divine endless empire. In keeping with time-honoured allegorical interpretations of Virgil, Dante imagines the transmission of empire and learning, as well as the pilgrim's progress toward salvation, as a movement from ruin to repair, and he uses strategies of locational memory, places and images of the past, to remind readers of this essential pattern. Even as Dante distinguishes Rome's secular empire from the Roman Catholic Church, he nevertheless affirms the providential place of Rome within history. Dante does so, in part, by representing his own poetry theologically, specifically by rewriting Augustine's *Confessions* as an allegory of Virgil's *Aeneid*.

Dante depends upon Augustine to authorize the *Comedy's* sanctification of epic and empire – ironically, given Augustine's critique of Virgilian allegories. In *Paradise*, Augustine is one of the last figures that Dante the Pilgrim meets and his profound influence can be felt in the poem's final stanzas, which recount Dante's final vision. Whereas Augustine imagines a book of memory that is incomplete until death or time's end, Dante glimpses the entire book of memory:

> In its profundity I saw – ingathered
> and bound by love into one single volume –
> what, in the universe, seems separate, scattered:
> substances, accidents, and dispositions
> as if conjoined – in such a way that what
> I tell is only rudimentary.[89]

This vision of Revelation may represent, in a sense, the scriptural completion of Augustine's art of recollecting the ruins of the past, which he only begins to imagine in the *Confessions* by reading the book of Genesis. Like Augustine, Dante concludes by calling for a vision of future recollection and repair of all that is scattered and fragmentary in this world. But unlike Augustine, Dante implicitly seeks to grant poetry a status similar to scripture. The impossibility of fully remembering what he saw – "at such a sight, [speech] fails – / and memory fails when faced with such excess" (56–7) – admits the impossibility of poetry to fully reveal divine truth: "and so, on the light leaves, beneath the wind, / the oracles the Sibyl wrote were lost" (65–6). Yet Dante opens the possibility that his poetry is a form of divine truth. "O Highest Light," he writes:

> to my memory
> give back something of Your epiphany,
> and make my tongue so powerful that I
> may leave to people of the future one
> gleam of the glory that is Yours, for by
> returning somewhat to my memory
> and echoing awhile within these lines,
> Your victory will be more understood. (68–75)

If the "Highest Light" has heard Dante's epic apostrophe, then his writing proceeds under divine inspiration, making it – even as a vision – like scripture itself. Whereas Augustine deliberately separates the art of memory from its use in epic in order to demonstrate its importance to theology, Dante makes his epic a vehicle for divine revelation by reincorporating Augustine's journey of the reformed soul back into an epic structure. Dante thus frames his *Comedy* as a place for recollecting Augustine's complaints about epic and empire, even as he depends upon Augustine's authority in order to deify the poetry and power of Rome's empire, past and present.

Petrarch's poetic recollections of Roma and Amor in effect "ruin" what Dante has repaired.[90] Perhaps to distance himself from the anxiety of Dante's influence, Petrarch's writing remembers – or rather fashions – another Augustine, one who refuses to sanctify Petrarch's love of Laura or his laureate ambitions. In the *Secretum*, Petrarch imagines a dialogue with Augustine, who berates him for memorizing Virgil's *Eclogues* (an echo of Augustine's confession of memorizing the *Aeneid*) with a memento mori: "Pray heaven you have as many recollections of your own death . . . And good those examples are not, if their effect is to take you off the trouble of remembering how time flies, and to lead you to forget your own last hour; to the recollection of which the whole of my discourse is entirely and without ceasing directed."[91] Confessing to and even embracing perversion over conversion in the *Rime Sparse* – scattered rhymes that contrast with monumental epic – Petrarch's persona remains in ruins, even as his poetry remembers Augustine's art of memory in the *Confessions*.[92] Divided between the competing demands of God and country, this world and the next, secular and sacred loves, ephemeral and eternal immortality, Petrarch makes being of two minds, his poetic persona's notorious ambivalence, into an internal and external dialogue about how to remember the past.

Petrarch's gathers his "scattered rhymes" into a book of memory that remains incomplete, a textual edifice that lies in ruins. He treats his poetry, which he calls *ruinae*, as pieces of a mosaic that never fully coheres but that paradoxically attains immortality by virtue of this same partiality: as literary remains translated across space and time, foundational to new literary edifices. In so doing, Petrarch implies that poetry's place always lies in ruins, metaphorical and otherwise. Rejecting the fantasy of Rome's imperial permanence, he takes Ovid as his primary guide, who in his *Metamorphoses* subjects both the immortality of poetry and power to profound scepticism. "If truth at all / Is established by poetic prophecy," Ovid concludes here, "My fame shall live to all eternity."[93] Throughout his mock epic, Ovid repeatedly suggests that Rome's so-called endless empire is destined for destruction, like poetry itself; however, he also suggests that poetry, like history, survives in ruins that inevitably metamorphosize into new forms and fictions. In Ovidian fashion, Petrarch famously laments the fall of Rome's so-called "empire without end," even as he positions ruin itself (rather than its repair) as the space of immortal memory – albeit, within the limits of time and history itself.

Unlike Dante's *Divine Comedy*, Petrarch's *Rime Sparse* begins and ends with his soul in a state of disrepair. The *Rime* starts with an Augustinian confession of ruin – "You who hear in scattered rhymes . . . when I was in part another man from what I am now" – and concludes in the same vein: "help my strayed frail soul and fill out with your grace all that she lacks."[94] The circularity of his journey mirrors Augustine's own in many respects, and in a larger sense reflects the circular pattern of history that Augustine charts for poetry and power, as well as the soul, within time. Unlike Dante, Petrarch ends his poetic collection not with a vision of complete recollection at time's end, but rather with a reaffirmation of his place within time. Making death the only apocalypse for now, he closes with a paean of love to the "Virgin" who "among all earthly dwellings [was] chosen" (like Laura) to be a memorial conduit between heaven and earth (366). But, the Virgin is not God, just as Laura is no Beatrice. Petrarch thus slyly confirms his own status as a sinner to the end, a human prone to idolatry. In contrast to Dante's synthesis of epic and scripture, Virgil and Augustine, Petrarch's poetry seems irredeemably, even gleefully, unrepentant. That Petrarch remains ambivalent – divided between earthly and divine love, Roma and Amor – and thus a "failed Virgil" ultimately appears to be more a conscious aesthetic choice and rhetorical strategy than an interior, subjective state. Petrarch made space for himself artistically in ruins, ironically counterpointing Dante's vision of cultural and spiritual rebirth. If Dante did evoke in Petrarch a powerful anxiety of influence, he nevertheless responds by making such anxiety the subject of his poetry.[95] And after Petrarch, to recollect the ruins of poetry and the past was to be such an ambivalent artist, in dialogue with one's self and with many others.

Spenser's Edification in Ruins

Van der Noot's *Theatre for Worldlings*, the scene of Spenser's earliest ruins poetry, participates in the early modern reception of the art of memory tradition that I have been exploring. On the most basic level, as previously suggested, the *Theatre* can be viewed as a memory the-atre: a location for locational memory, which represents places and im-ages according to the classical rules of the art associated with the poet Simonides, credited with both discovering the art of memory and the related analogy between words and images as "speaking pictures." However, Van der Noot treats mnemonics as more than a method of composition designed to aid the reader's recollection. On a more com-plex level, his use of the art relates to matters of memory, for he tells a story of history, of ruin and repair, as an epic allegory of the reformed Church. Forecasting the impending destruction of the Roman Catho-lic Antichrist, he locates England as a place where the remains of the true church have been recollected: "Almightie God of his diuine proui-dence hath . . . raised vp diuers good and godly princes and states, and prouided certaine places, wherto the elect and faithfull haue resorted & bene preserued . . . to the ende that his holy name myght there be glori-fied . . . and his Churche dispersed, in a manner restored" (sig. A6v). He further suggests that his poetry also represents such an edifice, as a the-atre where future denizens can discover a place in the City of God. And as the Protestant Van der Noot describes the ruin of Rome's church, he reinscribes a Virgilian allegory of empire for England, ironically on "Saint Augustine's" (sig. E1v) implied authority – Augustine as recon-ceived in Dante's epic. The *Theatre*'s intricate weaving together of Vir-gilian epic and Augustinian theology falls squarely within the tradition epitomized by *The Divine Comedy*. Yet even as the *Theatre* recasts and re-enacts earlier Christian allegory for Protestants, it also reveals irrec-oncilable tensions between the imperatives of the two cities, between scripture and storytelling, and, at least in the terms articulated by Van der Noot, between poetry and power.

From one perspective, such contradictions can be observed in Van der Noot's uses of poetry. He relies upon Petrarch's and Du Bellay's ruins poetry for visual and verbal proof of impending apocalypse. Al-though their poetry provides ample evidence of ruinous falls – a "so-daine flash of heauens fire" destroys Petrarch's representation of fame, his "Laurell" tree (sig. B3v), just as Du Bellay's vision of "The auncient glorie of Romane" empire is "broken all to dust" (sig. C2v) – Van der Noot frames their poetry as apocalyptic, positioning Petrarch and Du Bellay as poets less concerned with time than its end. Van der Noot reinforces this eschatological view by moving from Petrarch's poetry of personal ruin, to Du Bellay's poetry of Rome's ruin, to Van der Noot's poetry of ruin and revelation, depicting the fall of the City of Man and the rise of the City of God. Organized in a progression from this world to the next, this poetry illustrates Van der Noot's polemical point: true "empire without end" depends upon the final ruin of Rome.

As previously suggested, this type of Protestant allegory ironically perpetuates the fiction of Rome's "empire without end" until time's end, and its place on the path to salvation. Van der Noot's *Theatre* recapitulates Dante's response to Augustine in Protestant terms, which proves problematic in the context of his polemic. England can look to itself for evidence of Rome's impending ruin, Van der Noot asserts: "Call to remembrance," he writes, "and compare this place with the haling & plucking downe of Abbays, Frieries, and other religious houses (as they cal them) in . . . *England*, and in other places, and make your accompts, that more . . . [will] surely fal" (sig. L1v). As Van der Noot argues, the destruction of Rome's church in England heralds, writ small, the final ruin of the Antichrist and time itself. Yet his example serves as an odd reminder. If readers in fact "call to remembrance" that the Tudors consolidated their political power through the wealth extracted from despoiling the Roman Catholic Church's "religious houses," then England's ruins might gesture as much to Tudor imperial ambitions than to any lesson about the inevitable ruin of all earthly empires. In effect, Van der Noot tacitly tries to have it both ways, to serve God and Mammon: in one breath he castigates worldlings who pursue "greedie desires of earthly and transitorie riches" in the "seruice of wicked *Mammon*" (sig. D8), while in another he applauds England for its "abundance of treasure, as well golde and siluer," and "trafike of all kinds of marchandise" (sig. A5v). Such contradictions reveal the central problem with fashioning poetry as divine allegory: it inevitably produces competing claims to "empire without end" in this world and the next. After all, how can the movement of empire and learning truly be reconciled with eternal power, or Gloriana's myth with *sic transit gloria mundi*?

With the *Complaints*, Spenser rejects the moral of Van der Noot's story, insinuating that the *Theatre* taught him by negative example: an allegory that half-veils its use of poetry to flatter power, to fashion empire as divine, to represent transparent political fictions as the truth. Appropriating Van der Noot's methods for other matters of memory, Spenser suggests that his poetic ruins ultimately reveal only human truths within time. Returning to and reforming the place of his own edification, Spenser rebuilds the *Theatre*, retranslating Du Bellay's and Petrarch's ruins poetry and replacing Van der Noot's poetry about Revelation with a new poem, the "Visions of the World's Vanity." By retranslating and reordering Petrarch's and Du Bellay's poetry, Spenser recovers their more complex views of ruin. In the *Complaints*, both poets appear to be resolutely anti-apocalyptic, positioning ruin as a location for examining tensions between Rome's stories and its history. Neither poet remembers Rome's empire providentially, as the "Visions" poems suggest; rather, both poets situate Rome's ruin within the cycles of history – for now, if not forever. And both sceptically examine Rome's remains as physical evidence and mythic matter, with a clear ambition to make something new of Rome's ruins rather than either rebuild or revile them. Through translation, Spenser reimagines how empire and learning translate over time and space, rooting his vision in the here and now rather than the hereafter. Reversing the order of the *Theatre*'s poetry, his moves from visions of worldly ruin, to visions of imperial ruin, to visions of human ruin as memento mori. Spenser thus constructs the *Complaints* as a new theatre for worldlings concerned with the ruins of time rather than time's end.

Spenser's addition of Du Bellay's *Les Antiquitez de Rome*, translated as *Ruines of Rome: by Bellay*, restores the bigger picture of ruin ignored by Van der Noot.[96] Spenser locates the *Ruines of Rome* at the centre of the *Complaints* because it lies at the heart of this volume and, in many respects, Spenser's poetic vision of ruin. Carefully attributing this poetry to Du Bellay in the title (even as he explores his own entitlement to these ruins), Spenser suggests how this translation represents his own poetry: that is, as the literary fragments that he incorporates into his body of writing.[97] Du Bellay's negative capability on the *topos* of ruin provides an important model for Spenser, offering a theory and practice of poetics grounded in ruin itself, the significance of which Spenser makes explicit in *The Ruines of Time*, his reply to Du Bellay's poem (discussed in chapter 3). The *Ruines of Rome* allows Spenser to dramatize his own method as a poet, for Du Bellay's ruins mark not time's end but a place for remembering the past anew.

The poem begins with a desire to speak with the dead, as Du Bellay's speaker – like a new Aeneas – beckons forth the spirit of Virgil's Rome from the depths of history's underworld. Calling to ancient Rome's "heavenly spirites, whose ashie cinders lie / Under deep ruines," Du Bellay initiates the excavation of the past that frames the *Ruines of Rome* as a whole.[98] He constructs this symbolic catabasis through an internal dialogue that explores his persona's divided responses to Rome's legacy: the promise of "empire without end" and its evident failure. Du Bellay's speaker confronts the problem that Virgil's Rome cannot be found among the ruins – "Thou stranger, which for *Rome* in *Rome* here seekest, / And nought of *Rome* in *Rome* perceiv'st at all, / These same olde walls, olde arches, which thou seest, / Old Palaces, is that which *Rome* men call" – calling Virgil to guide him through Rome's history (3.29–32). On the one hand, Du Bellay's speaker assumes the posture of a Petrarchan lover, one who laments the loss of his imperial mistress and poignantly longs to recall the dead back to life, as though "a corse drawn forth out of the tombe / By Magicke skill out of eternall night."[99] On the other hand, Du Bellay's speaker acknowledges that such rebirth is an impossible fantasy, for "The corpes of *Rome* in ashes is entombed," evidenced by the sight of its burial within its own ruins (5.65).

To be sure, Du Bellay expresses nostalgia for Virgil's Rome even as he despairs of its re-edification. But more than expressing pathos, as Thomas Greene and others have argued, Du Bellay's ambivalence functions rhetorically, reflecting the dialogic structure of the poem.[100] Indeed, the *Ruines of Rome* demonstrates how Du Bellay eagerly grapples with problems of Virgilian imitation, particularly through his imitation of Petrarch's sonnet sequence. Crucially, Du Bellay inverts Petrarch's use of the *topos* of *amor summus roma*, the palindrome that figures Rome *as* Love (and vice versa), in order to explore how Rome's ruins defy its myth of endless empire. In so doing, he unearths the subtext of Petrarch's poetry: his Amor recollects Roma's ruins as story and history. Du Bellay unveils Petrarch's allegory in order to appropriate his poetic *ruinae*, to translate them in every sense for his poetry and for France's edification. Both poets use their ambivalence – being of two minds, divided and fractured themselves – as a way to construct a dialogue (within the self and with readers) about how literary architects can make use of Rome's remains, how old methods of fiction-making can be reborn in poetry's new places.

Such ambivalence allows Du Bellay to compare Rome as a fictional and historical construct, to explore dialogically how ruin relates to translation and transmission, to imagine how history marches on. Calling Rome "The peoples fable, and the spoyle of all," Du Bellay considers Rome as both story and history in the context of its ruins: the spoils that represent Rome's former glory, both its power and poetry (7.92). As he intimates here, Rome's "empire without end" only ever existed as a historical fiction. This acknowledgment of Rome's open secret implicitly answers the poem's central questions about why Rome fell, why Virgil's vision of Rome decayed, and more broadly, why nothing lasts. Rehearsing the conventional gamut of reasons – malicious gods, jealous fate, unrelenting and undiscerning nature – Du Bellay's speaker ultimately deems all his explanations insufficient to have caused Rome's ruin:

> Nor ruthlesse spoyle of souldiers blood-desiring
> . . . Ne stroke on stroke of fortune variable,
> Ne rust of age hating continuance,
> Nor wrath of Gods, nor spight of men unstable,
> Nor thou opposd' against thine owne puissance
> . . . [nor] thy pride so much abaced. (13.171–80)

Nor does he find solace in the inevitability of mutability – "I say not, as the common voyce doth say, / That all things which beneath the Moone have being / Are temporall, and subject to decay" – despite knowing "all this whole shall one day come to nought" (9.121–6). The speaker's knowledge of end time helps to explain why Rome "should not her name and endles honour keep": because *no* earthly city endures forever, even Rome.[101] Rather than either fashioning Rome as an idol reborn, or making claims for its divine empire, Du Bellay's poetic persona instead situates Rome's fall within the larger patterns of history. By tacitly denying Rome's "endles honour," her providential place in the path to eternity, its empire instead becomes exemplary, its ruins commonplace. In so doing, Du Bellay also implies that poetry – including his *Ruines of Rome* – can reveal only the truth of history in the present tense.

Although Du Bellay's speaker begins by promising to "erect to Memorie" an immortal monument in poetry – to "sing above all moniments, / Seven *Romane* Hils, the worlds seven wonderments" – he also repeatedly suggests the ironic implications of this boast (2.24–8). Rome's "moniments" come to signify less a divide between ancient glory and modern dissolution than their common building materials, and the matter of memory that Du Bellay builds upon ("above") in his own poetic monuments. Reviving ancient Rome represents a fantasy, Du Bellay suggests, except in memory: "her brave writings, which her famous merite / In spight of time, out of the dust doth reare," though his speaker ambiguously adds, "Doo make her Idole through the world appeare" (5.68–70). These "brave writings" might suggest a means of resurrecting Rome, but not as an immortal monument that forever repairs the ruins of the past. Rather, Du Bellay concludes that Rome's ruins *will* be rebuilt (in fact are being rebuilt), not as Virgil's "empire without end" but as the "spoil of all": the matter that future poets can use for new literary edifices. So even as Du Bellay's speaker longs to reconstruct Rome "by paterne of great *Virgils* spirit divine" (25.347), he finally settles on another pattern: "These olde fragments are for paternes borne," he observes of Rome's ruins, observing as well "how Rome from day to day, / Repayring her decayed fashion, / Renewes herselfe with buildings rich and gay" – continuing on a "pouldered corse" that marks the inevitable rise and fall, life and death, of all empires (27.372–8):

> So grew the Romane Empire by degree,
> Till that Barbarian hands it quite did spill,
> And left of it but these olde markes to see,
> Of which all passers by doo somewhat pill:
> As they which gleane, the reliques use to gather,
> Which th' husbandman behind him chanst to scater. (30.415–20)

Far from performing a heroic effort, Du Bellay's speaker gleans these spoils incidentally, gathering what "th' husbandman behind him chanst to scater" to create something novel. By identifying with Rome's accidental pilgrims, he also brings the *Ruines of Rome* full circle. Du Bellay begins as a stranger seeking "*Rome* in *Rome*" – that of Virgil's fabled eternal empire – and he ends as one of the "passers by [who] doo somewhat pill" Rome's ruins metaphorically. In this way, poetry participates in a larger pattern of history and transmission of culture, one perhaps intentionally reminiscent of Augustine's notion of despoiling "Egyptian gold": the fall of empires caused by despoliation in turn produces the spoils for new cultural edifices. Such despoliation marks a historical process by which empire and learning translate, and a process that at once describes and dramatizes Du Bellay's complex use of literary ruins for his fictional construction.

In this light, Du Bellay's pathos can be seen as pragmatic: as he dismantles Rome's legacy, he authorizes his own poetry. Divided from this persona (or perhaps exploring his other half) in *Defense and Illustration of the French Language*, Du Bellay here asserts the impossibility, even absurdity, of trying to rebuild Rome, a central cliché of the Renaissance. Mocking those who attempt to reconstruct the past as though "replasterers of walls," Du Bellay warns that "not thinking on the fall of so superb edifices . . . one part becomes dust and the other must be in many pieces . . . not thinking besides that many other parts did remain in the foundations of the old walls, or being lost through the long centuries . . . coming to rebuild this construction, you will be far from restoring it to its first greatness."[102] Imitating the ancients, he argues, requires renovation. Du Bellay then ends with a half-serious call to arms: "There then, Frenchmen, march courageously upon that pious Roman city . . . Attack this lying Greece . . . Pillage without scruple the·sacred treasures of the Delphic shrine as you have done in former times" (107). Exhorting the French to despoil again, if only metaphorically, Du Bellay celebrates ruin as part of a cycle of rebirth, recollecting Rome's gold for new literary and cultural edifices.

Castiglione in England

The process by which Du Bellay's pilgrim despoils the ruins of Rome, as both an observer and a participant in history, speaks to Spenser's poetics – his own art of recollecting ruin. By inflecting this chapter with the *Complaints*, I have tried to suggest how and why Spenser remembers others' complaints about ruin as his own. I will conclude by discussing the art of memory in the context of Castiglione's *The Book of the Courtier*, a work that profoundly influences Spenser's poetics of recollection, and which brings this chapter full circle. Modelled explicitly on Cicero's *On the Orator*, *The Courtier* charts an intertextual dialogue about ruin and recollection from Plato through Petrarch mirrored in my discussion throughout this chapter. Castiglione's portrait of the art provides an ongoing frame of reference for Spenser's writing, from *The Shepheardes Calender* to *A Viewe of the Present State of Ireland*, that recalls and responds to Castiglione's dialogue by revisiting its sources for the *ars memorativa* tradition and reforming them anew.

Thomas Hoby's 1561 translation of *The Courtier* into English also symbolically translated the Italian Renaissance to English shores; such was Castiglione's reception in England, where *The Courtier* was received as a glittering ideal of urbane Italianate humanism in a country that often perceived itself as a cultural backwater.[103] Fittingly, Castiglione's journey from Italy to England provides the pretext for his absence during the four-day discussion and debate at the Court of Urbino about the education of an ideal courtier. Like Cicero before him, Castiglione begins his memorial by confessing that his recollections come second-hand. "At the time when they were debated, it was my chaunce to be in Englande, yet soone after my retourne, I heard them of a person that faythfullye reported them unto me," he explains at the start of the dialogue, promising to "endevoure my selfe, for so much as my memorye wyll serve me, to call them particularly to remembraunce."[104] In keeping "with

Plato . . . and M. Tullius [Cicero]," Castiglione endeavours to preserve the "memorye" of the "perfect Courtier" as fashioned through this dialogue (17). Castiglione's engagement with locational memory connects with the location of the dialogue, Urbino and its court. "Provoked by the memorie" of the Duchess and her courtiers, now dead or dispersed, Castilgione hopes to preserve "the memorye of so excellent a Ladye, and the rest that are no more in lief" (13). Rather than a singular ideal, the court as a whole – with all the diverse members of its collective body – creates his picture of a perfect courtier. Indeed, dialogue itself represents the ideal of courtliness that he aspires to memorialize.

The Italian wars provide a context for Castiglione's remembrance of a Golden Age now ruined, resulting in "alterations . . . brought up both of the tunge, buildinges, garmentes and maners" – and providing the raw materials that Castiglione reconstructs in memory (16). As both the partial and provisional nature of his memorial suggests, this frame tale also derives from *On the Orator*, and, I would suggest, Castiglione frames his dialogue as another new tale of Simonides. To build this symbolic edifice to edification, he appropriates Cicero's (and Plato's) old method for new matters. *The Courtier* revives the ancient art of memory in order to tell a recent story of history, but one that also recalls the history of memory. In part, Castiglione reveals this as an art of concealing art. When introducing each day of the dialogue, he addresses both his desire to reconstruct the past and its impossibility, confessing the incompleteness of his memory in ways that speak indirectly to the art of memory as an art of storytelling. In a preface to the second day, Castiglione evokes the tale of Themistocles, whose rejection of the art of memory introduces Antonius' retelling of the tale of Simonides and review of mnemonics in *On the Orator*. Complaining about the burden of memory and the weight of the past, he laments (as though Antonius himself) the tendency toward romantic nostalgia, the natural inclination to "commend the times past, and blame the times present"; because of this, he longs "to find out (as Themistocles sayth) an art to teach us to forget" (100). This inversion of Antonius' sentiment, that Themistocles' rejection of the art should not discourage others from learning it, sounds ironically throughout *The Courtier*; after all, Themistocles' supernatural natural memory represents the impossible ideal that Antonius rejects, and a mistaken idea of Platonic recollection that Cicero later corrects. Castiglione at once reveals and conceals this art's source, not least of all when he describes this as an aesthetic ideal: "I remember that . . . that there were some most excellent Oratours, which among their other cares, enforced themselves to make every man beleve that they had no sight in letters, and dissemblinge their conning, made semblant that their orations to be made very simply, rather as nature and trueth lead them, then study and arte, the whiche if had bene openly knowen, would have putte a doubt in people's minde, for feare least he beguiled them" (53–4). Alluding to Cicero's revelation of Antonius' and Crassus' self-fashioned identities, Castiglione partly draws back the curtain on his own imitative performance.

As though performing multiple roles in Cicero's dialogue, Castiglione appears to favour modernity over antiquity. Introducing Book 3, he negatively compares the "auntient antiquities" of "praise" with "the livinge conversation of such as times past excelled in that Court" at Urbino (209), while again denying that his attempt "to defende this famous memorie from mortall oblivion" and "make it live in the mindes of our posteritie" can reconstruct the past (210). Just as Cicero argues that the character of Socrates in Plato's dialogues must represent only part of the picture, so Castiglione asserts that readers should remember to "conceyveth a certain greater opinion of them that are written upon, then it appeareth in those bookes can expresse" (210). More than a conventional expression of ineffability, such sentiment points the way to Book 4, where he most fully embodies the role of a new Cicero and Simonides. Interrupting the dialogue, Castiglione announces that "bitter . . . remembraunce [of] worldlie miseries" causes him to "remember that not long after these reasoninges where had, cruell death bereved our house" of certain interlocutors (292). Asserting that "trulye there never issued out of the horse of Troy so many great men . . . as there have come menne out of this house," Castiglione nevertheless clarifies that this dialogue represents a new story of history rather than ancient myth, and that Urbino's ruins – rather than Troy's – represent the symbolic space of his art of recollection (292).

Castiglione reproduces the shadow-box structure of *On the Orator* within *The Courtier* by recalling and repositioning Plato's *Phaedrus* and *Symposium* in the dialogue's conclusion. In the context of a debate about how a courtier ideally should advise and thus edify a prince, the interlocutors take up the topic of "temperance" in ways that return to the *Phaedrus'* central debate about love, a discourse whose only semi-veiled subtext relates to relationships of power. When an interlocutor complains that "the beautye of women is many times cause of infinit evilles in the worlde, hatred, warr, mortality, and destruction, wherof the rasinge of Troye can be a good witnesse," the poet-cum-courtier Peter

Bembo replies with a re-enactment of Socratic storytelling. Because "beawtie . . . is a holy thinge," he warns, so "any of us as prophane and wicked shoulde purchase him the wrath of God" and "lose . . . their sight, as Stesichorus did" for his dispraise of Helen (346–7). In what follows, Bembo reframes their dialogue about love, describing how "beawtie commeth of God," and echoing Socrates' love stories in the *Phaedrus* and *Symposium* (347). "Let him turn within himself to contemplate what he sees with the eyes of the mind," Bembo exhorts, describing how "remembraunce" causes the soul to ascend to heaven:

> Therfore the soule rid of vices, purged with the studye of true Philosophie . . . throughe the perticular beawtye of one bodye he guydeth her to the universall beawtue of all bodies: evenso in the last degree of perfection throughe perticular understandinge he guideth her to the universall understandinge. Thus the soule kindled in the most holye fire of true heavenlye love, fleeth to coople her selfe with the nature of Aungelles . . . And [thus] severed from oure selves, may be chaunged like right lovers into the beloved, and after we be drawen from the earth, admitted to the feast of the aungelles, where fed with immortall ambrosia and nectar, in the ende we maye dye a most happie and livelye death, as in times past died the fathers of old time. (357–8, 361)

When the other interlocutors laugh at his description of bodiless bliss and point out that "the way . . . that leadeth to this happines is so stiepe" that it would "be harde to gete up for men, but unpossible for women," they gesture to the underlying point of the performance, suggesting their understanding of *sprezzatura* (362). Bembo's palinode ultimately speaks to power, and indirectly to his own political theory. Having just already expressed a preference for the greater freedom and justice of republican rule over that of monarchy, Bembo's imitation of Plato represents art that simultaneously reveals that which it conceals: an argument against idolatry, in poetry or politics. In another sense, Bembo recalls Socrates' method as well as his matter, implying that just as a courtier can be a poet, so a poet can be a courtier, and that both can be philosophers.

The dialogue ends by emphasizing precisely what makes this rewriting and re-enactment of Plato novel: the possibility of female power, represented in *The Courtier* through Elizabeth Gonzago, the Duchess of Urbino, who rules (if only symbolically) in the place of the ailing and absent Duke. When debating the question of whether women are capable of such divine love, Bembo is reminded that "Socrates him selfe doeth confesse that all the misteries of love which he knew, were oped unto him by a woman, which was Diotima," and to "remembre moreover that S. Mari Magdalen had manye faultes forgeven her, bicause she loved much: and perhappes with no lesse grace then Saint Paul" (363). These remarks mark the end of the dialogue, with the promise to find "manye other" such examples unfulfilled, but it also marks the beginning of a conversation clearly intended to be continued (363). From another perspective, though, this conversation has been taking place all along. Castiglione dedicates *The Courtier* to the memory of the Duchess, and on more than one occasion suggests that she herself embodies the ideal courtier – even if he frames this (as Bembo does, unsurprisingly) in blatantly idolatrous terms.

Spenser himself continues this dialogue throughout his writing, raising the subtext of Castiglione's work to new levels: specifically, the reality of female power and the role of the poet-courtier in edification of princes and readers alike. In effect, Spenser's writing repeatedly translates *The Book of the Courtier* and its vision of cultural *translatio* into English (and within his own book of memory), drawing upon its portrait of poetry and power, emulating its method of memorializing for other matters, places, and times: for another Elizabeth and for England. As a would-be courtier-poet himself, Spenser lavishes Elizabeth with encomiastic poetry and yet takes this issue of idolatry-as-flattery seriously throughout his career, pursuing the problem of fashioning love poetry idolatrously (rather than temperately) in the context of stories of the soul from Plato to his present day, most notably in Alma's allegorical Castle of the Soul. In so doing, he extends Castiglione's dialogue about self-fashioning, reading *The Courtier* not as a guide to performing the part of an ideal courtier (a commonplace interpretation), but rather as an ideal representation of dialogue about the edification of the self and others, of princes and ordinary people. *The Courtier* marks one starting point for Spenser as he explores the place of poetry in culture: its ability to remember the past, to shape the present, to create a space for conversation.

My principal intention in this chapter has been to show the complexity of Spenser's edification in matters of memory: the broad range of methods available to him, the complex reception histories of his models, and the depth and scope of a dialogue in which Spenser sought to include himself. Moving from Spenser's edification to his literary edifices, the chapters to follow will further explore the materials discussed here: Castiglione, Plato, Cicero, and Petrarch in the context of *The Shepheardes Calender*; Augustine and Dante in the context of *The Faerie Queene*; Du Bellay in the context of *The Ruines of Time* and the *Complaints* volume as a whole. I will discuss other significant intertexts, Sidney's *Apology for Poetry* and Chaucer's *House of Fame*, as the signal texts of the English art of memory tradition that Spenser sought to continue. More than context for Spenser, such writing represents the matter he appropriates, takes and makes his own, in his double life as colonial and career poet. Throughout his writing, Spenser remembers and rewrites a history of the art of memory in all its varied conceptions, as translation, despoliation, conversion, reformation, re-edification, and recollection – and as ruins.

Chapter Two

The Death of the "New Poete": Ruin and Recollection in *The Shepheardes Calender*

Critics working in the field of English Renaissance literature have often celebrated Spenser's pastoral poetry as the birth of a sacred cow: a new Virgil for a renewed era. Why is not surprising – after all, Spenser seemingly names himself as such in *The Shepheardes Calender*. His first character-cum-critic, E.K. (whose scholarly introduction and glosses play a crucial part in the fiction), begins by christening the anonymous author with a name he deems more worthy of fame than Spenser's pseudonym, "Immeritô." What "so very well taketh place in this our new Poete," E.K. writes in the opening "Letter to Harvey," is the "worthines of the Roman Tityrus Virgile."[1] Thus endowed with Virgilian authority, Spenser could embody an entire nation's cultural aspirations, becoming a spokesman for some dearly held truths about what the very word "renaissance" means: a desire for cultural rebirth, to repair the ruins of the past in poetry – that is, to emulate Virgil. Yet *The Shepheardes Calender*, though a work intended to launch the career of the "new Poete," instead ironically explores the anxiety of Virgil's influence. More than expressing ambivalence about this literary inheritance, the *Calender* radically reforms the architecture of immortality by locating poetry's "place" not in monuments of either epic or empire but in ruins. As I argue, Spenser's poetry pursues the issue of edification, what it means to build a house of fame from the ruins of time, by recollecting a dialogue about the art of memory from Plato to his present. In so doing, Spenser's inaugural collection challenges the idea that England needs a new Virgil to usher in a new era, positioning the fantasy of renaissance itself as the central subject of this remarkably self-conscious work.

For not a few reasons, Spenser's *Calender* marked a strange debut on the English literary stage. This calendric collection of bucolics with its illustrative rough woodcuts adapted a popular medieval form that made it appear neither very old nor very new, as did its accompanying critical apparatus, a series of glosses by the professorial E.K., whose commentary attempted to cover the *Calender* with the patina of antiquity it otherwise lacked. Despite clear evidence of Spenser's catholic tastes and medieval influences, E.K.'s assertions of the *Calender's* Virgilian ambitions have historically dominated interpretation of this work; indeed, critics have often echoed these claims for Spenser's fame. "It is part of the fiction of *The Shepheardes Calender* that E.K.'s glosses and commentary are not part of the fiction," Michael McCanles writes, neatly encapsulating the work's reception history: "this fiction's success shows it to have been through the centuries a kind of *trompe l'oeil*, since editors, critics, and readers have usually taken it for the real thing."[2] Although this is no longer the case, E.K.'s desire to construct Spenser as England's new Virgil continues to speak to critical assumptions – not least of all, the belief that Virgil's example represented the necessary (perhaps the only) path to literary immortality and laureate renown – while also illuminating how Spenser's poetry challenges them.

How E.K. and the shepherds remember Virgil speaks, above all else, to his complex historical reception. Spenser's engagement with the poet's legacy is considerably more nuanced than that of his characters, and by constructing the *Calender* as a pastoral place for debate and dialogue about epic authority, he draws attention to the multiple Virgils available for literary imitation. But for E.K., as for the shepherds, Virgil is only the poet of epic. They focus on the idea of the Virgilian *rota*, the career trajectory whose most important point they locate as its end: the cultural and literary immortality promised in the *Aeneid* as the translation of Troy's ruins into "empire without end." E.K. introduces the *Calender* by strenuously arguing that Spenser's poem effects just such a translation, repairing ruinous old words into an immortal literary monument, erecting a house of fame for himself and England. However, the fluctuating manner by which E.K. describes Spenser's archaic language – at times as authoritative antiquities, at other times as undignified remains – speaks to the *Calender's* insistent questioning of its own Virgilianism. As this chapter argues, E.K.'s struggle to construct Spenser's authority in Virgilian terms – and his failure to accomplish this effort – enacts the *Calender's* central drama: a dialogue between E.K. and Spenser about *how* to remember the ruins of the past. The central issue of this dialogue concerns less Virgil per se than the varied uses – poetic, pedagogic, and political – of Trojan stories.[3] Thus even as the shepherds and E.K. look for a new Virgil to repair England's ostensible cultural ruin, Spenser looks to dialogue – specifically, I will argue, a dialogue about the art of memory – to create a place for poetry in English culture. Far from reconstructing a fiction of permanence, the *Calender* locates immortality in the space of ruin.

How *The Shepheardes Calender* examines fantasies of renaissance and their association with Virgil is suggested in the fuller context of E.K.'s opening remarks about the "new Poete": "Uncouthe unkiste, Sayde the olde famous Poete Chaucer: whom for his excellencie and wonderfull skil in making, his scholler Lidgate, a worthy scholler of so excellent a maister, calleth the Loadestarre of our Language: and whom our Colin clout in his Aeglogue calleth Tityrus the God of shepheards, comparing hym to the worthines of the Roman Tityrus Virgile. Which proverbe . . . as in that good *old Poete* it served well Pandares purpose, for the bolstering of his baudy brocage, so very well taketh *place* in this our *new Poete*" (13, my emphasis). With rhetorical sleight of hand, E.K. provides a Procrustean interpretation of "uncouthe, unkiste." This proverb, taken from Chaucer's *Troilus and Criseyde* (though only remembered half correctly), works to substitute the "new Poete" for the "old Poete" as England's Virgil. Whereas Colin suggests that England has already found (and lost) its answer to Virgil in Chaucer, E.K. evokes Chaucer precisely – paradoxically and perversely – in order to erase his influence. Instead, E.K. reasons, if Chaucer is called "Tityrus the God of shepheards," and if Colin compares him to "the Roman Tityrus Virgile," then Spenser (in some strange equation) also equals Virgil. The point is re-emphasized in E.K.'s gloss on Colin's name in *Januarye*: "Under which name this Poete secretly shadoweth himself, as sometime did Virgil under the name of Tityrus" (33). Throughout his commentary on the *Calender*, E.K. ignores or elides the ways that Spenser emulates "the olde famous Poete" Chaucer in order to construct the "new Poete" as comparable to "the worthines of the Roman Tityrus Virgile" (13). Crucially, though, Colin never connects the two Tityruses. Rather, E.K. does so on his own authority, placing himself in an analogous role to Lydgate as the "scholler" champion of a poet. Does E.K. mean to suggest that the "old" and "new" poets are both panderers, selling themselves in order to be known and loved rather than "uncouthe, unkiste"? Probably not. Writ small, though, this demonstrates the amusing ways that he continually denies Chaucer's central role in the *Calender*, attempting – albeit in vain – to reframe the medieval elements of this work as classical and as specifically Virgilian.

E.K. persistently misreads the *Calender*, evidenced in his anxiety about Chaucer's influence, and such misprisions lie at the heart of Spenser's dialogue in this witty yet serious investigation of literary authority. Scholars have long observed that Chaucer stands as Spenser's primary model of authorship and authority in *The Shepheardes Calender*; as John Watkins observes, "shifting conceptions of Virgilian authority are a function of shifting constructions of Chaucer as a principal mediational influence."[4] The significance of Chaucer's location in the poem, I will argue, relates to his novel treatment of locational memory in *The House of Fame*. *The Shepheardes Calender* remembers a history of the art of memory in which *The House of Fame* represents the culmination of a native tradition upon which Spenser builds and through which he reforms Italian influences. Castiglione's *The Courtier* also provides an important model for the *Calender*, initially as a source of E.K.'s defence of the "new Poete's" unorthodox style for a would-be court poet. More significantly, Spenser both appropriates and alters *The Courtier*'s two primary intertexts – Cicero's *On the Orator* and Plato's *Phaedrus* (as well as *Symposium*) – in order to explore the question of poetry's place, and poetry's relationship to power, as matters of memory. Through Chaucer, *The Shepheardes Calender* translates Castiglione into English, so to speak, reshaping the art of memory for a new time and place.

The first part of the chapter considers how *On the Orator* and the art of memory therein inform E.K.'s "Letter to Harvey" (and in ways that reflect Harvey's own "Letters to Spenser"). As discussed earlier, Cicero's dialogue rewrites the art of memory as a novel story of Rome's history, its ongoing ruin and recollection; for Cicero, as for Spenser, this tale serves to frame the work itself as a ruined edifice, a place in which the pastoral dialogue is recollected. The second part of the chapter considers how, just as Cicero's speakers re-enact the dialogue of Plato's *Phaedrus*, so Spenser's characters also re-enact this seminal dialogue about love. Platonic love holds a centrally important place in all of these works, for Plato transforms the art of memory in radical ways, using it not to remember old tales of Troy's ruin but to recollect new tales of love – and to tell a new story about what edifies both individually and collectively. As I argue, the *Calender* explores architectural mnemonics as a decidedly un-Virgilian method for remembering the ruins of the past. Rather than locating fame in the symbolic repair of Troy's or Troynovant's ruins, Spenser fashions poetic immortality as an ongoing art of recollecting ruin.

"O pierlesse Poesye, where is then thy place?":
The Anxiety of Virgil's Influence

The desire to locate a new Virgil for English culture, and the anxiety that no such author exists to fill Virgil's place, finds expression throughout *The Shepheardes Calender*. E.K. introduces the "argument" to the *October* eclogue as indirectly concerning the problem of Virgilian imitation, writing that "In Cuddie is set out the perfecte paterne of a Poete, which finding no maintenaunce of his state and studies, complayneth of the contempte of Poetrie" (170). Although E.K. ostensibly uses the phrase "perfecte paterne of a Poete" to refer to Cuddie, its importance lies in the ideal of authorship it represents – that is, a Virgilian ideal. By contrast to Virgil, the shepherds believe they write in the wrong genres, sing of the wrong muses, and live at the wrong time. Cuddie and Piers rehearse clichés of authorship, debating whether poetry is "a divine gift and heavenly instinct," or "to bee gotten by laboure and learning," or "adorned with both" inspiration and erudition (170). While disputing whether women or wine best inspires song, the shepherds can nevertheless agree on one point – poetry's woeful decline since its Golden Age in antiquity. The current "contempte of Poetrie" (55) has produced no new "Romish *Tityrus*" for England. Piers punningly describes poetry's sad state:

> O pierlesse Poesye, where is then thy place?
> If nor in Princes pallace thou doe sitt:
> (And yet is Princes pallace the most fitt)
> Ne brest of baser birth doth thee embrace.
> Then make thee winges of thine aspyring wit,
> And, whence thou camst, flye backe to heaven apace. (79–84)

Far from an isolated concern, Piers' complaint that England's orphaned and impoverished poetry can find a "place" in neither palace nor pub articulates *The Shepheardes Calender*'s central concern with the problem, and process, of situating poetry in English culture.

E.K.'s catchy alliterative phrase, "the perfecte paterne of a Poete," encapsulates Cuddie and Piers' expectations about poetry, exemplifying their mutual construction of authorship through Virgil's authority – an ideal whose influence pervades the *Calender*. Both Cuddie and Piers optimistically imagine that the right poet could build a place for poetry, housing it, repairing what the shepherds perceive as England's state of cultural ruin. Virgil's example proves crucial here because it provides all of their hopes and fears about poetry: their passionate conviction that poetry should rightly inhabit the architecture of power, the "Princes pallace," and their accompanying belief that the peerless poet occupies the position of heroic architect, one capable of constructing a monumental literary edifice. Both remember Spenser's poetic persona, Colin, as someone with the potential to play or perform Virgil's part in culture, suggesting that "*Colin* fittes such famous flight to scanne" in the same way that poetry's "place" is in "Princes pallace the most fitt" (88, 81). Yet Piers and Cuddie further concur that Colin, because distracted by love (or, more accurately, by the wrong kind of love), fails to fulfil this vital authorial role. Mired in hopeless Petrarchan romance and the love lyrics it provokes, Colin rejects the pressure to move on to epic poetry and thus, according to Cuddie and Piers, damns his chances at lasting fame. Without following Virgil's career path from pastoral to epic, Colin holds little hope of fulfilling what, to Piers and Cuddie, constitutes poetic perfection: Virgil's "paterne."

But a still more important issue remains at stake, one submerged within this authorial paradigm: how the shepherds imagine Virgil's "paterne" of cultural and imperial transmission, *translatio imperii et studii*. Piers suggests the significance of epic poetry when exclaiming, "There may thy Muse display her fluttrying wing, / And stretch her selfe at large from East to West" (43–4). The movement from East to West exemplified by Virgil's epic, which charts the imaginary path for the translation of empire and learning, suggests to Cuddie and Piers the path by which an imperial poet builds a house of fame for himself and his culture. Their inability to reconstruct Virgil's career in their pastoral world fills them with a powerful sense of belatedness and fin-de-siècle cultural decay. But if these shepherds cannot recognize their part in fashioning a place for poetry and Colin's house of fame, the very fact of their dialogue suggests that "poesye" cannot be not entirely "pierlesse," for they represent at least a small community of friends concerned with poetry's ostensible decline into oblivion. Through dialogue, indeed through the very fact of dialogue, Spenser mediates Cuddie and Piers' polarized perspectives on the past and the present: on the one hand, their impossibly idealistic conception of authorial construction and, on the other hand, their equally pessimistic notion of England's own lack of cultural edification. Their dialogue ultimately suggests how the *Calender* takes Virgil's authority as a cultural commonplace, positioning Virgil less as a guide than as a subject of debate.

In a sense, the *Calender* presents itself as a kind of literary case study for how readers respond to Virgil's legacy, especially the belief that Renaissance writers necessarily sought to reconstruct the ruins of the past according to his "perfecte paterne" of antiquity. Describing the humanist's desire to emulate Virgil as residing in "the paired intuitions of rupture and continuity," Thomas Greene writes that ruins necessarily produced a desire to rebuild the past, that ruins "inspired a will to form" because "to see the fragments was already instinctively to see how they had been or might be made whole"; he portrays this response to ruin as a "double gesture," by which "one first stoops, digs, gropes downward into the disorder of the past and then one rises and constructs upward by imitation."[5] But this impossible effort inevitably leads to failure, Greene also observes: "Renaissance culture is full of the failures resulting from the double phases of imitation . . . failures that in a sense justify the fear it inspired."[6] Understood this way, the ambivalence produced by ruin and its association with imitation – where optimistic ambition and pessimistic despair collided with paralysing uncertainty – inevitably leads to Virgil as the hallmark of imitative success or failure. Greene concludes that "personal adaptations" of the "double gesture" are only "distortions of the pattern" which authors followed, but these differences in patterns matter.[7] To explore the kind of creative imitation that Greene seeks means considering both how authors examined the anxiety of Virgil's influence and sought to make new "places" for themselves within the space of ruin. As Richard Helgerson argues, "Though Spenser was called "our Virgil" and Sidney "the English Petrarch," he observes, "neither much resembles his presumed model."[8] Rather, "each presents himself in opposition to a set of contemporary expectations – expectations similar enough to those against which Virgil and Petrarch presented themselves to make these earlier poet usable, but different enough to alter significantly the resulting pattern."[9] Through his characters' fixation with Virgil's "paterne," Spenser examines the anxiety that Virgil's paternal presence evokes in the shepherd world and, presumably, in Renaissance England. *The Shepheardes Calender* undermines the expectation that Virgil's career pattern (and paternal authority) represented the path that a poet seeking fame had to follow, and in the process seeks out other patterns of authorship to imitate.

Through dialogue about imitating Virgil's "paterne," Spenser explores the problem of pursuing permanence as either a literary or an imperial ideal. Nostalgically, the *Calender*'s inhabitants imagine building

immortality in exclusively Virgilian terms. While the apparent irre-
trievability of the past frustrates them, Spenser answers their ambivalence in a surprising way: with another vision of Rome's ruin. Turning
from the shepherds' debate about finding a "new Poete" who can fill
Virgil's place in England, I will trace E.K. and Spenser's dialogue about
the architecture of immortality in the introductory "Letter to Harvey."
Here, E.K. attempts to fashion the "new Poete" according to Virgil's
"perfecte paterne of a Poet" by evoking another "paterne" of authority
in Cicero's "paterne of a perfect Oratour" (15). The differences in these
phrases matter, for a "perfecte paterne of a Poete" implies that a poet
achieves perfection through a specific pattern, while "a paterne of a
perfect Oratour" leaves open the question of whether there is just one
pattern of perfection. These competing "paternes" exemplify Spenser
and E.K.'s tacit debate about authority, I argue, because they recall an
intertextual dialogue about the art of memory.

Broadly, E.K.'s epistle remembers the art of memory's use from Cicero to Castiglione, reflecting Spenser's early and continued interest in
the art of memory. Spenser's "Letter to Harvey" resembles Harvey's
own published Letters to Spenser – appropriately, given his fascination with, and study of, Cicero and Castiglione.[10] Harvey's arch and
artificial epistles are studded with allusions to rhetoric broadly and the
art of memory specifically. Harvey's first letter begins with reference to
the art: "*Immeritô*, in good soothe my poore Storehouse will affourd me
nothing" as much as your "large, lavish, Luxurious, Laxative Letters,"
but "I shall be faine to supplye the office of the Arte Memorative, and
putte you in minde of a pretty Fable in *Abstemio*"; and Harvey's last
letter ends with another elliptical allusion to the art: "But, see, how I
have the *Arte Memorative* at commaundement ... I had once againe nigh
forgotten your *Faerie Queene*."[11] On another level, E.K.'s epistle can be
read as a parodic misreading of *The Book of the Courtier*. In his introductory letter to this work, Castiglione defends the dialogue against those
who would say "it is so hard a matter and (in a manner) impossible to
finde out a man of such perfection, as I would have the Courtier to be":
"To these men I answere," he writes, "I am content to err with Plato ...
and M. Tullius [Cicero]," who created "the Idea or figure conceyved in
imagination of a perfect commune weale ... and of a perfect Oratour ...
so is it also of a perfect Courtier."[12] With E.K.'s epistle, Spenser indirectly extends this dialogue to the pursuit of the "perfecte ... Poete," at
once recalling Castiglione's primary source, Cicero's *On the Orator*, and
translating it, in a variety of respects, into English. Although Castiglione

embraces this ideal as a matter of dialogue and debate, as well as multiplicity over unity, E.K. takes the idea literally. He reads Castiglione, so to speak, as a how-to manual for would-be courtiers in search of patronage and preferment, fashioning the "new Poete" according to a clichéd "perfecte paterne of a Poete": as a flattering Virgilian poet who deifies English epic and Elizabethan empire. Spenser corrects his comic creation's ambitions, in part, by letting *The Courtier* speak for itself. As though addressing E.K.'s paired patterns of poetic and rhetorical authority, Castiglione's interlocutor mocks defences of style (like E.K.'s defence of the "new Poete's" style) that depend upon authorities about whom they know little: "Manye will judge of styles . . . [who] have small understanding in it, and praise Virgil and Cicero, because they heare them praised of many, not for that they knowe the difference betwene them" (73–4).

Relatedly, Spenser makes light of E.K.'s desire for England's cultural rebirth by having the introductory letter to the *Calender* echo Thomas Hoby's introductory epistle to his English translation of *The Courtier*.[13] Hoby laments the absence of an English renaissance – "(I knowe not by what destinye) Englishemen are muche inferiour to well most all other Nations" (6) – while insinuating that his translation may effect just such a desired *translatio imperii et studii* from Italy to England. Speaking against those who argue that translations "hurteth memorie and hindreth learning," Hoby asserts that "to be skilfull and exercised in authours translated, is no lesse to be called learning" (6). Despite the "rudeness" of his style – a problem he attributes to the English language itself – Hoby hopes that his translation of *The Courtier* will mean that "we alone of the worlde maye not bee styll counted barbarous in our tunge . . . And so shall we perchaunce in time become as famous in Englande, as the learned men of other nations have ben and presently are" (8, 7). Spenser clearly agrees with Hoby that *The Courtier* "is become an Englishman," and with the *Calender* he remakes this work – though not in E.K.'s image (3). More than a parody, E.K.'s letter recalls Castiglione's *Courtier* in order to return to their common source in Cicero's *On the Orator*, creating a multilayered dialogue about how style relates to memory and how both speak to poetry.

The "perfecte paterne of a Poete" and the "paterne of a perfect Oratour'

E.K.'s "Letter to Harvey" attempts to place new wine in an old bottle, portraying Spenser not simply as a soon-to-be-famous poet but more portentously as England's new and improved Virgil. Investing Spenser with a heroic model of authorship, the same authorial pattern that Cuddie and Piers chart for Colin in *October*, E.K. devotes the better part of his commentary to the sometimes explicit, sometimes implicit argument that Spenser has followed the "perfecte paterne of a Poete" in composing his inaugural work. And where Colin may fall short of expectations, E.K. implies that the "new Poete" himself succeeds brilliantly.[14] More than filling a vacant seat of authorship, he argues that Spenser has built a place for English poetry with the *Calender*. Like Cuddie and Piers, E.K. describes literary authority in monumental terms, intimating that it requires the kind of edifice that Virgil's epic fashioned for Rome.

The juxtaposition of E.K.'s opening and closing commentaries makes such architectural ambitions (and Spenser's response to them) apparent. Indeed, perhaps the best introduction to this character's place in *The Shepheardes Calender* lies in his departure from it. E.K.'s triumphant final commentary ironically glosses a missing emblem – a blank space at the end of *December*'s eclogue where Colin's last words should be – and thereby creates an intriguing paradox: an assertion of Spenser's poetic immortality in the absence of his (or, indeed, any) actual poetry. Inadvertently, E.K. praises the non-existent emblem as a poetic monument:

> The meaning whereof is that all thinges perish and come to theyr last end, but workes of learned wits and monuments of Poetry abide for ever. And therefore Horace of his Odes a work though ful indede of great wit and learning, yet of no so great weight and importaunce boldly sayth.
> Exegi monimentum aere perennius,
> Quod nec imber nec aquilo vorax etc.
> Therefore let not be envied, that this Poete in his Epilogue sayth he hath made a Calendar, that shall endure as long as time etc. folowing the ensample of Horace and Ovid in the like. (212)

The breezy tone and facile manner with which E.K. offers Spenser a classical pedigree, a genealogy of poetic immortality, marks this allusive claim as somehow inevitable. Directing readers to *December*'s vacant emblem (whatever it said prior to its mysterious disappearance), E.K. contends that the "new Poete" has been "folowing the ensample of Horace and Ovid" in staking his final claim to fame. Yet E.K.'s attempt to avert "envie" about such authorial boasts ultimately appears less an offer of literary context than a pretext for him to brag as well.

While this passage concludes E.K.'s critical annotations, it also affords us a glimpse at his foundational assumptions. With this comparative reading, E.K. conceals differences behind "etc's," portraying Spenser's ostensible declaration that "he hath made a Calender, that shall endure as long as time" as a mere reconstruction of Horace's claim to having "built a monument more lasting than bronze" (212). This interpretation, the "meaning" E.K. sees in the Horatian formulation, constitutes a clear inverse relation between material ruin and memorial survival: "all thinges perish and come to theyr last end, but workes of learned wits and monuments of Poetry abide for ever," which to E.K. presumably means that literary edifices memorialize best because they never fall to ruin. Though he clearly intends to fashion the *Calender* as an immortal monument, as Spenser's house of fame, E.K.'s interpretive elisions and omissions confer upon the *Calender* a status that the work itself then complicates. The absence of Colin's emblem, in other words, offers a further commentary on E.K.'s commentary. Since the promise of permanence forms the premise of poetic immortality, the missing words paradoxically undercut the work's claim to endurance, intimating that the *Calender* has fallen into the very state of ruin that E.K. claims it transcends. The *Calender*'s immortality is profoundly contradicted by its textual context (or lack thereof), yet this empty space on the page provides an important perspective on E.K himself. Readers can see him interpretively "fill in the blank," constructing Spenser's authority according to E.K.'s own desired pantheon.

The tension here, between judging the *Calender* as an immortal monument while conceding its ruinous appearance, forms the crux of E.K.'s strange defence of Spenser's poetry. E.K. at once asserts that Spenser built his literary monument by imitating Virgil's authorial pattern, repairing the ruins of the past, and attempts to reconcile this claim with the pervasive presence of ruin in the *Calender*. His vast ambitions for Spenser encompass reconstructing what he perceives as the linguistic and literary rotting of England's cultural fabric. Announcing that the *Calender* marks only the pastoral beginning of Spenser's Virgilian career path, he argues that Spenser "follow[s] the example of the best and most auncient Poetes, which devised this kind of wryting, being both so base for the matter, and homely for the manner, at the first to trye theyr habilities" (18). Spenser's "homely" origin in the pastoral is merely the start of something epic, because, as E.K. explains, "as young birdes, that be newly crept out of the nest, by little first to prove theyr tender wyngs, before they make a greater flyght . . . So flew Virgile, as

not yet well feeling his winges" (18). While directing this accomplish-
ment more to the future than the present, he implies all the same that
Spenser has already achieved his Virgilian ambitions.

However, much of E.K.'s preoccupation with the architecture of immortality involves his anxiety that the *Calender*, far from meeting this
restorative ideal, remains in ruins. This apparent conflict, between
wanting to introduce Spenser as England's new Virgil and sensing that
Spenser performs his role incorrectly, plays out in E.K.'s linguistic analysis of the *Calender*. Behind E.K.'s eagerness to inaugurate Spenser's
fame lurks an apprehension about the "new" poet's use of "old" language. If Spenser's Chaucerian language seems decidedly unclassical,
E.K. nevertheless attempts to portray it as such. Yet clear reservations
about Spenser's liberal use of old words, words that E.K. describes as
ruins, shape his introduction – even though he presents these doubts
as those of Spenser's audience. Anticipating readers' anxieties about
Spenser's antiquated language thus forms the critical role that E.K.
fashions for himself.

To defend Spenser's unorthodox style, E.K. asserts that his "old"
words have reconstructed England's decaying language, which E.K.
describes as a ruined edifice: "our Mother tonge, which truely of it self
is both ful enough for prose and stately enough for verse, hath long
time ben counted most bare and barrein of both . . . when as some ende-
voured to salve and recure, they patched up the holes with peces and
rags of other languages, borrowing here of the french, there of the Italian, every where of the Latine, not weighing how il, those tongues ac-
corde . . . with ours" (16). Previous authors "patched up the holes" of
the English language with "peces and rags of other languages," which
resulted not in a restored linguistic edifice but one, as E.K. puts it, with
a "disorderly and ruinous" appearance (15). Complaining that earlier
authors "made our English tongue, a gallimaufray or hodgepodge of al
other speches," E.K. only heightens this linguistic Tower of Babel with
his choice of words. To previous authors' failures E.K. pins a lack of
faith: not believing English "ful enough for prose and stately enough
for verse" produced their translative dereliction and, in turn, the cultural degeneration that he so deplores (16).

Yet the "new Poete," E.K. tells us, is a literary architect par excellence,
"for what in most English wryters useth to be loose, and as it were
ungyrt, in this Authour is well grounded, finely framed, and strongly
trussed up together" (17). Such architectural skill stands Spenser in
sharp contrast to "the rakehellye route of our ragged rymers," who,

E.K. hyperbolically rails, "without learning boste, without judgement jangle, without reason rage and fome . . . [and who] seeme to be so pained and traveiled in theyr remembrance, as it were a woman in chil-debirth" (17). Lavishly commending Spenser for laboring "to restore, as to theyr rightfull heritage such good and naturall English words, as have ben long time out of use and almost clear disherited," E.K. then exhorts none to "rashly blame" Spenser for his "choyse of old and unwonted words" (16). At the same time, he acknowledges that such archaisms may strike a jarring note, that Spenser's words "the which of many thinges which in him be straunge, I know will seeme the straungest, the words them selves being so auncient . . . so grave for the straunge-nesse" (14). Describing the words as "something hard, and of most men unused, yet both English, and also used of most excellent Authors and most famous Poetes" (14), E.K. paints the author as a linguistic archae-ologist and architect, heroically recovering forgotten English words.

E.K. piles on the architectural analogies, making his polemic meta-phorically plain to see: unlike authors who in "theyr remembrance" produced only crumbling hovels, Spenser recollected the ruins of the past into the *Calender*'s lasting monument (17). Yet while insisting that Spenser's poetry repairs the damage of less skilled literary architects, he argues his case in a peculiar and counter-intuitive fashion. To discredit England's native literary tradition, the one that Spenser ostensibly re-stored to classical form, E.K. summons tired clichés for the recovery of antiquity – disinterment, reconstruction, even rebirth – while produc-ing a diatribe against foreign words that ironically might apply equally to Spenser since, as he knows all too well, Spenser's own "old" words require some translating. This dismissal of past English authors (some very recent) seems directed less at translation per se than at an idea (or ideal) of cultural *translatio*.

E.K.'s architectural metaphors thus reveal a paradoxical argument: on the one hand, his own doubts about Spenser's status as a new Virgil and, on the other hand, his evident attempts to fit him into a Virgil-ian mould anyway. Filling in the symbolic empty spaces of the English language with foreign words once produced a dilapidated linguistic edifice, E.K. argues, while Spenser's use of seemingly decayed native words helped to render the English language a complete and sturdy structure. In other words, E.K. indirectly and uncomfortably admits that Spenser's "old" words still look like relics. But if E.K. worries that the *Calender* appears more like a ruinous edifice than an immor-tal monument, he nevertheless attempts to justify the value of these words *as* ruins and in a manner as "straunge" as the words themselves:

by praising Spenser's "dewe observing of Decorum" in "handeling his matter, and framing his words" (13–14). For E.K., Spenser's distinction from England's earlier and ostensibly inauspicious lot of authors hinges, in short, on how his "remembrance" shapes this memorial edifice (17).

E.K. looks to rhetorical decorum in order to explain why Spenser's *Calender*, presumably already an immortal monument, has been fashioned from linguistic ruins that remain visible in its structure. E.K. argues that decorum constructs the *Calender* as a classical unity (all appearances to the contrary). If counting a poet worthy of immortality for his deft use of "decorum" seems like damning with faint praise, decorum still forms the crux of E.K.'s defence of the *Calender*'s "aunciant" language. Rhetorical decorum, that is, generates and frames E.K.'s efforts to persuade readers that Spenser seamlessly adapted "old," undesirable words for his "new" literary edifice – that is, followed Virgil's pattern of translating ruin into repair. Yet a contradictory portrait emerges as E.K. attempts to rationalize the *Calender*'s appearance as a matter of just memory.

To explain the usefulness and beauty of Spenser's "hard" dialect, E.K. invokes rhetorical authorities on such matters. Cogitating aloud, E.K. muses, "sure I think, and think I think not amisse, that [these words] bring great grace and, as one would say, auctoritie to the verse," even if "amongst many other faultes it specially be objected of Valla against Livie . . . that with over much studie they affect antiquitie" (14). Lest critics consider Spenser a mere antiquarian, a mere collector of linguistic curiosities, E.K. asserts, "I am of the opinion, and eke the best learned are of the lyke, that those auncient solemn wordes are a great ornament" (14–15). But his discourse of decorum quickly bleeds from considerations of stylistic appropriateness into trickier questions of imitation. "Whenas this our Poet hath bene much traveiled and throughly redd," he explains, "how could it be, (as that worthy Oratour sayde) but that walking in the sonne . . . and having the sound of those auncient Poetes still ringing in his eares, he mought needes in singing hit out some of theyr tunes" (14). For his vexed defence of Spenser's *Calender*, E.K. thus seeks authority in "that worthy Oratour" Cicero and his portrayal of decorum in *On the Orator*:

> For if my memory fayle not, Tullie in that booke, wherein he endevoureth to set forth the paterne of a perfect Oratour, sayth that ofttimes an auncient worde maketh the style seeme grave, and as it were reverend . . . yet nether every where must old words be stuffed in, nor the commen Dialecte and

maner of speaking so corrupted therby, that as in old buildings it seme disorderly and ruinous. But all as in most exquisite pictures they use to blaze and portraict not onely the daintie lineaments of beautye, but also rounde about it to shadow the rude thickets and craggy clifts, that by the basenesse of such parts, more excellency may accrew to the principall; for oftimes we fynde ourselves, I knowe not how, singularly delighted with the shewe of such naturall rudenesse, and take great pleasure in that disorderly order. Even so doe those rough and harsh termes enlumine and make more clearly to appeare the brightesse of brave and glorious words. (15)

In this very selective memory of *On the Orator*, E.K. draws a portrait (reminiscent of his picture of the English language) of how "old" words paradoxically render a structure whole. To E.K., Ciceronian "decorum" means that Spenser's visibly archaic language somehow frames the *Calender* and thereby demonstrates its unity: so "those rough and harsh termes enlumine . . . the brightness of brave and glorious words." Yet he remembers Cicero's "paterne of a perfect Oratour" only partially at best. Indeed, this faulty recollection ultimately casts E.K., rather than Spenser, as the sunburnt figure stumbling through the landscape of antiquity, "much traveiled and thoroughly redd," hearing "the sound of those auncient [authors] still ringing in his eares" while he unconsciously "hit[s] out some of theyr tunes" (14). E.K. conflates two of classical Rome's greatest authorities – Virgil and Cicero – in order to suggest that Spenser pursued Virgil's "perfecte paterne of a Poete" through Cicero's "paterne of a perfect Oratour." Yet E.K. casts about wildly to link these patterns, to merge them in his overarching argument that the *Calender*'s immortal monument has repaired the ruins of England's past poets. With his assortment of arguments defending the work's decorum – ranging from conscious emulation, to unconscious simulation, to imitation in its most prudish sense of apt decoration or "ornament" – E.K. suggests his own struggle to interpret the author's intentions for the *Calender*.[15]

E.K.'s attempts to recall Cicero's *On the Orator* gesture to a memory tradition that he apparently only half remembers. What his memorial reconstruction of Cicero forgets proves crucial, however, for it frames a debate between E.K. and Spenser about *how* to remember the past. Given that Cicero was *the* authority on all matters of style in the Renaissance, E.K. seeks in Cicero's authority evidence of the *Calender*'s classical lineage, indirect proof of the "new Poete's" ambitions to follow

Virgil's ideal "paterne." Yet his allusions to Cicero contradict this Virgilian ideal, offering another vision of Rome's edification and repair, a different pattern for authorial and cultural formation. Cicero's authority backfires on E.K., whose two references to *On the Orator* recall not one ideal of style but rather a debate between the dialogue's two main speakers about matters of style and substance that E.K. has clearly forgotten. When he refers to Spenser "walking in the sonne," E.K. halfrecalls Antonius' discussion in Book 2 of the value of ancient writing to modern oratory. When E.K. describes the relation between "rough and harsh terms" and "the brightness of brave and glorious words," he halfrecalls Crassus' discussion of the mechanics of style in Book 3. Rather than being two unrelated fragments of the larger discourse, these two citations capture a debate between Antonius and Crassus about how the past should be remembered, and the purposes to which it should be put. What falls between E.K.'s allusions to *On the Orator* serves as an ironic reminder of what he forgets or misremembers: that Cicero rewrites the tale of Simonides as a story of Rome's history, the ruin of its republic, and his literary recollection of it. The tale of Simonides comes between these allusions to Antonius and Crassus, a positional order that suggests Cicero's place in the dialogue: he rewrites the tale of Simonides as a way to mediate the opposed views of his speakers. Spenser similarly creates an implied dialogue with his characters, particularly E.K. E.K.'s references to an ideal Ciceronian style introduce an intertext that ultimately undermines his own argument, for these allusions serve to remind readers about two different, even opposed, patterns of edification. Through Cicero's dialogue, Spenser answers E.K.'s vision of Virgilian literary immortality, suggesting that poetry's "place" lies in ruins as a symbolic location for ongoing recollection and renovation.

Forgetting and Remembering Cicero's *On the Orator*

Like *The Shepheardes Calender*, Cicero's *On the Orator* concerns itself both with creating a literary monument to the fame of its interlocutors and with building a "place" or location for cultural memory, endeavours that Cicero figuratively connects through techniques of locational memory.[16] Yet Cicero less appropriates the rules of this art than recasts the art's apocryphal origin as a frame tale, a fictional narrative through which his dialogue reconstructs the ruins of Rome's republic into a textual edifice. Renovating the tale of Simonides as a story of Rome's history, Cicero imagines building immortality as an art of memory, an art in which ruins function as places for recollecting the past anew. Extending my earlier discussion of *On the Orator*, this section focuses on how Cicero's adaptation of the art of memory negotiates Antonius' and Crassus' divided perspectives on the ideal pattern of an orator.

The art of memory colours Antonius and Crassus' dialogue about language and decorum and, more broadly, their debate about the ideal orator, for it inflects their opposed ideas of what an orator should know, particularly as it relates to the value of ancient Greek learning. Antonius provocatively proclaims that he can "only understand such of the Greek writings as their authors wished to be understood by the generality of people," as his "custom is to read these books . . . when I have leisure," only for "amusement" but not for the business of oratory:[17] "What profit is there from it, then? I own that there is not much; yet there is some; for as, when I walk in the sun, though I may walk for another purpose, yet it naturally happens that I gain a deeper color; so when I have read those books attentively at Misenum (for at Rome I have scarcely the opportunity to do so), I can perceive that my language acquires a complexion, as it were, from my intercourse with them" (98). For Antonius, engaging in disciplines outside the field of rhetoric has limited value. His "language acquires a complexion" or "deeper color" from reading "Greek writings," but he represents this "intercourse" as superficial, cosmetic, and fundamentally irrelevant to the substantial matters of Roman oratory. Such imitation is merely incidental, accidental colouring, which Antonius emphasizes when he dismisses ancient philosophy and poetry as merely leisure-time activities: "If I ever fall in with the philosophers, deluded by the titles to their books . . . I do not understand a single word of them, so restricted are they to close and exact disputations" (98–9). In the same breath, he dismisses "the poets" who, "as speaking in a different language, I never attempt to touch at all" (99). Antonius makes an exception for "those who have written history," but only to "amuse" himself and only historians "who adopted such a style that they seem to wish to be familiar to us who are not of the deepest erudition" (99).

Whereas Antonius acquires only a sunburned "complexion" from imitating the past, from all things Greek, in Book 3 Crassus responds that "both our language and the nature of things allows the ancient and excellent science of Greece to be adapted to our customs and manners" (219). Crassus continues by recasting Antonius' framing of style as accidental "deeper color":

A speech, then, is to be made becoming in its kind, with a sort of complexion and substance of its own . . . but that it be, as it were, strewed with flowers of language and thought, is a property which ought not to be equally diffused throughout the whole speech, but at such intervals that, as in the arrangement of ornaments, there may be certain remarkable and luminous objects disposed here and there. Such a kind of eloquence, therefore, is to be chosen, as is most adapted to interest the audience, such as may not only delight, but delight without satiety (for I do not imagine it to be expected of me, that I should admonish you to beware that your language be not poor, or rude, or vulgar, or obsolete; both your age and your geniuses encourage me to something of a higher nature). (219–20)

Because each speech is unique, "with a sort of complexion" of its own, "eloquence" necessarily entails decorum: language "adapted to interest the audience." To describe this decorum, Crassus returns to the language of painting that Antonius used earlier to describe the art of memory. Recall from chapter 1 that Antonius explains how "this faculty of *artificial memory* practice will afford (from which proceeds habit), as well as the derivation of similar words converted and altered in cases, or transferred from particulars to generals, and the idea of an entire sentence from the symbol of a single word, after the manner and method of a *skillful painter, who distinguishes spaces by the variety of what he depicts*" (188, my emphasis). In describing the "method" of artificial memory, Antonius connects this art with the visual arts and with the other tale of Simonides as the origin of the saying that painting is silent poetry, poetry a speaking picture.

Yet whereas Antonius dismisses other fields as irrelevant to the business of oratory, Crassus suggests how their matter and method meet in a common place: the art of memory. Book 2 closes with Crassus' complaint that "Antonius . . . left me nothing but words, and took the substance for himself," but he connects substance with style through the art of memory (191). Crassus radically expands what the art of memory means, such that it describes not only a memorable style of speech or delivery but also the very remembrance of antiquity. Locational memory thus works as the vehicle whereby a more complex view of style can emerge: "It is difficult to tell what the cause is why, from those objects which most strongly strike our sense with pleasure, and occasion the most violent emotions at their first appearance, we should soonest turn away with a certain loathing and satiety. How much more florid, in the gayety and variety of coloring, are most objects in modern pictures than in ancient ones; which, however though they captivate us at first sight, do not afford any lasting pleasure; whereas we are strongly attracted by rough and faded coloring in the paintings of antiquity" (220). The question of *how* poetry acts as a "speaking picture" relates to decorum, as Wesley Trimpi has argued; that is, decorum describes in verbal and visual terms how to accommodate an audience's vision depending on the degree of distance.[18] Crassus' language suggests that such spatial accommodation applies to time as well, the distance between past and present. When he compares the limited pleasure of brightly painted "modern pictures" with the lasting pleasure of the "rough and faded coloring in the paintings of antiquity," Crassus does not favour one but rather describes an ideal that would integrate the two styles – modernity and antiquity – and, in so doing, enhance the understanding and memory of the audience. The connection between the art of memory and the visual arts, then, constitutes more than the creation of images that speak to an audience; rather, the deeper connection between memorial arts and plastic arts has to do with the importance of adapting sightlines to an audience's vision. As Crassus explains, "We should the less wonder at this effect in language, in which we may form a judgment, either from *the poets or the orators*, that a style elegant, ornate, embellished, and sparkling, without *intermission*, without restraint, without variety, whether it be *prose or poetry*, though painted with the brightest colors, can not possibly give lasting pleasure" (221, my emphasis). Through visual and psychological accommodation, Crassus suggests, both poetry and oratory can speak across the "intermission" of time and space. This speaks directly to style and decorum. As he all but admits, so-called pure Latin is a fiction. Although speaking correctly is expected, Crassus argues that no single style is correct. Rather, there is a wide variety of styles to choose from, and so what makes for great speakers constitutes decorum: employing words appropriately and elegantly (Crassus must use multiple words to describe this ideal), fitting words to the occasion and matching matter with expression.[19]

By beginning Book 3 of *On the Orator* with his adaptation of the art of memory, Cicero indirectly asks us to consider its bearing on this book's stated topic: language and style. Just as Crassus expands the significance of the art of memory, so Cicero's "intermission" at the beginning of Book 3 works in a similar manner: the art of memory again acts as a vehicle to a new understanding of style and decorum. The lynchpin here is history. For Antonius, history has nothing to do with oratory:

"Do you see how far the study of history is from the business of the orator? . . . for who is ignorant that it is the first law in writing history that the historian must not dare to tell any falsehood, and the next, that he must be bold enough to tell *the whole truth*" (99, my emphasis). Presumably, orators (and certainly poets) cannot be held to such high standards of honesty. Crassus disagrees with Antonius on this point. History has everything to do with oratory, just as Athens has everything to do with Rome: "By what other voice than that of the orator, is history, the evidence of time, the light of truth, the life of memory, the directress of life, the herald of antiquity, committed to immortality?" (92). Despite their differences, Crassus and Antonius nevertheless seem to agree that history should tell the "whole truth."

Yet when Cicero interrupts their dialogue at the beginning of Book 3, he represents history not exactly as the "light of truth" but rather as a story about their history, and one that links poetry, rhetoric, and philosophy together in ways that these speakers cannot know. In remembering the events that "ruined the commonwealth" (194), Cicero casts himself in the role of Simonides, remembering their dialogue amidst the ruins of Rome's republic. "Bitter remembrance renewed in my mind," he writes, "for the genius worthy of immortality, the learning, the virtue that were in Lucius Crassus, were all extinguished by sudden death, within ten days from the day which is comprised in this and the former book" (192). Remember, though, that Cicero himself has *no* personal memory of this dialogue: "For I, who was not present at this dialogue, and to whom Caius Cotta communicated only the topics and heads of the dissertation, have endeavored to shadow forth in the conversation of the speakers those *peculiar styles of oratory* in which I knew that each of them was conspicuous" (196, my emphasis). This history is neither "the whole truth," as Antonius calls it, or "the light of truth," in Crassus' words. But history *is* what Crassus calls "the life of memory": the continuing process of recollecting and rebuilding the ruins of the past. In framing the work of history in such terms, through imperfect and partial recollection and through the fiction of the tale of Simonides, Cicero builds upon Plato's art of memory, suggesting that writing functions as a crucial reminder but not a static monument to memory. In place of Antonius' view that history does not matter to the present, and Crassus' view that ancient history is all-important, Cicero demonstrates the ongoing project of accommodating the past to the present. By telling Rome's history as a story, another tale of Simonides, Cicero creates a more complex perspective on the truth of history than that of his characters, Antonius and Crassus. Such broad decorum means not telling *the* truth of history, as both Antonius and Crassus assert, but acknowledging a larger truth: that history is always built upon stories, stories that reflect the multiple truths of the past that take place in dialogue. Differing styles and ideals of oratory, differing notions of knowledge and practice, dialogue itself, together represent the larger truth of history that *On the Orator* remembers.[20]

"Style" thus plays a crucial part in this dialogue, for it indicates not simply language but the unique way of using language that came to define these speakers. It is "style" that allows Cicero not to remember the exact words of the conversation but to imagine the way it might have occurred. Knowing a particular style thus becomes the marker of a whole person; it would seem that the "characters of style" can refer both to different types of style and to different types of people. In *On the Orator*, style thus represents character as both truth and fiction. Cicero suggests as much when he describes Plato's portrait of "the character of Socrates"; given that his dialogues cannot reconstruct the past or fully capture Socrates' character, imaginative invention is required in order to remember the past, however imperfectly. In rhetoric as in philosophy, style functions as reminder and spur to the stories that inevitably play a part in remembering the past.

By committing his characters' dialogue to writing, Cicero reveals that which lies beyond their field of vision, outside the garden where they debate the ideal education of the orator: Rome's ruin and with it their own. But the continued life of Cicero's dialogue makes the more important statement about the nature of continuity and adaptation. Just as no one "perfect" style exists, no one "paterne of a perfect Oratour" exists either; and rather than recovering *an* ideal of rhetoric, *On the Orator* recalls a dialogue or debate about *differing* ideals of rhetoric. Dialogue as a form of memorial accommodation, it seems, is the dialogue's only true ideal of decorum. "Here the recollection of an old tradition must be revived in my mind," Cicero explains, "adapted . . . [so that] you may understand what opinions the most famous and eloquent men entertained respective the whole art of oratory" (7). Nor does he presume to have the last word on the matter. Rather, by transforming the *ars memorativa* from a technique for individual memory into a story of collective memory, Cicero illustrates how the ruins of the past are continually refashioned through recollection. His portrait of the architecture of immortality as a process of cultural transmission therefore depends upon dialogue – dialogue that describes "decorum" in the sense of cultural change. As Mary Carruthers has argued, "By their very nature signs are sensible, practical, worldly, belong to the traditional realm of rhetoric and must be understood within its procedures, most particularly the process of decorum, of fitting a word to a thing in terms that an audience will understand."[21] When extended to history as well as language, such decorum describes the architecture of *On the Orator*, for in performing Simonides' role in order to recall Rome's ruin, Cicero implies that his literary edifice will remain incomplete – in ruins – changing with new times and places in renewed dialogue. This dialogue both remembers the dead and allows them to continue speaking, a conversation that necessarily changes to suit the perspectives of new audiences as they join this dialogue – as late arrivals to the banquet, so to speak – about cultural change and transmission. In performing Simonides' role, Cicero teaches future readers how to recollect his writing by continuing to make Simonides' discovery.

*   *   *

E.K. appears to forget as much of *On the Orator* as he remembers, as his justification of the "new Poete's" use of ruinous "old" words leans on a limited and distorted interpretation of Ciceronian decorum and authority. Overlooking the debate between Antonius and Crassus, E.K. attributes both allusions to a unified Ciceronian pronouncement on style. And though he clearly intends to exalt the "new Poete's" conscious imitation of antiquity, E.K. forgets the Ciceronian context for unconscious imitation as a sunburn of sorts: that is, Antonius' argument against the necessity of imitating antique learning. E.K.'s defence of the *Calender*'s linguistic "rudeness" also misremembers another key Ciceronian context: Crassus' admonishment to his students, "beware that your language be not poor, or rude, or vulgar, or obsolete" (220). Through half-remembered allusions, Cicero's dialogue reflects ironically on E.K.'s attempt to classicize Spenser's catholic literary style, to portray it as a return to so-called pure English – a fiction, indeed. By misremembering *On the Orator*, E.K. fails to see how readers themselves create the *Calender*'s "decorum."

How readers behold *The Shepheardes Calender* is E.K.'s greatest concern and the reason why he attempts to frame the poem as an immortal monument, an immutable house of fame. Yet his faulty memory and misprisions serve as reminders for readers, for he indirectly recalls what makes language memorable according to the principles of the art of memory – decorum – and he creates a space in which to recall the larger significance of decorum to *On the Orator*.[22] Cicero's dialogue suggests that decorum, adapting matter for new times and places, applies to the work as a whole. This point is given its full expression when Cicero interrupts the dialogue to narrate the death and decline of the interlocutors, creating the kind of break or "interval" that makes *On the Orator* memorable. Cicero rewrites the tale of Simonides in order to disagree with his characters about how they see history, as "the light of truth," and implies his story of Rome's history is at least partly fictional: the tale of Simonides itself is obviously a tall tale, and Cicero himself imagines this dialogue from limited information, suggesting that *On the Orator* is precisely the "old building" that "semes disorderly and ruinous" – the appearance that E.K. most wants to avoid for *The Shepheardes Calender*. Through E.K., Spenser imitates Cicero's style of dialogue, creating a cast of characters to debate these issues of style and decorum and how they relate to cultural transmission and history. For Cicero as for Spenser, it would seem, style and decorum speak to history – they are the principles by which he remembers the past.

Ultimately, E.K. calls upon Cicero's authority less to defend Spenser's "decorum" than to justify his own place in the *Calender*. With the analogy of poetry and painting, it appears that E.K. pictorially represents his own critical decorum, insinuating that his glosses gather Spenser's "old" words into a coherent monument, mediating the distance between near and far, old and new, past and present, completing the *Calender* and demonstrating that fashioning a literary edifice depends upon such authoritative remembrance. In this way, Cicero's "paterne of a perfect Oratour" would serve E.K.'s end, allowing him to paint his commentaries on Spenser's "auncient" language as the ruins that frame the *Calender* and, in effect, complete the portrait. In a sense this conflates and even creates a dependent relationship between E.K.'s and Spenser's authority. E.K. credits himself with exclusive knowledge and interpretive skill, claiming alone to know how Cicero's "paterne of a perfect Oratour" allows Spenser to fulfil a "perfecte paterne of a Poete." In so doing, he misses the point of Ciceronian "decorum," for he sees decorum as the duty of the author-cum-architect who builds his immortal monument once, if not for all. But *On the Orator*'s portrait of Rome provides another perspective on Virgilian fantasies of permanent repair: Rome is eternally falling and being remembered. E.K. misses precisely this pattern of edification, the cycle of ruin and recollection that marks poetry as well as history. He positions his commentary as the "light of truth" even as he accidentally recalls a dialogue between characters that replicates the dialogue within the *Calender*, drawing attention to Spenser's staging of disagreements with his characters. E.K.'s portrayal of the *Calender*'s architecture thus allows readers to see the "place" of ruin in it differently from him, to hear a debate between E.K. and Spenser around opposing "paternes" of authorial edification. Against E.K.'s passionate defence of his poetry, Spenser suggests that the *Calender* bears out another interpretation of Cicero, and another understanding of the architecture of immortality: not as an edifice that repairs ruin permanently, but as ruins that provide the space for continual recollection.

At the heart of this debate lies the question of exactly who builds literary immortality: the author or the audience? E.K. imagines a literary monument as an individual authorial construction, a private mnemonic that to be remembered requires another authority – ideally one like E.K., who claims to have been "made privie to [Spenser's] counsell and secret meaning" – and he thus performs his role in the *Calender* as Spenser's "translator" (19). By "glosing and commenting" on Spenser's poetry, E.K. hopes that England "might be equal to the learned of other nations" (19), but he rarely succeeds in effecting this kind of cultural *translatio* – one desired end of the Virgilian *rota* – because his glosses rarely hit the mark. While promising to reveal what Spenser "him selfe [is] labouring to conceale," his relationship to Spenser's "auctoritie" is clearly more complex than that of simple confidence and revelation (19). With many of E.K.'s seemingly erudite glosses, Spenser hints that E.K. knows less than he professes – nowhere more so than in his final commentary. His interpretation of *December*'s missing emblem, in asserting commonplaces about the immortality of this poetry, reveals the useful ways E.K. misreads the *Calender*. Spenser's epilogue replies with his own picture of the architecture of immortality – one that echoes Chaucer, England's older "new Poete," in *Troilus and Criseyde*:

Loe I have made a Calender for every yeare,
That steele in strength, and time in durance shall outweare:
And if I marked well the starres revolution,
It shall continewe till the worlds dissolution.
To teach the ruder shepheard how to feede his sheepe,
. . . Goe lyttle Calender, thou hast a free passeporte. (1–7)

The epilogue exposes E.K. and Spenser's dialogue, laying bare their contrasting notions of fashioning literary immortality. While E.K.'s analysis of this passage reiterates Horace's claim to permanence – that the *Calender* "shall endure as long as time etc. folowing the ensample of Horace" – reading further into the passage clarifies that Spenser's depiction of poetic immortality embraces change rather than defying it (212). "It shall continewe till the worlds dissolution" does not mean that the *Calender* stands as a monument to outwear time; rather, Spenser locates the *Calender*'s "strength," "durance," and ability "to continewe" within reach of time's scythe and with its ability "to teach": to edify. The epilogue emphasizes that poetry's life depends upon transmission, upon being relinquished by its author for future renovation, and that fame exists as a process of transmission. It explains how Spenser's work survives, in what form and fashion it persists, and thus elucidates a version of immortality that implicates Spenser's audience in his and the *Calender*'s continued memorial life. By depicting poetic immortality as movement rather than monument, the epilogue insinuates that E.K.'s final gloss constructs Spenser's authority only in partial terms; and against E.K.'s visions of a monumental edifice, Spenser implies that his literary edifice survives in ruins. With its echoes of Chaucer's conclusion to *Troilus and Criseyde*, the irony of E.K.'s defence of the "new Poete" fully emerges. Chaucer sends off his book with the anticipation that, even in English, it will require translation:

> Go little book . . .
> And since there is such great diversity
> In English, and our writing is so young,
> I pray to God that none may mangle thee,
> . . . I beg of God that thou be understood![23]

Unlike E.K., Chaucer (and Spenser) understands that translation depends upon reception.

E.K.'s introduction and commentary therefore affect Spenser's authority in ironic and unintentional ways, placing it effectively outside the text and into hands other than his own. As Spenser intimates, E.K. himself "ruins" *The Shepheardes Calender* in order to "repair" it, for without antiquity, how can there be renaissance? He thus constructs older English words as rare remains so that he, through the "new Poete," can claim to have ushered in cultural rebirth. While Spenser tacitly concurs that E.K.'s glosses frame the *Calender* like so many ruins, he also suggests that such ruin serves another end as the "place" for dialogue and continual recollection, by which the *Calender*'s edifice is adapted for new times and places: "decorum" that continues to build Spenser's monument anew. And Spenser repeatedly underscores the important place of ruin in his *Calender* as part of the larger "paterne of the perfect Oratour," suggesting that ruin and recollection constitute the very art of memory by which readers construct and reconstruct his *Calender*. By virtue of E.K.'s interpretive fallacies, Spenser engages readers in an ongoing dialogue about what decorum means to English poetry. As Kathy Eden observes, rhetorical accommodation "includes in its radical sense the act of "making to feel like one of the family," and the rhetorical tradition "thematizes the interpretive act, at its best, as the arduous journey home."[24] Decorum describes poetry not as an immortal monument but as the fashioning of a home through discourse and recollection. Ironically, E.K.'s glosses create space in the *Calender* where readers can act as the continuing architects of a house of fame at home: England.

The epilogue offers a reminder of Chaucer's important place in the *Calender* and the art of memory tradition that Spenser recollects through him. In his epistle, E.K. points to the place in the *Calender* where Colin names Chaucer as his original. "As for Colin," E.K. writes,

> under whose person the Authour selfe is shadowed, how furre he is from such vaunted titles and glorious showes, both him selfe sheweth, where he sayth.
>> "Of Muses Hobbin. I conne no skill." And,
>> "Enough is me to paint out my unrest, etc." (18)

E.K. omits the central point of this passage: Chaucer's influence. As Colin explains in the *June* eclogue, his authorial ambitions follow the path of this other "Tityrus." Affirming that he does not "followe flying fame" and defending his "rough" rhymes in ways that undermine E.K.'s defence of Spenser's old words, Colin says: "I wote my rymes bene rough, and rudely drest: / The fytter they, my carefull case to frame" (75–9). He then explicitly attributes this rude style to lessons learned from Chaucer:

> The God of shepheardes *Tityrus* is dead,
> Who taught me homely, as I can, to make . . .
> Nowe dead he is, and lyeth wrapt in lead . . .
> And all hys passing skil with him is fledde,
> The fame whereof doth dayly greater growe. (81–92)

This allusion to Chaucer suggests that England's older Tityrus and earlier "new Poete" has already died, puncturing E.K.'s fantasies of rebirth. But it also suggests how Chaucer illuminates Spenser's sense of "decorum," helping to explain the *Calender*'s architecture of immortality. Acknowledging the "rymes bene rough, and rudely frame" makes them all the "fytter" to "frame" his poetry, as his "case" for poetry. As critics have observed, Spenser's language is neither especially medieval nor Chaucerian. Yet E.K. correctly (if inadvertently) views Chaucer's language as ruins. The complex notion of how words are ruins that the poet recollects will be explored in the second part of this chapter. Spenser models his vision of fame on Chaucer's *House of Fame*, where poetry and language are imagined as ruins: the matter of memory upon which new structures like *The Shepheardes Calender* are built. Asserting that Chaucer "taught me homely, as I can, to make," Spenser implies that his model of edification relates fundamentally to writing about England as their shared home and location for memory.

The "Labyrinth of Love": Remembering the House of Tudor and *The House of Fame*

The question of poetry's "place" finds a compelling answer in E.K.'s "Letter to Harvey," where he describes *The Shepheardes Calender* as a whole – "the generyll dryft and purpose of [the] Æglogoges" – through Colin's painful journey as an "unstayed yougth [who] had long wandred in the common Labyrinth of Love" (19). For the shepherds as well as E.K., the "Labyrinth of Love" refers to a Petrarchan prison of love lyrics that holds Colin captive, and which he must escape to pursue his literary destiny. Yet this "common Labyrinth of Love," I will suggest, is a commonplace in more ways than one.[25] Just as the speakers in Cicero's *On the Orator* perform Plato's *Phaedrus* in a pastoral place where "friends have all things in common," so the shepherds and E.K. reenact (albeit unwittingly) Plato's dialogue through their debate about Colin's divided loves. This shadow-box narrative structure extends the *Calender*'s pursuit of poetry's location in culture through locational memory, from Plato to Petrarch and beyond, at once reminding readers of the frame for Castiglione's dialogue and translating this model into English. As in *The Courtier*, the tale of Stesichorus figures centrally in the *Calender*'s complex treatment of poetry and power.[26] Finally, I suggest that Chaucer's *House of Fame* provides an alternative way to view the commonplace "Labyrinth of Love": as an ideal place for recollection. Even as the shepherds complain about the absence of a "place" for poetry, they fashion Colin's house of fame in ways that reform a Chaucerian model of memory.

Januarye finds Colin in a state of personal and poetic ruin, visible in the eclogue's woodcut, which reveals a broken pan pipe and a broken Colin, forlornly gazing toward the place representing his love.[27] E.K. explains how "Colin cloute a shepheardes boy complaineth him of his unfortunate love, being but newly (as semeth) enamoured of a countrie lasse called Rosalinde," and "fynding himselfe robbed of all former pleasaunce and delights, hee breaketh his Pipe in peeces, and casteth him selfe to the ground" (29). *Januarye* thereby casts Colin in the role of a failed love poet, and Rosalind as the perfect Petrarchan mistress. If Rosalind initially encouraged Colin's amorous advances and therefore inspired him poetically, her transformation into a cold, distant, disdainful mistress places Colin securely within a Petrarchan tradition of longing for an irretrievable past. Unlike Petrarch's Laura, Rosalind's rejections make her a discouraging muse, deflating Colin's poetic and amorous inspiration. Colin's broken "pipe" implies a reason for his impotence: following too closely on Petrarch's heels has resulted in clichéd poetry and frustrated desires; as Louis Montrose puts its, "the pain of longing and denial impels Petrarchan creativity, but it renders Colin poetically sterile."[28] "Ah God, that love should breede both joy and payne," Colin laments, though observing this paradox offers his burning heart cold comfort (54). Rosalind "laughes [at] the songes, that *Colin Clout* doth make," holding his "rurall musick [in] scorne" (66, 64), and readers might chuckle too at his poor imitation.

Lest readers interpret this merely as the complaint of a mediocre poet, E.K. once again labors to reveal what Spenser "him selfe labour[s] to conceale" (19). Providing a series of glosses on the characters' names, E.K. attempts to establish the *Calender*'s central debate: "Rosalind) is also a feigned name, which being wel ordered, wil bewray the very name of hys love and mistresse, whom by that name he coloureth. So as Ovide shadoweth hys love under the name of Corynna, which of some is supposed to be Julia, themperor Augustus his daughter . . . [for] this generally hath bene a common custome of counterfeicting the names of secret Personages" (34–5). Striking a knowing tone, E.K. confides that Rosalind's "feigned name" conceals an important person. In offering examples of authors who protected their poetic muses with pseudonyms for reasons both personal and political, he means to reveal *the* truth: that Spenser's "counterfeicting" of Rosalind's true identity implies a titillating truth behind this fictional relationship, that this veil demonstrates Spenser's use of important literary conventions. Yet what E.K. leaves out of this gloss paradoxically points the reader in a different interpretive direction: toward understanding Rosalind's identity as a more complex allegory than simply as a thin disguise for Spenser's own "love and mistresse." The palindrome *amor summus roma* is central here: the idea that remembering love necessarily means recollecting Rome and its ruins.[29] That Rosalind's love represents an Amor that definitively equals Roma seems clear, especially given *Januarye*'s woodcut: this image represents Rosalind's "neighbor towne" as a place where the ruined Roman coliseum looms in the background. Just as Petrarch recollected his love of his imperial mistress, Rome, so Spenser implies a similar link between Colin's poetic and cultural endeavours.

As E.K. and the shepherds reason, Colin's obsession with Rosalind produces love lyrics that prevent him from praising Elizabeth in epic terms. In other words, Colin's "long wandrying" in the "common Labyrinth of love" means that he stays stuck in the role of a Petrarch rather than assuming the heroic role of a Virgil. By composing Petrarchan lyric rather than epic, indeed by giving up on poetry altogether by breaking his pipe, Colin appears to neglect his shepherd community; after all, to be England's new Virgil ultimately requires valuing duty over desire, love of country over all else. As England's "new Poete," Spenser seems to chart a path that love prevents Colin from pursuing. Spenser thus transcends his alter ego's limitations, some critics argue, moving beyond lyric into the realm of epic. (Recall that E.K. prefers "Tityrus" to "Colin" because it speaks to his epic ambitions for Spenser.) In effect, Spenser subverts the terms of such an opposition via a larger perspective on the "Labyrinth of Love." Colin's problem energizes the shepherds' dialogue about Platonic love via a series of oppositions between "wrong" and "right" kinds of love, associated with specific genres and authors. More than a commonplace, Plato's *Phaedrus* stands as an intertext that suggests another answer to their debate.

When E.K. introduces Hobbinol (a character he clearly identifies with, if only in part), he attempts to explain Platonic love and, in the process, introduces an important intertext:

> Hobbinol) is a fained country name, whereby, it being so commune and usuall, seemeth to be hidden the person of some his very speciall and most familiar freend, whom he entirely and extraordinarily beloved, as peradventure shall be more largely declared hereafter. In thys place seemeth to be some savour of disorderly love, which the learned call pæderastice: but it is gathered beside his meaning. For who that hath red Plato his dialogue . . . of Socrates opinions, may easily perceive, that such love is muche to be allowed and like of, specially so meant, as Socrates used it: who sayth, that

in deede he loved Alcybiades extremely, yet not Alcybiades person, but hys soule, which is Alcybiades owne selfe. And so is pæderastice much to be præferred before gynerastice, that is the love whiche enflameth men with lust toward woman kind. But yet let no man thinke, that herein I stand with Lucian or hys develish disciple Unico Aretino, in defence of execrable and horrible sinnes of forbidden and unlawful fleshlinesse. (33–4)

With his anxious gloss on "Hobbinol" and hysterical comparison of two forms of love, E.K. unwittingly points to another path through the "Labyrinth of Love," one where Platonic love dovetails with, and alters, the dichotomy of Amor and Roma. E.K.'s marginal invocations of "place," his attempt to frame Hobbinol within Greek paideia, mixed with his awkward attempts to explain Platonic love as the movement from the corporeal to the spiritual, from human love to divine love, are important reminders of Plato's *Phaedrus*. Through his misunderstanding of Platonic love, E.K. ironically gestures to its important role in the *Calender*. If only through the subject of sexuality, E.K. suggests the "Socratic" role that Hobbinol plays in the *Calender*. Indeed, Hobbinol motivates the central debate of the *Phaedrus* by encouraging Colin to give up Rosalind for Eliza (or himself), lyric for epic poetry, Rome for England.[30] The commonplace of friendship, so frequently evoked by E.K., points to the Platonic commonplace that matters most: the common place that Socrates and Phaedrus construct at the end of the *Phaedrus*, the place of their dialogue where "friends have all things in common."

The issue of "place" relates to the art of memory throughout *The Shepheardes Calender*, framed through debates about the architecture of immortality. Although E.K. describes the poem as a "Labyrinth of Love," he suggests that Colin-cum-Spenser escapes this place for another, the house of fame and eternal monument to poetry that his epic will construct. Colin's progress as a poet and lover depends upon the Virgilian career "paterne," but also upon a commonplace "paterne" of love: so-called Platonic love, which charts a progression from human love, idolatry, to divine love that recollects a place and the past simultaneously. Against this romantic idea of Platonic love, Spenser integrates the *Phaedrus* as another way in which poetry recollects history and the past. In so doing, Spenser reminds us of another way to interpret the *Phaedrus*, not as a story of divine love per se but rather as a new tale of love that is explicitly contrasted with Trojan tales of love, ruin, and recollection. Spenser also reminds us of Chaucer's reception of Platonic love and the stories of Troy in *The House of Fame*. Chaucer chooses to remain in a labyrinth of love in *The House of Fame*, and this decision is the foundation upon which Spenser constructs his *Shepheardes Calender*. Following Plato's example, both Chaucer and Spenser recall Trojan tales of love while refusing to worship its gods – or the idols of poetry, power, and politics made in their name. In so doing, Spenser announces that his love of the Tudors will remain a secular comedy rather than a·divine one.

The *Aprill* Eclogue: "O quam te memorem virgo? O dea certe"

With its clear echoes of Virgil's *Fourth Eclogue*, the *Aprill* eclogue seemingly reproduces a Golden Age prophecy for England: the return of the Virgin Astraea in the form of Queen Elizabeth and, with her, peace and prosperity. Just as Virgil's poetry seemingly attributed divinity to Caesar, so Spenser seems to deify the Tudors here, endowing them with the same divine justification for empire. For good reasons, then, critics have often read this eclogue as evidence of Spenser's Virgilian aspirations.[31] Yet the intertextual presence of the *Phaedrus* creates a strong counter-narrative, a dialogue within *Aprill*'s dialogue about the relationship of poetry to power. This layered debate turns on the question of how Colin's poetry represents the Tudors. E.K. introduces *Aprill* by announcing that "This Æglogue is purposely intended to the honor and prayse of our most gracious souvereigne, Queene Elizabeth" (70), but the precise nature of this "prayse" forms the true subject of the eclogue. In his glosses, E.K. casts Colin-cum-Spenser in the role of a new Virgil, arguing that Colin's poetry deifies the Tudors in architectural terms; as E.K. asserts, the House of Tudor repaired England's political ruin, wrought by decades of civil war, achieving in English history the imperial and cultural pattern that Virgil imagined for Rome. But even as E.K. celebrates the divine right of Tudor monarchy, *Aprill* challenges the truth of his interpretation and, more broadly, of related fictions. Spenser undermines E.K.'s claims to Tudor divinity by recalling Plato's *Phaedrus* and the art of memory therein, particularly Socrates' palinode, which refuses to worship idols of poetry or power.

    Aprill resumes *Januarye*'s debate about love, framed again as recollection: that is, the recollection of an ideal pattern of ruin and re-edification. In his "Argument," E.K. explains how the "two shepheardes" Hobbinol and Thenot return to the subject of Colin's "great misadventure in Love, whereby his mynd was alienate and with drawen . . . from all former delightes and studies," "complayning" that Colin has turned his back on love and poetry – the "pleasaunt pyping . . . ryming and singing" of an earlier, happier time which *Aprill* remembers (70). In Colin's absence, Hobbinol "taketh occasion . . . to recorde a songe, which the sayd Colin sometime made in honor of her Majestie, whom . . . he termeth Elysa" (70). Like E.K., the shepherds remember Colin's poetry along with their desire for a new Virgil. Unlike Virgil's *Fourth Eclogue*, however, Colin's poetry is presented as past rather than prologue. Moreover, Hobbinol ironically projects a glorious future for Colin's poetry that Colin himself rejects, and the truth of Colin's Golden Age past or future comes under scrutiny as his poetic *ruinae* are recollected and re-enacted.

With this dialogue, the shepherds re-enact the central debate of the *Phaedrus* about the "right" versus "wrong" kind of love, and a comparison of Rosalind and Elizabeth framed by architectural tropes structures the dialogue. Hobbinol reiterates his complaint that "the ladde, whome long I lovd so deare, / Nowe loves a lasse, that all his love doth scorne" (10–11), blaming Rosalind for the tragic repercussions of Colin's misplaced love: "Hys pleasaunt Pipe, whych made us meriment, / He wylfully hath broke, and doth forbeare" (14–15). Thenot responds by reminiscing about Colin's ability "to make" or fashion with poetry, asking why "hath he skill to make so excellent" and "Yet hath so little skill to brydle love?" (19–20). His question recalls the *Phaedrus*, the attempt to bridle uncontrollable passions of the soul as a charioteer driven by two horses, good and bad, temperate and intemperate. When Hobbinol blames Rosalind for this love sickness – "So now fayre *Rosalind* hath bredde his smart" (27), he laments – E.K. provides a gloss ostensibly defending Rosalind as a muse worthy of "immortalitie" (78). But while calling her "a Gentle womane of no meane house," he nevertheless damns her with faint praise:

> neede nether Colin be ashamed to have her made knowne by his verses, nor Hobbinol be greved, that so she should be commended to immortalitie for her rare and singular Vertues: Specially deserving it no lesse, then eyther Myrto the most excellent Poete Theocritus his dearling, or Lauretta the divine Petrarches Goddesse, or Himera the worthye Poete Stesichorous hys Idole: Upon whom he is sayd so much to have doted, that in regard of her excellencie, he scorned and wrote against the beauty of Helena. For which his præsumptuous and unheedie hardinesse, he is sayde by vengeaunce of the Gods . . . to have lost both his eyes. (78)

On the face of it, E.K. praises Rosalind as "deserving" of poetic "immortality." Yet by comparing her with other presumably worthy muses like "Lauretta the divine Petrarches Goddesse" and "the worthye Poet

Stesichorous hys Idole," he implies that Rosalind is similarly a false "Idole." Reading between the lines of this defence, E.K.'s apology for Colin's poetry in fact elaborates on Hobbinol's initial argument: both imply that Colin serves Rosalind as a false rather than a true "Goddesse," unlike Eliza-cum-Elizabeth. Indirectly, E.K. portrays Rosalind's love as a form of ruinous spiritual blindness that incites the wrath of the gods. The reason why becomes clear: constructing Rosalind as an idol allows E.K. to fashion Elizabeth as truly divine. In a broader sense, this gloss allows him to contrast a false Petrarchan pattern with a true Virgilian one.

Yet E.K. misinterprets – or more precisely, half-remembers – the tale of Stesichorus in ways prove productive. He asserts that Stesichorus initially chose the wrong love, choosing "Himera" over "Helena" and thus human rather than divine love; were this true, Stesichorus' blinding would provide something of an object lesson for Colin. However, "Himera" is not a person but a location, Stesichorus' home – a misprision that speaks to E.K.'s inability to read Rosalind in terms of place (e.g., as Rome) rather than as a "feigned name" for a real person.[32] E.K. misremembers the cause of Stesichorus' punishment and the palinode that followed it in Plato's tale, in effect reversing the point of Socrates' story: E.K. attributes the gods' blinding wrath to Stesichorus' refusal to worship Helen truly rather than to the falseness of Trojan tales themselves. As with the Ciceronian references in his "Letter to Harvey," E.K.'s apparently authoritative allusion to "Stesichorus" and "hys Idole" opens up a counter-discourse that returns to the art of memory. Socrates' exploration of the relation between love and idolatry, which culminates in a sharp critique of the gods of state, forms the necessary subtext for *Aprill*.

Divining Power in Plato's *Phaedrus*

With the tale of Stesichorus, as previously discussed, Socrates performs the role of poet, reforming both the method and matter of poetry as his own philosophical art of recollection.[33] As part of a larger debate about the right and wrong kinds of love and, specifically, in response to Lysias' sophistic argument that love should be avoided because it leads to destruction, Socrates ostensibly recollects Stesichorus' palinode – a palinode itself about the process of divine recollection, which enables him to recover "the sight of his eyes" lost "because of his defamation of Helen" (490). As Socrates recollects this palinode to recollection, however, he suggests that this poem represents his own creation and, in so doing, dramatizes his ironic use of the art of memory – his imitation of the mnemonic method of oral poets – in order both to criticize an old story of history and, further, to fashion a new allegory of love and edification.

Socrates initially agrees with Lysias' argument, asserting that "a man who is dominated by desire and enslaved to pleasure" is "bound to be jealous," striving to keep his love object submissive by keeping him from anyone or anything that would "increase his wisdom – by which I mean divine philosophy" (486). He also agrees that this kind of love would lead to ruin, that such an "offensive captor" would "*ruin* his [lover's] property, *ruin* his physique, and above all *ruin* his spiritual development, which is assuredly and ever will be of supreme value in the sight of gods and men alike" (488, my emphasis). But Socrates also intimates that this kind of speech and sentiment sounds like fiction: epic fiction, to be precise. He has, he suggests in conclusion, merely performed commonplaces about love. "Let that then, my boy, be your lesson," he tells Phaedrus, but then adds: "My dear good man, haven't you noticed that I've got beyond dithyramb, and am breaking out into epic verse, despite my faultfinding?" (489). Socrates implies the triteness of his "lesson": it represents *the* commonplace of "epic verse," which orators and actors, poets and politicians alike perform as though the truth.

Therefore, Socrates quickly recants as though for telling lies about the gods: "The fact is, you know, Phaedrus, the mind itself has a kind of divining power, for I felt disturbed some while ago as I was delivering that speech . . . But now I realize my sin" (489). "That was a terrible theory," Socrates confesses, calling it "foolish, and somewhat blasphemous" (489). "Do you not hold Love to be a god, the child of Aphrodite?" Socrates asks Phaedrus; he affirms this, "but not according to Lysias," Socrates rejoins (490). Re-enacting Stesichorus' palinode forms a shared rebuttal to Lysias. "For such as offend in speaking of gods and heroes there is an ancient mode of purification," Socrates recalls, "which was known to Stesichorus, though not to Homer," who remains blind to the truth (490). "As a true artist he understood the reason" and thus produced his palinode: "False, false the tale. / Thou never didst sail in the well-decked ships / Nor come to the towers of Troy" (490). This ambiguous defense of Helen offers an implied critique of Trojan tales, raising the question of Helen's very existence even while defending her virtue.

This critique of Trojan tales serves as the point of departure for Socrates' new tale about love: the story of the soul's fall to ruin and forgetfulness, and how love serves as a reminder by which the soul recollects itself. Against Lysias' sophistries, Socrates argues that love, far from posing a threat to happiness, offers a path back to divinity. As though performing the role of a poet, Socrates attributes his new tale about love to Stesichorus – "That which I shall now pronounce is by Stesichorus" (491) – framing this as his recollection or, indeed, his art of memory, his recuperation of Stesichorus via a Golden Age tale about the prehistory of the soul. Yet despite Socrates' professed fear of blasphemy and the wrath of the gods, his love story serves an ironic end, allowing him to address the problem of idolatry at the heart of Trojan tales and the use of these tales to construct idols of love and power. Rather than defending the truth of the gods, he challenges Phaedrus' desire to worship idols like Lysias (and Socrates himself) as though divine. Socrates paradoxically defends the divinity of love in order to show that "divine philosophy" or the love of wisdom does not pretend to idolatry and is therefore unlike the self-made gods of poetry, politics, and pedagogy. The point of his tale is to expose fictions – including Socrates' own – as such: stories that must be questioned, especially when they leave this pastoral place and re-emerge in Athens. Socrates plays the part of poet but uses lies to tell the truth, and in so doing recalibrates the relationship between humanity and divinity.

Before relating Stesichorus' divine revelation, Socrates qualifies the truth of this tale. The "soul is immortal," he explains, but adds that "'immortal' is a term applied on no basis of reasoned argument at all, but our fancy pictures the god whom we have never seen, nor fully conceived, as an immortal being, possessed of a soul and a body united for all time" (492–3). Such divinity, because it can never be known, is necessarily a work of the imagination. Presumably putting aside the issue of his tale's truth, "let these matters, and our account thereof, be as God pleases" (493), Socrates then offers an origin myth of human forgetfulness, rewriting the epic places of memory, both the underworld and the place that he claims no poet has ever written about: the heavens. Describing the "many spectacles of bliss upon the highways whereon the blessed gods pass to and fro," Socrates asking Phaedrus to "behold, there in the heaven Zeus, mighty leader," where he "drives his winged team" (494). As Socrates explains, whatever "soul has followed in the train of a god, and discerned something of truth . . . shall remain always free from hurt," but "when she is not able to follow, and sees none of it, but meeting with some mischance comes to be burdened with a load of forgetfulness and wrongdoing," the winged chariot of the soul then "sheds her wings and falls to the earth" (495).

How can a soul reascend to the heavens, recapturing this Golden Age of bliss in the train of Zeus? Only through "a recollection of those things which our souls beheld aforetime as they journeyed with their god" (496). This process of recollection is dialectical, "passing from a plurality of perceptions to a unity gathered together by reasoning" (496), by which Socrates defines himself and philosophy: "Believe me, Phaedrus, I am a lover of these divisions and collections, that I may gain the power to speak and to think, and whenever I deem another man able to discern an objective unity and plurality, I follow 'in his footsteps where he leadeth as a god'" (511–12). Yet this allusion to Homer's *Odyssey* (5.193) underscores that his tale about recollection is itself a fiction, a heuristic tale about philosophy. The recollection that Socrates describes is ultimately less divine than human, less metaphysical than poetic, less atemporal than historical. The use of dialectic, "passing from a plurality of perceptions to a unity gathered together by reasoning," produces "understanding" represented as recollection: knowledge whose origin cannot be known but which can nevertheless be found through the process of thinking philosophically, the love of wisdom told as a love story.

Socrates' tale of how love leads to divine recollection turns on the issue of idolatry. His ironic praise of divinity works to reveal how humans by nature fashion themselves as gods, both wittingly and unwittingly, and specifically as the god of love – Cupid. His vision suggests how he appropriates a theory of poetry based on the use of places and images in the art of memory, for the vision of beauty serves as the crucial reminder in this process of divine recollection. "When one who is fresh from the mystery, and saw much of the vision, beholds a godlike face or bodily form that truly expresses beauty," Socrates explains, the lover experiences "reverence as at the sight of a god, and but for fear of being deemed a very madman he would offer sacrifice to his beloved as to a holy image of deity" (497). He describes how the sight of the beloved causes the soul, Psyche, to remember her former winged state and painfully begin to regrow her wings:

> even as a teething child feels an aching and pain in its gums when a tooth has just come through, so does the soul of him who is beginning to grow his wings feel a ferment and painful irritation. Wherefore as she gazes upon the boy's beauty . . . then has she respite from her anguish, and

is filled with joy. But when she has been parted from him and become parched, the openings of those outlets at which the wings are sprouting dry up likewise and are closed . . . and thereat the whole soul round about is stung and goaded into anguish. (497–8)

Torn between joy and anguish, driven mad by love, the lover alternately "remembers the beauty of her beloved and rejoices" and despairs at his absence, worshipping the beloved as though a god. But in the process of fashioning an idol to love, she falls into forgetfulness – into a state both erotic and blissful and, fundamentally, enslaved. "She forgets them all," everything except her beloved, seeking instead both her disease and its cure, "welcoming a slave's estate and any couch where she may be suffered to lie down close beside her darling, for besides her reverence for the possessor of beauty she has found in him the only physician for her grievous suffering" (498). This powerful portrait of lovesickness describes the painful regrowth of the soul's wings, enabling her to ascend again to divinity. Yet this part of the story truly concerns the relationship of humans to one another. Crucially, Socrates admits this tale is impossible to verify, and thus belongs in the same category as the other stories he has told. "You may believe that or not, as you please; at all events the case and the nature of the lover's experience are in fact what I have said," Socrates informs Phaedrus, and then wittily cites "Homeric scholars from the unpublished works" to support his argument (498). With his story, Socrates ultimately suggests that idolatry, fashioning human love as though divine, is a supremely human tendency.

If all people love idolatrously, as Socrates suggests, then the challenge is to worship the right kind of divinity. Describing how the lover treats the beloved, "as if the beloved himself were a god he fashions for himself," Socrates explains that humans chose the god they follow, but this path ideally leads to self-knowledge – to recollection rather than forgetfulness: "Thus the followers of Zeus seek a beloved who is Zeuslike in soul; wherefore they look for one who is by nature disposed to the love of wisdom and the leading of men . . . and as they follow up the trace within themselves of the nature of their own god their task is made easier, inasmuch as they are constrained to fix their gaze upon him, and reaching out after him in memory they are possessed by him, and from him they take their ways and manners of life, in so far as a man can partake of a god" (499). To underscore this human self-fashioning, he adds: "But all this, mark you, they attribute to the beloved, and the draughts which they draw from Zeus they pour out, like bacchants, into the soul of the beloved, thus creating in him the closest possible likeness to the god they worship" (499). Socrates' point seems clear: a true lover does not pretend to be a non-lover (as Lysias does in his speech) or fashion himself as a god. Lies about the gods are, finally, lies about people – or, rather, the lies that people tell about themselves. The beloved in turn comes to recognize this truth "with amazement": that he has found the highest love, "that all his other friends and kinsmen have nothing to offer in comparison with this friend in whom there dwells a god" (501).

"Divinity" in Socrates' terms connects with the "divining power" of the mind. Love can lead either to ruin or to recollection depending upon the ability to discern the difference between divinity and idolatry. The larger point here is political, as well as pedagogical and poetical. The danger of mistaking fiction for truth has to do with the world that exists outside of this dialogue's pastoral sweet spot. With a rhetorical question, Socrates asks, "Tell me then, when an orator, or a king, succeeds in acquiring the power of a Lycurgus, a Solon, or a Darius, and so winning immortality among his people as a speech writer, doesn't he deem himself a peer of the gods while still living, and do not people of later ages hold the same opinion of him when they contemplate his writings?" (503). This cuts to the heart of Phaedrus' own idolatry, his unquestioning belief in Lysias' arguments and his attempt to reiterate them. Socrates jestingly refers to the issue of idolatry at the start and end of the dialogue when Phaedrus challenges him to a little friendly competition: Phaedrus says, "You have undertaken to make a better speech than that in [Lysias'] book here," and "I in my turn undertake like the nine Archons to set up at Delphi a golden life-sized statue, not only of myself but of you also" (483). It is precisely this idolatry that Socrates refuses, not wanting to be a god or an idol but instead a lover known by another name: "To call [a philosopher] wise, Phaedrus, would, I think be going too far; the epithet is proper only to a god. A name that would fit him better, and have more seemliness, would be 'lover of wisdom,' or something similar" (524). The name that "would fit," that would be proper or apropos to his lesson, turns on the larger issue of poetry's place in culture.

Socrates concludes his story of love with a witty apostrophe: "dear God of love, I have offered the fairest recantation and fullest atonement that my powers could compass," adding that "some of its language, in particular, was perforce poetical, to please Phaedrus" (502). The propriety of the "poetical" in a story of divinity clearly relates to the imaginative truths that fiction can reveal. In the tale of Theuth, as discussed in the previous chapter, King Thamus stands as an exemplar, for he questions the gifts of the god Theuth, and determines the truth of their worth for himself. That Phaedrus recognizes the tale of Theuth as a fiction, as well as Socrates' other tall tales, represents the end of the lesson: the ability to tell the truth, or discern self-fashioned gods. As Socrates tells it, love of wisdom serves as a reminder of divinity as the god within. The *Phaedrus* redefines divinity as Socrates rewrites a cultural fiction, replacing old Trojan tales of love and ruin with a new story of history. The dialogue itself creates a new place through its revisionary art of memory: a common place where "friends have all things in common" in the pleasant place of the dialogue itself and, ultimately, in writing. Socrates' final prayer to the god Pan resonates throughout *The Shepheardes Calender*, which repeatedly refers back to Pan and the various kinds of divinity attributed to this mythic god – poetic, religious, political – by which Spenser also reveals how fictions find use in the world.

*   *   *

Through the *Phaedrus*, Spenser highlights the problem of idolatry: interpreting poetic fictions as divine truth, fashioning rulers as though gods. E.K.'s allusion to the tale of Stesichorus insinuates that Colin's songs for Rosalind are idolatrous fictions whereas his poems for Elizabeth represent true divinity. But the reminder of Socrates' palinode in *Aprill* raises the question of how Colin's poem to Eliza – itself a palinode, as a labour of love that he now silently repudiates – should be remembered, as truth or fiction. Although the poem asserts, "Shee is my goddesse plaine / And I her shepherds swayne" (97–8), Elizabeth's divinity is represented as mythology, as "*Syrinx* daughter without spotte, / Which *Pan* the shepheards God of her begot" (50–1). Colin never commits himself to naming either Elizabeth or her "heavenly race" as more than poetic gods (53).

E.K. shows no such restraint, and his gloss on "Syrinx" exposes his determination to shape Colin's poetry as prophetic, divine, and imperial. He identifies "Syrinx" as "the name of a Nymphe of Arcadie, whom when Pan being in love pursued" and, in Ovidian fashion, as the origin of pastoral poetry (79). "She flying from him, of the Gods was turned into a reede," E.K. explains, "So that Pan catching at the Reedes . . . made the Reedes to pype: which he seeing, tooke of them, and in remembrance of his lost love, made him a pype thereof" (79). But he refuses to see this as mere mythology and instead comically confuses truth with fiction, poetry with people: "But here by Pan and Syrinx is

not to bee thoughte, that the shephearde simplye meante those Poetical Gods: but rather supposing (as seemeth) her graces progenie to be
divine and immortal . . . So that by Pan is here meant the most famous
and victorious King, her highnesse Father, late of worthy memorye K.
Henry the eyght. And by the name, oftymes . . . be noted kings and
mighty Potentates: And in some place Christ himselfe, who is the verye
Pan and god of Shepheardes" (79–80). This invocation of Pan returns
once again to the *Phaedrus* and, indirectly, to pastoral poetry. Socrates
offers the dialogue's final prayer to Pan as a way of culminating their
literary activity, and to underscore what makes it edifying: that is, the
ability to recognize fictions of divinity as fictions of power. E.K.'s distinction between poetic fictions of divinity and true divinity serve as an
ironic reminder of Plato's dialogue, but what makes his commentary
comic also makes it profoundly serious. With tortured logic, E.K. fashions a divine genealogy from Pan, in effect authorizing himself to my-
thologize the divine right of Tudor rule, conflating Tudor divinity with
poetry's divine origins. This tale of Pan making reeds into a pipe "in
remembraunce of his lost love" casts Anne Boleyn as the nymph "Syrinx," who inspired the love leading to Pan's divine "remembrance": the
birth of poetry and Queen Elizabeth, too. But E.K. protests too much
about "Poetical Gods," and his narrative seems like little more than a
just-so story of Tudor divinity. Rather than reading Colin's praise for
Elizabeth poetically, E.K. takes it literally, affirming "Elisa" as divinity
itself. The bizarre trajectory of his gloss on "Syrinx" suggests Spenser's
own editorial comment on his learned commentator.

Spenser undercuts E.K.'s ambition to construct the House of Tudor
as a place where poetry and providence, story and history, meet. Some
of the most anodyne praise in Colin's poetry becomes fodder for E.K.'s
most adamant assertions. "Tell me, have ye seene her angelick face, /
Like *Phœbe* fayre?" Colin's poem asks (64–5), where "The Redde rose
medled with the White yfere, / In either cheeke depeincten lively
chere" (68–9). To these questions, E.K. replies: "By the mingling of the
Redde rose and the White, is meant the uniting of the two principall
houses of Lancaster and of Yorke: by whose longe discord and deadly
debate, this realm many yeares was sore traveiled, and almost cleane
decayed. Til the famous Henry the seventh, of the line of Lancaster, taking to wife . . . Elisabeth, daughter to the fourth Edward of the house of
Yorke, begat the most royal Henry the eyght . . . in whom was the firste
union of the Whyte Rose and the Redd" (80–1). E.K.'s interpretation
makes Colin's poetry (or its ambiguous recollection) into a political allegory, transforming past ruin into prophesied repair via the providential

rise of the divine House of Tudor. He credits the Tudors with uniting Lancaster's and York's "principall houses" as one edifice, with salvaging England from the civil wars, the "long discord and deadly debate" that threatened to leave its nation "almost cleane decayed." Here as throughout his glosses to *Aprill*, E.K. draws suggestive parallels with Virgil's *Fourth Eclogue*, in which the return of the Golden Age represents the hope for political peace after Rome's civil wars. Ironically, though, E.K.'s interpretations remind readers of how interpretation radically alters a work after the death of the author – in this case, Virgil. Clearly, Virgil did (or could) not intend his *Fourth Eclogue* to be read as Christian prophecy, as it came to be, though it set the stage for his prophecy of Rome's "empire without end" in the *Aeneid*. What the sanctification of empire means clearly changes with the reception of Virgil's works, especially through the relationship of the *Eclogues* to the *Aeneid*. By emphasizing the role of reception in constructing a work's meaning, Spenser implies similar complexities about the relation of *The Shepheardes Calender* to his future *Faerie Queene*.

E.K.'s interpretation of *Aprill*'s final two emblems reinforces his Virgilian view of authority, his vision of the poet as heroic cultural architect, but it also recasts Virgil's eclogue in light of his epic. Thenot's emblem in *Aprill* quotes Aeneas' question to his disguised mother (Venus dressed as the nymph Diana), "*O quam te memorem virgo?*" (163), as she guides him toward his destiny, his true love, Rome. In a sense, this articulates the central question of *Aprill*: how should this Virgin be remembered? This question clearly applies to the Virgin Queen, who fashioned herself as another Astraea, the Virgin who returns a lost time. Hobbinol's emblematic reply, "O dea certe," provides E.K. with the proof he needs that *Aprill* follows Virgil's *Fourth Eclogue* as a prophecy of a renewed Golden Age for epic and England (165):

> This Poesye is taken out of Virgile, and there of him used in the person of Æneas to his mother Venus, appearing to him in likenesse of one of the Dianaes damosells.. there most divinely set forth. To which similitude of divinitie Hobbinoll comparing the excelency of Elisa, and being through the worthynes of Colins song . . . Whom Thenot answereth with another part of the like verse, as confirming by his graunt and approvaunce, that Elisa is nowhit inferiour to the Majestie of her, of whome that Poete so boldly pronounced, O dea certe. (84)

In his gloss, E.K. reverses the order of things: he mistakenly attributes the question to Hobbinol and the reply to Thenot, "O dea certe." Yet

Hobbinol's answer to the question of how to remember this virgin, as "a goddess, certainly," is rendered ambiguous in the context of the *Aeneid*. In one sense, Venus – whether as herself or in disguise – should be remembered as a goddess. In another sense, Venus is clearly *not* the goddess – whether Astraea or the Virgin Mary – that later readers, like E.K., attributed to the poem. Spenser's positioning of Virgil's two key works has a profoundly deflating effect: rather than the *Aeneid* fulfilling the Golden Age prophecy of the *Fourth Eclogue*, both appear to be poetic fictions. As a Socratic figure, Hobbinol might endow this reply with an irony that Thenot could not capture: "a goddess, certainly" would carry the same sort of weight and meaning as Socrates' prayer to Pan at the end of the *Phaedrus* – a prayer meant to indicate the opposite of what it seems to, the absence of true divinity except as a poetic fiction. Nevertheless, E.K. presents Elizabeth as the divine fulfilment of Virgil's prophecy in the *Fourth Eclogue*, realized in the movement from pastoral to epic. To E.K., Colin and Spenser clearly remember Elizabeth just as Virgil would: surely, as a goddess. Yet this emblem reminds readers of *Aprill*'s decidedly un-Virgilian pattern of recollection, asking us to consider another, very different way of remembering Elizabeth and the Tudor line. Aeneas' demand, "O quam te memorem virgo?", poses other, more important questions: What authorizes Elizabeth as a "goddess"? How else might England remember her or the Tudors? Whether Elizabeth is called (or constructed as) a goddess in Virgilian fashion, or whether she is divinely recollected in the sense of Platonic dialogue, is central to *Aprill*'s eclogue. Since Colin prefers Rosalind's "meane house" to "Elisa's" House of Tudor, since he confounds all warnings to move from pastoral to epic, E.K.'s epic assertions of *Aprill*'s Virgilian ambitions are suspect.

Colin's poem promises that Elizabeth "shalbe a grace, / To fyll the fourth place, / And reigne with the rest in heaven" (115–17). Yet *Aprill* provides two competing ways of viewing this "place" and, more broadly, the place of poetry in culture. Building a House of Tudor from Colin's poetic remains in Virgilian fashion, past becomes prologue as E.K. asserts this poem is indeed divine prophecy. From another view, however, this pastoral dialogue remembers the past in every sense, in ways that reach beyond the dichotomy of Amor and Roma. Plato's *Phaedrus* serves as a reminder of sorts, presenting a third option (in the love triangle) for understanding how *Aprill* constructs a place in English culture, a memorial edifice, for both the Tudors and for Colin. As I have been arguing, Hobbinol's recitation of Colin's poem energizes dialogue about the "right" and "wrong" kinds of love in the sweet spot and thus recollects divinity not as truth but as a cultural fiction. With the tale of Stesichorus, Spenser recalls Socrates' art of recollecting ruin as precisely a fiction that stands against the Trojan tales that poets, pedagogues, and politicians usually remember.

June: "Such pierlesse pleasures have we in these places"

June returns to the question of poetry's proper "place" but with a new answer: that poetry's place lies in England's own pastoral places, the sweet spot that will mark the location of *The Faerie Queene*. In the "Argument" to *June*, E.K. summarizes Colin's continuing trials in the "Labyrinth of Love": Colin still complains of "being (as is aforesaid) enamoured of a Country lasse Rosalind, and having (as seemeth) founde place in her heart, he lamenteth to his deare frend Hobbinoll, that he is nowe forsaken unfaithfully, and in his steed . . . another shepheard received disloyally" (109). This eclogue thus introduces Spenser's epic in more ways than one. Chaucer's use of locational memory in *The House of Fame* provides a crucial model of authorship here, for he imagines the location of poetry within just such a "Labyrinth of Love." *June* announces Spenser's intentions for *The Faerie Queene* when Colin cites Chaucer's authorial "paterne" as the model for building his own house of fame. As I will suggest, Chaucer's obsession with place in *The House of Fame*, with the location for memory and locational memory, mirrors Spenser's own obsession with place in *The Shepheardes Calender*. Like Chaucer, Spenser draws upon the art of memory to describe how ruins – fragments of literary texts, old words – provide places for recollection by which new houses of fame are continually built and rebuilt.

Hobbinol begins *June* in Socratic fashion by praising the "place" of their discourse. "Here the place, whose pleasaunt syte / From other shades hath weand my wandring mynde," he exclaims, "The simple ayre, the gentle warbling wynde, / So calme, so coole, as no where else I fynde" (1–2, 4–5). This place, England itself, is an ideal location for writing poetry, and Hobbinol reminds Colin of this by recalling his past successes. But heartbroken Colin, who has been replaced in Rosalind's heart, describes himself as a homeless and failed hero: "But I unhappy man, whom cruell fate, / And angry Gods pursue from coste to coste, / Can nowhere fynd, to shroude my lucklesse pate" (14–16). It would seem that Colin's problem resides in his idea of home, located in classical epic, which proves too elusive to reach. *June* would also seem to represent a palinode of sorts in which Colin rebukes his former passion and poetry. He recalls how in the "carelesse yeeres" of his "youth," he had "in verses made" his "plaintive please" known, described as a kind of idolatry (33, 42). Although he once would "seeke for Queene apples unrype, / To give my *Rosalind* . . . / To Crowne her golden locks," his "yeeres more rype, / And losse of her" have taught him hard lessons (43–7). By treating Rosalind as his "Queene," by idolizing Amor and Roma, Colin seemingly remains trapped in the "Labyrinth of Love," unable to progress to the right kind of love for Eliza and England.[34] Despite this bleak picture, however, *June* ultimately creates a holographic image of Colin's progress through love's labyrinth. Spenser does so, paradoxically, by creating a false debate between Hobbinol and Colin about the ideal "place" for epic poetry – the kind of false debates, I will argue later in this book, that shape *The Faerie Queene*.

Countering Colin's pessimism, Hobbinol points in two temporal directions. Recollecting the "delight" of his scattered rhymes, the "rymes and roundelayes, / Which thou were wont on wastfull hylls to singe" (51, 49–50), Hobbinol suggests how past can also be prologue, for he recalls Colin's former epic greatness in this pastoral setting: "I saw *Calliope* wyth Muses moe, / Soone as thy oaten pype began to sound" (57–8), he exclaims, as "They drewe abacke, as halfe with shame confound, / Shepheard to see, them in theyr art outgoe" (63–4). Pointing toward the future, Hobbinol advises Colin that he needs both a different love and a change of place, symbolically exchanging Rome for England, Rosalind for Eliza, pastoral for epic. "Forsake the solye, that so doth thee bewitch: / Leave me those hilles, where harbrough nis to see," he pleads, "And to the dales resort, where shepheards ritch, / And fruictfull flocks bene every where to see" (18–19, 21–2). In this place, Colin will return to a Golden Age he never left, where

> frendly Faeries, met with many Graces,
> And lightfote Nymphes can chace the lingring night . . .
> Whilst systers nyne, which dwell on *Parnasse* hight,
> Doe make them musick, for their more delight:
> And *Pan* himselfe to kisse their christall faces,
> Will pype and daunce, when *Phœbe* shineth bright:
> Such pierlesse pleasures have we in these places. (25–32)

The place that Hobbinol describes, of course, is the place they already inhabit: England's green and pleasant land. This place of "frendly Faeries, met with many Graces," where "*Pan* . . . / will pype and daunce, when *Phœbe* shineth bright," is also the same place that *The Faerie Queene* will share. Implicit in the movement from Rosalind's and Rome's bewitching hills to Elizabeth's and England's enchanted dales (anatomy aside) is a revealing paradox: Colin must remain in the place of pastoral in order to advance to epic. Rather than needing to search for home, *June*'s eclogue ironically suggests that Colin is already there.

Colin's rejection of fame deepens the paradox, suggesting that *The Faerie Queene* will take place in this location and will be a poetic edifice fashioned by locational memory. "I play to please my selfe," he asserts, "Ne strive to winne renowne, or passe the rest: / With shepheard sittes not, followe flying fame: / But feede his flocke in fields, where falls hem best" (72–6).This "paterne" of poetry and fame belongs to the *Calender*'s other "Tityrus," Chaucer. "The God of shepheards *Tityrus* is dead, / Who taught me homely, as I can, to make," Colin laments, who "whilst he lived, was the soveraigne head / Of shepheards all," for "Well couth he ... lightly slake / The flames, which love within his heart had bredd / And tell us mery tales" (81–7). The English Tityrus' transformative power provides a model of edification:

Nowe dead is he, and lyeth wrapt in lead ...
And all hys passing skil with him is fledde,
The fame whereof doth dayly greater growe.
But if on me some little drops would flowe,
Of that the spring was in his learned hedde,
I soone would learne these woods, to wayle my woe,
And teache the trees, their trickling teares to shedde. (89–96)

In his gloss to this passage, typically, E.K. attempts to diminish Chaucer's influence on Colin and *The Shepheardes Calender*. Of "Tityrus" he writes, "That by Tityrus is meant Chaucer, hath bene already sufficiently sayde, and by thys more playne appeareth, that he sayth, he tolde merye tales. Such as be hys Canterburie tales. whom he calleth the God of Poetes for hys excellence, so as Tullie calleth Lentulus ... the God of hys lyfe" (117). This passage contrasts with E.K.'s gloss in *Aprill* to Pan, the god of shepherds, as a representation of divinity: if Pan represents both Christ and the Tudors, E.K. can interpret Colin's poetry as Virgilian and prophetic. When referring to the other Tityrus, however, E.K. denies Chaucer's divinity as a poetic commonplace, calling him "God of Poetes" in order to emphasize Chaucer's humanity.

Typically, E.K.'s gloss is half right for all the wrong reasons: Pan is always, only, a god of poetry in this poem – the same god to whom

Socrates and Phaedrus dedicate their common place where "friends have all things in common," including love poetry. Nevertheless, E.K.'s gloss ironically reminds readers of Chaucer's central place in the *Calender*. As previously discussed, E.K. misinterprets this important passage in the introductory "Letter to Harvey," where he associates Colin's demurral of fame with classical and Continental authors rather than Chaucer. By describing the poem as a "Labyrinth of Love," E.K. alludes to the poem in which Chaucer similarly refuses to be named by fame: *The House of Fame*. Although E.K. suggests that Chaucer's influence is limited to *The Canterbury Tales*, *The Shepheardes Calender* has much in common with this poem, which bears a similarly ambiguous relation to more epic work. Chaucer locates the matter for his memory in the labyrinth that lies beneath Fame's palace, the house of trees-cum-texts that he recollects as his house of fame. In so doing, Chaucer mediates the binaries of Amor and Roma, preparing the ground for new tales of love about England. Colin's eulogy for Chaucer remembers his art of memory, I suggest here, by recalling the organic, changing nature of England's poetry.

Thinking of England: Chaucer's *House of Fame*

Chaucer's *House of Fame* epitomizes the English art of memory upon which Spenser builds. As Beryl Rowland argues, "In the *House of Fame*, the explication of the art of memory is far more complex because it is central to the subject of the poem," suggesting further that "Chaucer's 'tresorye' of the mind is comparable to St. Augustine's 'palace of memory' in the *Confessions*."[35] Chaucer uses the Augustinian art of memory not only to demonstrate how he fashions the poem, I will argue, but also in order to tell a new story of history – his own and England's – built not upon the ruins of Troy but upon those of the English language.

On one level, Chaucer builds multiple houses of memory throughout the poem – from the Temple of Venus, to the Palace of Fame, to the labyrinthine house of love stories that forms its symbolic foundation – filled with vivid images that his poetic persona traverses; on another level, though, Chaucer's poem explores the art of memory as a method by which poets recollect the past, implicitly criticizing its uses and revising the matter of memory. This complex engagement with the art of memory amounts to a reception history that dovetails in crucial ways with the reception of different Trojan tales, including, it would seem, Chaucer's own. In this dream vision Chaucer seeks novelty, new tales of love, by reforming the art of memory; this includes Virgil and Ovid, Plato and Aristotle, but also the novel uses of these authors by the triumvirate of *amor summus roma*: Dante, Petrarch, and Boccaccio. As scholars have suggested, *The House of Fame* can be read as a playful parody of *The Divine Comedy* and poetry as divine revelation.[36] Divided into three locations like *The Divine Comedy*, Chaucer's poetic persona "Geffrey" begins at the Temple of Venus and is then carried to Fame's Palace by Jove's eagle, which gives him a preliminary lesson about this edifice and the process of edification related to the art of memory. Chaucer's humane comedy nevertheless makes a serious argument about the relation of poetry to power. *The House of Fame* locates the place for poetry in neither Temple nor Palace, places where lovers worship power and poetry idolatrously, but in a third location of Chaucer's design: the labyrinthine edifice illustrating this process of edification, the place where the speaker "Geffrey" discovers new matter of England's memory as new tales of love.

In the Temple of Venus, Geffrey discovers, worshipping love means remembering Trojan tales in all their variety. This "temple y-mad of glas" exemplifies the poetic use of the art of memory: an architectural space filled with vivid images, "curious portreytures / And queynte maner of figures."[37] As in the *Aeneid*, where Aeneas sees the story of Troy's fall on the walls in the Temple of Juno, Geffrey discovers the Trojan legend "wryten on a table of bras" hanging on a wall (142). But as he views competing tales of Troy, Virgil's and Ovid's, telling the truth about them proves impossible, for these tales differ in their depictions of Rome's founding legend based on their radically different account of Dido and Aeneas' affair. Chaucer laughs at his own persona's perplexity, a speaker who has an idolatrous fascination with Amor and Roma but proclaims his lack of experience with love. Turning away from describing Dido and Aeneas together, the speaker complains,

> What shulde I speke more queynte
> Or peyne me my wordes peynte
> To speke of love? It wol nat be;
> I can nat of that facultee. (245–8)

A deus ex machina in the form of the eagle arrives to clear up Geffrey's confusion, who informs him that Jupiter, though pleased that Geffrey "Hast served so ententifly / His blinde nevew Cupido, / And faire Venus" (616–18), also thinks he needs new material:

> thou has no tydinges
> Of Loves folk, if they be glade,
> Ne of nought elles that God made;
> ... of thy verray neighebores
> That dwellen almost at thy dores
> Thou herest neither that ne this. (644–51)

Instead of going home and reading another book, Jove (via the eagle) tells Geffrey that he must learn new tales of England – the "verray neighebores" that Geffrey has neglected in favour of tales of Troy. Jupiter directs him to the House of Fame, where he will learn new tales of love, both truth and lies: "Of Loves folke mo tydinges / Both sothe sawes and lesinges" (675–6). This rebuke may speak ironically to Chaucer's own poetic career, his rewriting of old Trojan tales with *Troilus and Criseyde*, just as the conjunction of new English tales and fame may speak to *The Canterbury Tales*.[38] That the king of the gods gives the author a lesson in writing about human rather than divine love also suggests how Chaucer makes light of Jove's divinity and, by extension, Dante's claims for the divinity of power and poetry, bound to Virgil's vision of Rome's "empire without end."

This tacit complaint about idolatry finds its fullest expression in Fame's palace where, instead of learning new stories of love, Geffrey witnesses the idolatrous worship of Fame – a fantastic figure at once monstrous and monarchial, and a blend of Virgil's and Ovid's creations.[39] Chaucer fashions Fame's Palace as a memory theatre and, crucially, as a court of power. From his "remembraunce" (1182) of "this riche lusty place / That Fames halle called was" (1356–7), Geffrey describes an edifice miraculously held together "withouten peces or joininges" (1187), crowded with "Imageries and tabernacles" (1190) and filled to overflowing with crowds of people seeking to win a name from Fame:

> Ful the castel, al aboute,
> Of alle maner of minstrales
> And gestiour, that tellen tales
> Bothe of weping and of game,
> Of al that longeth unto Fame. (1196–1200)

He describes Fame on her throne, "Sat in a see imperial, / That made was of a rubee al," as a larger-than-life figure drawn from Virgil's and Ovid's portraits: "A feminyne creature; / That never, formed by nature" is stretched such "That with hir feet she th'erthe reighte, / And with hir heed she touched hevene" (1361–2, 1365–6, 1374–5). Crucially, poetry supports the House of Fame, as Geffrey observes Homer "hye on a pilere / Of yren," along with Virgil, Ovid, Lucan, and so on (1465–6). With these famous authors thus transformed into literal pillars, "besy for to bere up Troye" (1472), Chaucer intimates that political ambition and tales of Troy are mutually supporting. Fame herself appears to be fashioned as an idol of gold with the power to confer immortality on those who worship her. Geffrey observes the "right greet company" that kneels before Fame and begs her to give them names: "Graunte us, lady shene / Ech of us, of thy grace, a bone!" (1528, 1536–7). Gold and riches pervade Fame's palace, suggesting a reciprocal relationship between legitimizing fictions and wealth. But Geffrey also witnesses the arbitrary judgments of Fame, who at a whim turns petitioners over to Slander, so that "every wight / Speke of hem harm and shrewednesse / In stede of good and worthinesse" (1626–8). Feeling sorry for those unjustly slandered, he seems to reject fame. When a voice suddenly asks, "Frend, what is thy name? / Artow come hider to han fame?" (1871–2), Geffrey replies that he has not come here to seek a name from Fame but to learn something new:

> The cause why I stonde here:
> Som newe tydings for to lere
> Som newe thing, I noot what,
> Tydinges, other this or that,
> Of love or swiche things glade. (1885–9)

From what he has seen, he says, "these be no swiche tydinges / As I mene of" (1894–5).

Geffrey's discontent with Fame's palace catalyses his movement to the third location of the poem, the edifice that provides his promised edification in new tales of love. Hearing that Geffrey has not yet heard "newe tydings," an unnamed man takes him to this other place:

> Com forth, and stond no longer here,
> And I wol thee, withouten drede,
> In swich another place lede
> Ther thou shalt here many oon. (1912–15)

From Fame's palace, he leads Geffrey to a place that lies below it: "An hous, that Domus Dedaly, / That Laborintus cleped is / Nas made so woderliche ywis" (1920–2). The Palace of Fame would seem to be built upon the Matter of Troy, the pillars of poetry, and yet there is new matter below its surface, where new tales rise and are gathered together. Woven of "twigges, falwe, rede, / And grene eek" (1936–7), showing thousands of entrances, and full of noise, this place both recalls and renovates earlier houses of fame. Penelope Reed Doob observes that this edifice "is woven of multicolored twigs: it is literally *textus*, like Virgil's labyrinth and like literature."[40] Yet Chaucer clearly remakes the labyrinthine underworld as a place for memory, in ways that speak as much to Dante as to Virgil.

This labyrinthine edifice represents Chaucer's method and matter of edification, his art of memory, and the location where he remembers England. As Geffrey recalls this dream vision from within "the tresorie it shette / Of my brayne" (524–5), he offers a portrait of faculty psychology that dovetails with and indeed demonstrates his poetics, which explores the relationship of poetry to "place" (719). The labyrinth is a place "fild ful of tydinges" (1957), pervaded by rumors and stories –

> Of werres, of pees, of mariages,
> Of reste, of labour, of viages,
> Of abode, of deeth, of lyfe,
> Of love, of hate, acorde, of stryfe. (1961–4)

It exemplifies the eagle's earlier lesson about how fame is built through the gathering and sorting of all spoken language: "every speche or noise or soun, / . . . Mot nede come to Fames Hous" (783–6). Explaining that "Soun is nought but air y-broken" (765), the eagle describes speech as being like pebbles thrown into a pond, spreading ripples in the air; because "every thing . . . Hath his proper mansioun, / To which it seketh to repaire" (753–5), even spoken words, "every speche of every man, / . . . Moveth up on high to pace / Kindely to Fame's place" (849–52). Geffrey observes this himself: how sounds enter the labyrinth, the imagination; move up into the House of Fame, a form of judgment and a filtering system; and then finally enter the memory. As already suggested, Chaucer appears to derive his story of language from Augustine's *Confessions*, a version of faculty psychology that finds a parallel in Alma's Castle of the Soul. Still more expansively, the Eagle attributes his heuristic explanation to "Aristotle and Daun Platon" (759). Chaucer combines a Platonic narrative of originary ruin and recollection with an Aristotelian portrait of the psyche that ultimately replaces Trojan tales. In this "new" tale of love, the House of Fame captures words – "air y-broken," symbolic ruins – every one of which find their proper "place" within "so juste a place," a place where words are remembered and then judged (in the double meaning of court, monarchial and judicial), and then given a name by fame – good or bad. The broken sounds or words that fill the edifice are continually edified in new ways, creating a house fashioned from tales and changing with every new story.

Significantly, the Eagle calls this lesson a work of "imaynacioun," and, like Socrates speaking to Phaedrus, tells Geffrey to "Tak it in ernest or in game" (728, 822). This advice about the larger truth of the tale applies to Geffrey's and the reader's edification. In *The House of Fame*, memory and imagination share a common place, both intimately related to the process of recollection. The inability to tell the truth in any absolute way suggests how history depends upon the imaginative construction of tales and also upon the recognition that such tales rely on fiction, at least in part. Chaucer implies that tales only lie when (as in the temple and palace) they pretend to tell truths, and that poetry's truth ultimately depends upon its use.

Amazed by the sight of a crowd, "a congregacioun / Of folk as I saw rome aboute" (2034–5), Geffrey hears a jumble of tales both true and false, yet this confusion of truth and fiction would seem to be the end of Geffrey's lesson about fame: he discovers the process by which tales are transmitted regardless of their truth and the effect their reception can have. This house illustrates the formation of myths, specifically what may be Trojan stories of history: the building of tall tales and their movement from "north and southe" and "fro mouth to mouthe," "encresing evermo" until "From a spark spronge amis / . . . al a citee brent up is" reminds readers of the development of Trojan tales of ruin and their recollection over time and across space (2075–80). With this vivid illustration of the translation of culture through poetry, this third house, though a constantly whirling edifice, encloses the matter of Chaucer's poetic recollection. Geffrey observes the house "Was ful of shipmen and pilgrymes / With scrippes bretful of lesings / Entremedled with tydinges" and watches "pardoneres, / Currours, and eek messageres / With boistes crammed ful of lyes" moving in all directions (2122–9). These shipmen, pardoners, and pilgrims carry tales mixing truth with fiction, providing Geffrey with his new "tydinges" of love:

And as I alderfastest wente
Aboute, and dide al myn entente

Me for to pleyen and for to lere,
And eek a tyding for to here
That I had herd of som contree
That shal nat now be told for me –
For it no nede is, redely. (2131–7)

The "contree" that Geffrey demurs from naming can be no other than
England, and, as he suggests, the new love stories discovered here will
shape his poetic memory. The multitude in the "Labyrinth" represents
the Matter of England (rather than the Matter of Troy, or Rome, or even
Britain) that he will continue to remember.

In the midst of the din and confusion of the labyrinth, Geffrey sees
"a man, / Which that I nevene nat ne can, / But he semed for to be /
A man of great auctoritee" (2155–8), at which point the poem ends, an
abrupt conclusion that has led many readers to assume that Chaucer
never completed it. Yet it is significant that the poem ends without returning to the dream vision frame, with the speaker still wandering
through the labyrinth. The obvious parallel for this concluding sight
of "A man of great auctoritee" would be Dante's vision of divinity at
the end of *The Divine Comedy*, rendered in a more homely and perhaps
parodic style; Chaucer catches a glimpse of himself here, and his future
authority. Yet much as Geffrey declines a name from Fame, so Chaucer
refuses to name himself here. Unlike Dante, who makes himself the
subject/author of his pilgrimage, Chaucer represents himself as one
of many pilgrims telling tales of love in English and about England.
Ceasing to idolize Venus or Fame, books or monarchs, Chaucer in effect
authorizes himself in his own "contree," recollecting these tales in no
typical epic but as a story about home all the same, and a voyage that
extends the pilgrimage of *The House of Fame*.

As Lee Patterson argues, Chaucer's poem criticizes poetry's idolatrous relationship to power: "the *House of Fame* presents a trenchant
commentary on both the vagaries of service in the prince's court and
its effect on literary ambition. In Fame's court writers become mere
agents of the powerful . . . their mutual task is simply to bear up the
fame of the mighty. In this world, even the greatest of poets are simply
propagandists."[41] Chaucer's poem clearly seeks to distinguish between
fame that depends upon fashioning rulers as gods and fame that insists upon remaining human, refusing to worship the idols of power,
poetry, and pedagogy. It matters that Geffrey chooses to remain in the
labyrinth at the end of the poem, for while Petrarch may long to emerge

from his labyrinth of love but cannot because he is torn between poetry and divinity, Chaucer remains undivided in a space of ambiguity: he has found his place. With this labyrinth, Chaucer rewrites the place of memory not as heaven, purgatory, and hell, but as the place he calls home: England. Rather than fashioning a monument to fame, Chaucer creates a house of memory that remains in ruins, an edifice fashioned from earlier texts that can grow and be grafted onto new family trees. Just as Plato relocates poetry in the space, the sweet spot, of philosophical dialogue, so Chaucer imagines *The House of Fame* as a place where "broken sounds" are perpetually remembered.

*   *   *

Chaucer's poem holds a centrally important place in the *June* eclogue: as Chaucer recollects new tales of love in (and for) England, he suggests that Amor does not always or necessarily equal Roma. *The House of Fame* provides an alternative architectural model that answers E.K.'s and the shepherds' Virgilian fantasies of poetic immortality, including their belief that poetry's place belongs in the "Princes pallace." Colin's rejection of fame findsat least a partial reflection in Geffrey's rejection of "Fama": Chaucer's persona begins by idolizing Venus and her offspring Aeneas, but Geffrey ultimately refuses to worship Fame at her court of power. This refusal to deify monarchy speaks to the central if unspoken debate between E.K. and Spenser about how poetry speaks to power and, specifically, about how *The Shepheardes Calender* represents the Tudors. In contrast to Dante, Chaucer refuses to attribute to poetry any capacity for divine revelation; moreover, unlike Virgil and Ovid, Chaucer's portrait of fame revels in the inextricability of truth and lies, story and history, which marks poetry and, finally, which makes fame the product of collective memory – the crowd that fills the labyrinth with love stories – rather than either prince or poet per se. Ultimately, Chaucer takes a very Socratic stance on his own Platonic love stories, suggesting that when fiction acknowledges its status as such, it teaches how to tell, or discern, complex truths. In a sense, *The House of Fame* allows Spenser to echo Colin's declaration of independence: he plays to please himself, not in order to divide poetry from power (clearly an impossibility) but in order to emulate Chaucer's perspective on truth-as-fiction, never pretending that his poetry can fashion any gods except as idols.

Chaucer's poem suggests how England represents a "place" for poetry in ways that E.K. fails, albeit amusingly and productively, to understand. Rather than following Virgil's career pattern, Spenser adopts Chaucer's paternity, a fact that E.K. remains blissfully ignorant of, evidenced by a series of glosses that take the meaning of "place" all too literally. Of Hobbinol's description of shepherd land as a "Paradise," E.K. identifies this not as England but as "Eden . . . Which of the most learned is thought to be in Mesopotamia" (114). He also fails to take Hobbinol's advice to Colin "Forsake the soyle" in figurative terms: "This is no poetical fiction, but unfeynedly spoken of the Poetic selfe, who for speciall occasion of private affayres (as I have bene partly of himselfe informed) and for his more preferment removing out of the Northparts came into the South, as Hobbinoll indeede advised him privately" (114). E.K. reads Hobbinol's description of "Those hylles" not as allegories for Rome's seven hills but as "the North countrye, where he dwelt" and "The Dales" as "The Southpartes, where he nowe abydeth" (114–15).

These glosses attempt to map the "place" of poetry onto England's geography but they miss the mark, most dramatically in the context of Spenser's English epic. E.K. offers a preposterous historicist commentary on the phrase "Frendly faeries," which he glosses with another time and place, "when all Italy was distraicte into the Factions of the Guelfes and Gibelins, being two famous houses in Florence," translated to England: "Which words nowe from them (as many thinge els) be come into our usage, and for Guelfes and Gibelines, we say Elfes and Goblins" (115). Despite his obsession with Spenser's eventual move to epic, and despite his claims to special knowledge and insider status, E.K. fails to observe what readers can easily recognize: an announcement of *The Faerie Queene*. Typically, he chooses to interpret the phrase "Frendly faeries" in the context of Italy and Dante's epic. Nevertheless, E.K.'s initial comments on this same phrase inadvertently suggest a more important context:

> Frendly faeries) the opinion of Faeries and elfes is very old, and yet sticketh very religiously in the myndes of some. But to roote that rancke opinion of Elfes oute of mens hearts, the truth is, that there be no such thinges, nor yet the shadowes of the things, but onely by a sort of bald Friers and knavish shavelings so feigned; which as in all other things, so in that, sought to nousell the comen people in ignorounce, least being once acquainted with the truth of things, they woulde in tyme smell out the untruth of theyr packed pelfe and Masspenie religion. (115)

E.K.'s gloss recalls the comic fairy tale with which the Wife of Bath begins her Arthurian story in *The Canterbury Tales*, but with a reversal.

The Wife claims that "In th'olde dayes of the Kyng Arthour . . . Al was this land fulfild of fayerye," but in the now disenchanted world "hooly freres" have driven them all out by blessing their dwellings.[42] E.K. instead argues that the fairies were lies told by these friars, indicative of the bad "Massepenie" or Roman Catholic religion. Revealing his Protestant leanings, E.K. also reveals his ignorance of Spenser's epic, which though a modern Protestant allegory will be set in medieval (and Roman Catholic?) England.

E.K.'s misinterpretations offer frequent, ironic reminders of Chaucer's place in Spenser's once and future poetry. The ideal of authorship that the "Romish *Tityrus*" represents clearly dominates the *Calender*, particularly because the shepherds (like E.K.) conceive of authority through Virgil's precedent. Moreover, for Hobbinol as for E.K. and the shepherds, the author alone builds his house of fame. Yet Chaucer's death and the subsequent development of his fame "teaches" Colin about how to remember the past; with the decay of Chaucer's physical and poetic corpus (his body "lyeth wrapt in lead," and "all hys passing skil with him is fledd") comes the growth of his fame – "the fame whereof doth dayly greater growe" (89–92). Hardly an immortal monument, this house of fame grows by degrees, building on the ruins of the past and, as Colin himself exemplifies, through the memory of others. "But if on me some little drops would flowe," presumably of Chaucer's inspiration and authorial example, Colin might continue this pattern: "I soone would learne these woods, to wayle my woe, / And teache the trees, their trickling teares to shedde" (93, 95–6). The ambiguity of this "woe" – whether it refers to Chaucer or Rosalind – suggests that Spenser shares the method and matter of Chaucer's poetry. Just as the *Phaedrus* is dedicated to the memory of Socrates, and just as Cicero's *On the Orator* is dedicated to the memory of its interlocutors, so Spenser dedicates his work to Chaucer's memory.

Colin's praise of England's Tityrus suggests that the "Labyrinth of Love" is less a place of entrapment than a place for continued recollection, for remembering the dead. For Spenser as for Chaucer, language-as-ruins forms the matter of memory and poetry's continued edification. Chaucer's *House of Fame* thus casts E.K.'s "Letter to Harvey," with its defence of Spenser's old words, in a new light: as "textus" – trees, twigs, texts – Chaucer's poetry indicates the family tree, and genealogical line, that Spenser seeks. Colin's poetic ruin and the old words of the "new Poete" will be recollected like Chaucer's: his own fame "doth dayly greater growe," though the shepherds and

Colin do not see their part in creating this fame. Nevertheless, precisely at the moments when they lament Colin's personal and professional ruin they also recollect the fragments of his poetry, adapting them for a new literary and cultural edifice and moving him inadvertently toward his house of fame, building a place for collective memory amidst the ruins of poetry and love. The pattern of the English "Tityrus," whom Colin calls the "God of shepheardes," parallels Colin's authorial path throughout the *Calender* and within the "Labyrinth of Love." This gradual edification through recollection describes Colin's sense of immortality – not as a permanent edifice that resists ruination, but one that is built and rebuilt in collective memory. *June* thus articulates a profound commonplace: to write epic is to write about home. Chaucer teaches Colin this, for as he declares of this English Tityrus, he "taught me homely, as I can, to make" (82). Hobbinol underscores this by exhorting Colin to go "home" at *June*'s end: "But now is time . . . homeward to goe: / Then ryse ye blessed flocks, and home apace . . . / And wett your tender Lambes, that by you trace" (117–20). Though Hobbinol and Colin disagree about fame, their debate is ultimately beside the point. Colin's house of fame is built even as they speak, precisely because he leaves his fate – and fame – in others' hands.

"O pierlesse Poesye, where is then thy place?": October, November, December

Returning to *October*, Cuddie's question – "O pierlesse Poesye, where is then thy place?" – takes on new meaning in light of the *Calender*'s broad exploration of "place" and "poesye" from Plato to Spenser's present. This brief history of locational memory provides another way to imagine poetry's location in culture, one neither limited to Virgil's "paterne" nor confined to the "Princes pallace." Recall that Cuddie and Piers, in E.K.'s words, "complayneth of the comtempte of Poetrie" in shepherd land (170). As I have been arguing, Spenser tacitly counters their anxiety about fin-de-siècle cultural decay by suggesting that poetry's "place" lies in the very ruins of Colin's poetry that they recollect in dialogue, the house of fame that they (along with the other inhabitants of shepherd land) unconsciously fashion. Particularly in its echoes of *Aprill* and *June*, the *October* eclogue affirms the architecture of immortality as an ongoing art of recollection.

The *October* eclogue explores the death of the "Romish *Tityrus*" and the anxiety that no poet has taken his place, for want of love or money

(55). Cuddie's complaints about his failing career provides the immediate context for their dialogue, but the conversation soon turns to Colin, directly and indirectly. Piers' advice that Cuddie give up lyric for epic – "Abandon then the base and viler clowne, / . . . And sing of bloody Mars, of wars, of giusts" (37–9) – recalls Hobbinol's advice to Colin in *June*. Much as Hobbinol suggests, Piers proposes that for Cuddie's "Muse" to "display her fluttrying wing, / And stretch her selfe at large from East to West," the flight path to fame that follows empire and learning, he must sing of "Elisa" (43–4). But unable to think of England, they instead remember Rome and the Virgilian career path that leads inevitably to epic. "Indeede the Romish *Tityrus*, I heare," Cuddie recalls, "Through his *Mecœnas* left his Oaten reede, / Whereon he earst had taught his flocks to feede, / And laboured lands to yield the timely eare," putting away his panpipe instead to "sing of warres and deadly drede" (55–60). For Cuddie and Piers, to write epic is to write like Virgil, yet they suggest that reconstructing Virgil's career constitutes an impossible ambition. To recreate this ideal of authorship ideally would require reproducing the conditions under which Virgil wrote:

> But ah *Mecœnas* is yclad in claye,
> And great *Augustus* long ygoe is dead:
> And all the worthies liggen wrapt in leade,
> That matter made for Poets on to play. (55–64)

Poets need love *and* money, Cuddie complains, the exchange of poetry for patronage that makes mutual immortality possible.

Piers and Cuddie lament the death of Virgil, but in a broader sense they despair of Rome's ruin as the broken promise of eternal empire and poetry. Their complaint about the glories of Rome now "long ygoe . . . dead" and "wrapt in leade" also, however, creates verbal echoes that serve as an ironic reminder of another time and place, and the death of another poet, Chaucer: the "God of shepheards *Tityrus* is dead," Colin despairs in *June*, and "lyeth wrapt in lead" (81, 89). This other Tityrus represents the pattern of edification that Colin has learned and that ultimately describes authority in *The Shepheardes Calender*. Although Cuddie and Piers lament the absence of "matter" on which poets can play – the Matter of Rome as well as the matter of a poet's sustenance – the matter of memory can be found in this place. Indeed, Cuddie and Piers *are* the matter of memory, in the manner of Chaucer's *House of Fame*, as they recollect Colin's poetry against a pastoral backdrop. The twigs-cum-*textus*

of Chaucer's labyrinthine house of fame also form Spenser's poetic genealogy, his adopted family tree. This reminder of Chaucer's paternal
presence points up another irony – the desire for a new Virgil, or a "new
Poete," has already been answered, thus reframing the fantasy of rebirth.

Chaucer's poem also undercuts how Cuddie and Piers understand
the relation between poetry and power, which they imagine as one of
exaltation, even deification – precisely the relationship that Chaucer
parodies in *The House of Fame*, largely in response to Dante's portrait of
Rome's divine imperium in *The Divine Comedy*. To make *"Cuddies* name
to Heaven sownde," Piers asserts, first entails singing of *"Elisa"* or *"Augustus'* (54, 53, 62). As in *Aprill*, their conversation turns to a debate
about love and its effect on Colin, whom they regard as England's only
hope. *"Colin* fittes such famous flight to scanne," they affirm, "were
he not with love so ill bedight" (88–9). Rehearsing clichés of poetic
inspiration – "O if my temples were distaind with wine, / And girt in
girlonds of wild Yvie twine," Cuddie muses, "How I could reare the
Muse on stately stage" (110–12) – they imagine that Elisa's love might
lift Colin "up out of the loathsome myre" and toward the "starry skie,"
moving him from secular love to divine love, allowing him to create
an "immortal mirrhor" in poetry (92–4). For Cuddie and Piers the poet
must play the part of Platonic lover. But Colin's refusal to give up his
idol, Rosalind, makes this hope seem hopeless. Without such a poet or
patron to extravagantly praise, Piers returns divine inspiration to its
source: "And, whence thou camst, flye backe to heaven apace" (84).

Yet with *October's* woodcut Spenser subtly challenges his characters'
views about authorship and culture, ironically suggesting less that poetry holds no place in English culture than that Cuddie and Piers may
be looking in the wrong place for it. Seemingly pointing in two directions at once, *October's* emblem offers two different ways of seeing their
dilemma. In this illustration, Piers probably gestures to the foreground
where Cuddie strides, pantomiming the "perfecte paterne of a Poete"
(170) – laurel crown aloft, poetic scroll in hand – likely in imitation of
the "Romish *Tityrus*" (55). But Piers simultaneously motions toward
a figure in the background, likely Colin, approaching what looks like
the very monumental architecture, the place for poetry, that they bemoan England lacks. While Cuddie plays at poet laureate he stands
practically alone (with Piers forming his only audience), whereas
Colin approaches not only this edifice but also a busily discoursing
crowd, whose very presence seemingly refutes Piers' assertion that no

one – neither "Princes" nor "brest of baser birth" – cares about poetry (80–2). Silently rebutting such dire pronouncements, Spenser draws attention to such a "place" for poetry: a house of fame. The Chaucerian context of *June* and the *Calender* writ large undercuts any monolithic vision of the "Princes pallace" as the "place" for poetry by suggesting what lies beneath the palace: the "Labyrinth of Love." The presence of the crowd can thus indicate what moves this figure toward a house of fame. Just as in Chaucer's vision, in which the crowd provides him with new tales of love that represent the matter of his poetic memory, so Spenser suggests a more complex role for poetic reception than either E.K. or the shepherds recognize.

As the *October* image may imply, dialogue rather than the poet alone builds a place or edifice for poetry in culture. The gradual integration of Colin's poetry and authorial renown into England's pastoral world, the spread of his fame and the consequent growth of his house of fame, follows the Chaucerian "paterne" that Colin describes in *June* but which is implemented throughout the *Calender*; indeed, Spenser suggests that his own fame also depends upon the continual conversation through which the fragments of love and poetry are recollected.[43] As Roland Greene observes, part of the "answer" to Colin's dilemma "is collective and cultural: the explorations of dialogic speech by pairs such as Cuddie and Thenot, the revivals and rehearsals of Colin's lyrics by surrogates, and the ritualized anatomy of lyric by Willy and Perigot all work to rediscover the values of an equivocal, self-examining discourse and to make it a habitable climate for it."[44] Rather than understanding Colin as trapped in the "Labyrinth of Love" because of his static, failed romance, his growing, edifying fame suggests how and why Colin might remain in such a labyrinth: it represents a place in which to continue recollecting the past anew. Although their romantic and nostalgic view of authorship prevent Cuddie and Piers from recognizing their own part in building Colin's house of fame, readers may nevertheless recognize the crucial place of their dialogue in recollecting just such an edifice. While unable to settle this pressing matter of poetry's "place" in culture, Cuddie and Piers resolve to enjoy their *locus amoenus*, the sweet spot of their dialogue: "But ah my corage cooles ere it be warme," a calmer Cuddie sighs, "For thy, content us in thys humble shade: / Where no such troublous tydes han us assayde, / Here we our slender pipes may safely charme" (115–18). As in Plato's *Phaedrus*, the shepherds remember within the place of poetry: the sweet spot that they reconstruct in dialogue. Like Hobbinol in *June*, they have begun transforming what epic means, accommodating it for a new time and place, and building Colin's fame, albeit unconsciously, through the very fact of their dialogue. By recollecting Colin's ruinous past and poetry, Piers and Cuddie do not achieve their authorial ideals, but they succeed as architects all the same.

The *November* eclogue offers another, still more pointed reply to the question of poetry's "place" in culture. Whereas *October* mourns the death of the "Romish *Tityrus*" and the ruin of the Rome that made his glory possible, *November* mourns the death of a maiden named "Dido." Scholars have long debated how this "weeping for Dido," to borrow Augustine's phrase, speaks to Spenser's epic ambitions for *The Faerie Queen*.[45] The death of Dido, I suggest, stands for the death of an ideal: that Spenser will write a Virgilian epic for England. The *November* eclogue undermines E.K.'s attempts to fashion the "new Poete" as England's new Virgil or to construct the *Calender* as a monument to Virgil's career path. Writ small, *November* portrays what will become the central problematic of *The Faerie Queene* – the question of how to remember Elizabeth in poetry, an issue that turns on Dido's identity.

Once again, this debate can be heard amid the ironies of E.K.'s glosses. He states that Colin "bewayleth the death of some mayden of great bloude, whom he calleth Dido," but adds that this "personage is secrete and to me altogether unknowne" (187). In another gloss, E.K. asserts that the "person both of the shephearde and of Dido is unknowen and closely buried in the Authors conceipt," though he adds: "But out of doubt I am, that it is not Rosalind, as some imagin" (195–6). Explicitly denying that Dido represents Rosalind, E.K. instead identifies her with Elizabeth, describing her as "the greate shepehearde his daughter sheene"; this "great shepheard," he further argues, "is some man of high degree, and not as some vainely suppose God Pan" (195). With this gloss, E.K. confirms his triumphant declaration of Elizabeth's divine genealogy through Henry VIII-as-Pan in the *Aprill* eclogue. It seems clear why E.K. would deny that Dido stands for Rosalind; it allows him to suggest that she represents Elizabeth, and indeed that *November* presents a Tudor allegory. After all, if Rosalind symbolizes Dido, then weeping for her signals Colin's inability to renounce his love of Rome for England, or trade lyric for epic. But if Elizabeth equals Dido, then she stands as the impediment to Colin-cum-Aeneas' pursuit of endless empire and, further, her death would be a reminder of the tragic cost of empire-building.

Here as elsewhere, E.K. is partially right for the wrong reasons. "Dido," whom Virgil also names "Elisa," seems to represent both Colin's Elisa and Queen Elizabeth. *October*'s "Elisa" would also seem to double for *November*'s "Elisa," for as Piers argues when urging Cuddie to sing an epic song, "Whither thou list in fayre *Elisa* rest, / Or if thee please in bigger notes to sing, / . . . All were *Elisa* one of thilke same ring" and either way "mought our *Cuddies* name to Heaven sownde" (45–54). This appears to be the role Colin plays in *November* as he sings Elisa's praises to the heavens, but in ways that create a double vision of his future. Colin memorializes the death of his muse – "*Dido* my deare alas is dead, / Dead and lyeth wrapt in lead" – whom he makes immortal in poetry: "O heavie herse . . . / O carefull verse" (58–62). As he sings to "Heaven," nevertheless, his verse transforms from a human tragedy to divine comedy:

> Dido nis dead, but into heaven hent.
> > O happye herse,
> Cease now my Muse, now cease thy sorrowes sourse,
> > O joyfull verse.
> Why wayle we then? why weary we the Gods with playnts,
> As if some evill were to her betight?
> She raignes a goddesse now emong the saintes;
> That whilome was the saynt of shepheards light:
> And is enstalled nowe in heavens hight.
> > I see thee blessed soule, I see,
> > Walke in *Elisian* fieldes so free. (169–79)

Punning on Elisa's name, he places her in the "Elisian" fields of the underworld, a "Heaven" paradoxically pagan and Roman Catholic: "She raignes a goddesse now emong the saintes." The woodcut accompanying *November* seems to reinforce this allegorical mingling of epic and Christian elements. It shows Colin crowned poet laureate in a pastoral place, with a church in the background, a tree in the foreground, and a funeral procession behind him. As *November*'s image might imply, *The Faerie Queene* will be such an allegorical mixture: a Christian epic, with all the complex layering that such a genre must essay.

If readers interpret *November* as an expression of Spenser's Virgilian ambitions, then Dido's death marks a shift for Colin as lover and poet. Like an epic hero, Colin says goodbye to the destructive passion that distracted him from epic destiny, but like a Christian knight, Colin promises to keep remembering love of God even as he pursues love of country. However, there are other more critical reasons why Colin (and Spenser) might weep for Dido. As critics have argued, *November* alludes to Augustine's role in *The Faerie Queene*, especially the *Confessions* where he "learned to lament the death of Dido, who killed herself for love."[46] For Leslie Whipp, weeping for Dido signifies "the identification of Colin as a Petrarchan lover-poet," and signals the place where Colin and Spenser truly part company: "Spenser, unlike Colin, will not be a poet who weeps for Dido."[47] And certainly, Augustine ultimately repents of his love of Dido as idolatrous. Yet in another register weeping for Dido may be understood as an anti-epic position, and thus aligned with Augustine's implied critique of Virgil and epic. After all, Aeneas never weeps for Dido – a point driven home by Dido's impassive greeting in the underworld. In *The House of Fame*, Geffrey is strongly on the side of Dido, criticizing Aeneas' actions in harsh terms: "he to hir a traitour was" (267). For Aeneas, giving up Dido signalled the victory of duty over desire, the collective over the individual, love of country over all else, and Colin in a sense erases this dichotomy with his poetic elegy: desire and duty merge for Colin in his memory of Dido. Weeping for Dido means not simply being a new Virgil, despite the epic allusion. Instead, it means something like recanting a form of epic idolatry – a Dantean idea of epic that would put Dido "in heavens hight," deified as a conduit to divinity and immortality. In this respect *November* seems to close the door (or coffin) on the possibility that Spenser will follow Virgil's path through Dante, turning epic into divine truth. How we interpret Spenser's allegory depends a great deal on how we interpret Augustine's. As I argue at length in chapter 4, Spenser builds Augustine's anti-epic stance into *The Faerie Queene*'s allegory and critique of allegory. Spenser thus introduces *The Faerie Queene* – which he never calls an "epic," just as he never calls *The Shepheardes Calender* "pastoral" – by drawing the pattern of allegory that he symbolically kills off in the *November* eclogue, the place where Colin (who having broken his pan pipe) ceases to be recollected by others and finally composes a "new" poem in the present.

From another perspective, Spenser here redefines what it means to be a "new Poete." This eclogue emphasizes the "endles souvenaunce" (5) of Colin's poetry and memory as he laments the death of a Dido, thus suggesting the possibility of immortality through poetic recollection. In a sense, Spenser affirms his Platonic love for Elizabeth by emphasizing that his continued recollection of her, in the sweet spot that represents England's green and pleasant land, aspires to reveal human truths. This same truth speaks to Colin and Spenser's memory. The desire and duty to remember the past, whether accomplished consciously or unconsciously, constitutes a conversation that affects the social world of the shepherds in profound ways: not through the heroic poet alone but heroically all the same. Here as elsewhere, Spenser constructs the truth of his poetry as inevitably double. It thus seems a mistake to judge Colin as either a success or failure; instead, he exemplifies the pattern that Spenser's shepherds illustrate throughout *The Shepheardes Calender*. Just as Colin builds a "hearse" in "verse," as a location for the continued memory of Dido, so Colin's own poetry serves similarly as a "place" for collective recollection, a location in which the shepherd world can continue to live and speak.

Colin begins and ends the *Calender* in a state of personal and poetic ruin, pictured in the woodcuts to *Januarye* and *December*, both of which contain images of his broken pan pipe. To this extent, his progress as a lover is circular. If viewed in Petrarchan terms, then Colin tragically never finds his way out of the "Labyrinth of Love." In *Januarye*, Rosalind has broken his heart and in turn his poetic inspiration; she "laughes the songs, that *Colin Clout* doth make," leading him to break "his oaten pype" (66, 72). In *December*, Colin despairs that his "spring is spent, [his] sommer burnt up quite" (129). But if viewed in Chaucerian terms, his choice to stay in the "Labyrinth" becomes redemptive, even comic. Colin's refusal to play a Virgilian role, his apparent passivity and self-destructiveness in the face of his own ruin, implies that his house of fame is fashioned less through his own volition than through the memory of others. Spenser suggests as much through the absence of Colin's emblem in *December*, the very place where E.K. ironically praises *The Shepheardes Calender* as an immortal monument. The missing emblem serves as a symbolic space of ruin, and thus a place for the ongoing dialogue that continues Colin's immortality. The *Calender* suggests a reorienting not only of epic values but also of epic ends: not the fantasy of "empire without end" that Virgil's hero pursued, nor a static monument to the fame of its author, but rather the hope of "endles souvenaunce," by which this edifice might be forever built and rebuilt from the ruins of time. *The Faerie Queene*, Spenser clarifies through his shepherds' continuing dialogues, will not conform to Virgil's "perfecte paterne of a Poete" but rather will follow a new architectural pattern, fashioning a new "place" for poetry from the ruins of the past. *The Shepheardes Calender* "continewes . . . to teach," just as Colin praises Chaucer's poetry for continuing to teach, how immortality is fashioned within the cycles of ruin and recollection. Colin intones, "Gather ye together my little flocke," but his "flocke" have already been doing this throughout the *Calender*, gathering his scattered rhymes in their memory (145). The process of recollecting Colin's poetry moves him closer to his house of fame, because the very act builds a place for poetry in culture. Spenser also points *The Shepheardes Calender* in the direction of home, toward the poetic edifice that he will fashion from Colin's ruins – the house of fame that will continue to be built, even after the death of the author.

Chapter Three

The Ruines of Time and the Art of Recollection

In a calculated move, one of many designed to make a name for the "new Poete," E.K. reminds readers in his introductory epistle to *The Shepheardes Calender* that the anonymous author dedicated his poem to none other than "the Noble and worthy Gentleman, the right worshipfull Ma. Phi. Sidney, a special favourer and maintainer of all kind of learning."[1] Who better to defend the "new Poete's" new work than Sidney? Naturally, E.K. insists on sharing the spotlight, referring Harvey to "this my labour, and the maydenhead of this our commen frends Poetrie," and imploring him to "Defend" the *Calender* (and E.K.'s own "labour" of love) "with your mighty Rhetorick . . . against the malice and outrage of so many enemies, as I know wilbe set on fire with the sparks of his kindled glory" (20). In so doing, E.K. appears to choose the patron he prefers – despite the author's intentions. In this instance, though, E.K. may be correct. In the war against enemies of poetry and other critics, Sidney would turn out to be a strange ally, famously damning the *Calender* with faint praise in his *Apology for Poetry*. Though sometimes taken in earnest, this chapter argues that Sidney's criticisms of Spenser turn on a jest, albeit a serious one. Sidney's disparaging remarks about the "new Poete's" old style reflect his witty parody of E.K.'s style, revealing what Sidney and Spenser as "frends" hold in "commen": a mutual art of memory. Moreover, Sidney's performance as an upstart poet-courtier can remind readers of their common source (at least in part) for the art of concealing art: Castiglione's *Courtier*. Tracing their intertextual dialogue, I suggest that Sidney's *Apology* recalls Spenser's *Calender* in order to define and defend their shared vision of poetics, and that Spenser in turn recalls this exchange in his memorial for Sidney, *The Ruines of Time*.

Long considered a minor (and not very good) poem, *The Ruines of Time* has been read as a defence of poetry that imitates Sidney's, but their common wealth – poetry's spoils – suggests a more complex relationship.[2] Millar MacLure has observed the art of memory at work in *The Ruines of Time* as, he writes, "a process of imprinting on the mind virtues, vices, states of being, as in the tradition described by Frances Yates."[3] Spenser constructs the poem as a kind of memory theatre, drawing attention to his use of mnemonic methods through architectural places and vivid images, both fashioning *The Ruines of Time* as a symbolic edifice and demonstrating how he does so. However, Spenser also engages with the art of memory in a significantly more expansive way. Indeed, Spenser's method of recollection reflects the central matter of the poem: the paradoxical notion that poetry survives not as an immortal monument but rather as "the ruines of time." For Spenser and for Sidney, the "ruines" of poetry are metaphoric in a very precise sense, as vehicles for cultural transmission that translate the past for the present. As Spenser recollects his and Sidney's literary dialogue about poetry as an art of memory, he positions poetry's "ruins" (including his own) as their common place of recollection. Here as in the *Calender*, Spenser presents poetry not through permanence but perpetuation, not through stasis but change, not as univocal but dialogic. Even as it celebrates the immortality of poetry, *The Ruines of Time* speaks to the contingent nature of all edifices, material or memorial, within time. To the question of what happens to poetry given time's scythe and the inevitable death of the author – in this context, Sidney's death – Spenser suggests that immortality lies in ruins.

This chapter follows a circuitous route – from *The Ruines of Time*, to Sidney's *Apology for Poetry*, which engages with Cicero's *On the Orator* and Plato's *Phaedrus* partly through *The Shepheardes Calender*, and back again to *The Ruines of Time* – with a specific end in mind: to suggest how and why both poets situate poetry's ruins as the best place for England's edification and collective memory. Through its intertexts, *The Ruines of Time* marks a dialogue about locational memory and the location of poetry in culture, which the poem itself dramatizes. Even as he upends ideals of permanence, Spenser creates a space where England can remember itself.

Poetry's "Place" in *The Ruines of Time*

Where do readers find the art of memory in *The Ruines of Time*? One answer lies in the poem's place in Spenser's career. As previously discussed, the *Complaints* volume interrupts the two parts of *The Faerie Queene* and thus Spenser's presumed Virgilian career path, by returning to his first work as a translator of ruins poetry for Jan Van der Noot's *Theatre for Worldlings*.[4] Yet as the title itself suggests, *The Ruines* of *Time* tacitly rebuts Van der Noot's apocalyptic vision. Self-consciously reflecting upon what it means to imagine building upon the ruins of the past after Virgil, and the legacy of Rome's ruin, Spenser remembers Du Bellay's and Petrarch's poetry in ways that fundamentally reform the *Theatre*: whereas Van der Noot represents poetry as prophecy and theology, drawing a line from Virgil's *Fourth Eclogue* to the book of Revelation, Spenser explicitly avoids making any such claims for poetry here and throughout his *Complaints*. Indeed, his criticisms relate to such political and theological fictions: those that reproduce fictions of "endless empire" in present-day politics. Ironically, though, *The Ruines of Time* has been interpreted in this way, as a poem that exchanges imperial for poetic immortality.[5] As I argue, Spenser complains (so to speak) about translating fiction as history – specifically, as tales of Troy's ruin – in part through the act of translation itself: by translating Du Bellay's *Les Antiquitez de Rome* as the *Ruines of Rome* and placing it at the centre of his *Complaints*. As Hassan Melehy has argued, "*The Ruines of Time* presents a poetics" that should be understood as "no less than a manifesto for a renewed English poetry, founded on the ruins of the past," and which builds upon Du Bellay's model of imitation: "imitation [which] involves borrowing pieces of text from models from the past, reordering them, transforming them, and writing a test that addresses and contributes to the present context."[6] I locate this process of imitation in the specific context of the art of memory, situating ruin as a space of recollection.

Recall that the *Ruines of Rome* creates an intricate dialogue about the anxiety of Virgil's influence.[7] Although some critics have argued that Du Bellay's hope for poetic immortality expresses mostly hopelessness, this could be reframed as an acceptance of history.[8] Du Bellay places poetry within the context of the rise and fall of empires: "If under heaven anie endurance were," he asserts, "These moniments, which not in paper writ, / But in Porphyre and Marble . . . / Might well have hop'd to have obtained it."[9] These poetic "moniments" indicate the status of the poem: no immortal monument by virtue of permanence, the *Ruines of Rome* itself remains in ruins. In effect, Du Bellay realigns poetry and history not through Virgilian fictions of permanence but rather through ruin and the need for continual remembrance. "Cease not to sound these olde antiquities," he charges readers, intimating that future remembrance or gleaning represents the best (and maybe only) immortality possible (32.444). By the poem's end, Du Bellay's ambivalence leads him to a new conclusion, away from epic aspirations of endless empire or poetry and toward a more georgic sense that immortality lies in the endlessly renewed labours of recollection. Spenser confirms this sense in his envoy to the *Ruines of Rome*: "Well worthie thou of immortalitie," he writes, adding that "he all eternitie survive, / That can to other give eternall dayes" (451, 455–6). Du Bellay's "days therefore are endles," immortal in continuity, because his "learned writs" have created a foundation for new poets (457, 452).

The Ruines of Time registers the significance of Du Bellay's resolution to make new use of poetry's ruins. A.E.B. Coldiron encapsulates Spenser's complex appropriation of Du Bellay, writing that "his is an excavation not just of Rome, not just of Du Bellay's Rome, but of Du Bellay's way-of-excavating."[10] Spenser's poem begins where Du Bellay's leaves off – with a city that "time in time" has destroyed: its "fable" and "spoyles," monuments and memory. Whereas Du Bellay's "stranger" seeks "*Rome* in *Rome*," Spenser's finds Verlame as an accidental tourist:

> It chaunced me on day beside the shore
> Of silver streaming *Thamesis* to bee,
> Nigh where the goodly *Verlame* stood of yore,
> Of which there now remaines no memorie,
> Nor anie little moniment to see,
> By which the travailer, that fares that way,
> This once was she, may warned be to say.[11]

From the outset, Spenser draws attention to Verlame's paradoxical plight: while Du Bellay's speaker sees in Rome's ruins mutability, pride, glory, to name a few of his contradictory responses, Spenser's speaker sees nothing – only imagined, remembered ruins. "There now remaines no memorie, / Nor anie little moniment to see," the speaker warns, lest future travellers miss the invisible Verulamium. The fact that Verlame, the unhappy spirit of a former outpost of the Roman Empire in Britain, has no *visible* ruins forms the central crux of *The Ruines of Time*.

This absence figures centrally in how Spenser reimagines the architecture of immortality, though modern visitors do not always notice the absence of Verlame's physical ruins. "The ruins of Rome and of Verulam as the visible and material signs of the past introduce the problem which the immortality-of-poetry *topos* solves as a national key," Anne Janowitz writes, adding: "the lesson Spenser intends to teach . . . is that the image of the nation is made in poetry, and that poetry can ensure national immortality, repairing the ruins of previous empires and shifting the locus of the *translatio imperii* into the domain of poetic structure."[12] These remarks gesture to an opposition between empire and poetry inscribed in the immortality of poetry *topos*; as Horace (among others) boasted, empire falls to ruin but monuments of poetry last forever. To exchange "endless empire" for poetry without end, to argue that poetry achieves the permanence denied to history, seems like a solution to the problem of a fallen Rome or any empire, and certainly Verlame desires exactly such an exchange.[13] As I will argue, though, Spenser tacitly engages Verlame in dialogue, challenging her view of poetic immortality by locating it in another place – that is, within the ruins of time, and within the cycles of ruin and re-edification that mark both history and poetry. In its rise and fall, poetry mirrors history; like monuments of stone, monuments of poetry also inevitably decay. The ghostly Verlame represents a poem in search of a place for memory, unaware that she already occupies that very place within her ruins. Spenser's poem thereby overturns the basic opposition between material and memorial structures underwriting the commonplace of poetic immortality: the fantasy that poetry can mirror, or replace, the fiction of endless empire. Instead of stones, "the ruines of time" represent poetry's ruins: both the remains of a fallen house of fame and places for re-edification and remembrance. Rather than building an immortal monument, Spenser embraces the contingency of all structures.

Where "the goodly *Verlame* stood of yore" matters less than the fact that she lacks a location for her memory, a problem that finds an answer, appropriately, in locational memory. "*Verlame* I was," she declares in the past tense, and thus describes her present paradox:

> I was that Citie, which the garland wore
> Of *Britaines* pride, delivered unto me
> By *Romane* Victors, which it wonne of yore;
> Though nought at all but ruines now I bee,
> And lye in mine owne ashes, as ye see:
> *Verlame* I was; what bootes it that I was,
> Sith now I am but weedes and wastfull gras? (36–42)

Does the poem's speaker see anything but "weedes and wastfull gras?" In one sense, he sees no city, no ruins, no remains of any kind. He does, however, see an image of Verlame:

A Woman sitting sorrowfullie wailing,
Rending her yeolow locks . . .
In her right hand a broken rod she held,
Which towards heaven shee seemd on high to weld. (9–14)

Reminiscent of Du Bellay's spirit of Rome and of biblical weeping widows, Verlame cuts a familiar figure.[14] As the spoil of *"Romane* Victors" and "that Citie . . . of *Britaines* pride," she comes by her ambivalence naturally. Just as two Romes exist for Du Bellay, "Rome in Rome," so Verlame has something of a split personality, a double identity, so to speak. Like Du Bellay's speaker, she vacillates between nostalgia for empires past and an awareness that all empire is vanity, destined for ruin. As Verlame remembers herself, she reconstructs her house of memory and, some critics have argued, builds a house of pride.[15] Though at first she demurs "to tell the beawtie of my buildings fayre," as "but lost labour, that few would beleeve, / And with rehearsing would me more agreeve," she ultimately cannot resist doing so (85, 90–1). As though an orator using the method of architectural mnemonics, Verlame remembers herself as places – "High towers, faire temples, goodly theaters" – suitably divided by intervals – "wrought with faire pillours" – and filled with "fine imageries," providing practically an overview of the rules of artificial memory (92, 96). These structures have fallen, "turnd to dust, / And overgrowen with blacke oblivions rust," and so has her house of memory (97–8). However, a more complex understanding of the art of memory emerges in Verlame's complaint. Throughout *The Ruines of Time*, Verlame remembers herself historically and poetically and in so doing her complaint inadvertently draws a portrait of Spenser's complex, dialogic art of memory. By recollecting the ruins of history and fiction, what Du Bellay divides into the "fable" and "spoyle" of the past, Verlame builds a place for memory even as she laments the absence of such a space.

Unlike Du Bellay's speaker, Verlame's contradictory views have vexed and perplexed her critics to no end.[16] In Verlame's defence, I will suggest that such contradictions ultimately serve a similar rhetorical end: through her divided state, Spenser constructs a dialogue about poetry and history much like that of the *Ruines of Rome*. As Verlame shifts between lamentations for glorious empire and lamentations for earthly vanity, echoes of Du Bellay's ambivalence resound. "O *Rome* thy ruine I lament and rue," she despairs, remembering when "of the whole world as thou wast the Empresse, / So I of this small Northerne world was

Princesse" (78, 83–4). Further, Verlame's historical recollections make a subtle but crucial point that undermines her forceful nostalgia: Rome was only one chapter in her history. Nor does she fictionalize her story: that is, Spenser does not have her reconstruct Trojan fictions in *The Ruines of Time*.[17] As a city led by the female warrior Boadicea, famous for resisting Roman conquest – "In *Britannie* was none to match with mee," she boasts, "Ne *Troynovant*, though elder sister shee" (100, 102) – Verulamium stands as a force opposed to Roman idealization, a de facto anti-Troynovant.

To see Verlame as merely self-pitying, or her lamentation for past glory as merely a pagan perspective, is to miss (or mistake) her personal history lesson: time has taught Verlame that all things fall to ruin, monuments and memory alike. As Graham Hammill observes, "Verlame personifies a lack of memory . . . that bespeaks history as the relentlessly destructive force of decay and ruin."[18] Aware of such destructive forces, Verlame can even sound strangely like an irate theologian when warning against the "trustlesse state of miserable men, / That builde your blis on hope of earthly thing, / And vainly thinke your selves halfe happie then," and urging a righteous path: "Living, on God, and on thy selfe relie; / For when thou diest, all shall with thee die" (197–9, 209–10). More significantly here, Verlame learns that memory requires a location, and thus her doleful invocation of the *ubi sunt topos* can in some sense be taken literally. While bemoaning the decay of her city into desolation – "Where my high steeples whilom usde to stand . . . / There now is but an heap of lyme and sand, / For the Schriche-owl to build her balefull bowre" (127–30) – Verlame also points to the broader implications of her decimation. "Where be those learned wits and antique Sages," she asks, and "Where those great warriors, which did overcomme / The world with conquest of their might and maine, / And made one meare of th'earth and of their raine?" (59–63). Verlame supplies her own answer: "They all are gone, and all with them is gone," she complains, and "Ne ought to me remaines, but to lament / My long decay, which no man els doth mone" (155–7). Ultimately, Verlame grieves less for the fall of empire, of which Rome is only part, than for its consequences. Cultural transmission, once epitomized by the river Thames, has ceased: "where the christall *Thamis* wont to slide / In silver channell, downe along the Lee, / . . . There now no rivers course is to be seene."[19] Memory requires a place, it seems, even as it continues to move (like culture itself) from place to place.

The *genius loci* Verlame represents poetry as a form of locational memory, though Spenser finesses just what this means. For Verlame, poetry can counteract time's ruinous power. Instructing rulers to make sure "That of the *Muses* ye may friended bee, / Which unto men enternitie do give" (366–7), she makes a strong claim for the immortality of poetry that proves deceptively simple:

> For deeds doe die, how ever noblie donne,
> And thoughts of men do as themselves decay,
> But wise wordes taught in numbers for to runne,
> Recorded by the Muses, live for ay;
> Ne may with storming showers be washt away,
> Ne bitter breathing windes with harmfull blast,
> Nor age, nor envie shall them ever wast. (400–6)

Although such claims for poetry seem utterly conventional – indeed, a near paraphrase of Horace or Ovid – a more complex view of immortality comes into focus when she praises Camden's history as the exception to the charge that "Nor anie lives that mentioneth my name / To be remembered of posteritie" (164–5). Camden, "the nourice of antiquitie, / And lanterne unto late succeeding age," able "To see the light of simple veritie, / Buried in ruines" (169–72), would seem to offer Verlame the very kind of immortality she seeks: "*Cambden*, though time all moniments obscure, / Yet thy just labours ever shall endure" (174–5). In an act of renaissance itself, Camden recollected Verulamium's history, disinterring the ruins of time and gathering them together in a "moniment" that ideally "ever shall endure." But if Camden's *Britannia* (which gently questions England's Trojan legend) answered Verlame's prayers for historical immortality, why has she been forgotten? Verlame answers this indirectly with a question:

> But whie (unhappie wight) doo I thus crie,
> And grieve that my remembrance quite is raced
> Out of the knowledge of posteritie,
> And all my antique moniments defaced?
> Sith I doo dailie see things highest placed . . .
> Forgotten quite as they were never borne. (176–82)

Even Camden's history could not preserve Verulamium's memory eternally, as A. Leigh DeNeef observes: though "Camden . . . constructs an eternal mnemonic monument" of Verlame, her "continued existence is not in fact "redeemed" by his mnemonic text."[20] Instead, Camden only participated in the *process* of remembering history's ruins that others must continue, since immortality demands more than writing – it demands that people recall this writing. But if Camden's monumental history failed to secure forever Verlame's memory, it nevertheless serves as a spur to Verlame's own historical recollections of herself: the repair of her ruin in memory. More than an anodyne hope for eternal fame, this clear call to "cease not to sound these old antiquities" illustrates Spenser's vision of poetry as an art of recollecting ruin.

The paradoxes of Verlame's defence of poetry surface again in her eulogy for Sidney. She rejoices that Sidney now has joined "that blessed throng / Of heavenlie Poets and Heroes strong," asserting the immortality of his poetry: "So there thou livest, singing evermore, / And here thou livest, being ever song . . . / . . . So thou both here and there immortall art" (337–42). "Will I sing" Sidney's praises, Verlame promises, but then qualifies this by questioning its necessity. After all, as Verlame asks, "who can better sing" of Sidney:

> but who can better sing
> Than thou thy selfe, thine own selfes valiance,
> That whilest thou livedst, madest the forrests ring,
> And fields resownd, and flockes to leap and daunce . . .
> To runne thy shrill *Arcadian* Pipe to heare. (323–8)

This reminder of Sidney's poetry, however, prompts another question: why has he been forgotten? *The Ruines of Time* itself complicates Verlame's idealization of Sidney's poetic immortality by providing him with a memorial that, presumably, he does not need. Neither poetry nor patronage would seem to ensure immortality, Verlame suggests when she recalls Sidney's uncle Leicester, also dead and presumably forgotten: "Ne anie Poet seekes him to revive," Verlame laments, despite the fact that "manie Poets honourd him alive" (223–4). If unintentionally, she observes the transience of memory for both poets and their protectors alike.

Of course, Sidney (though dead) had hardly been forgotten, least of all by Spenser. Yet here as elsewhere in Spenser's poetry, the *topos* of forgetfulness serves as a reminder in more ways than one. When Verlame accuses Spenser's poetic persona of exemplifying England's collective amnesia – "Ne doth his *Colin*, carelesse *Colin Cloute*, / Care now his idle bagpipe up to raise," she chastises, "Wake shepheards boy, at length awake for shame" (225–6, 231) – she makes space for Sidney's memorial: the poem within the poem, and memory theatre within the larger memorial structure of the poem. That Verlame charges "Colin Clout" with the task of remembrance matters both because Spenser dedicates *The Shepheardes Calender* to Sidney, and because Sidney demonstrates a similar dedication to Spenser in the *Apology for Poetry*. For both writers, poetic immortality resides in the art of recollection that the ruins of poetry themselves elicit.

Where the Truth Lies: Sidney's *Apology for Poetry* as an Art of Memory

Does poetry ensure immortality? Sidney affirms as much when concluding his *Apology for Poetry*, though perhaps the poet affirms too much. "Thus much curse I must send you in behalf of all poets," Sidney tells poetry haters, "that while you live, you live in love, and never get favor for lacking skill of a sonnet; and when you die, your memory die from the earth for want of an epitaph."[21] Those who spurn the muses remain "uncouthe" and "unkiste" in life and in death (to borrow E.K.'s use of Chaucer's words) (*Shepheardes Calender*, 13) – forgotten, a fate perhaps worse than death. As Sidney would know, though, to "live in love" *and* have "skill of a sonnet" offers no guarantee of "favor" either personally or professionally, and so his curse seems at least partly self-directed: an ironic reflection on his own life and legacy. Playfully giving the lie to literary immortality thus allows Sidney to make an example of himself: even for a devoted courtier and star-lover, passion and poetry alone cannot ensure that "memory" will not "die from the earth for want of an epitaph." That Spenser provides Sidney with just such an epitaph in *The Ruines of Time* confirms that even immortal poetic monuments must be recollected from ruins, the matter of memory upon which poetry's dream houses are continually built and rebuilt. Neither poet indicts poetry for failing to memorialize permanently; rather, they defend poetry on the very ground of its mutability.

The necessity of an epitaph even for poets like Sidney, the need to keep remembering, suggests one reason that he defines poetry both as an "art of imitation" and an art of memory (18). Sidney's conclusion slyly echoes the end of Castiglione's introductory letter to *The Courtier*, a work that similarly blurs truth and fiction, and similarly conceals and reveals the art of memory. As Castiglione writes, "if the booke shall generally please, I wil count him good, and think that he ought to live: but if he shall displease, I will count him naught, and beleave that the memorye of him shall soone perish."[22] As another courtier-poet *par excellence*, Sidney characterizes *mimesis* not through the famous Horatian phrase *ut pictura poesis* but according to Simonides' saying that painting is silent poetry, poetry a speaking picture. "To speak metaphorically," Sidney says, poetry can be characterized as "a speaking picture" – circular logic, to be sure, but an apt demonstration of poetry's fundamentally pictorial nature (18). As discussed, Simonides represents two related discoveries: the relation between visual and verbal arts and the art of memory.[23] Together, these tales of Simonides suggest that poetry and rhetoric share a common method and a common ground, a point that Sidney clarifies:

> Even they that have taught the art of memory have showed nothing so apt for it as a certain room divided into many places, well and thoroughly known. Now that hath the verse in effect perfectly, every word having his natural seat, which seat must needs make the words remembered. But what needeth more in a thing so known to all men? Who is it that ever was a scholar that doth not carry away some verses of Virgil, Horace, or Cato, which in his youth he learned, and even to his old age serve him for hourly lessons? (54)

Sidney first describes poetry as a kind of architectural mnemonic, a literary house of memory. Poetry's pretty rooms naturally offer fitting places for memory, "seats" in a double sense: locations for words and the visual images they provoke, or heads or topics represented by people at a banquet, as in the tale of Simonides. The passage slides into a still more expansive way of understanding poetry as an art of memory. Even as Sidney coyly wonders why he should repeat the well-known rules of artificial memory, he suggests an answer that reframes the question: "Who is it that ever was a scholar that doth not carry away some verses of Virgil, Horace, or Cato, which in his youth he learned, and even to his old age serve him for hourly lessons?" With this rhetorical question, Sidney subtly shifts perspectives on the ideal place of memory: from rhetoric to poetry, from edifice to edification, from whole to part, from permanence to perpetuation. Sidney reimagines poetry as an art of memory, representing poetry less as images that cohere as a fixed edifice but rather as fragments or remains that readers "carry away," transport from youth to old age, as "some verses" that translate across time and space. In pieces and parts, indeed as symbolic ruins, poetry acts as a vehicle for transmission, edifying both individually and collectively. Crediting the "fitness [poetry] hath for memory" and, in a larger sense, to knowledge – the "delivery of the arts . . . from grammar to logic, mathematics, physic, and the rest" – Sidney explains how "the rules chiefly necessary to be borne away are compiled in verses" (55). This expansion of the art of memory from "rules" to "verses" depends upon learning being "borne away" and then reborn, fashioned anew, within the space of poetry.

Because of poetry's evident virtues, "verse being in itself sweet and orderly, and being best for memory, the only handle of knowledge," Sidney concludes that "it must be in jest that any man can speak against it" (55). Yet his *Apology for Poetry* ironically depends on just such a jest. Sidney "speak[s] against" the style of *The Shepheardes Calender* "in jest," I suggest, by mimicking the style of Spenser's first character-cum-critic, E.K., and challenging the substance of E.K.'s ambitious defence of poetry. Sidney's criticism of the *Calender* thus proceeds *serio ludens*.[24] Reversing E.K.'s defence of Spenser's poetry, Sidney enters into Spenser's implied dialogue with his fictional critic about the architecture of immortality. Whereas E.K. asserts that fame requires heroic authorship, a new Virgil to fashion a permanent monument to poetry and culture from the ruins of the past, Spenser suggests that immortality lies in poetry's figurative ruins that create places for dialogue and the continued reformation of any house of fame. With the *Apology*, Sidney elaborates upon Spenser's defence of poetry as an art of memory.

Echoing E.K.'s rhetoric of ruin and his desire for cultural rebirth, Sidney describes the state of English poetry as a cultural wasteland. "Why," he demands, should "England . . . be grown so hard a stepmother to poets, who certainly in wit ought to pass all other," and why "poesy, thus embraced in all other places, should only find in our time a hard welcome in England"? (68–70). To the question of whither England's laureates, Sidney despairs, "I think the very earth lamenteth" their absence "and therefore decketh our soil with fewer laurels than it was accustomed" (70). This barren landscape "should seem to strew the house for poets," he complains, figuring England as a fallen house of fame and thus without a place for poetry (70). When Sidney cites *The Shepheardes Calender* as a partial exception to Britannia's sad decline and fall, he does so without ever naming the poem's author, who thus remains "unkiste":

> *The Shepherd's Calendar* hath much poetry in his eclogues, indeed worthy the reading if I be not deceived. That same framing of his style to an old rustic language I dare not allow, sith neither Theocritus in Greek, Virgil

in Latin, nor Sannazzaro in Italian, did affect it. Besides these, do I not remember to have seen but few (to speak boldly) printed that have poetical sinews in them: for proof whereof, let but most of the verses be put in prose, and then ask the meaning, and it will be found that one verse did but beget another, without ordering at the first what should be at the last; which becomes a confused mass of words with a tingling sound of rhyme, barely accompanied with reason. (74)

As Sidney complains that contemporary poetry is "a confused mass of words with a tingling sound of rhyme, barely accompanied by reason," he recalls E.K.'s "Letter to Harvey" in *The Shepheardes Calender*, where E.K. lambastes "the rakehellye route of our ragged rymers" who "without learning boste, without judgement jangle, and without reason rage and fome" (17). Yet Sidney disparages the *Calender*'s "old rustic language," the same "old words" that E.K. defends in his introductory letter. Remember that E.K. praises this "kind of wryting," as discussed in the previous chapter, because though "being both so base for the matter, and homely for the manner," it has been used by "young birdes . . . by little first to prove theyr tender wyngs, before they make a greater flyght. So flew Theocritus . . . So flew Virgile . . . So Marot, Sanazarus, and also divers others excellent both Italian and French Poetes, whose foting this Author every where followeth" (18). In reply, Sidney riddles prettily as he reverses the "new Poete's" famous flight. Whereas E.K. promotes the author's style – "his dewe observing of Decorum everye where . . . in al seemly simplycitie of handeling his matter, and *framing* his words" (13–14, my emphasis) – because it endows him with a classical pedigree, Sidney rejects the *Calender*'s structure for the opposite reason: because it lacks classical precedent. "That same *framing* of his style to an old rustic language I dare not allow," Sidney avers authoritatively, "sith neither Theocritus in Greek, Virgil in Latin, nor Sannazarro in Italian, did affect it" (*Apology*, 74, my emphasis).

Through his criticism of the *Calender*'s style and his elaborate parody of E.K.'s style, Sidney in fact defends the "new Poete's" old words and, moreover, joins in Spenser's defence of poetry. Precisely how Sidney remembers the "new Poete" – who as in the *Calender* remains anonymous, still without a name (other than Immeritô) if not without some claim to fame – creates an implied dialogue with E.K. (and his creator) about poetry's "place" in culture. The issue of "framing" holds a central place in this dialogue about how poetry edifies. Recall that E.K. constructs the *Calender* as nothing less than the rebirth of culture in

England, the realization of renaissance after the darkness of the Middle Ages, a work that repairs the ruins of the past and, in linguistic terms, the damage inflicted to English by lesser literary architects: "For what in most English wryters useth to be loose, and as it were ungyrt," E.K. claims, "in this Authour is well grounded, finely *framed*, and strongly trussed up together" (17, my emphasis). Remember, E.K. most wants readers to view the *Calender* as an immortal monument that not only resists ruin but that also repairs the ruins of the past. Never concealing his desire to make a new name for Immeritô, he attempts to conceal the author's medieval model of authorship, Chaucer, in place of classical and modern patterns of authority. Emulating Spenser's relationship with his character-cum-critic, Sidney indirectly refutes E.K.'s estimation of Chaucerian language and reputation as the dark age before the Renaissance: "Chaucer undoubtedly did excellently in his *Troilus and Criseyde*," he writes in the *Apology*, "of whom truly I know not whether to marvel more, either that he in that misty time could see so clearly, or that we in this clear age walk so stumblingly after him" (73). Sidney and Spenser both laugh, it seems, at E.K.'s fantasy of cultural rebirth.

These parallels point to more than mockery, though. Sidney gets the joke at the heart of the *Calender* – Spenser's witty exploration of authorship and its attendant anxieties through the figure of E.K. – and makes it his own. Like Spenser, Sidney expands what the art of memory means in order to claim it (or perhaps reclaim it) for poetry. His dramatic impersonation of E.K., moreover, underscores their shared view of poetry by continuing a fiction of authority. Sidney's legendary irony suggests why the *Apology* represents fiction as truth and vice versa. In effect, Sidney puts his theory into practice, providing a map of misreading by misconstruing and even ruining the *Calender* in order to remember it. Against E.K.'s will to construct Spenser's poetry monumentally, Sidney reminds readers that the poem's symbolic ruins create a "place" for its continued recollection. In so doing, his defence of the *Calender*'s poetry – and, indeed, all poetry – as an art of memory serves as a reminder: Sidney remembers a history of poetry, from Plato to his present, in which critics and advocates alike locate a "place" for poetry in locational memory.

That Sidney finds fiction's defenders in unlikely places – the fields of philosophy, rhetoric, history, and, indirectly, theology – speaks to the larger ambitions of the *Apology*: to extend fiction-making not only to prose but also to all disciplines.[25] Sidney defines verse, against prose, as the ideal location for memory and vehicle for knowledge, for its rooms provide both an order and the possibility of new orders: poetic spaces that can be both traversed and transported themselves from place to place, representing fixity and mobility. Yet this definition contradicts a central argument of the *Apology*: that so-called poetry is not limited to verse but includes *any* form of fiction-making – anything, that is, which speaks to the mind's eye and thus to memory. More expansively, Sidney explains that "indeed the greatest part of poets have apparelled their poetical inventions in that numbrous kind of writing which is called verse; indeed but apparelled, verse being but an ornament and no cause to poetry, sith there have been many most excellent poets that never versified" (21). Of such poets that "writ in prose," he argues, "I speak to show, that it is not rhyming and versing that maketh a poet, no more than a long gown maketh an advocate . . . But it is that feigning notable images of virtues, vices, or what else, with that delightful teaching, which must be the right describing note to know a poet by" – even if, "indeed the senate of poets hath chosen verse as their fittest raiments" (21). Any writing that feigns "notable images of virtues, vices, or," Sidney adds playfully, "what else," can be counted as poetry; any writing that dresses itself in the "raiments" of poetry uses the strategies of fiction-making. As Sidney suggests, his own prose *Apology for Poetry* can therefore be considered poetry (or fiction) in that he too uses the techniques of the poets, making "speaking pictures," thereby defining and demonstrating poetry as an art of memory in any form of writing.

Sidney's repeated allusions to the *Calender* also evoke its central intertexts, Cicero's *On the Orator* and Plato's *Phaedrus*. The *Apology* remembers the prose of Cicero and Plato as poetry that speaks as an art of memory, setting the stage for Sidney's witty prosopopoeia of the prosaic E.K., and reminding readers that Spenser's pastoral dialogues (both poetry and prose) locate poetry's "place" in a range of fields. As I discussed in the previous chapter, E.K. defends the *Calender*'s old and obsolete words through Cicero's authority, yet forgets Antonius and Crassus' differences about style as well as the subtext of their debate: the art of memory, and Cicero's rewriting of the tale of Simonides. Just as Spenser undermines E.K.'s view of Ciceronian decorum (and indeed E.K.'s own sense of decorum), so Sidney similarly challenges E.K.'s authority by citing Cicero. Too many metaphors overwhelms the ear, eye, and memory, Sidney complains, calling this vice "a most tedious prattling, rather over-swaying the memory from the purpose whereto they were applied" (83). Like E.K., Sidney turns to *On the Orator* on stylistic decorum and other matters of art:

For my part, I do not doubt, when Antonius and Crassus, the great
forefathers of Cicero in eloquence, the one (as Cicero testifieth of them)
pretended not to know art, the other not to set by it, because with plain
sensibleness they might win the credit of popular ears; which credit is the
nearest step to persuasion; which persuasion is the chief mark of oratory;
I do not doubt (I say) but that they used these knacks very sparingly. . .
Undoubtedly (at least to my opinion undoubtedly) I have found in divers smally learned courtiers a more sound style than in some professors
of learning; of which I can guess no other cause but that the courtier, following that which by practice he findeth fittest to nature, therein (though
he know it not) doth according to art, though not by art: where the other,
using art to show art, and not to hide art (as in these cases he should do)
flieth from nature, and indeed abuseth art. (84)

"But what?" Sidney asks rhetorically, "Methinks I deserve to be pounded
for straying from poetry to oratory" (84). Through this wry conclusion, Sidney reveals that which E.K. conceals (or forgets), the larger
context of rhetorical decorum: Cicero's new tale of Simonides, which
frames the dialogue. Hiding the art of memory in plain sight, a gesture inscribed within both *On the Orator* and *The Courtier*, speaks to
Sidney's characteristic *sprezzatura*, as he both postulates and performs
ars celare artem. "Art" ostensibly refers to style, to oratorical "knacks"
used to make language seem artful without trying too hard, but Sidney
also suggests the "art" of memory in Cicero's dialogue, the fullest use
of which is necessarily concealed from his interlocutors. Through stylistic mimicry, Sidney mocks E.K. as a "professor of learning" who
clearly knows less than he professes, while styling himself as a "smally
learned" courtier who knows better. Recall that E.K. promises to reveal what the "Authour [him] selfe" concealed, who "chose rather to
unfold great matter of argument covertly, then professing it," which
he professes having "by meanes of some familiar acquaintaunce [been]
made privie to his counsell and secret meaning" in the *Calender* and
"in sundry other works of his" (18–19). As "friends have all things in
common," as the *Phaedrus* puts it, E.K.'s "friendship" serves as a foil for
Sidney's friendship with Spenser, and a way to articulate what these
"friends" hold "in common" in their related defenses of poetry, the "secret meaning" that is an open secret.[26]

Nevertheless, Sidney and E.K. can agree that the English language
has been underestimated, and both vigorously defend their vernacu-
lar. "Our Mother tonge, which truely of it self is both ful enough for

prose and stately enough for verse," E.K. argues, "hath long time ben counted most bare and barrein of both" (16). Sidney concurs: "For the uttering sweetly and properly the conceits of the mind, which is the end of speech," he writes, English should be regarded "equally with any other tongue in the world" (*Apology*, 85). But here they part company, fundamentally disagreeing about what style and decorum mean. E.K. denies that English should be a "mingled language" and his praise of Spenser never attempts to conceal this desire for linguistic purity: "we speak no English, but gibbrish," E.K. argues, praising the "new Poete's" "old words" as a revival – indeed, a rebirth – of pure English: "he hath laboured to restore, as to theyr rightfull heritage such good and naturall English words, as have ben long time out of use and almost cleare disherited" (*Calender*, 16). By contrast, Sidney praises the eclecticism of the English language. "I know some will say it is a mingled language," he confesses, but "why not so much the better, taking the best of both the other?" (*Apology*, 85). Making good use of the "mingled" English language necessitates decorum in the broadest sense: "we may bend to the right use both of matter and manner; whereto our language giveth us great occasion, being indeed capable of any excellent exercising of it" (85). Contrasting the courtier's urbane style with the pompous professor's, Sidney playfully undermines E.K.'s self-professed authority on poetry, challenging him on matters of both style and substance.

Sidney's impersonation of E.K. returns readers to the central issue of *The Shepheardes Calender*: the question of poetry's "place" in English culture and beyond. In so doing, Sidney reimagines the relationship between poetry and oratory, what E.K. calls the "paterne of a perfect Oratour" (*Calender*, 15) and "the perfecte paterne of a Poete" (170), and which he imagines as one ideal pattern for the "new Poete" and his persona, Colin Clout. As if answering Piers' plaintive plea in *October*, "O pierlesse Poesye, where is then thy place?" Sidney locates poetry in a common place with rival disciplines, even as he asserts poetry's pride of place:

> Now doth the *peerless poet* perform both: for whatsoever the philosopher saith should be done, he giveth a *perfect picture* of it in someone by whom it presupposeth it was done, so as he coupleth the general notion with the particular example. A *perfect picture*, I say, for he yieldeth to the powers of the mind an image of that whereof the philosopher bestoweth but a wordish description, which doth neither strike, pierce, nor possess the sight of the soul so much as that other doth . . . So no doubt the philosopher,

with his learned definition, be it of virtue, vices, matters of public or private government, replenisheth the memory with many infallible grounds
of wisdom, which, notwithstanding, lie dark before the imaginative and
judging power if they be not illuminated or figured forth by the *speaking
picture of poesy*. (*Apology*, 27–8, my emphasis)

Although ostensibly comparing poetry to history, Sidney surrepti-
tiously connects fiction to philosophy and rhetoric, suggesting how
poetry's "perfect picture[s]" unite these disciplines. This passage again
brings together the two tales of the poet Simonides: as inventor of the
art of memory, and as the origin of the analogy between poetry and
painting as "speaking pictures." As Sidney suggests, in Platonic fashion, the art of memory has value only when it exceeds simple rules for
memorization. "To a man that had never seen . . . a gorgeous palace,
the architecture, with declaring the full beauties, might well make the
hearer able to repeat, as it were by rote, all he had heard, yet it should
never satisfy his inward conceits with being witness to itself of a true
lively knowledge," he explains; "But the same man, as soon as he might
see . . . the house well in model, should straightways grow without
need of any description, to a judicial comprehending of them" (27–8).
Rhetoric alone provides only a partial view of the art of memory, Sidney suggests, and Cicero provides the example that proves the rules
of art matter less than their creative use: "Tully taketh much pains and
many times not without poetical helps to make us know the force love
of our country hath in us" (28). The use of poetry's perfect pictures in
any discipline, be it philosophy, rhetoric, or poetry itself, thus can tell a
story about history. "If the poet do his part aright," Sidney writes, "he
will show you in Tantalus, Atreus, and such like, nothing that is not
to be shunned; in Cyrus, Aeneas, Ulysses, each thing to be followed;
where the historian, bound to tell things as things were, cannot be liberal (without he will be poetical) of a *perfect pattern*" (32, my emphasis). Because of this, he argues, the historian often "must be poetical"
– and the poet historical (33). The art of memory teaches how to "see
through" such veiled truths: "So no doubt the philosopher, with his
learned definition, be it of virtue, vices, matters of public or private
government, replenisheth the memory with many infallible grounds of
wisdom, which, notwithstanding, lie dark before the imaginative and
judging power if they be not illuminated or figured forth by the speaking picture of poesy" (28). If Sidney's ambiguous praise seems at least
partly directed at poetry's rivals, his "perfect pattern" unites rather

than divides the different disciplines, showing how poetry shares a place (perforce, if not by choice) with other fields.

Like the *Calender*, the *Apology* draws not one "perfect pattern" but rather ways of adapting patterns to make them "perfect" in any given situation or context, as it draws attention to the larger role that "speaking pictures" can play in learning. Even as he asserts poetry's superiority over philosophy on the ground of their essential difference – that philosophy teaches through abstract "wordish description[s]" that cannot, unlike poetry's moving pictures, stir the "sight of the soul" – Sidney simultaneously inverts this argument, implying that both poetry and philosophy create "perfect pictures" that make matter memorable. In this context, Plato matters most of all. Plato was indeed a poet, Sidney passionately professes, who he holds in the greatest "reverence . . . sith of all philosophers he is the most poetical" (63). When offering an apology for Plato, Sidney intimates that poetry never left the Republic, where it always held a central place. Although philosophers cannot educate as well as poets – after all, Sidney reminds us, "certain poets, as Simonides and Pindar, had so prevailed with Hiero the First, that of a tyrant they made him a just king, where Plato could do so little with Dionysius, that he himself of a philosopher was made a slave" (64–5) – he appears to take seriously Plato's complaints about poetry:

> Plato found fault that the poets of his time filled the world with wrong opinions of the gods, making light tales of that unspotted essence, and therefore would not have the youth depraved with such opinions . . . [Yet] the poets did not induce such opinions, but did imitate those opinions already induced. For all the Greek stories can well testify that the very religion of that time stood upon many and many-fashioned gods, not taught so by the poets but followed according to the nature of imitation. (65–6)

In jest and in all seriousness, Sidney broaches the touchy subject of poetry's lies about the gods, the reason why Plato ostensibly banishes poets from his ideal Republic. But Sidney intentionally if coyly misinterprets Plato's complaints about poetry as a matter of faith rather than idolatry in the mundane realms of pedagogy and power. He does so by focusing on poetry's ability to represent divinity truly rather than what is truly at stake: the uses of poetry's "perfect pictures" as political fictions, enacted and re-enacted by self-fashioned gods of state. All the same, the real issue comes to the fore. With his art of concealing and revealing art fully on display, Sidney contends that Plato objected to the "many-fashioned gods" of pagan antiquity – not to poetry itself – reasoning that since he "only meant to drive out those wrong opinions of the Deity," and since "Christianity hath taken away all the hurtful belief), perchance (as he thought) nourished by the then esteemed poets," Plato should be given a place of honour in the Republic of Poetry (66). "So as Plato, banishing the abuse, not the thing, not banishing it, but giving due honor unto it, shall be our patron and not our adversary," Sidney affirms, explaining why a lover of wisdom might think as much: "For indeed, I had much rather (sith truly I may do it) show their mistaking of Plato (under whose lion's skin they would make an ass-like braying against poesy) than go about to overthrow his authority" (67).

E.K., clearly, is one such "ass." In correcting the common "mistaking of Plato," Sidney performs a parody of E.K.'s misinterpretations of Platonic love poetry, as a way to remember the "many-fashioned gods" of power, politics, and pedagogy. Sidney thus slyly takes up a central issue of the *Calender*: the use of poetry's gold to fashion idols, in E.K.'s case, to celebrate Tudor divinity. "The wiser a man is," Sidney says in E.K.'s voice, "the more just cause he shall find to have in admiration" in Plato's dialogues, "especially sith he attributeth unto poesy more than myself do, namely, to be a very inspiring of divine force, far above man's wit" (67). Yet Sidney implies the opposite of what he claims – that Plato both "giveth high and rightly divine commendation to poetry" – and with Socratic irony tacitly rebuts such "mistaking" views (66–7). Indirectly, he corrects E.K.'s view of poetry's "place" in Plato's dialogues, and specifically one of his glosses in the *October* eclogue. Describing the sweet spot of the shepherds' dialogue, E.K. writes that "This place seemeth to conspyre with Plato," whom he erroneously claims describes the divine origin and subsequent degradation of poetry in his dialogue on the *Laws*: "al men being astonied and as it were ravished, with delight, thinking (as it was indeed) that he was inspired from above, called him vatem: which kind of men afterwarde framing their verses to lighter musick . . . found out lighter matter of Poesie also, some playing wyth love, some scorning at mens fashions, some powred out in pleasures, and so were called Poetes or makers" (*Calender*, 177–8). E.K.'s history of poetry inverts the Greek and Roman terms for poets, "vatem" and "makers," but Sidney sets him straight on this and other mistakes in the *Apology*. "Among the Romans a poet was called *vates*," he explains, "which is as much as a diviner, foreseer, or prophet . . . so heavenly a title did that excellent people bestow upon this heart-ravishing knowledge" (10). Moreover, Sidney admonishes any claim to poetry's divinity as a mistake in itself. Virgil's poetry proves exemplary in this regard, and Sidney cites the tradition of Virgilian lots as a prophetic practice: the "*Sortes Virgilianae*, when by sudden opening Virgil's book they lighted upon any verse of his making, whereof the Histories of the Emperors' Lives are full" (10–11). Although Sidney calls this a "very vain and godless superstition" and dismisses it as ancient history (11), "Virgil's book" continued to be used as political prophecy, to stake claims to endless empire for Aeneas' alleged descendants. The use of poetry to create the "many-fashioned gods" of empire, Sidney implies, continues in present-day England. Poetic "lies about the gods," he would seem to suggest, have little (if anything) to do with religious differences.

Sidney suggests as much when he corrects E.K.'s other mistaken definition of poetry. In contrast with the Romans, he explains, the Greeks named their poets "makers," separating the human from the divine where poetry is concerned. Sidney then identifies himself with this name: "The Greeks called him a poet, which name . . . cometh of this word *poiein*, which is, to make, wherein I know not whether by luck or wisdom we Englishmen have met with the Greeks in calling him a maker: which name, how high and incomparable a title it is, I had rather were known by marking the scope of other sciences than by my partial allegation" (13). His preference for "maker" to "seer" positions poetry as only human. Some poetry could be considered divine, Sidney carefully suggests, yet even as he allows for sacred poetry he worries about profanity: "And may not I presume a little further . . . and say that the holy David's Psalms are a divine poem?" Yes, he answers, for "even the name Psalms will speak for me, which being interpreted is nothing but songs; then, that is fully written in meter" and "which is merely poetical."[27] How else could you understand the Psalms except as "heavenly poesy, wherein almost he showeth himself a passionate lover of that unspeakable and everlasting beauty to be seen by the eyes of the mind, only cleared by faith" (12)? Having worshipped poetry as though divine, Sidney offers a partial apology: "But truly, now having named him, I fear me I seem to profane that holy name, applying it to poetry, which is among us thrown down to so ridiculous an estimation. But they that with quiet judgments will look a little deeper into it, shall find the end and working of it such, as being rightly applied, deserveth not be scourged out of the Church of God" (13). Despite his palinodic retraction, Sidney's point remains the same: scriptural praise of divinity may be read poetically, but this is different from using poetry to fashion divinity.

Nevertheless, Sidney willingly attributes a kind of divinity to poetry, and to this end he refashions commonplace ideas about Platonic (and Ciceronian) love of wisdom:

If the saying of Plato and Tully be true, that who could see virtue would be wonderfully ravished with the love of her beauty, this man sets her out to make her more lovely in her holiday apparel, to the eye of any that will deign not to disdain until they understand. But if anything be already said in the defence of sweet poetry, all concurreth to the maintaining the hero-ical, which is not only a kind, but the best and most accomplished kind of poetry. For as the image of each action stirreth and instructeth the mind, so the lofty image of such worthies most inflameth the mind with desire to be worthy, and informs with counsel how to be worthy. Only let Ae-neas be worn in the *tablet of your memory*, how he governeth himself in the ruin of his country; in the preserving his old father and carrying away his religious ceremonies, in obeying the god's commandment to leave Dido. (48–9, my emphasis)

This passage draws on a Platonic art of memory – established in the *Phaedrus*, imitated by Cicero and others, including Sidney – in which beauty forms the ultimate reminder, leading the soul from its state of ruin to recollection, which Plato defines as true love of wisdom. Through Plato's and Cicero's dialogues, Sidney challenges Trojan tales of love's ruinous effects, replacing them with new stories of history. At the same time, he suggests just what these forms of edification hold in common. The art of memory creates a commonplace for different versions of how beauty spurs the recollection of divinity, the movement from human to divine love – the love of wisdom that can apply to pagans and Christian poets alike. Further, Sidney connects rhetoric and philosophy to poetry as the matter to be "worn in the tablet of your memory" when he links "Plato and Tully" to Virgil's *Aeneid* as models of edification: specifically, how the hero "governeth himself in the ruin of his country," conveying and thus "preserving" the remains of the past. Epic poetry, Virgil's in particular, answers the need for a "heroical" education in virtue, Sid-ney argues, thus ironically answering E.K.'s (and perhaps Spenser's) anxieties about Virgilian influence. But rather than remembering the *Aeneid* as history, this epic becomes the exemplar of poetry as an edi-fying fiction, one that depends upon the art of memory. This passage epitomizes Sidney's definition of poetry, his sense that "even they who have taught the art of memory" have recognized how "verse in effect perfectly" fits the requirements of usefulness and beauty; this passage both anticipates and answers the question, "Who is it that ever was a scholar that doth not carry away some verses of Virgil, Horace, or Cato, which in his youth he learned, and even to his old age serve him for hourly lessons?" (54).

Historicizing Virgil's legacy throughout his *Apology*, Sidney underscores the difference between writers and reception – as when, for example, he winks at the godless tradition of Virgilian lots. He further deflates the Trojan legend as a model of translating empire or learning by tacitly denying the legend of Brutus in his description of Wales, where "the true remnant of the ancient Britons" has survived despite invaders who "did seek to ruin all memory of learning from among them, yet do their poets even to this day last" (10). The past survives in ruins of poetry, and when readers "carry away" poetry's ruins like so many epic heroes, these "verses" will continue to edify. When Sidney writes "Only let Aeneas be worn in the tablet of your memory" (49), he implies that there is only one story of history – Virgil's version of Troy's ruin – but then he suggests the opposite when recalling a longer history of diverse Trojan tales: "Let us but hear old Anchises speaking in the midst of Troy's flames, or see Ulysses in the fulness of all Calypso's delights bewail his absence from barren and beggarly Ithaca . . . and our Chaucer's Pandar, so expressed that we now use their names to signify their trades; and finally, all virtues, vices, and passions so in their own natural seats laid to the view that we seem not to hear of them, but clearly to see through them" (28–9). The multiple versions of Trojan tales underscores the impossibility of taking such stories as the truth of history (or divinity), and the example of Aeneas' virtue in leaving Dido stands out as one such clearly ambiguous example. Sidney's call serves as an injunction to remember the ruins of Troy as a place for recollection, not as truth but as transparent fiction, reminding readers "clearly to see through them." In language reminiscent of the tale of Simonides, Sidney praises poetry's "natural seats" or places as a way to teach "virtues, vices, and passions," in part, by teaching readers how to recognize fiction. Sidney thus joins Spenser in reforming the art of memory for poetry, showing and telling how this art can do far more than merely build castles in the air.

As a final test, Sidney also demands that readers "see through" his own fictions. When answering the charge that poets "be the principal liars," Sidney famously replies with Socratic irony – a liar's paradox that reveals how fiction's lies (including his own) paradoxically tell the truth. "For the poet, he nothing affirms," Sidney affirms, "and therefore never lieth" (57). Qualifying this assertion, he muses: "I answer paradoxically, but truly, I think truly, that of all writers under the sun the poet is the least liar, and, though he would, as a poet can scarcely be a liar . . . For, as I take it, to lie is to affirm that to be true which is false" (56–7). Despite his doubletalk, Sidney makes a crucial distinction that elides the boundaries between truth and fiction. To lie is to affirm, as Plato suggests, to pretend to know the truth and to offer this truth for sale, but this does not mean that poetry should be exiled from the Republic. Fiction that announces itself as such, without the intent to deceive, in effect tells the truth about its own lies – and indirectly, those of others. "And therefore," Sidney reasons, "though he [the poet] recount things not true, yet because he telleth them not for true, he lieth not," a point he illustrates with a question directed to enemies of theatrical performance: "What child is there that, coming to a play, and seeing Thebes written in great letters upon an old door, doth believe that it is Thebes?" (57). Not surprisingly, Sidney supplies his own answer: "If then a man can arrive at that child's age to know that the poet's persons and doings are but pictures what should be, and not stories what have been, they will never give the lie to things not affirmatively but allegorically and figuratively written" (57). This speaks to Sidney's own semi-veiled fiction. As Margaret Ferguson explains, the word "apology" derives from the Greek "*apologos*, meaning 'story' or 'fable' " as well as defence.[28] As she argues, Sidney's *Apology* ideally should be read "not only as an important work of literary theory, but also as a work of quasi-autobiographical allegory"; noting that "Sidney's contemporary Puttenham called [allegory] "the courtly figure,' " she terms it "an important weapon of defense for an Elizabethan aristocrat" – especially a master of "deep dissimulation" like Sidney (137–8). As Sidney suggests, all poets – whether they write in prose or verse, whether in the field of fiction or in other places – depend upon allegory to express matters "not affirmatively but . . . figuratively written." Writing "allegorically" (and thus "speaking other" than the so-called literal truth) is lying that reveals a truth worth knowing: self-knowledge. By presenting matter ironically and indirectly, poets teach readers how to recognize multiple, competing truths and, most importantly, how to discern among them. Sidney implies that his own *Apology* represents such truth "under the veil of fables" (88).

Sidney dramatizes this truth throughout the *Apology*, ironically, by affirming it too much. Whereas "other artists, and especially the

historian," who by "affirming many things, can, in the cloudy knowledge of mankind, hardly escape from many lies," the poet "citeth not
authorities of other histories, but even for his entry calleth the sweet
Muses to inspire into him a good invention," a poetic paradox that Sidney puns upon: "therefore, as in history looking for truth, they [read-
ers] go away full fraught with falsehood, so in poesy looking for fiction,
they shall use the narration but as an imaginative ground-plot of a
profitable invention" (57–8). Indirectly, Sidney makes fiction the disciplinary common ground, or "ground-plot," for edification: the basis of
"profitable invention" for poets and ordinary people. The *Apology*, as
both a history of stories and a story of histories, ultimately recognizes
the value of fiction-making in any field or form. "In troth," Sidney affirms again, the poet is "not laboring to tell you what is or is not," and
so he identifies himself with "the poet [who] . . . never affirmeth," who
"never maketh any circles about your imagination to conjure you to
believe for true what he writes" (57). But naturally, Sidney does just
that in the end – conjure readers to believe the truth of what he writes:
"I conjure you all that have had the evil luck to read this ink-wasting
toy of mine, even in the name of the nine Muses, no more to scorn the
sacred mysteries of poesy, no more to laugh at the name of poets, as
though they were next inheritors to fools, no more to jest at the reverent
title of rhymer" (87). Sidney cannot resist just one more "jest" when he
affirms the divine right of rhymers. Urging readers "to believe . . . that
it pleased the heavenly Deity, by Hesiod and Homer, under the veil
of fables, to give us all knowledge, logic, rhetoric, philosophy natural
and moral," and "to believe with me that there are many mysteries contained in poetry, which of purpose were written darkly, lest by profane
wits it should be abused," Sidney thus ruins sacred truths, including
his own (88). And if readers don't believe him? They can go to hell – or,
poetry's perpetual underworld: "Thus doing, your soul shall be placed
with Dante's Beatrix or Virgil's Anchises," he swears, confusing the
places for heaven and hell in order to bring poetry down to earth (88).
Rather than divine revelation, poetry reveals human truths that Sidney
makes memorable: to those who "cannot hear the planet-like music of
poetry . . . thus much curse I must send you in the behalf of all poets,
that while you live, you live in love, and never get favor for lacking
skill of a sonnet; and when you die, your memory die from the earth for
want of an epitaph" (89). Sidney's profound jest suggests that he might
have known this life lesson would apply to him, too.[29]

Remembering Sidney in *The Ruines of Time*

With *The Ruines of Time*, Spenser remembers Sidney, providing him with the epitaph that even poets require, and a memorial that turns on their shared art of memory. Constructing this poem within the place of ruin (Sidney's as well as Verlame's), though less as a new Virgil than as a new Simonides, Spenser implies that even his own poetic monument is not "without end." Fittingly, he answers Sidney's call for "the heroical" with Sidney's own life story. Just as Aeneas exemplifies the heroic for Sidney, so Sidney fills that role – as the heroic figure that England should remember – in Spenser's vision of poetic immortality. By remembering Sidney, Spenser remembers what these friends hold in common: a defence of poetry's place in ruins.

Through Verlame's and Sidney's stories, Spenser expands the art of memory from the pictorial into the narratival: a story of history that translates the past for the present, continuing to build upon the ruins of time. *The Ruines of Time* presents the art of memory in the broadest possible terms, offering readers multiple ways of thinking about locational memory. The oratorical display by which Verlame reconstructs her "High towers, faire temples, goodly theaters," demarcating spaces "with faire pillours," and filling them with "fine imageries," can be seen as a literary method: the use of spaces and images designed to aid in the recollecting of key topics (92–6). Similarly, the final visions produce an emblematic memory theatre very like Van der Noot's *Theatre for Worldlings*. But Spenser draws attention to how he uses the art of memory to tell a story about history, one that can be seen in Ciceronian and Platonic terms: as in *On the Orator*, the ruins of Verlame's city are places for recollection; as in the *Phaedrus*, the art of memory is reimagined as a story of recollecting divinity. Like Sidney, Spenser never affirms and therefore never lies: instead, he has Verlame argue that poetry is immortal because it derives from divinity, while drawing attention to the fact that Verlame herself is only a poetic fiction.

As he does with E.K., Spenser engages in a tacit dialogue with Verlame, a debate about the immortality of his own poetry. When Verlame asserts that "deeds do die, how ever noblie donne, / And thoughts of men do as themselves decay, / But wise wordes taught in numbers for to runne, / Recorded by the Muses, live for ay," she makes an absolute statement of poetry's permanence (400–3). Yet she also radically qualifies this praise. In comparing those who die "In foule forgetfulnesse, and nameles lie" and those who "live for aye above" with "the Gods" and "on *Nectar* and *Ambrosia* do feede" (378, 396, 399), Verlame implies that place matters to memory. Spenser makes her statements about poetic permanence deeply ambiguous, such that they can be read as either an absolute claim of poetic incorruptibility or as a qualified assertion of perpetuation. The purpose of this anamorphic image becomes clear. The shape immortality takes – whether whole or ruined – depends upon the location of memory. Poetry may be immortal in heaven – realm of "*Jove* the father of eternitie*" (369) – but not necessarily on earth, as the title of Spenser's poem suggests. Verlame's claim that "fame with golden wings aloft doth flie, / Above the reach of ruinous decay" can be taken literally; immutable immortality heads to heaven, but poetry remains in ruins within time (421–2). Her double blessing on Sidney – "so there thou livest, singing everymore, / And here thou livest, being ever song" (337–8) – suggests the difference between immortality in heaven and on earth: in heaven Sidney sings for ever, but on earth he must be continually sung in order to be immortal. Within the earthbound world of England, in other words, immortality must be continually recalled from oblivion. In this place, at least, monuments of memory would seem to be as fragile as monuments of marble.

Verlame's final assertion of poetic immortality clarifies how place matters to memory:

> The seven fold yron gates of grislie Hell,
> And horrid house of sad *Proserpina*,
> They able are with power of mightie spell
> To breake, and thence the soules to bring awaie
> Out of dread darknesse, to eternall day,
> And them immortal make, which els would die
> In foule forgetfulnesse, and nameles lie . . .
>
> So raisde they eke faire *Ledaes* warlick twinnes,
> And interchanged life unto them lent,
> That when th'one dies, th'other then beginnes
> To shew in Heaven his brightnes orient. (372–89)

For Verlame, the place of poetry matters to memory in a very literal sense – whether in heaven or on earth – but readers can understand this insistence upon location in figurative terms. Poetry makes immortal what otherwise would "in foule forgetfulnesse, and nameles lie," not

because it fashions a monument that never falls to ruin but because poetry's ruins are places for refashioning and remembering anew. Spenser
thus portrays immortality as a kind of reciprocity: poetry both bestows
immortality and partakes of it, creating an exchange between past and
present, the living and the dead – but never permanently. In each case,
recalling the dead to life occurs temporarily: Persephone must return
to the underworld, Eurydice to death, and in the case of Castor and
Pollux, "when th'one dies, th'other then beginnes" (388). Through the
example of Castor and Pollux, "faire *Ledaes* warlick twinnes," who play
a key role in the tale of Simonides, Spenser suggests how poetry recalls
the dead from the ruin of forgetfulness, if only temporarily. The story of
Castor and Pollux reflects the theory and practice of poetics that Sidney
and Spenser as friends hold in common, for by remembering one another, they effect an exchange between heaven and earth (or England),
continuing the cycle that constitutes immortality.[30] The passage thus
illustrates how poetry's ruin can be at once a reminder and a place for
remembrance.

As Spenser suggests, though, readers should question Verlame's id-
iosyncratic theology.[31] Naturally, she draws her examples of "heaven"
and immortality entirely from classical myth; and of course, as the
poem in ruins that longs for immortality, Verlame has faith in her own
stories. However, her vision of heaven and hell, earthly and everlasting poetry, are manifestly fictions, which Spenser uses paradoxically to
deny poetry-as-revelation, reframing its truths as human. By treating
Sidney's apotheosis as a complex fiction, Spenser demands a certain
scepticism from readers – an awareness that poetic immortality is only
ever a fantasy. After all, how can poetry be permanent when, as part of
history, it is also subject to mutability?

Spenser's poem brings commonplaces of poetic immortality down to
earth, so to speak, by remembering Sidney in ways that remind readers
of his *Apology for Poetry*. Moreover, Sidney's divine apotheosis locates
his memory in his own poetry's pretty rooms. As he writes in the
Apology, "The grammarian speaketh only of the rules of speech" and
"theron gives artificial rules, which are still compassed within the circle
of a question," whereas "only the poet . . . goeth hand in hand with
nature, not enclosed within the narrow warrant of her gifts, but freely
ranging only within the zodiac of his own wit" (13–14). The "zodiac of
[Sidney's] wit" figures pictorially as the "heavens" in the visions that
follow. With these visions of ruin, Spenser creates a memory theatre fashioned after Sidney's own art of memory, making the stars themselves

the location for remembering the star-lover Astrophil. Drawing upon Sidney's language of artificial memory – from "artificial rules" to the "zodiac," which simultaneously evokes both humanist and hermetic commonplaces of locational memory – Spenser remembers Sidney in the location most fitting or apropos for his fame: the heavens. In these celestial spaces of memory, Spenser fashions a memory theatre in which the ruins of time are places for recollecting the past: not a monument per se but a space of immortality all the same. If remembering *is* immortality, then the story of Sidney's history illustrates this crucial idea: both the inevitability of ruin and the necessity of continued recollection forms the education in edification for the speaker and readers alike. As the state of Sidney's memory suggests – at once permanent and contingent, whole and ruined – poetic immortality depends upon location. Poetry can translate immortality from heaven to earth only temporarily in a process of exchange illustrated by Sidney's and Spenser's remembrances and revisions (as well as defences) of each other's poetry.

The poem concludes with another memory theatre of visions. Verlame again demands that readers see her absent presence, her invisible ruins:

Let them behold the piteous fall of mee . . .

And his owne end unto remembrance call;
That of like ruine he may warned bee,
And in himselfe be moov'd to pittie mee (461–9)

At this point, she disappears; "Thus having ended all her piteous plaint, / With dolefull shrikes shee vanished away," Spenser's speaker laments, though he continues to seek out her image in vain: "Looking still, if I might of her have sight" (470–1, 476). Busy recalling her "passion strong" and "renewing her complaint," the speaker then sees a series of visions that validate the poem's double vision of poetic immortality (479). On the one hand, these emblems of ruin translating into recollection reinforce Verlame's vision of poetry as immortal in the heavens; on the other, Spenser draws the poem's heavens from Sidney's own poetry. "Before mine eies strange sights presented were," he says, "Like tragicke Pageants seeming to appeare" (489–90). These "tragicke Pageants" symbolically enact the drama of Spenser's poem, a memory theatre that teaches how to continue recollecting and refashioning the ruins of time.

With two sets of mirroring emblems, Spenser illustrates both ruin and re-edification. The first set of emblems portrays images of edifices falling to destruction, including Spenser's own poetic monuments:

> Then did I see a pleasant Paradize
> . . . Made for the gentle squire, to entertain,
> His fayre *Belphœbe* . . .
> But ô short pleasure bought with lasting paine,
> . . . I sawe this gardine wasted quite (519–29)

With this vision of *The Faerie Queene* itself falling to ruin, Spenser suggests that even his own poetry is not without end. Viewing these scenes of destruction, Spenser's troubled persona asks why "time doth greatest things to ruine bring?" (556), a question answered by a kind of deus ex machina who clarifies the meaning of the visions: "all is vantie and griefe of minde, / Ne other comfort in this world can be, / But hope of heaven" (583–5). Yet the vision that follows frames these statements neither in terms of immediate apocalypse, nor as a rejection of all things worldly. The speaker sees "a goodly Virgine" asleep in a sumptuous matrimonial bed, as a voice tells her to awake: "For lo her Bridegrome was in readie ray / To come to her, and seeke her loves delight" (636, 640–1). But this allegorical marriage of Christ and Church remains unconsummated: "With that she started up with cherefull sight, / When suddeinly both bed and all was gone, / And I in langour left there all alone" (642–4). The fact that unveiled truth remains a dream here is central to Spenser's visionary poetics.

Rather than depicting ruin at the *end* of time, Spenser illustrates how memory survives *in* time. With Sidney's apotheosis in the next set of emblems, Spenser demonstrates how memory translates to heaven as "spoyles" and, through recollection, translates memory back to earth, repairing the ruins of time, if only for a time. The first three images translate memory from earth to heaven, where memory finds a final resting place in "heavenly signe[s]" (601). Sidney's memory also finds a place among the heavenly constellations: "th'Harpe of *Philisides* now dead . . . / . . . So now in heaven a signe it doth appeare, / The Harpe well knowne beside the Northerne Beare" (609–16). Such locations for memory are pictured as

> A curious Coffer made of *Heben* wood,
> That in it did most precious treasure hide . . .

So now it is transform'd into that starre,
In which all heavenly treasures locked are. (618–30)

This image finally encloses Sidney's memory:

A Knight all arm'd, upon a winged steed . . .
Fully mortally this Knight ywounded was,
That streames of blood foorth flowed on the gras.

Yet was he deckt (small joy to him alas)
With manie garlands for his victories,
And with rich spoyles, which late he did purchas
Through brave atcheivements from his enemies:
Fainting at last through long infirmities,
He smote his steed, that straight to heaven him bore,
And left me here his losse for to deplore. (646–58)

Spenser allows Sidney to translate his "manie garlands" to heaven (as the memory of Sidney's "brave atcheivements") and, by extension, to offer England these "victories" to remember. With this image of Sidney's apotheosis, the material remains or "rich spoyles" – the stuff of history – are transformed into the "ruines of time," the stuff of immortal memory: "an Arke of purest gold / . . . Which th'ashes seem'd of some great Prince to hold, / Enclosde therein for endles memorie" (659–62). Spenser's speaker observes that it "Seemed the heavens with the earth did disagree, / Whether should of those ashes keeper be," a dispute solved by the "wing footed *Mercurie*" (664–6). But lest Sidney be mistaken as a god himself, Spenser evokes the messenger god, Hermes.[32] Here and throughout the poem, Spenser suggests that his poetry reveals human truths, not divine.

With these visions, Spenser builds his own theatre for worldlings, one that recalls Van der Noot's *Theatre* but with key differences. Whereas the *Theatre* teaches worldlings to forget this world for the world to come, Spenser teaches how to fashion a theatre for memory by recollecting the ruins of time, a process that his poem reveals "by demonstration" (488): depicting poetry as both an edifice and a means of edification. Yet by drawing attention to fictions of poetic immortality, Spenser denies his own poetry divine status and, indirectly, criticizes poetry that would attribute divine truth to itself or those it praises. Discerning lies about the gods – discerning fiction from history – lies at the heart of Spenser's complaints, here and throughout his work. The poem's negative theology, the need to recognize fictional, even self-fashioned gods, and the issue of "telling the truth" when fiction and history inevitably mingle, points readers inevitably toward *The Faerie Queene*.[33]

By calling his poem *The Ruines of Time*, Spenser emphasizes the work's location within time and history. The struggle to retrieve Sidney's heavenly memory continues even for Spenser, who concludes that he has built this poetic edifice by recollecting the "riche spoyles" of memory:

> Immortal spirite of *Philisides*,
> Which now art made the heavens ornament,
> That whilome wast the worlds chiefst riches;
> Give leave to him that lov'de thee to lament
> His losse, by lacke of thee to heaven hent,
> And with last duties of this broken verse,
> Broken with sighes, to decke thy sable Herse . . .
> Vouchsafe this moniment of his last praise. (673–82)

On earth, poetry remains in ruins – "broken verse" that must continued to be remembered. As Spenser directs Sidney's sister (as a patron of poetry) to "vouchsafe this moniment of his last praise," he reminds readers that *The Ruines of Time* must be remembered to live on after the death of its author. Clearly, Spenser's own immortality depends not only upon his ability to remember others but also upon being remembered himself. With this final tentative invocation of the immortality of poetry *topos*, Spenser makes his poem the place that Verlame claims England lacks. This poetic edifice, built from ruin and destined to return to ruin, encloses Spenser's vision of immortality as remembrance. *The Ruines of Time* thus remains in ruins, a contingent edifice meant to be renovated in future dialogue. In this regard, the process of recollecting matters more than the product, the poetic monument less than what remains of it. Spenser creates a memory theatre for Sidney and England that demonstrates the art of memory, exploring how poetry builds and rebuilds immortality from the ruins of time. Poetry would seem to offer no guarantee of memorial permanence, witnessed by the ostensibly ruinous state of the poem itself. Here as elsewhere, Spenser refuses to invest poetic structures with static immortality. But he nevertheless champions poetry's ruins as places in which to recollect the past anew – a view that reflects Spenser's desire as well as duty to make something new of inevitable decay.

Chapter Four

"The Methode of a Poet Historical [and] . . . an Historiographer": Recollecting the Past in the 1590 *Faerie Queene*

Philip Sidney's witty portrait of a "historian" in the *Apology for Poetry* bears a striking resemblance to the memorable court historian Eumnestes in the allegorical Castle of Alma:

> loaden with old mouse-eaten records, authorizing himself (for the most part) upon other histories, whose greatest authorities are built upon the notable foundation of hearsay, having much ado to accord differing writers, and to pick truth out of partiality, better acquainted with a thousand years ago than with the present age, and yet better knowing how this world goeth than his own wit runneth, curious for antiquities and inquisitive of novelties, a wonder to young folks and a tyrant in table talk, denieth in a great chafe that any man, for teaching of virtue and virtuous actions, is comparable to him.[1]

A historian may claim to be "the witness of time, the light of truth, the life of memory, the directress of life, the herald of antiquity," Sidney asserts (on Cicero's authority), but he also notes, "even historiographers . . . have been glad to borrow both fashion and perchance weight of poets. So that truly neither philosopher nor historiographer could at the first have entered into the gates of popular judgments if they had not taken a great passport of poetry" (24–5, 9). If, as Sidney suggests, historians can "borrow both fashion and perchance weight of poets," then the reverse should be true as well: poets can also "borrow" the "fashion" and "weight" or style and substance of historians, and for similar ends – "for teaching of virtue and virtous actions." Yet here as elsewhere, Sidney's authoritative distinctions collapse under the weight of his irony. Indirectly, he tells this truth: historians and poets have always been

"comparable" in both the method and the matter of storytelling, as witnessed nowhere more clearly than in epic. Moreover, just what each
teaches of virtue has never been transparent, Sidney jestingly suggests.
The "lies of the poets" are also the "lies of the historians," in other
words: "authorizing" themselves on other "authorities" by reconstructing narratives already "built upon the notable foundation of hearsay,"
living in the past (or "better acquainted with a thousand years ago than
with the present age") while claiming to teach "virtuous action" in the
present. If Sidney makes a joke at the expense of E.K., who embodies
the desire to construct "antiquities" as "novelties" and vice versa, he
also seriously suggests why this matters: the complex intertwining of
story and history, in writing as in the world, speaks to the process by
which all people must "pick truth out of partiality" amidst the "antiquities" – or ruins – of time. To tell the truth, especially given that the
truth itself always changes, entails reforming old matters of memory
into something new.

The subtext that Sidney so artfully conceals and reveals, the closely
related roles of poets and historians, also provides an important context
for the 1590 *Faerie Queene*. Here as in *The Shepheardes Calender*, the larger
issue at stake concerns a central question of Castiglione's *Courtier*,
which Sidney-as-courtier intimates: the question of how to fashion
princes and ordinary people alike, and the best method for achieving this end. As I argue, the art of memory plays a central part in how
Spenser imagines the relation between story and history, and its role in
edification. In his prefatory letter to Walter Raleigh, Spenser turns to
the topic of what poets and historians hold in common, how they "borrow both fashion and . . . weight," method and matter, of storytelling
from one another, by alluding to their common place in memory and
in Spenser's poem: Alma's Castle.[2] At once veiling and unveiling his
allegory, Spenser acknowledges "how doubtfully all Allegories may be
construed," and how "this booke of mine, which I haue entitled the
Faery Queene, being a continued Allegory, or darke conceit," should be
clarified for Raleigh and readers alike: "for your better light in reading
therof" (737). As though E.K. himself, Spenser purports to reveal what
otherwise might be concealed, and thus misconstrued, by his readers.
"I haue thought good aswell for auoyding of gealous opinions and mis-
constructions . . . to discouer vnto you the general intention or meaning, which in the whole course thereof I haue fashioned," says Spenser
in baroque fashion: "The generall end therefore of all the booke is to
fashion a gentleman or noble person in vertuous and gentle discipline"

(737). Yet the "Letter to Raleigh" engages in the kind of ironic misdirection found in E.K.'s "Letter to Harvey," specifically in how Spenser defines his method – and implicitly, his motive – as poet. Distinguishing poets from historians, presumably to assert his rightful poetic licence with history, Spenser explains that the "Methode of a Poet historical is not such, as of an Historiographer": "For an Historiographer discourseth of affayres orderly as they were donne, accounting as well the times as the actions, but a Poet thrusteth into the middest, euen where it most concerneth him, and there recoursing to the thinges forepaste, and diuining of thinges to come, maketh a pleasing Analysis of all" (738). Spenser's distinction between poets and historians echoes Sidney's in the *Apology*, where he writes that "if they" – poets – "will represent an history, they must not (as Horace saith) begin *ab ovo*, but they must come to the principal point of that one action which they will represent" (*Apology*, 77). Yet this seemingly trivial difference clearly speaks to the poem as an allegory, paradoxically by "speaking other," suggesting why Spenser never calls *The Faerie Queene* an "epic" (just as he never calls *The Shepheardes Calender* a "pastoral").[3] In one sense, Spenser leads neither Raleigh nor reader astray. *The Faerie Queene* indeed begins in "the middest," illustrated with an innuendo: a "Gentle Knight . . . pricking on the plaine" thrusts readers into the proverbial midst of action (1.1.1). In a more important sense, though, Spenser slyly misleads both reader and Raleigh by suggesting that historiography holds no place in Faerie Land.

Spenser reveals this disingenuousness in his "methode" of ordering his three-part story of English history. If read according to its *narrative* order, *The Faerie Queene*'s history of England begins in "the middest" – in Book 2, the middle of three books, in Eumnestes' chamber in Alma's Castle – before advancing to the end and beginning of England's story, both of which take place in Book 3. When read in this order, the history offers an apparently flattering portrait of England: England appears as a nation built according to a "perfect" (as E.K. would say) Virgilian pattern, the ancestral origins of Troy's ruins repaired and reformed, translated and transformed into a new Troy and, ideally, an endless empire. But when read in *chronological* order, this same history paints a less perfect picture: England appears as a nation built upon the "foundation of hearsay," stories of history grounded in tales of Troy's ruin, whose continual re-enactment belies fictions of eternal empire. Read either way, Spenser constructs his story like history itself: as a circular pattern of ruin and re-edification that undermines teleological tales of permanence. Underscoring this double vision, Spenser ends his letter by circuitously sending readers and Raleigh back to his history in "the middest" in Alma's Castle: "Thus much Sir, I haue briefly ouerronne to direct your vnderstanding to the wel-head of the History, that from thence gathering the whole intention of the conceit, yet may as in a handfull gripe al the discourse" (738). The "wel-head of the History" points to the Castle of Alma as the place where Spenser identifies his "methode" for "al the discourse": the art of memory.[4] In this chapter, I explore how Spenser uses this art to fashion a new story of ruin and recollection, even as he recollects old Trojan tales, and why this matters. By creating a holographic image of history, Spenser both represents self-fashioning and criticizes its uses in poetry and politics: that is, the use of fiction to fashion epic or empire as divine.

Since Frances Yates' *The Art of Memory*, scholars have seen the art at work in *The Faerie Queene*. Writing that "the art of memory . . . begun by Simonides and elaborated by classical rhetoricians" found early modern literary use as "a kind of unspoken allegory," Michael Murrin links the art of memory with the historiography depicted in the Castle of Alma, a place where Spenser's heroes "find their national histories written in the memory of the human soul, as Spenser himself finds the stories of *The Faerie Queene* in his Muses' document chest."[5] As Murrin explains, the art of memory provides a method of "recalling both the past and the future."[6] Yet the art of memory's significance extends beyond Alma's Castle, and not simply to the many other houses of memory that populate Faerie Land. Rather, I argue, the Castle of Alma emblematizes a history of memory that Spenser recalls throughout his career; it also represents Spenser's "methode" of edification – self-fashioning as self-knowledge, poetically figured as the ongoing recollection and reformation of the past – for the whole of *The Faerie Queene*. In a sense, this particular allegory answers Sidney's complaint that historians alone believe themselves capable of the "teaching of virtue and virtuous action," despite their use of poetic methods and matters, and clearly speaks to Spenser's desire "to fashion a gentleman or noble person in vertuous and gentle discipline" (737). The allegory of Alma offers an unsentimental education, unveiling the kind of self-fashioning that turns rulers into gods, empire into a fantasy of permanence and providence. Spenser's use of the art of memory relates to this deeply ambiguous portrait of history, addressing the issue of both what and how readers remember.

The issue of self-fashioning returns to the broader question of poetry's relation to power: whether (or to what degree) Spenser fashions himself as England's new Virgil – a cause alternately for praise and blame, as discussed earlier in this book. Yet from both vantages scholars construct similar narratives: whether Spenser condones or challenges imperial myths, critics tend to see him in a Virgilian role, for better and for worse.[7] Michael O'Connell, describing "the Vergilian nature of Spenser's methods and motives toward history," writes that "in the historical dimension of *The Faerie Queene* . . . [readers] can recognize Spenser's most profound imitation of Vergil."[8] However, this argument depends upon a particular view of allegory: namely, that Christian writers corrected Virgil by supplying the true origin and end of history, transforming the journey from ruined Troy to eternal Troynovant into an allegory of the soul's journey from time to timelessness. "His knowledge of history, the Renaissance poet believes, permits him to rewrite the *Aeneid* – in effect to complete it," Andrew Fichter has argued, given that Renaissance poets "could see the whole of what Virgil knew only in part."[9] For many scholars, Augustine's authority resolves tensions between pagan epic and Christian allegory, allowing for religious rewritings of Virgil. "On a literal level, history had already refuted Virgil's prophecy of Rome as . . . *imperium sine fine*," John Watkins contends, "but taken allegorically as a promise of Christian salvation, the prophecy might be revived and Virgil's cultural prestige preserved," such that "the quest for a future *imperium* becomes the quest to transcend time altogether and enter the City of God."[10] As Patrick Cheney argues, the notion that "for the Renaissance poet, the Virgilian political *telos* of the earthly city fulfils the Augustinian, salvific *telos* of the heavenly city" applies powerfully to Spenser's writing, suggesting that "the great Church father influences Spenser to reinvent the entire Virgilian wheel."[11]

There can be no doubt about Augustine's profound influence on *The Faerie Queene*, but the implications of this influence remain a matter of debate. Kenneth Gross observes that "Augustine at least makes plain how difficult it is to distinguish allegory as a mode of unveiling from allegory as a mode of mystification, usurpation, and idolatry," and my argument builds upon this fundamental insight.[12] By imitating Augustine, I argue, Spenser challenges the model of Virgilian epic and, more broadly, the reception of Trojan tales as Christian allegory, especially that of Europe's most recent new Virgil: Dante. Spenser suggests as much in his "Letter to Raleigh" through the sin of omission. He claims to have followed "all the antique Poets historicall" – naming Homer and Virgil, as well as contemporaries like as Tasso and Ariosto – but omits the most obvious example of an allegorical epic, *The Divine Comedy* (737). More than mere forgetfulness, this serves as an indirect reminder of Spenser's reformation of allegory-as-*anamnesis*. In effect, critics (like E.K.) fashion Spenser as a "new" Dante, mapping his reconciliation of Virgilian epic and Augustinian theology in the *Comedy* onto Spenser.[13] Yet Dante's poetic journey from sin to salvation stands in stark contrast to Spenser's journey through Faerie Land. In this regard, Chaucer's influence once again can be felt: as Chaucer parodies Dante's pilgrimage and claims for poetry in *The House of Fame*, so Spenser follows his path in *The Faerie Queene*, especially on the road to and from Alma's Castle, which suggests a parodic revision of Dante's epic. Spenser divides that which Dante unites – Virgil and Augustine, epic and empire, story and history – in order to make a paradoxical argument: even allegorically, fiction cannot tell *the* truth or offer divine revelation, whether in a pagan or a Protestant world.

Most broadly, Spenser's poem revises and reforms what it means to read (or write) epic as an allegory of the soul.[14] In this regard, Augustine plays a double role in *The Faerie Queene*. Spenser at once reminds readers of Augustine's complaints about the matter of allegory – especially about turning Virgil's epic into a Christian allegory of empire or eternity – and imitates Augustine's reformed method of allegory, his art of memory. For Spenser, as I suggest in chapter 1, Augustine's use of the art of memory represents the culmination of an alternative tradition (which builds upon Plato's and Cicero's writing) of using the "methode" of the poets to both criticize old stories of history and to construct new stories of history about the soul's ruin and re-edification. Moreover, recalling Augustinian intertexts allows Spenser to undermine readerly expectations about allegory itself. As David Galbraith observes, "Spenser explicitly sets the poem in the context of a genealogy of allegorical interpretation and literary imitation."[15] Although we often think of allegory as veiling deeper truths, these truths can be multiple and ironic, producing different irreconcilable meanings rather than layers of meaning that are coherent – truths that serve to both unveil *and* veil.[16] Spenser's allegory doubles as an anti-allegory, I argue, one particularly visible in Book 2, where juxtaposed allegories of the "Poet historical" and "Historiographer" illustrate their shared "methode" and matter of memory, and yet result in opposed versions of history.

A tension between story and history structures this chapter, which explores Spenser's art of memory as a way to think of, and remember, England. At stake is the promise and problem of erecting imperial power and permanence upon Troy's ruins. Spenser draws attention to the problems – political, historical, theological, artistic, and even ethical – of fashioning history upon Trojan tales of divinity and empire, especially as religious allegory. Even as he reproduces a Trojan lineage for England's monarchs, he reveals how Troy's legendary ruins mask the foundation of empire, the ruins of war, and allow rulers to fashion themselves as gods. Taking Spenser's history out of order, I begin with the end (and origin) of England's history in Book 3: here, a parodic re-enactment of Trojan tales paints a circular portrait of history, and also points the narrative in a circle – back to the competing visions of history found in Books 1 and 2. Turning to Book 1, I examine Spenser's ironic representation of the two cities in the context of Augustinian historiography in *City of God*. Next, I explore the juxtaposed allegories of English history found in Book 2, beginning by reading the debate about gold in Mammon's Cave in the context of Augustine's *On Christian Doctrine*. I then consider the allegory of Alma's Castle of the Soul, where historical ruins become the stuff of England's historical memory, in the context of Augustine's *Confessions*, exploring how Augustine's recollection of his ruined soul bears upon Spenser's remembrance of history's ruins. Here, a "Historiographer" reveals how the "Poet historical's" fictions are incorporated into English history, including Spenser's Faerie Land tale. Returning to Book 3, I suggest how the end of English history ironically marks its continued ruin. As I argue, Spenser's allegorical method unveils paradoxical truths about his allegory: that tales of endless empire belie the perpetual ruin in history but also make up history, as the ideological fictions repeated and re-enacted by self-fashioned gods of state.[17]

As Sidney argues in the *Apology*, fiction can never "give the lie to things" if an audience recognizes "things not affirmatively but allegorically and figuratively written" (57). This is not mere sophistry on Sidney's part: to tell the truth, for Socrates as for Sidney, amounts to discernment, that is, recognizing fictions as such. Such recognition given, as Sidney calls it, the "cloudy knowledge of mankind" entails the ability to read critically, sceptically, and indeed allegorically – precisely the Spenserian lesson in "self fashioning" (*Apology*, 57). In his "Letter to Raleigh," Spenser apologizes for his "methode" (much as E.K. does when defending old-fashioned words in *The Shepheardes Calender*), which "will seeme displeasaunt" for some who would "rather haue good discipline deliuered plainly" rather than "thus clowdily enwrapped in Allegoricall deuises" (737). But he tacitly defends his "methode," too, when, by affirming that nothing can be found here "that is not delight-full and pleasing to commune sence," he gestures once again to the al-legory of the mind's own place, or common place, Alma's Castle (737). In examining the related "methode" of "Poet historical" and "Histori-ographer," Spenser remembers ironic truths of history: that Virgilian fictions have been taken as the truth of history, even divine revelation; that Trojan tales are the matter of both poets and historians; and that stories of Troy's ruin and repair are endlessly re-enacted, belying the larger truth of history and empire – its ongoing ruination.

The Beginning and End of History: Britomart's and Paridell's Tales of Troy

Spenser concludes *The Faerie Queene*'s history of England at its nominal point of origin: with Britomart's and Paridell's tales of Troy's ruin, the stories of their nations' Trojan ancestries. In Canto 9 of Book 3, both characters relate how Troy's ruin symbolically translates into their new Troynovants, forming foundations for their respective nations, France and England, grafting members of the Trojan family tree in new soil. But the episode presents less a vision of imperial genealogy than a glimpse at how imperial leaders reproduce fictions of history. Even as Britomart and Paridell assert the westward migration of Troy's ruins, the continental drift of empire and learning toward France and En-gland, their dialogue raises rather than resolves questions of how to remember history. By ending England's three-part history at its mythi-cal beginning – with Trojan tales, the origin of history – Spenser ar-ticulates the problem of narrating history through fiction. This episode highlights the seemingly endless multiplicity of Trojan legends and the paradox at the heart of *translatio imperii et studii*: if empire and learning are always moving westward, then how can any nation stake a claim to endless empire except in a provisional, temporary sense? Britomart's and Paridell's tales of Troy's ruin and re-edification emerge as parodic literary conflations, mingling Homeric, Virgilian, and Ovidian elements that suggest, though never articulate, the ideal end of "empire without end." This omission itself becomes significant. Their histories imply fic-tions of endless empire yet manifest only the endless reproduction of Trojan narratives and new Troynovants. This ironic treatment finds a mirror in the order of the narrative itself, which points the reader in a circle, back to Book 2, where England's history begins in "the middest." This narrative circularity, I will suggest, mirrors the circularity of empire within history: the ongoing ruin that belies fictions of permanence.

Past is indeed prologue when Paridell remembers his Trojan lineage. Assuming a heroic posture that quickly slides into burlesque caricature, Paridell performs his epic role – enchanting his host's wife, Hellenore, with tales of war – while reducing Troy's mythology to a ploy for seduction. In lamenting Troy's tragic end, he recounts the famous city's fall with high drama:

> Troy, that art now nought, but an idle name,
> And in thine ashes buried low dost lie,
> Though whilome far much greater then thy fame,
> Before that angry Gods, and cruell skye
> Vpon thee heapt a direfull destinie,
> What boots it boast thy glorious descent,
> And fetch from heauen thy great Genealogie,
> Sith all thy worthy prayses being blent,
> Their of-spring hath embaste, and later glory shent. (3.9.33)

In this passage, dramatic commonplaces about Troy's ruin slip into a kind of unintentional self-parody. While criticizing Troy's pride in its "glorious descent" as a hubristic boast fully answered by the "angry Gods," Paridell unwittingly describes himself. After all, he too claims a place in that "great Genealogie" through his ancestor "Sir *Paris*" (34), and by implication represents one of those offspring who "hath embaste" the city's fame. Epitomizing this history, Paridell then gives a literal version of *translatio imperii*: his ancestor Paris "Gathred the *Troian* reliques sau'd from flame, / And with them sayling thence, to th'Isle of *Paros* came" (36). When Britomart chimes in to ask, "what to *Aeneas* fell?" (40), Paridell's account of Aeneas' wanderings offers an epic digest of Rome's origin, albeit an account devoid of any end. Aeneas "with a remnant did to sea repaire," Paridell recounts, literalizing the reconstruction (or repairing) of ruin, "Where he through fatall errour long was led / . . . From shore to shore" (41). Most of Paridell's description concerns war and violence that, significantly, he justifies as the work of fate alone; "the fates ordaind" for Rome "Wedlock contract in bloud, and eke in blood / Accomplished" (42). Despite Paridell's clear deference to this unhappy fate, the "fatall errour" that begins Aeneas'

wanderings and allows him to conquer Italy never indicates any special destiny for Rome, and he omits any reference to Aeneas' divine
imperative. Paridell instead segues into Rome's other foundational
myth, the story of Romulus and his place in "renewing" Troy: Aeneas'
son "in long *Alba* plast his throne apart, / Where faire it florished, and
long time stoud, / Till *Romulus* renewing it, to *Rome* remoud" (43). The
omission of prophecy reveals much: without Jove's promise of eternal
empire to justify Troy's ruinous end, Paridell points to the pointlessness
of Rome's bloody origins.

As with many of *The Faerie Queene*'s pairings, this episode's dialogue has often been viewed from a split perspective: Paridell's version of Virgil has been seen as a laughably mindless imitation, while
Britomart's vision of history has been regarded as a redemptive solution to Paridell's botched effort. Richard McCabe, for example, argues
that "for Paridell history forms a repetitive sequence of tragic falls oc-
casioned by wild, undisciplined passion," while "for Britomart, seeking the legitimate creative union of marriage, disaster heralds rebirth
and renewal."[18] Yet Paridell and Britomart only *seem* to construct competing versions of history. More important is what their tales share:
both legendary genealogies illustrate the bankruptcy of Trojan claims
to empire. Paridell's narrative acts as a reminder, spurring Britomart
to remember England's origins in Troy's fall, and she recalls "that she
was lineally extract: / For noble *Britons* sprong from *Troians* bold, /
And *Troynouant* was built of old *Troyes* ashes cold" (38). Britomart's
depiction of cultural transmission, building Troynovant from Troy's
ruins, is a pure fantasy of rebirth. However, her triumphal account
contains multiple ironies. When mapping Troy's destiny onto yet another Troynovant – a "third kingdome," England – Britomart gestures
in two directions as she predicts that England's empire will "equalise"
the glory of old Troy:

> There there (said *Britomart*) a fresh appeard
> The glory of the later world to spring,
> And *Troy* againe out of her dust was reard,
> To sit in the second seat of soueraigne king,
> Of all the world vnder her gouerning,
> But a third kingdome yet is to arise,
> Out of the *Troians* scattered of-spring,
> That in all glory and great enterprise,
> Both first and second *Troy* shall dare to equalise. (44)

Each Troynovant has the lustre of a special providential end, yet an end that each fails to achieve. To "equalise" the first or second Troy could be taken in two opposed ways: either that England would also become an "empire without end" or that England would fall to ruin. Britomart's language underscores such a cyclical rise and fall of empires: Rome sprang out of Troy's "dust," became "soueraigne king / Of all the world," but returned to dust. The repetition of "Troynouant" prompts the question of whether this refers to England now or an England to come (45). The description of England as "a wonder of the world," a "song [sung] in forreine lands," an imperial giantess who "threates the skye," exacerbates the confusion (45). Unintentionally, Britomart im- plies that England's "third kingdom" may have already come to pass.

Britomart inadvertently broaches the problem of reconciling Rome's myth with England's own, the irony of endlessly reproducing new Troys. This infinite regress of Troynovants thus nudges readers to recog- nize what Britomart and Paridell do not: the gap between the promise of eternal empire and its failure for Rome, a fissure between hoped- for immortality and the apparent inevitability of ruin. Humorous bumbling, however, turns serious as Spenser reminds readers that the stories of the "Poet historical" are only one way to remember history. Paridell's struggle to recall the parts of history that do not accord neatly with epic fiction illustrate this clearly. Apologizing for having forgotten about England's branch of the Trojan family tree, Paridell gestures to a source of history – Eumnestes' chamber of memory:

> Ah fairest Lady knight, (said *Paridell*)
> Pardon I pray my heedlesse ouersight,
> Who had forgot, that whilome I heard tell
> From aged *Mnemon*; for my wits bene light.
> Indeed he said (if I remember right,)
> That of the antique *Troian* stocke, there grew
> Another plant, that raught to wondrous hight,
> And far abroad his mighty branches threw,
> Into the vtmost Angle of the world he knew. (47)

Having forgotten what he "heard tell / From aged Mnemon," Alma's allegorical historiographer, Paridell recalls history only as the Trojan fictions of the "Poet historical." Even his belated remembrance sani- tizes "Mnemon's" historiography by recalling it merely as myth: Pa- ridell recounts how "that same *Brute*" had "by fatall course" discovered

England, deemed "fittest soyle for their abode," which he describes as a place empty save "an huge nation of the Geaunts broode" (48–9). Omitting what happens in the middle of England's history, Paridell instead relates how Brutus "through wearie wars and labours long, / Subdewd with losse of many *Britons* bold" (50). He concludes by gesturing to what he omits here: a "famous history . . . enrold / In euerlasting moniments of brasse, / That all the antique Worthies merits far did passe" (50).

Crucially, this reference points readers back to Book 2 and the middle portion of England's history, in "the middest" where it begins, reminding readers of what Paridell and Britomart forget: the repetition of Trojan tales throughout England's history and the seemingly endless ruin that accompanies these stories. The history written in Alma's Castle of the Soul reveals the "moniments," and admonishments, to complex truths of history that Paridell misremembers. But his confusion also gestures to another direction too, back to Book 1:

> His worke great *Troynouant*, his worke is eke
> Faire *Lincolne*, both renowmed far away,
> That who from East to West will endlong seeke,
> Cannot two fairer Cities find this day,
> Except *Cleopolis:* so heard I say
> Old *Mnemon*. (51)

While Paridell's praise of London and Lincoln is on one level wholly conventional, the context of imperial failure and succession gives this reference to "two . . . Cities" a specific valence: he substitutes the two cities, the City of Man and the City of God, for those of Faerie Land (and thus England). In essence, both characters can only think of history in terms of Cleopolis, the city of earthly glory. Their dialogue circles a profound absence that nevertheless serves as a reminder, for the allusion to the "two . . . Cities" points to two places in *The Faerie Queene* – the Castle of Alma in Book 2 and the House of Holiness in Book 1 – where Cleopolis might be called "Cliopolis": a city of history destined for ruin, a city that builds its history upon the very fictions that Britomart and Paridell remake. Not knowing the difference between the City of Man and the City of God leaves Britomart and Paridell free in Book 3 to see history *as* fiction, to view Cleopolis as the end of history. In Book 1, by contrast, Redcross Knight appears to learn the difference between the two cities. However, as I argue, this episode in fact establishes the problem of reading and writing allegorically. Turning to Augustine's *City of God*, I will suggest how this crucial intertext illuminates what these characters remember, and forget, about the past.

City of God and the Ruins of Rome

In *City of God*, Augustine plays the role of "Historiographer," working to reveal the stories that make up history.[19] Structured through a complex dynamic of separation and connection, this work attempts to differentiate between historical facts and fictions, to reveal how Rome's perpetual cycle of ruin belies its mythic promises of eternal repair. Augustine attempts to distinguish fact from fiction, story from history, and eternity from empire. He nevertheless builds his work upon the premise that the two cities are one.[20] He explains, "I shall go on to say . . . what I think needs to be said regarding the origin, history, and deserved ends of the two cities, which, as already remarked, are in this world commingled and implicated with one another."[21] "In this world," in the midst of time, the City of God and the City of Man are inextricable. Augustine differentiates historiographically between the two cities not in order to demonstrate their fundamental separation but to demonstrate the challenges of their mutual implication: "I promised to write of the rise, progress, and appointed end of the two cities . . . in order that . . . the course of that city which is God's might be made more distinctly apparent, without interpolation of foreign matter from the history of the other city, although down to the revelation of the new covenant it ran its course, not in light, but in shadow . . . [and] so that attentive readers may compare the two" (609). Augustine's argument that the City of God and the City of Man exist simultaneously until time's end fundamentally shapes his historiographic work. Rather than seeing Rome as either an endless empire or the empire that ushers in end time, *City of God* exposes the historical fictions that underwrite Rome and indeed all empires.

Specifically, Augustine attempts to tell the truth about the fiction of Rome's eternal empire and its history of ruin, at once asking readers to recognize the historical fallacy of Rome's permanence and yet to see Rome's ruin within the context of the City of God. "I have to defend the city of God," he writes, not only from those who attribute the sack of Rome in 410 to Christianity but also from those who believe that Rome should exist as an eternal empire (4). Admonishing the "escaped multitudes who now reproach the Christian religion and impute to Christ the ills that have befallen their city" (4), Augustine chastises those "whose morals are in ruins" but who blame Rome's ruin on Christianity (37). Rome's ruin is not the end of the world, he argues; instead, the sack of Rome represents only the latest chapter in the empire's ongoing history of ruination. Repeatedly reminding readers that Rome fell to ruin not once but many times, Augustine portrays Rome's history as a cycle of despoliation: "All the spoiling . . . which Rome was exposed to in the recent calamity – all the slaughter, plundering, burning, and misery – was the result of the custom of war" (9). Having fashioned a god of empire, Romans worshipped only "the mammon of iniquity," Augustine asserts, and now mourn only the loss of "silver and gold" (15). Such greed for gold forms Rome's true foundation, he argues. "What are kingdoms but great robberies?" Augustine asks: "this evil increases to such a degree that it holds places, fixes abodes, takes possession of cities, and subdues peoples, [while] it assumes the more plainly the name of a kingdom, because the reality is now manifestly conferred on it" (112–13). Rome built its empire upon the spoils of war, he argues, and upon a mythology of permanence.

To demonstrate the perpetuation of stories both within and as history, Augustine writes against an allegorical tradition that by the fifth century had already become commonplace – a tradition of interpreting epic tales, especially Virgil's, as the truth of history. To see the Roman Empire as divinely sanctioned, as a representation of the City of God, meant that the story of Troy's ruin and permanent repair could be slotted into the alpha and omega of scripture as the soul's journey from earthly empire to endless empire. Augustine attacks this allegorical tendency, particularly in political fictions, from the twin perspectives of secular and sacred historiography. To argue that historians and poets have colluded to repeat the same tales of Rome's origins, Augustine both criticizes and emulates the Roman antiquarian Varro. Augustine observes that Varro "wrote forty-one books of antiquities . . . divided into human and divine things," yet "these divine things were instituted by men: 'As the painter is before the painted tablet, the mason before the edifice, so states are before those things which are instituted by states'" (187–8). Through this method, Varro attempts to divide fact from fiction, story from history, in a manner that Augustine imitates here. Varro's historiographic method of dividing "antiquities into human and divine things" allows Augustine to similarly pursue the separation of secular and scriptural historiography, even as he repeatedly asserts that the two cities are intertwined. However, Augustine-as-historiographer also vehemently admonishes "Varro's opinion, that it is useful for men to feign themselves the offspring of the gods" (76), examining the motivating hypocrisy:

> Some one will say, But do you believe all this? Not I indeed. For even Varro, a very learned heathen, all but admits that these stories are false, though he does not boldly and confidently say so. But he maintains it is useful for states that brave men believe, though falsely, that they are descended from the gods; for that thus the human spirit, cherishing the belief of its divine descent, will both more boldly venture into great enterprises, and will carry them out more energetically, and will therefore by its very confidence secure more abundant success. (76–7)

Such fictions, he implicitly argues, have consequences in the world as well as in writing. By swearing that "empire is the gift of Jove," Romans simply named their desire for domination, Augustine sneers, and so Jove "himself might be called Empire . . . For what part could Jove have here when those things which might be thought to be his benefits are held to be gods, called gods, worshiped as gods, and are themselves invoked for their own parts?" (123). Not only does this kind of interpretation give Rome more historical significance than it deserves, but it also represents a patently false vision of Rome's history, masking its continual rise from and fall to ruin, the fate of all earthly empires in "the middest" of time. After all, how could any soul travel the linear route from a ruined Troy to a permanent Troynovant, like Aeneas en route to Rome, given the cyclical instability of all political structures?[22] Such a mapping of epic stories onto history, Augustine emphasizes, are fictions of power made by self-fashioned gods of empire.

In denying Rome's endless empire, Augustine also denies it a place in the path to eternity. He takes aim at those who interpret scripture as allegorical proof of Rome's imperial myth, particularly through the book of Revelation and the book of Daniel.[23] "Some have interpreted these four kingdoms as signifying those of the Assyrians, Persians, Macedonians, and Romans," Augustine argues, "But he who reads this passage, even half-asleep, cannot fail to see that the kingdom of Antichrist shall fiercely, though for a short time, assail the Church before the last judgment of God shall introduce the eternal reign of the saints" (748). Scripture makes the "end" of history clear, he argues: Rome cannot be either an "empire without end" or the last kingdom on earth. But even as Augustine argues that scripture should not be interpreted as an allegory of epic, he asserts that scripture represents historiography that must nevertheless be read allegorically. Far from rejecting secular history and looking forward only to timelessness, Augustine concerns himself with the importance of being historical – with all of history. Writing of the New Jerusalem of Revelation, he comments, "This city is said to come down out of heaven . . . It is indeed descended from Heaven by its commencement, since its citizens during the course of this world grow by the grace of God . . . Was not the Apostle Paul himself a citizen of the heavenly Jerusalem, and was he not so all the more when he had heaviness and continual sorrow of heart for his Israelitish brethren?" (736–7). Like Paul, Augustine sees himself as already "a citizen of the heavenly Jerusalem."[24] Here as in his other works, Augustine attempts to replace epic with scripture as his culture's "book of memory," as the writing that should be interpreted both allegorically and historically, precisely because divinity encompasses all of history.[25]

Because the City of God is here and now, Augustine argues, self-fashioning means continually recollecting and reforming history's gold for a new spiritual edifice. He describes this process of ruin and recollection in *On Christian Doctrine* and *Confessions*, where he contrasts the spoils gained by praying to the "mammon of unrighteousness" and "money or wealth which has been unjustly acquired," with the "true riches" received by those "eternal habitations" (808). The intermingling of the two cities until their separation at history's end provides Augustine's most potent rationale for why epic fictions of endless empire cannot be understood as the truth of history, even in allegorical terms. Because the two cities exist simultaneously in "the middest" of time, the path from one city to the other cannot be like the journey from Troy to Troynovant. And, still more significantly, because their twinned histories cannot be separated, Augustine repeatedly draws distinctions between story and history and asks readers to do the same.

Tales of Two Cities: Cliopolis and the New Jerusalem

Book 1 locates Cleopolis – as a microcosm of Faerie Land and, in a larger sense, *The Faerie Queene* – in "the middest" of history.[26] Here, even as Spenser articulates the "ends" of epic history he also subverts them, exposing his own history as fiction. By demonstrating the inextricability of fiction and history, I will suggest, Spenser discerns ways of remembering reminiscent of Augustine's complaint in *City of God*: that stories of history, whether in poetry or historiography, are used to rename human desire as divinity, turning humans into gods. After his harrowing trial with Despair, Una leads Redcross to the "House of Holiness" and the holy figure of Contemplation, whose "mortall life he learned had to frame / In holy righteousnesse" (1.10.45). Contemplation presumably teaches Redcross how to "frame" the relation between "mortall life" and "holy righteousnesse" through a glimpse of the future – a New Jerusalem – and offers a path to get there. In this location, sacred memory and secular memory mingle, and indeed merge. Contemplation leads Redcross "to the highest Mount," which is first compared to Mount Sinai and the Mount of Olives, "For euer with a flowring girlond crownd" in "endlesse memory / Of that deare Lord, who oft thereon was fownd," and then to "that pleasaunt Mount" Parnassus, where "the thrise three learned Ladies play / Their heauenly notes" (53–4). This convergence of secular and sacred memory, emblematized by a poet laureate's crown and a crown of thorns, marks the episode's central point: in the midst of time, the two cities exist simultaneously, which necessitates reading allegorically.

When Contemplation offers up the New Jerusalem for Redcross Knight's view – that "goodly Citie . . . / Whose wals and towres were builded high and strong / Of perle and precious stone" – Redcross realizes his error: like Paridell and Britomart, he had mistaken Cleopolis for the New Jerusalem, confusing the two cities (55). "Faire knight," Contemplation announces,

> *Hierusalem* that is,
> The new *Hierusalem*, that God has built
> For those to dwell in, that are chosen his,
> His chosen people purg'd from sinfull guilt. (57)

Contemplation then maps Redcross Knight's journey between the two cities: "The Citie of the great king . . . / Wherein eternall peace and happinesse doth dwell" (55). Amazed by eternity, Redcross exclaims that he had believed that "great *Cleopolis* . . . / In which that fairest *Faerie Queene* doth dwell, / The fairest Citie was" (58). But now his ambitions are all redirected to a far greater glory: "this great Citie that does far surpas, / And this bright Angels towre quite dims that towre of glas" (58).

If the episode ended here, it would supply a tacit correction to Britomart's and Paridell's histories: Cleopolis is *not* the end of history or an empire without end. But this is the middle of the episode, and what follows complicates the allegory considerably. Although Redcross seems to supply the correct Christian response, rejecting the City of Man for the City of God, Contemplation puts Cleopolis on the path to salvation, reiterating Paridell's basic error. "*Cleopolis* [is] for earthly frame," he says, "The fairest peece, that eye beholden can," exhorting Redcross to "couet" a place "in th'immortall booke of fame" through "seruice to that soueraigne Dame," the Faerie Queene: "For she is heauenly borne, and heauen may iustly vaunt" (59). In one sense, Contemplation is correct: serving "that soveraigne Dame" and working for her "glorie" – either Una's or the Faerie Queene's – will earn Redcross a place in "th'immortal booke of fame," the kind found in the back chamber of the Castle of Alma. But the episode ultimately suggests that Contemplation's vision of history also represents an historical fiction that self-consciously reflects Spenser's "methode" as a "Poet historical." After linking the Faerie Queene and Redcross genealogically, Contemplation says: "And thou faire ymp, sprong out from English race . . . / Well worthy doest thy seruice for her grace, / To aide a virgin desolate foredonne" (60). He assures Redcross "a blessed end" (61), but only if he follows a prescribed path to glory by moving from labour to rest, from war to peace:

> But when though famous victorie hast wonne,
> And high emongst all knights hast hong thy shield,
> Thenceforth the suit of earthly conquest shonne,
> And wash thy hands from guilt of bloudy field:
> For bloud can nought but sin, and wars but sorrowes yield. (60)

Contemplation then reveals Redcross Knight's identity:

> Then seeke this path, that I to thee presage,
> Which after all to heauen shall thee send;
> Then peaceably thy painefull pilgrimage
> To yonder same *Hierusalem* do bend,
> Where is for thee ordaind a blessed end:
> For thou emongst those Saints, whom thou doest see,
> Shalt be a Saint, and thine owne nations frend
> And Patrone: though Saint *George* shalt called bee,
> Saint *George* of mery England, the signe of victoree. (61)

The future Saint George's georgic labour makes it difficult to interpret this episode as a Protestant allegory. The simultaneous necessity and repudiation of good works in the name of salvation serves as a creation myth for England's patron saint, himself a remnant of Roman Catholicism. Crucially, however, Redcross himself questions this vision of history, for he no longer sees Cleopolis as history's end. "What need of armes," he asks, "where peace doth ay remaine, / . . . and battailes none are to be fought?" (62). Pleading to take this journey out of order, so to speak, he begs:

> O let me not . . . then turne againe
> Backe to the world, whose ioyes so fruitlesse are;
> But let me here for aye in peace remaine,
> Or streight way on that last long voyage fare. (63)

Redcross further challenges Contemplation about his origins. "But now aread, old father, why of late," he asks, "Dist though behight me borne of English blood, / Whom all a Faeries sonne doen nominate?" (64). Redcross wonders, in other words, whether this is a case of mistaken identity.

Contemplation's reply ironically underscores the episode's double vision, at once allaying and confirming Redcross Knight's suspicions about his Faerie Land genealogy:

> For well I wote, thou springst from ancient race
> Of *Saxon* kings, that haue with mightie hand
> And many bloudie battailes fought in place
> High reard their royall throne in *Britane* land,
> And vanquisht them, vnable to withstand:
> From thence a Faerie thee vnweeting reft,
> There as thou slepst in tender swadling band,
> And her base Elfin brood there for thee left.
> Such men do Chaungelings call, so chaungd by Faeries theft. (65)

With a remarkable shift from English history to historical fiction, from Saxon England to Faerie Land, Contemplation inadvertently portrays Redcross Knight's genealogy as a kind of theft, a poetic fiction claimed as the spoil of war. Spenser thereby offers a glimpse of history, which he then exchanges – like the story of Redcross as a changeling – for a fiction of England as Faerie Land. As a "chaungeling" stolen by faeries, Redcross Knight's lineage connects him to the Faerie Queene only "by Faeries theft," a fabricated origin that exposes the fictions it reproduces.

This revealing description locates war and conquest as the forces motivating history and empire – the "*Saxon* kings" who, Contemplation narrates, had "vanquisht" the "royall throne" in England – the very facet (and fact) of history that divine, genealogical fictions serve ultimately to conceal.

Redcross Knight's meeting with Contemplation appears to follow a Christianized pattern of epic history: the hero discovers his lineage and with it his nation's destiny, whose history finds a place in the structure of eternity. Yet his sceptical attitude – he must fight to preserve an empire that he knows must end – suggests the problem with fashioning English history as a divine allegory. Redcross ultimately yields to Contemplation's greater wisdom: "he looked to the ground, / . . . His feeble sence, and too exceeding shyne. / So darke are earthly things compard to things diuine" (67). But his questioning spurs readers to challenge Contemplation's prophecy. What seems like divine revelation turns out to be a problem of reading and writing allegory. Although Redcross accepts this prophecy, readers may see this allegory less as truth than as fiction, or rather as the melding of the two. Spenser demonstrates the creation of historical fictions used, on the one hand, to mask despoliation and, on the other hand, to justify the end of imperial desire: this "ancient race . . . high reard their royall throne in *Britane* land" with "many bloudie battailes." He thus produces a double vision of history: Redcross must fulfil his destiny to become the patron saint of England and, at the same time, he justly challenges his dubious genealogical destiny to "fight" for England, to serve the Faerie Queene. The darkness of "earthly things" noted by Redcross suggests that *in medias res*, readers also see as through a glass darkly: the veil of allegory necessarily present in writing and the world. If this episode indicates how allegory reconciles epic and Christian visions of history, it also suggests their irreconcilability.

The extent to which the characters remember and forget the relation between the two cities reflects upon the readers of these allegories.[27] The stories of history in Book 1 and Book 3 tacitly build upon a similar foundation: a divine genealogy that carries with it the silent promise of inheriting "empire without end." Contemplation makes Redcross' place in the New Jerusalem contingent upon fighting for Cleopolis, and this paradoxically recalls Augustine's argument in *City of God*: that God's city depends upon no earthly empire. Spenser's comments on his description of the New Jerusalem provide an apt illustration of the limits of epic:

Whose wals and towres were builded high and strong
Of perle and precious stone, that earthly tong
Cannot describe, nor wit of man can tell;
To high a ditty for my simple song;
The Citie of the great king hight it well,
Wherein eternall peace and happinesse doth dwell. (55)

More than mere modesty, such ineffability suggests how and why Spenser undermines his own religious allegory. By examining differences between epic and scripture as forms of history, Spenser provides different answers than the ones Contemplation offers, and, in so doing, he intimates that his poem cannot be read as divine revelation but rather as the characteristic blend of truth and fiction that exists not only in allegory but also in "the middest" of history.[28]

Allusions to the two cities in Books 1 and 3 may remind readers of Augustine's *City of God*, thereby gesturing to the central problem of how to read and write allegorically. How readers might interpret the episode with Redcross depends upon its historical frame. If imagined in a Protestant context, it makes sense allegorically: England represents the City of God, or the closest thing to it on earth, and the Roman Catholic Church is the Antichrist. But Spenser also complicates this general allegory of Book 1. The episode can be interpreted as an allegory of Protestant England that destroys Duessa (for Roman Catholics the Antichrist of the book of Revelation and for Protestants the biblical representation of the Roman Catholic Church), but the double historical time frame here and throughout Book 1 problematizes this. Does Book 1 take place "now" in Renaissance England or "then" in medieval England? One aswer, of course, is both, and this would seem to affirm a typological reading of *The Faerie Queene* as a whole. But another reading suggests a very different interpretation. After all, there is not *one* image or episode of revelation in Book 1 but a *series* of encounters with the beasts of Revelation. Does Duessa therefore represent the demonic Roman Catholic Church at war with Protestant England, or does Duessa represent the Saracen threat, the Islamic "other" of the medieval period that fits with the Arthurian context of the poem, engaged in a series of holy wars with the once holy Roman Catholic Church? Given the two simultaneous historical moments, Spenser offers competing views of Book 1's allegory. This points to a still more significant problem that *City of God* helps to illuminate. The sheer multiplicity of scenes ripped from the book of Revelation and given a modern allegorical gloss intimates that scripture, like Trojan stories of history, can and has been repeatedly used for political fictions, supplying ambition with divine justification. The repetition of this story of history points to a parallel critique of political fictions in Book 3 in which Britomart and Paridell re-enact Trojan tales for their own national and imperial ends. The manipulation of allegory to fashion gods of state, whether pagan or Christian, is at stake, and Spenser uses his own allegory in order to unveil self-justifying fictions of divine self-fashioning. The anti-allegories embedded within Books 1 and 3 suggest that allegory itself has a history on the page and in the world that Spenser's poem explores and, in a larger sense, attempts to reform.

Book 2: From Cave to Castle

The various stories of history in Books 1 and 3 build upon a similar foundation: a divine genealogy that carries with it the tacit promise of "empire without end." By contrast, Book 2 – the middle history of England, which Paridell half-recalls as "Mnemon's" scrolls and which takes place in the mnemonic space of Alma's castle – represents history as a cycle of ruin and re-edification. Spenser's proem to Book 2 famously asks his "most mighty Soueraine" whether

> All this famous antique history,
> Of some th'aboundance of an idle braine
> Will iudged be, and painted forgery,
> Rather then matter of iust memory. (2.Proem.1)

On the face of it, Elizabeth's glorious lineage reflects and legitimates Spenser's work: "In this faire mirrhour maist behold thy face, / And thine owne realmes in lond of Faery, / And in this antique Image thy great auncestry" (4). But the beginning of Canto 10 provides another perspective, one that links the "matter of Just memory" to the art of memory in complex ways. Spenser first plays the "Poet historical," building upon the "ruines" of the past by imitating epic:

> Argument worthy of *Mæonian* quill,
> Or rather worthy of great *Phœbus* rote,
> Whereon the ruines of great *Ossa* hill,
> And triumphes of *Phlegræan Ioue* he wrote,
> That all the Gods admird his loftie note.

> But if some relish of that heauenly lay
> His learned daughters would to me report,
> To decke my song withall, I would assay,
> Thy name, O soueraine Queene, to blazon farre away. (2.10.3)

British history, "the famous auncestries / Of my most dreaded Souer-aigne" (1), is a matter "worthy of *Mœonian* quill," Apollo's imagined epic in praise of Jove's triumphs (3). Yet in the next stanza Spenser also plays the role of "Historiographer," gesturing to the chamber of Eumnestes and Anamnestes where Elizabeth's less glorious history can be found:

> Thy name O soueraine Queene, thy realme and race,
> From this renowmed Prince deriued arre,
> Who mightily vpheld that royall mace,
> Which now thou bear'st, to thee descended farre
> From mightie kings and conquerours in warre,
> Thy fathers and great Grandfathers of old,
> Whose noble deedes aboue the Northerne starre
> Immortall fame for euer hath enrold;
> As in that old mans booke they were in order told. (4)

By telling the story "in order," Spenser reminds readers of the "Letter to Raleigh" where he distinguishes the "methode" of the "Poet historical" from the "Historiographer" based on how they order their narratives. As I have been arguing, this also alludes to the "methode" by which Eumnestes orders his history and Spenser orders his poem. The allusion to Eumnestes, the historiographer in Alma's Castle of the Soul, and to his books of memory – indeed, to the art of memory – alerts readers to a tension that unfolds in Book 2, as an allegory of the "Historiographer" unveils an allegory of the "Poet historical." "The matter of Just memory" evokes the legendary Matter of Troy, the Matter of Rome, and the Matter of Britain remembered in the Castle of Alma, as well as the method of recollection that produces two visions of history.

The journey from Mammon's Cave to Alma's Castle, the dominant narrative of Book 2, tells England's history in "the middest." Although Spenser nominally begins England's history in the Castle of Alma, this episode is linked to the Cave of Mammon, most obviously because they are locations that follow upon each other in Guyon's

symbolic catabasis and anabasis. But the episodes are also linked because they demonstrate the tensions between the "Poet historical"
(evident in the Cave of Mammon) and the "Historiographer" (evident
in the Castle of Alma). The difference between these episodes lies not
in their method of creating places and images for recollection – both
rely on the art of memory – but rather in the kinds of stories about history they construct. The Cave of Mammon and the Castle of Alma are
allegories that reflect upon the issue of *what* and *how* to read allegorically, an issue that Spenser broaches through Augustine's *On Christian Doctrine* and *Confessions*. At the same time, both demonstrate the
presence and persistence of stories both *in* history and *as* history. The
pattern of England's history that emerges is one of ongoing ruination,
concealed and revealed in repeated tales of Trojan offspring. Characteristically for Spenser, what appear to be clear oppositions between
Cave and Castle, epic and history, become increasingly problematic.
Yet the oppositions remain vitally important, for it is by the process
of teasing out the complex relation between opposed terms that the
reader proceeds through the hermeneutical labyrinth of *The Faerie
Queene*.

The "Legend of Temperance" reframes a quintessentially Aristotelian
virtue in Augustinian terms. Spenser suggests that the golden mean
bears an intimate relationship to gold itself, figured both materially and
memorially in Book 2's central allegories; further, he illustrates how
the link between temperance and gold runs through the art of memory
tradition. In part, this tradition can be observed in Castiglione's treatment of temperance. The golden mean of courtly behaviour discussed
in Book 2 of *The Book of the Courtier* (appropriately enough) finds its
fullest expression in Book 4, as the dialogue turns to the question of
how a courtier can best edify a prince.[29] To make the case for temperance as the signal ideal of princely edification, the courtier-poet Peter
Bembo offers a Golden Age narrative in which he re-enacts the central
stories of Plato's *Phaedrus*. Replacing the soul's winged chariot with
a metaphorical ship of state, Bembo describes how reason must "de-
fendeth herself from the tempestuous Seastormes" of "incontinencie,"
against which temperance provides the "maner help of Pilott for her
safegard" (304). Just as one would "breake horses," he further suggests
(returning in part to Plato's original example), so those vices "tried by
temperance" are similarly tamed, leading to justice, "queen of all other
vertues," and good governance, "sufficient to make men happie, and
to bring once again into the world the golden age" (306–8). Yet lest it

seem that he has fashioned his prince as an idol of gold, "a Demy God" (312), Bembo recollects Socrates' palinode of Stesichorus, returning to the art of memory as a method by which poets and philosophers, as well as courtiers, can tell the truth about matters of idolatry, in poetry as in politics.[30]

Spenser again returns to one of Castiglione's central intertexts, the *Phaedrus*, in effect translating *The Courtier* for England and Elizabeth's edification. However, Spenser frames his treatment of temperance in "the middest" of time, pursuing the relationship of story to history, and poetry to power, in the context of Augustinian temperance – specifically, Augustine's recollection of Platonic temperance as an art of memory. For Plato, temperate love provides one answer to the problem of idolatry. Temperance, a quality emphasized throughout the *Phaedrus* in particular, promotes a sceptical engagement with the world, a dialogic and dialectical one. Phaedrus begins the dialogue with a promise to erect a golden statue of Socrates if he can outperform Lysias, but he ends with an indirect retraction of this juvenile idolatry through his final prayer to "Pan" and all the "other gods . . . in this place," that "outward things . . . may not war against the spirit within": "May I count him rich who is wise and as for gold, may I possess so much of it as only a temperate man might bear and carry with him" (525). This prayer marks the end of his education in love – with an understanding that the "gold" he carries lies within. Such an opposition between an intemperate desire for golden idols and the tempering of "gold" for new uses is paramount in Augustine's *On Christian Doctrine*, where he describes reading scripture allegorically through his famous phrase "Egyptian gold." For Augustine as for the Platonic tradition he reinterprets, writing represents this "gold" when tempered, transmuted, converted. Augustine's *Confessions* pursues the ideal of temperance not only as a reining in of the body's desires but also as the soul's recollection of itself through divine love. This model of reading allegorically in *On Christian Doctrine* and writing allegorically in the *Confessions* takes centre stage in Book 2 and the allegorical journey from Cave to Castle.[31] The journey from Mammon's Cave to Alma's Castle presents allegories that unveil themselves, in part by gesturing to the history of allegory. Through Augustine's works, I argue, Spenser tells the truth about his own epic, discerning *his* story from history, revealing repeat performances of Trojan stories throughout history. Spenser incorporates Augustine's reformation of allegory into his own, turning the art of memory into a spur to recollection, for readers if not for the heroes.

Serving Gods and Mammon: A Parodic Underworld

The Knight of Temperance, Guyon, encounters Mammon when looking for adventure, like a hero in search of an epic: "So long he yode, yet no aduenture found, / Which fame of her shrill trompet worthy reedes" (2.7.2). Guyon instead finds Mammon, who holds up a mirror to his ambitions, showing him his own desires in the form of gold. From the beginning of the episode, Mammon's gold clearly represents more than wealth. Rather, the temptations Mammon offers Guyon are emblematic of history's seductiveness, and Guyon's vulnerability lies precisely in his ambition to be a part of history: the desire for fame that he as yet unsuccessfully seeks. Mammon himself exhibits a curious conflation of gold and decay; like a relic, his "yron coate all ouergrowne with rust" conceals an interior "enueloped with gold" that has lost its lustre and become "darkned with filthy dust" (4). This coat "Wouen with antickes and wild Imagery" makes Mammon indistinguishable from the "masse of coyne" upon his lap, which he gazes at with "couetous desire" (4): "Round about" Mammon "lay on every side / Great heapes of gold that neuer could be spent" (5). In ruinous condition – "withouten moniment" – these metals serve as worldly admonishments: "most were stampt, and in their metall bare / The antique shapes of kings and kesars straunge and rare" (5). With the figure of Mammon, readers thus glimpse the god to whom Augustine says the Romans prayed, a personification of greed who tempts Guyon with gold and promises immortality through empire. Guyon initially rejects Mammon's wealth as though an epic hero who, in Virgilian and Dantean fashion, curses the "hunger for gold" and instead embraces the promise of a renewed Golden Age associated with empire.[32] But famously, this seemingly virtuous response does not prevent Guyon from satisfying his curiosity about the gold that leads to his descent into Mammon's Cave.

This episode can be interpreted as both a classical and Christian allegory, with Guyon's descent into Mammon's Cave representing both a journey to the underworld and a harrowing of hell, as well as a scriptural allegory of Satanic temptation. As I suggest, though, Spenser does not reconcile layers of secular and sacred meaning but instead problematizes their conflation. Rather than representing epic allegory as divine truth, Spenser evokes Augustine's view of allegorical interpretation in *On Christian Doctrine* in order to suggest their fundamental incommensurability. In a broader sense, Spenser explores the history of allegory, the tradition of epic underworlds as places of both remembering and forgetting history; specifically, this episode can be understood as a parodic response to Dante's *Divine Comedy* and the problem of idolizing poetry or power, deifying epic or empire. By recalling an Augustinian model of reading allegorically, Spenser offers a powerful critique of allegory within the allegory itself.

Reading epic as Christian allegory fashions human rulers into gods of gold, Augustine argues in *City of God*, and in *On Christian Doctrine* he describes how better to reform history's gold through conversion. This question of how to use gold – and, ultimately, how to understand its place in history – underpins the dialogue between Guyon and Mammon. "What art thou man, (if man at all thou art)" Guyon asks, "That here in desert hast thine habitaunce, / And these rich heapes of wealth doest hide apart, / From the worldes eye, and from her right vsaunce?" (7). Mammon replies that he is "God of the world and worldlings," an idol fashioned from his own gold, who promises "riches, renowme, and principality, / Honour, estate, and all this worldes good" (8). The desire for gold motivates history, he argues, a desire reproduced "in the hollow earth['s] eternall brood" (8). However, Guyon resists Mammon's offer "to serue" him and insists instead upon a chivalric ideal of service, valiantly praising "the high heroicke spright, / That ioyes for crownes and kingdomes to contend"; "Faire shields, gay steedes, bright armes be my delight," Guyon asserts, for "Those be the riches fit for an aduent'rous knight" (10). Moreover, Guyon rebukes the deity of greed with apparent temperance, telling Mammon "thy godheades vaunt is vaine" (9), and arguing that he ruins rather than raises empires: "Ne thine be kingdomes, ne the scepters thine; / But realmes and rulers thou doest both confound" (13). Irritated but not deterred by his naive virtue, Mammon replies that all of Guyon's desires can be bought.

Guyon's seemingly virtuous rejection of Mammon's gold serves as a prelude to his vision of history and the place of gold within it, a narrative of the Golden Age that ultimately reveals Guyon's innocence (and ignorance) about the world. "The antique world, in his first flowring youth, / Found no defect in his Creatours grace," he asserts, "But later ages pride, like corn-fed steed, / Abusd her plenty" (16). Placing the desire for gold at the centre of this fall into history, Guyon relates how "a cursed hand the quiet wombe / Of his great Grandmother" tore open from the earth's "sacred tombe," a symbolic rape that inspired more lust for gold:

> Therein he found
> Fountaines of gold and siluer to abound
> . . . his huge desire
> And pompous pride eftsoones he did compound. (17)

Calling this avarice a "life-deuouring fire" (17), Guyon distances himself from what seems, after all, to be ancient history. Yet his refusal to believe that gold still motivates history (or himself) in the end exposes Guyon's guilelessness. Superficially, he declines Mammon's gold until he knows its origin: "till I know it well be got," or whether Mammon "didst these goods bereaue / From rightfull owner by vnrighteous lot" (19). However, this focus on the source of the gold, and whether or not he gained it through theft, belies Guyon's curiosity (as many scholars have observed) about the cave itself. He wonders "What secret place . . . / . . . where has thou thy wonne, that so much gold / Thou canst preserue from wrong and robbery?" (20). It seems that Guyon's interest in the gold lies neither in its origins or its uses. Rather, the place itself tempts Guyon precisely because Mammon represents it as a version of Guyon's Golden Age tale: the womb of mother earth still filled with gold and yet unspoiled by human hand. In other words, Guyon is tempted by the possibility of glimpsing his own fiction of history – a time before virgin gold found "use." Throughout the episode, Guyon substitutes stories for history, conflating poetry with power, forgetting any religious reasons not to serve Mammon. The reason why becomes clear: Guyon cannot see beyond his worship of the Faerie Queene.[33] Spenser thus challenges Guyon's idealistic sense that his chivalry remains untouched by a desire for gold, suggesting that he may already serve Mammon.

Promising to reveal what "yet neuer eye did vew," Mammon

> by and by
> Through that thicke couert he him led, and found
> A darkesome way, which no man could descry,
> That deepe descended through the hollow ground,
> And was with dread and horror compassed around. (19–20)

With its demarcated spaces and vivid images, and fashioned according to the "methode" of the "Poet historical," Mammon's Cave represents a mnemonic place for both remembering and forgetting the past. Relatedly, the very structure of the house conflates gold with ruin:

That houses forme within was . . .
Embost with massy gold of glorious gift,
And with rich metall loaded euery rift,
That heauy ruine they did seeme to threat . . .

Both roofe, and floore, and wals were all of gold
But ouergrowne with dust and old decay. (28–9)

Labouring for gold conquers all in the house that Mammon built, where
tempering applies not only molten metal – "By euery fornace . . . /
Deformed creatures, horrible in sight, / And euery feend his busie
paines applide, / To melt the golden metall, ready to be tride" – but also
indirectly to a virtue of self-temperance (35). In one sense, Mammon
does not lie when he tells Guyon that he has been permitted to glimpse
forbidden knowledge. "Behold, thou Faeries sonne, with mortall eye,
/ That liuing eye before did neuer see," Mammon swears, presenting
"the fountaine of the worldes good" and asserting, "Loe here the worldes blis, loe here the end, / To which all men do ayme, rich to be made:
/ Such grace now to be happy, is before thee laid" (38, 32). In another
sense, though, the allegory of the cave permits readers to see what
Guyon fails to recognize: that is, how Mammon is related to fictions of
power. Guyon remains willfully and happily ignorant, turning to look
away: "Another blis before mine eyes I place, / Another happinesse,
another end . . . / in armes, and in atchieuements braue" (33). He questions this gold's "use," asking "Money God . . . what needeth mee /
To couet more, then I haue cause to vse?", but remains oblivious to what
this gold truly represents (39). Guyon's inability to interpret this gold
reflects the central problem of this allegory, and in ways that speak to
The Faerie Queene as a whole. Augustine's *On Christian Doctrine* points
up the underlying irony of Guyon's seeming virtue: because he refuses
to *use* despoiled gold, he remains blind to his reflection in the mirror of
Mammon's seduction. The question of gold, at the centre of Guyon and
Mammon's debate, recalls Augustinian allegory in ways that unveil the
"methode" and matter of the "Poet historical."

Reading Allegorically in *On Christian Doctrine*

In *On Christian Doctrine*, "gold" figures centrally in Augustine's attempt to replace epic with scripture as his culture's central "book
of memory": the story that he interprets allegorically. His central

contention in *City of God*, that the two cities exist simultaneously and are intertwined in the present, informs *On Christian Doctrine* in the context of scriptural interpretation. Given the intermingling of the two cities within time, Augustine argues that scripture must be interpreted historically. In both works, allegory could be identified as his central concern: how and, more to the point, what to read allegorically. The desire to read epic as Christian allegory, to see Aeneas' journey from ruined Troy to eternal Troynovant as the soul's journey from the City of Man to the City of God, is precisely the form of allegory that Augustine attempts to refute – though also, ironically, precisely the kind of allegorical reading most often attributed to him. Yet Augustine does not so much read epic allegorically as borrow allegory as a method for reading scripture. In a broad sense, this appropriation of allegory represents a disciplinary competition of sorts. On the one hand, he asserts the value of poetry to theology: "There are thousands of imagined fables and falsehoods by whose lies men are delighted, which are human institutions . . . but all this part of human institutions helpful to the necessary conduct of life is not to be shunned by the Christian; rather, as such institutions are needed, they are to be given sufficient notice and remembered."[34] On the other hand, he inverts the position of poetry in culture, using poetry to interpret scripture rather than vice versa. Augustine thus salvages the method but not the matter of the "Poet historical," embracing allegory as a vehicle even as he rejects epic stories of history per se.

As if answering Tertullian's infamous challenge, "what has Athens to do with Jerusalem?", Augustine explains both why and how scripture should be read not only as Christian history but also as encompassing the whole of history. Since all of history is divine, he argues, all of history's riches must be brought to bear on the interpretation of scripture: "whatever evidence we have of past times in that which is called history helps us a great deal in the understanding of the sacred books, even if we learn it outside of the Church as part of our childhood education" (63). Those who dismiss the past as irrelevant demonstrate a contempt for all forms of knowledge, he further argues, for even "those who exult in divine assistance and who glory in being able to understand and treat the sacred books without precepts" nevertheless "should remember that they have learned at least the alphabet from men" (4). What and how readers remember the past forms the crux of this treatise. To describe the pilgrim's progress from Athens to Jerusalem, Augustine adapts an epic metaphor for understanding scripture:

Suppose we were wanderers who could not live in blessedness except at home, miserable in our wandering and desiring to end it and return to our native country. We would need vehicles for land and sea which could be used to help us reach our homeland . . . But if the amenities of the journey and the motion of the vehicles itself delighted us, and we were led to enjoy these things which we should use, we should not wish to end our journey quickly, and, entangled in a perverse sweetness, we should be alienated from our country, whose sweetness would make us blessed. Thus in this mortal life, wandering from God, if we wish to return to our native country where we can be blessed we should use this world and not enjoy it, so that . . . by means of corporal and temporal things we may comprehend the eternal and the spiritual. (9–10)

Augustine uses the epic journey as a pedagogical tool; the pleasurable poetic metaphor prepares his readers for the serious study of scripture. But the metaphor itself carries temptations. Only readers who avoid becoming "entangled in [its] perverse sweetness," who can avoid being lured from home by poetry's siren song, can discover how to use poetry as a vehicle, a way of translating the past for the present. At the same time, Augustine capsizes his own epic metaphor, punctuating the distance between secular and spiritual journeys by asserting that "[they] do not come to Him who is everywhere present by moving from place to place, but by good endeavor and good habits" (13). Here as in his other works, Augustine makes going home, the end of the epic journey, less as a matter of finding home than fashioning home within the self.

The epic simile invites a comparison between two books of memory – poetry and scripture – as vehicles of edification. To reimagine the role of ruin in edification, Augustine draws his central analogy from scripture rather than epic, describing the spoils of Egypt rather than those of Troy. Just as the Israelites despoiled Egyptian "gold" on their exodus, so Christians should seize and convert history's gold on their continued exodus from the City of Man:

If those who are called philosophers, especially the Platonists, have said things which are indeed true and are well accommodated to our faith, they should not be feared; rather, what they have said should be taken from them as from unjust possessors and converted to our use. Just as the Egyptians had not only idols but grave burdens which the people of Israel detested and avoided, so also they had vases and ornaments of gold and silver and clothing which the Israelites took with them secretly when they fled, as if to put them to a better use . . . In the same way all the teachings of the pagans contain not only simulated and superstitious imaginings and grave burdens of unnecessary labor . . . but also liberal disciplines more suited to the uses of truth, and some most useful precepts concerning morals. These are, as it were, their gold and silver, which they did not institute themselves but dug up from certain mines of divine Providence, which is everywhere infused, and perversely and injuriously abused in the worship of demons. (75)

In this famous depiction, Augustine describes how cultural transmission takes place not as the literal despoliation of empires but as the symbolic and memorial despoliation of history's gold. As he concludes, readers "should take this treasure" not for its own sake but "held to be converted to Christian uses" (75). He thus pursues an implicit contrast between material and memorial spoils: the spoils of empire building and of spiritual edification. Rather than having intrinsic value, the value of history's gold depends precisely upon its use, and precisely how Augustine imagines edification marks his radical departure from epic. In contrast to the City of Man, built upon spoils of war later deemed prophetic ruin, a retrofitted divine justification for empire building, the soul's edification represents a memorial pillaging of history writ large. The gold of Athens can thereby become the foundation of the New Jerusalem within time itself.

The necessary conversion – or tempering – of history's gold ultimately relates to the reading of scripture. Augustine reminds readers that "when the student of Holy Scripture . . . begins to approach his text, he should always bear in mind the apostolic saying, 'Knowledge puffs up; but charity edifies'" (76). Therefore, "to the extent that the wealth of gold and silver and clothing which that people took with them from Egypt was less than that they afterwards acquired at Jerusalem . . . the knowledge collected from the books of the pagans, although some of it is useful, is also little as compared with that derived from Holy Scriptures" (77–8). Augustine concludes that when "prepared by this instruction," readers will be "built up in charity" (78). This interpretive attitude emphasizes the necessity of converting rather than merely collecting history's gold: the former leads to edification, whereas the latter leads to arrogance and the false arrogation of divinity. Augustine's object lesson in the proper use of gold embeds these two possibilities: the Israelites may have despoiled Egyptian gold on God's injunction, but they also misused it to fashion an idol, the Golden Calf. The attraction of gold can never be its own end, in other words. By embracing all of history as the tools with which to interpret scripture, readers avoid being arrogantly "puffed up" and are instead "edified." This process of edification describes how history's gold becomes the foundation for Augustine's reformed soul.

*   *   *

Augustine's work suggests the ways in which the Cave of Mammon is an allegory of allegory, or more specifically, an allegory about reading allegorically. *City of God*, which rebukes the fantasy of Rome's divine endless empire and traces its history of ruination, figures prominently in the Cave of Mammon episode, as does *On Christian Doctrine*, where the use and misuse of history's spoils takes centre stage. *On Christian Doctrine* serves as an ironic reminder in this episode about using gold to fashion idols – precisely what Mammon consciously and Guyon unconsciously effect. The temptations Mammon offers Guyon ultimately serve only to reinforce his own fiction of history, his idolatry of the Faerie Queene, though he cannot recognize this. This inability to distinguish between story and history, or poetry and power, ultimately aligns Guyon with Mammon's version of history. In the broadest sense, this episode holds up fictions of empire to scrutiny by suggesting that kingdoms are built upon despoiled gold. Mammon's kingdom, to paraphrase Augustine, is nothing less than a great robbery. Yet Guyon remains oblivious because his perspective on history, like Paridell's, does not extend beyond Cleopolis. Guyon's perception of himself as an epic hero and his reiteration (and re-enactment) of Golden Age fictions prevent him from seeing that he too worships a god of gold. In a sense, Spenser suggests that Guyon has fallen prey to Mammon's temptations – the desire for fame, glory, power – long before he enters Mammon's Cave.

Rather than serving God over Mammon, Guyon chooses to serve the Faerie Queene, blind to his own ambitions even when Mammon presents them in the form of his daughter: sitting in "a stately seige of souereigne maiestye," surrounded by pillars decked "with crownes and Diademes, and titles vaine / Which mortall Princes wore, whiles they on earth did rayne" (2.7.44, 43). This episode darkly reflects Chaucer's *House of Fame* by representing both the desire for fame, for immortality in epic and empire, and its price. "Deriued" from Philotime (the love of glory and perhaps Gloriana) "are [all] this worldes blis" (48), Mammon boasts:

There, as in glistring glory she did sit,
She held a great gold chaine ylincked well,
Whose vpper end to highest heauen was knit,
And lower part did reach to lowest Hell;
And all that preace did round about her swell,
To catchen hold of that long chaine, thereby
To clime aloft, and others to excell:
That was *Ambition*, rash desire to sty,
And euery lincke thereof a step of dignity. (46)

Mammon creates a paternity for history, personified and allegorized by his daughter, that works against the idealized genealogy delineated in Book 3. The urge to despoil has fathered history, and the desire for her reflects a desire for gold that Guyon can only imagine as ancient history. "Thy spouse I will her make, if that thou lust," Mammon promises, "That she may thee aduance for workes and merites iust" (49). And when he offers Guyon his daughter to serve, both Guyon's immortal longings and his courtly values are implicated in the "ambition" of those who seek advancement by becoming linked to the queen's "great gold chaine." Surrounded by gold and riches, by people of every nation, Philotime's image suggests the power to reproduce others in her image. Yet whereas Guyon sees Philotime as "gorgeous," readers see her differently, having been told that her appearance masks a fallen state: "most heauenly faire indeed and vew / She by creation was, till she did fall; / Thenceforth she sought for helps, to cloke her crime withall (45). From his limited perspective, Guyon clings to an ideal of chivalric service. But while Mammon's cynicism evidently juxtaposes Guyon's idealism, Mammon also clearly mirrors Guyon's desire to idolize the queen he serves. When Guyon rejects Mammon's offer to serve Philotime, he does so for all the wrong reasons, calling himself an "vnworthy match for such immortall mate" (50). Albeit indirectly, this rejection paradoxically demonstrates how Guyon's and Mammon's seemingly competing versions of history hold a great deal in common: both fashion idols of gold in order to satisfy the desire for power, wealth, and immortality.

Without recognizing himself in Mammon's seduction, Guyon remains fundamentally unenlightened by this experience, his apparent fall into history, a point that Spenser reinforces at the episode's end. In the final cantos, Spenser offers Guyon and readers a tour of secular and sacred, fictional and historical reminders of the fall into history.

Through "that famous golden Apple . . . / The which emongst the gods false *Ate* threw," the fall of man is linked with the fall of Troy as a matter of worshipping "the gods false": "Till partiall *Paris* dempt it *Venus* dew, / And had of her, faire *Helen* for his meed, / That many noble *Greekes* and *Troians* made to bleed" (55). This connection eludes Guyon completely, even when he meets twin exemplars of arrogating divinity: Tantalus, who tested Jove's godliness, and Pilate, who "Deliuered vp the Lord of life to die."[35] Equating Guyon's Aeneas-like ambitions as "Pilot" to this "Pilate," Spenser suggests that the act of producing fictions of divinity represents the origin of humanity's fall. When Mammon charges, "Thou fearfull foole, / Why takest not of that same fruit of gold?" (63), Guyon tries to make a virtue of his ignorance. Having been warned of the apple's power – "through sinfull bayt; / To which if he inclined had at all . . . / Would him haue rent in thousand peeces strayt" – he abstains from the very knowledge that might save him from repeating history's mistakes (64). His seemingly virtuous ability to resist temptation amounts to not remembering the uses of gold within history. Spenser thus depicts history in more complex ways than Guyon can comprehend, even when he feels tempted by that tree's "golden apples glistring bright" (54). His originary myth of the fallen Golden Age contrasts with these histories of fallen humanity. But without noticing Mammon's true temptation, the appeal to Guyon's own idolatry, he remains blind to all but his vision of history. What Guyon cannot see in Mammon's Cave or in himself is the human desire to fashion gods of gold. In Augustinian fashion, Spenser thereby demonstrates the misuse of gold, identifying imperial leaders as Mammon's progeny.

In the end, Guyon and Mammon only *seem* to hold opposing versions of history; indeed, their debate discloses their similar views. This episode offers less a double vision of history than a double vision of Guyon, as both virtuous hero and flawed anti-hero, depending upon whether one views him as an allegory or as the participant in an allegory. Guyon's inability to see himself in the mirror of Mammon's temptation literally causes him to fall, as the episode's conclusion ironically suggests. Guyon faints upon his departure from Mammon's Cave – a faint reminiscent of Dante's hero in the *Comedy* – as his "vitall powres gan wexe both weake and wan . . . / Like mightie pillours, this fraile life of man" (65). Guyon appears dead when robbers attempt to despoil his gold armour. But they advance no further than a debate about the legitimacy of sacking dead bodies; it is "enuie base, to barke at sleeping fame," "to spoile the dead of weed / Is sacrilege, and doth all sinnes ex-ceed," and they are warned to "leaue these relicks of his liuing might" (2.8.13, 16). In the midst of this mock-continuation of Guyon and Mam-mon's debate about gold, Arthur arrives to chase away the would-be robbers. When the two heroes discover their linked bonds of love and knighthood, Arthur questions Guyon about the image on his golden shield, asking "Why on your shield so goodly scord / Beare ye the pic-ture of that Ladies head?" (2.9.2). Guyon responds with what could only be called intemperate passion:

> She is the mighty Queene of *Faerie*,
> Whose faire retrait I in my shield do beare; . . .
> Throughout the world renowmed far and neare,
> My liefe, my liege, my Soueraigne, my deare,
> Whose glory shineth as the morning starre,
> And with her light the earth enlumines cleare;
> Far reach her mercies, and her prayses farre,
> As well in state of peace, as puissance in warre. (4)

Proclaiming her "bountie, and imperiall powre" a "thousand times fairer then her mortall hew," Guyon exclaims to Arthur that her sight will "infinite desire into your spirit poure!" (3). Guyon's "infinite de-sire" for the Faerie Queene, of course, parallels Philotime's lustful courtiers. As with Philotime's lovers, Guyon's and Arthur's love is intemperate not just in the private sense but also in the public realm of politics and power. With apparently no greater consciousness than Guyon, Arthur calls him a "happy man" because the Faerie Queene has "made thee souldier of that Princesse bright, / Which with her bounty and glad countenance / Doth blesse her seruants, and them high adaunce" (5). At the same time, Arthur alludes to the price of this ap-parently noble desire for service: "sufficient were that hire / For losse of thousand liues, to dye at her desire" (5). This sexual pun belies a seriousness about what it means to serve the Faerie Queene. What does being linked to the queen's "great gold chain," as are Philotime's ambi-tious servants, mean for these knights? "My whole desire hath beene, and yet is now," Arthur vows, "To serue that Queene with all my powre and might" (7). Their mutual love of the Faerie Queene shapes their vi-sions of history. As Guyon promises Arthur, "I labour would to guide you through all Faery land" (8). Book 2 offers just that: a guided tour of Faerie Land's competing stories of history.

Alma's Castle of the Soul and the Art of Recollection

After emerging from his fall into Mammon's Cave, Guyon ascends to Alma's Castle, where he encounters an allegorical answer to Mammon in "aged Mnemon": the mnemonic personification of memory who recollects history in, and as, England's soul. In this place, Spenser relates England's history in "the middest," offering a Trojan narrative that spans from Brutus' arrival in Britannia to the once and future King Arthur, a story of history that epitomizes Geoffrey of Monmouth's medieval history of the kings of Britain. Yet more than anywhere else in *The Faerie Queene*, here Spenser criticizes the reiteration of Trojan tales – including, it would seem, his own – for reasons that speak indirectly to allegory itself. Readers might see Guyon's journey from Cave to Castle as a redemptive narrative, a religious allegory of epic that charts the soul's pilgrimage from the City of Man to the City of God, from a space of forgetting to one of remembering, from ruin to repair.[36] Yet Spenser undermines such an allegorical interpretation, which would ignore the dark vision revealed in Mammon's Cave: how he and Guyon use poetic fictions to worship power, fashioning idols of gold that serve their ambitions. Similarly, Spenser punctures the overly redemptive aura of Alma's Castle with a profound irony: despite presenting England's Trojan origins, the episode suggests that they represent Mammon-like constructions of divinity, political fictions repeated and re-enacted throughout history that never end in "empire without end" but rather perpetuate ongoing ruin.

In the journey from Mammon's Cave to Alma's Castle, Spenser juxtaposes allegories of the "Poet historical" and the "Historiographer." Whereas the "Poet historical" of Mammon's Cave creates an allegory about the fiction of endless empire, the allegory of the "Historiographer" in Alma's Castle illustrates the place of fiction in the continual rise and fall of empire. In both allegories, nevertheless, Spenser works to unveil the stories that shape history in writing and in the world. Despite the division Spenser establishes in the "Letter to Raleigh" about the differences between the "methode" of a "Poet historical" and a "Historiographer," he ultimately suggests – and in terms reminiscent of Sidney's *Apology for Poetry* – how they intersect, and why this matters. By artificially dividing poets from historians, Spenser paradoxically demonstrates what they hold in common: they share a "methode" of ordering the symbolic spoils – or gold – of the past into narrative, the art of memory, and a common matter of memory, tales of ruin and endless empire.

As I argue, Augustine's art of memory plays an important if ironic role in the allegory of Alma's Castle. Augustine's method of reading allegorically, despoiling history's gold as described in *On Christian Doctrine*, is also his method of writing allegorically in the *Confessions*, where he recollects such historical gold for his soul's edification and reformation, and where Augustine's personal history allegorically represents a larger story of history, that of everyman. Spenser similarly transports the gold from Mammon's Cave to Alma's Castle, converting it into the foundation of the soul's edification, an allegory of self-fashioning at once individual and collective. As Spenser recalls and rewrites the *Confessions*, he positions Augustine as his model for reforming the roles of both "Historiographer" and "Poet historical." In Alma's Castle, Spenser plays both parts, creating a heuristic tale about a new story of history built upon the fragments of older ones: Geoffrey of Monmouth's history of Britain's kings. Yet Augustine's religious meditations ironically allow Spenser to remind readers of his complaints about fashioning Trojan tales as divine revelation. In so doing, Spenser distances himself from his presumed Virgilian role models – especially the new Virgil of *The Divine Comedy*.[37] Recollecting Augustine's "book of memory" within his own book, as well as the books of memory written and read in the soul's edifice, Spenser refuses to deify poetry or power, epic or empire. Alma's castle instead becomes a place for readers to recognize and remember fictions of divine self-fashioning within history.

Throughout this episode, Spenser makes implicit comparisons between Alma's Castle and Mammon's Cave, particularly through the *topos* of ruin. How the two allegories represent the architecture of immortality can be seen in their representations of female power. Whereas Mammon invites Guyon to immortality through marriage with Philotime, to reproduce his empire by becoming "lincked" to her "great golden chain," Alma tempts with no such link: "*Alma* she called was, a virgin bright ... / [whom] many a Lord of noble parentage, / ... sought with her to lincke in marriage" – but none successfully (2.9.18). And whereas in Mammon's Cave gold conceals Philotime's fallen state and creates the illusion of imperial immortality, in Alma's Castle the threat of imminent ruin speaks to the contingency of all structures of power: a "thousand enemies about vs raue," Arthur and Guyon are warned upon entering this edifice (12). Far from an immortal monument, Alma's Castle is built "of thing like to that Ægyptian slime, / Whereof king *Nine* whilome built *Babell* towre"; and like that monument, is destined to fall: "O great pitty, that no lenger time / So goodly worke-manship should not endure: / Soone it must turne to earth; no earthly thing is sure" (21). The inevitability of mutability marks Alma's Castle and, by analogy, the human body; as Spenser suggests, both structures are ultimately subject to time. Although called a "worke diuine," Al-ma's Castle – an edifice at once "imperfect [and] mortall" as well as "immortall [and] perfect" – mingles human and divine elements, both ruin and its repair, in its very structure (22). Moreover, the same intem-perate desires that motivate history in Mammon's Cave exist as well in Alma's Castle. A place where labour also conquers all, "*Appetite*" works over "a caudron wide and tall, / Vpon a mighty furnace . . . / day and night it brent, ne ceased not" (28, 29). Like the smelting of gold in Mam-mon's Cave, appetite also needs tempering here. One such desire, for fame, connects these places, evidenced by "*Prays-desire*"; dressed "in a long purple pall, whose skirt with gold / Was fretted all about," she confesses to being "sad in mind, / Through great desire of glory and of fame" (39, 37–8). Just as Philotime mirrors Guyon's "great desire of glory and of fame," so Arthur's ambitions are implicated in this meet-ing with allegorical royalty, mirroring his desire for glory by serving the Faerie Queene.

In a sense, the materials of memory in the Cave of Mammon – the spoils of history that represent either ruin or gold, depending upon their use – find parallels in the Castle of Alma, though they are given a new order and shape through the process of recollecting the past. Memory reshapes intemperate desire by providing a "goodly order," apparent to Arthur and Guyon when they enter the castle's highest three rooms (33). Proceeding through the mind's own places, they pass through foresight, knowledge, and finally arrive at "a stately Turret" of memory (44). This place of recollection is also a space of ruin: "That chamber seemed ruinous and old / And therefore was remoued farre behind," yet behind its decayed appearance "were the wals, that did the same vphold / Right firme and strong, though somewhat they de-clind" (55). Significantly, the structure of the "Turret" is contrasted with "that proud towre of *Troy* . . . / From which young *Hectors* bloud by cruell *Greekes* was spilt" (45). The soul itself is not like the "towre[s] of *Troy*" and yet, as readers see, it is edified by recollecting the ruins of such structures. The difference between material and memorial ruins, rather than clearly demarcated, is radically elided.

Such memorial ruins of history are embodied by "aged Mnemon," or Eumnestes, himself. In Memory's chamber, the knights discover

> an old oldman, halfe blind,
> And all decrepit in his feeble corse,
> Yet liuely vigour rested in his mind . . .
> Weake body well is chang'd for minds redoubled forse. (55)

Memory has a body ruined by age but a mind that recollects ruin:

> This man of infinite remembrance was,
> And things foregone through many ages held,
> Which he recorded still, as they did pas,
> Ne suffred them to perish through long eld,
> As all things else, the which this world doth weld,
> But laid them vp in his immortall scrine,
> Where they for euer incorrupted dweld. (56)

Instead of portraying memory's "immortal scrine" as an edifice that stands in contrast to ruin, Spenser describes Eumnestes' chamber as continually fashioned from the ruins of of time:[38]

> His chamber all was hanged about with rolles,
> And old records from auncient times deriu'd,
> Some made in books, some in long parchment scrolles,
> That were all worme-eaten, and full of canker holes. (57)

In the midst of this decaying historical matter, Eumnestes recollects the past:

> Amidst them all he in a chaire was set,
> Tossing and turning them withouten end;
> But for he was vnhable them to fet,
> A litle boy did on him still attend,
> To reach, when euer he for ought did send;
> And oft when things were lost, or laid amis,
> That boy them sought, and vnto him did lend.
> Therefore he *Anamnestes* cleped is,
> And that old man *Eumnestes*, by their propertis. (58)

The chamber "seem[s] ruinous and old," like Eumnestes himself, but such ruins are the matter of his memory "withouten end."[39] With his helper "*Anamnestes*," recollection, the "man of infinite remembrance" gathers the ruins of the past as the books of England's collective memory.[40] The disrepair of these histories – "Some made in books, some in long parchment scrolles . . . all worme-eaten, and full of canker holes" – implies that memory also falls to ruin and that recollecting ruin represents a process that must continue throughout time. Eumnestes' "immortal scrine" thus achieves a strange immortality, one that seems counterintuitive; after all, the *topos* of literary immortality is typically associated with edifices that can *withstand* ruination. Yet since material ruin persists in history, it cannot therefore be written out of historical memory. Eumnestes fashions immortality by "tossing and turning" these ruinous old texts "withouten end," illustrating a dynamic art of memory that indirectly undermines ideas of permanence as stasis.

In the Castle of Alma, Spenser presents an allegory of the soul – body and mind – built by and as an art of memory. "Spenser's picture of Memory . . . contains a considerable amount of information about the mnemonic process and is crucial for our understanding of Renaissance theory," Michael Murrin writes, explaining the relation between the art of memory and allegory: "The specific techniques by which the poet affected the memories of his audience were themselves invented by a poet," Simonides, and "since Renaissance critics habitually identified allegory with poetry, a series of equivalences is suggested: memory with allegory and both with poetry."[41] Explaining that "Mnemosyne concerns herself essentially with historical events, while in anamnesis the individual recalls a prehistorical situation, something [before] time and history," Murrin suggests that "Poets do "much the same thing when," as he argues, "by recalling both the past and the future" they participate "in a viewpoint somehow beyond time, concerned though it may be with events in time or expressing itself through them."[42] As I will argue, "anamnesis" in Alma's Castle refers to prior knowledge not as metaphysics but as a matter of historical memory. Spenser's art of memory is used to explore both *how* to remember and *what* to remember, in what amounts to a critique of historical fictions. The art of memory thus works in different ways in the allegory of Alma's Castle. As a method of edification, Spenser draws upon the poetic uses of locational memory – places and images – in order to make this edifying location memorable; in so doing, he illustrates how to recollect the ruins of the past, drawing an analogy between individual and collective memory, the fashioning of the self and society. But Spenser also uses the art of memory to explore history and, further, as a reminder that memory itself has a history.

Turning to the *Confessions*, I will suggest how Augustine's work sheds light on Spenser's allegory of the soul. The relevance of Book 10 of the *Confessions* to Canto 10 in Book 2 of *The Faerie Queene* is made clear by Spenser's framing topic, "The Legend of Temperance." Augustine explores his authorial method as a matter of fashioning memory: by tempering history's gold, he gives it a new order in narrative. Yet this reformation of history's gold for and within his soul is, as Augustine suggests, an endeavour that mingles story and history, fact and fiction, in ways that speak to the art of memory broadly and to the *Phaedrus* specifically. For Plato as for Augustine, *anamnesis* – the recollection of *a priori* knowledge – represents a means of both challenging and constructing origin stories about the past, of using tales to tell truths. The art of memory represents the historical gold that Augustine converts into an allegory of self-fashioning, precisely the operation performed by Eumnestes and Anamnestes, and for a similarly paradoxical end: to reveal the place of stories both *in* history and *as* history.

Augustine's *Confessions:* Truth and Method

The art of memory is both the method and the matter of Book 10 of Augustine's *Confessions*. As though he were the court historian in his own castle of the soul, Augustine portrays himself as a memorial edifice. Describing how places and images aid in recollection writ large, he relates how each memory "is admitted through its own special entrance" in the body – "light, color and shape are admitted through the eyes; sound of all kinds through the ears; all sorts of smell through the nostrils; and every kind of taste through the mouth" – and how "all these sensations are retained in the great storehouse of the memory," memories which "can be brought out and called back again when they are needed" but each of which "enters the memory through its own gateway and is retained in it" (214–15). Even metaphorically speaking, Augustine's portrait of recollection clearly recalls Aristotle's tract *Memory and Recollection*, appended to his work *On the Soul*, which grounds faculty psychology – the soul as a composite of both mind and body – in mnemonic theory. What Aristotle calls a "method of recollection" applies here, but only in part.[43] The old saw that Augustine converts to Platonism is also partly true, for he reforms Plato's fictional allegory of love in the *Phaedrus* in order to replace Trojan tales of ruin and recollection with his own. In Book 10 of the *Confessions*, a break in the narrative in which Augustine describes both his method and motive for this memoir, he also suggests the work's more radical reformation of the art of memory into a story of history.

Augustine converts the art of memory into an art of salvation, as discussed in chapter 1, confessing that his soul is a "house . . . in ruins" and describing the process of its re-edification.[44] Although scholars have sometimes argued that the *Confessions* turns Virgil's *Aeneid* into a Christian allegory, this would seem to confuse Augustine's poetic method with his matter. He begins Book 10 by indirectly reminding readers why epic cannot be his book of memory. Augustine begins by confessing both his love of God – it "is you whom I love and desire" – and those loves that divide him from divinity (207). "As for the other things in life, the more we weep for them, the less they merit our tears," he writes, thereby recalling the role that the *Aeneid* once played in his psyche as he wept for Dido while forgetting himself, in effect, idolizing poetry (207). Nevertheless, a poetic art of memory itself represents the gold that Augustine tempers for a new edifice (146). As he collects his "scattered and unheeded" memories and refashions his soul, Augustine remembers earlier transformations of the art of memory, in particular that of Plato. Appropriating the method of the poets as mediated through the "books of the Platonists" (154), Augustine writes an allegory of himself that also doubles as a Christian defence of poetry. This work relates dialectically to *City of God*, where he argues against reading fictions of endless empire as the truth of history, and tacitly contrasts epic and scripture as opposed "books of memory"; as well as to *On Christian Doctrine*, where he demonstrates how to interpret scripture allegorically (or even poetically) as a matter of converting history's gold for the soul's edification. With the *Confessions*, Augustine dramatizes how to both read and write allegorically, replacing Trojan tales with a story of his own soul's ruin and reformation.

Suggesting that his *Confessions* mingles truth and fiction, Augustine in effect justifies his own method as a "Poet historical." Questioning why readers might "wish to hear from me what sort of man I am," he also questions the boundaries between story and history in this work: "When [readers] hear me speak about myself, how do they know whether I am telling the truth, since no one knows a man's thoughts, except the man's own spirit that is within him?" (208). Augustine answers this question with another: "if a man recognizes his true self, can he possibly say "This is false", unless he is himself a liar?" (208). He thereby suggests that the literal truth of the story is less important than its larger truths: "Although I cannot prove to them that my confessions are true, at least I shall be believed by those whose ears are opened to me by charity."[45] Such a charitable hermeneutic amounts to reading for the truths that belie fiction – spiritually or allegorically – and he explores the role that fiction plays in telling complex truths.

If, as Augustine suggests, the writing of virtuous pagans symbolizes the gold that he despoils and converts on his symbolic exodus from the City of Man, this gold nevertheless carries its own temptations. Here as throughout Augustine's writing, the value of history's spoils (as with writing itself) depends upon its use – appropriating history's gold *and* making it appropriate for new uses. Temptation and temperance are paired terms when Augustine describes his motives and method; indeed, despite his professed desire to edify, he also explores less altruistic reasons for writing his memoir. In ways reminiscent of the *Phaedrus*, Augustine enumerates the temptations, both physical and psychological, that his love story incites.[46] The "more dangerous" kinds of "temptations," he writes, speak to his own writing: the desire for fame, glory, praise, to fashion himself or others as idols of gold. Augustine confesses too that although "gratified . . . less by praise than by the truth," that "the love of praise tempts me," what he calls "vainglory" (246–7). And finally, he fears the outcome of a temptation, the "self-complacency" that marks "the vanity of those who are pleased with themselves" (248). These temptations threaten Augustine, making him vulnerable to "the fallen angels" who, Mammon-like, could seduce him: the "devil" who "pretends to be like God," who "tries to represent himself as immortal" (250). "The human tongue is a furnace in which the temper of our souls is daily tried," Augustine writes, implying that such self-glorifying temptations are as much internal demons as external ones (245). Converting history's gold requires tempering both the mind and body, and he anatomizes how "to control our desires" so that we "can . . . master" ourselves (233). But rather than constructing either the mind or the body as inherently sinful, Augustine approaches them together as a vehicle, so to speak, for self-mastery, whose value finally depends upon use.

The same is true of Augustine's writing, as well as the writing that he remembers. Indeed, Augustine's allegory of self-fashioning models the tempering or conversion of history's gold for a new edifice, and nowhere more than in Book 10. Indirectly here, he acknowledges himself as a creative artist, even a poet, who brokers in a love of knowledge, images of beauty, a desire for fame – all the temptations that he acknowledges as part of writing his *Confessions*. Like Plato, Augustine offers readers poetry as palinode. But even as he appropriates the method of the poets (Cicero's and Plato's, as well as Homer's and Virgil's), he nevertheless thoroughly reforms the matter of memory. Book 10 recalls the *Phaedrus* by reforming its central narrative, taking seriously the issue of remembering and forgetting divinity that in Plato's dialogue (159). Specifically, Augustine examines the issue of prior knowledge as relating to the truth of origins. As scholars have argued, he clearly rejects Plato's tales of the soul's continued rebirth, the transmigration of souls that would allow for the recollection of knowledge that cannot be otherwise explained, as told in the *Phaedrus* and other key dialogues.[47] However, if Plato's tales of the soul's fall and re-edification are understood in literary rather than literal terms, then Augustine's investigations of the paradoxes of forgetfulness and recollection align in many respects with Plato's. Both writers position the soul's recollection of the past, prior knowledge, as related to writing which prompts the mind's own divining power.

As Augustine investigates his method as an historiographer of the soul, he transforms Plato's tale of how the fallen, forgetful soul reforms itself by recollecting the divine within. "What, then, do I love when I love God," he asks, a question that leads into his investigation of the self, time and history, memory and recollection (213). Describing "the great storehouse of the memory," he writes, "In it I meet myself as well. I remember myself" (215). Portraying locational memory as both a natural and artificial faculty, Augustine praises how "memory captures" both images and facts "with astonishing speed and stores them away in its wonderful system of compartments, ready to produce them again in just as wonderful a way when we remember them" (217). But even as Augustine praises this faculty, he also acknowledges its fundamental mystery: "Although it is part of my nature, I cannot understand all that I am," and "I am lost in wonder when I consider this problem" (216). Because "the power of the memory is prodigious . . . a vast, immeasurable sanctuary," Augustine explores the paradox of recollecting divinity. But even as he ponders the mystery of memory – asking, "How, then, did these facts get into my memory? Where did they come from?" (218) – he also demystifies recollection:

> learning these facts, which do not reach our minds as images by means of the senses but are recognized by us in our minds, without images, as they actually are, is simply a process of thought by which we gather together things which although they are muddled and confused, are already contained in the memory. When we give them our attention, we see to it

that these facts, which have been lying scattered and unheeded, are placed ready to hand, so that they are easily forthcoming . . . once they have been dispersed, I have to collect them again, and this is the derivation of the word *cogitare*, which means *to think* or *to collect one's thoughts*. For in Latin the word *cogo*, meaning *I assemble* or *I collect*, is related to *cogito*, which means *I think* . . . But the word *cogito* is restricted to the function of the mind. (218–19)

Here as elsewhere, Augustine transforms the remembrance of things past by returning to earlier uses of locational memory. As in the *ars memorativa* tradition in which he locates himself, all the mind's faculties – imagination, reason, and memory – participate in the labour of recollection. Like Socrates, Augustine represents himself as a "lover of divisions and collections" that allow him to think and speak and, most broadly, to remember the past as self-knowledge. The creative process of recollection requires change, decorum, or, put another way, conversion.

Augustine realizes that recollecting his sin, his soul does mean simply reconstructing the past. "I remember myself and what I have done," he explains, as well as "all that I have ever learnt of the liberal sciences," but that cannot explain the mystery of remembering things whose origin cannot be located (215–16). Augustine thus puzzles how recollecting relates to forgetting:

what is forgetfulness but absence of memory? When is it present, I cannot remember. Then how can it be present in such a way that I can remember it? . . . Who can understand the truth of the matter? O Lord, I am working hard in this field, and the field of my labours is my own self. I have become a problem to myself, like land which a farmer works only with difficulty and at the cost of much sweat. For I am not now investigating the tracts of the heavens, or measuring the distance of the stars, or trying to discover how the earth hangs in space. I am investigating myself, my memory, my mind. (222–3)

The paradoxical labour of "remembering forgetfulness" links the metaphysical to the historical. The truth of the past, like the truth of the self, is a "space" as unfathomable as the "tracts of the heavens" yet the place where Augustine finds "myself, my memory, my mind." He explains this paradox with a parable: "the woman who had lost a coin searched for it by the light of a lantern, but she would never have found it unless she remembered it" (224). A similar search for things "lost and found" (literally and figuratively) impels Augustine's search for history's gold, impelled by the memory of "happiness" whose origin he cannot place (227). As in the *Phaedrus*, Augustine observes the profound limits of locational memory as a method of recollection. "In which part of my memory are you present, O Lord?" he asks, "What cell have you constructed for yourself in my memory? What sanctuary have you built there for yourself?" (230). However, Augustine also acknowledges the futility of such questions, and ultimately reframes them: "Why do I ask what place is set aside in my memory as your dwelling, as if there were distinctions of place in the memory? Truly you do dwell in it, because I remember you ever since I first came to learn of you, and it is there that I find you when I am reminded of you" (231).

Augustine finds divinity within himself and his memory when "reminded" by writing – Cicero's, Plato's, and most of all, scripture – which he recollects within his book of memory, enabling him to remember the past. The best example of this is Augustine's interpretation of the book of Genesis in the last books of the *Confessions*, which exemplifies the paradoxical recollection of *a priori* knowledge. As his glosses on scripture make clear, however, even the truth of scriptural history is never transparent. To suggest this, Augustine interprets "In the Beginning God made heaven and earth" in an extravagant allegorical fashion: "Scripture does not say on which day you made them, and I understand the reason for this to be that "heaven" here means the Heaven of Heavens – that is, the intellectual heaven, where the intellect is privileged to know all at once, not in part only, not as if it were looking at a confused reflection in a mirror, but as a whole, clearly, face to face" (289). This interpretation builds the inevitability of partial knowledge into itself: in time people see through a glass darkly, and thus only the fragments of truth. Chastising those who claim to know *the* truth of scripture or divinity, Augustine writes: "there are others, not opponents of the book of Genesis but acclaimers of it, who say, 'This is not what the Spirit of God, who wrote these words through Moses his servant, meant us to understand by them. He did not mean them to be understood as you explain them. He meant them to be taken in another way, the way that we say is right'" (290). Augustine's fullest answer to such criticisms comes later in the *Confessions*:

> I know that a truth which the mind understands in one way only can be materially expressed by many different means, and I also know that there are many different ways in which the mind can understand an idea that

is outwardly expressed in one way. Take the single concept of the love of God and our neighbour. How many different symbols are used to give it outward expression! How many different languages have words for it and, in each of them, how many different forms of speech there are by which it can be conveyed! The creatures of the sea increase and multiply in this way. On the other hand, consider the verse "In the Beginning God made heaven and earth." Scripture presents this truth to us in one way only, and there is only one way in which the words can be shaped by the tongue. But it may be understood in several different ways without falsi-fication or error, because various interpretations, all of which are true in themselves, may be put upon it. The offspring of men increase and mul-tiply in this way . . . in all these [interpretations] we find the process of multiplication at work. In all of them we find fertility and increase. (335–6)

So Augustine concludes, where writing is concerned – "in the case of signs outwardly given," even scripture – "a single truth can be expressed by several different means . . . a single expression can be interpreted in several different ways" (336). Discovering the truth of history means accepting the paradox of partial truths that are gathered together, collected and recollected in endlessly imaginative interpreta-tions, even wondrous stories. These represent the ongoing reproduction of meaning, suggesting that truth, like life, can be fruitful and multiply. Framed as recollection, all knowledge (including the knowledge of his-tory) becomes self-knowledge, a way of internalizing authority. Fol-lowing Plato's path, Augustine frames truth not as doctrine per se but as knowledge of the self, by the self, and for the self – and the only truth worth having. Like Socrates, he asks, "What man can teach another to understand this truth?" (347). "We must knock at your door," Augus-tine replies, and "only then shall we receive what we ask and find that we seek; only then will the door be opened to us" – that is, to the castle of the soul (347).

*   *   *

What is the place of the art of memory in the Castle of Alma? In one sense, the art of memory in this space represents the culmination of a tradition that Spenser traces throughout his writing. In Alma's Castle, Spenser not only remembers Augustine, Cicero, Plato, and Aristotle, but he also remembers Augustine remembering these earlier writers. In so doing, Spenser returns the art of memory to epic, not in order to reconcile Trojan tales with Christianity, or Virgil with Augustine, but rather to remind readers of the history of memory *within* the memory of history. As Spenser intimates in his "Letter to Raleigh," Eumnestes' chamber illustrates the art of memory as the "methode" of storytelling that shapes the matter of his memory: the Matter of Britain, writ small in Alma's Castle, but also *The Faerie Queene*, writ large. Augustine's *Confessions* provides Spenser with his seminal model for reforming the "Poet historical" as a "Historiographer," bringing together the method and matter of memory in new ways. In effect, Spenser elides the very dichotomy between poets and historians established in the poem's explanatory letter, yet this conflation paradoxically speaks to his poetic reformation: it marks the Castle of Alma's crucial distinction from the Cave of Mammon and, still more importantly, defines Spenser's fundamental difference from the "Poet historical" he never names, Dante. Spenser's allegorical portrait of the soul's self-fashioning thereby both remembers and answers Augustine's objections to epic: that its stories of history are taken as truths, turning rulers into gods. This speaking picture, in the broadest sense, most fully expresses Spenser's vision of how poetry might speak to, and perhaps fashion, power.

The distinction between the allegory of a "Historiographer" and that of a "Poet historical" ultimately collapses in the space of Eumnestes' chamber, where the three "Augustines" discussed in this chapter meet, so to speak: Augustine the "Historiographer," Augustine the "Poet historical," and, perhaps most significantly in this context, Augustine the allegorist. What these Augustines hold in common is a determination to mine *all* of history's gold, including stories, in the service of fashioning the self and society. In one sense, the Augustine of *City of God* seems to be resolutely anti-epic, rejecting tales of Troy's gods insofar as the prophecy of Rome's "empire without end" serves to mask the truth of Rome's history: its ongoing ruin. Similarly, the Augustine of *On Christian Doctrine* would replace epic with scripture as the common book of memory, even as he borrows his method of allegorical interpretation from poets. Yet the Augustine of *Confessions*, though he rejects myths of empire and its gods of gold and indirectly replaces scripture with epic, nevertheless also plays the part of "Poet historical" when he constructs his own story of history. He appropriates the art of memory precisely as a method common to all writers: just as Plato proposes that philosophers can be poets, and as Cicero suggests that orators and storytellers are intimately related, so Augustine associates theologians with allegorists. For Augustine, as for the Platonic tradition of *anamnesis* that he recollects and rewrites, telling new stories of history is a way of examining old ones, whether those of epic or scripture, as well as a way of teaching others how to discern truth from fiction, both in writing and in the world. To question the truth of origin tales matters not only because, as Augustine suggests, story and history are inextricably entwined, but also because the past is continually re-enacted in the present as fictions of power: as new Troys, new endless empires.

The space of Eumnestes' chamber thus recalls Augustine's "methode" as a "Poet historical" in the *Confessions*: just as he despoils the gold of history for his memoir, tempering and refashioning these materials into the matter of his allegorical "book of memory," so Spenser despoils the gold of Mammon's Cave, symbolically transporting it to Alma's Castle, where he tempers it as an Augustinian "Poet historical" and dramatizes this process of edification as an art of recollection. In so doing, Spenser simultaneously plays the part of an Augustinian "Historiographer," and hence the irony of the books read in Alma's Castle. Spenser does not locate scripture as the book of memory in his castle of the soul, instead filling the room of memory with Trojan histories. As a response to Augustine, this works on several levels. It suggests a recuperation of epic from the charges Augustine lays against it in both the *Confessions* and *City of God*. Yet, as the particular histories read by Arthur and Guyon make clear, Spenser suggests that the only way for epic to answer Augustine's critique is to build an Augustinian historiography into itself, unmasking the fictions of empire on which it itself is built. The histories read in Alma's Castle unveil its own allegory, illustrating the rise and fall of empires, built upon despoliation, which the fiction of endless empire and its gods work to conceal. In this memorable allegory of saving the soul and mending the psyche, readers observe how Spenser recollects and reforms the stories that shape memory, individually and collectively, as history: he remembers Geoffrey of Monmouth's history in such a way that it ultimately exposes its own fictions. Furthermore, by putting secular history at the heart of his allegory, Spenser tacitly rejects the claims to divine inspiration that characterize epic.

As both "Poet historical" and "Historiographer," Spenser explores the complex inter-implication of story and history – how the truths of the "Historiographer" cannot be separated from the fictions of the "Poet historical." This demonstrates (as Augustine underscores in the *Confessions*) the impossibility of knowing absolute truth in this world. The histories read in Alma's Castle illustrate the intermingling of story and history, not only because historiography relies on the lies of the poets (as Sidney would argue) but also because fictions of empire are themselves part of history (as Augustine would argue): what history chronicles is the repeated use of imperial fictions to legitimate claims to endless empire and permanent repair of the ruins of time. Spenser's strong opposition in the "Letter to Raleigh" between "Poet historical" and "Historiographer" becomes increasingly problematic as readers delve further into its implications, particularly in Book 2. To understand the ways in which story and history at once conjoin and divide requires an active, vigorous, uncertain process of reading – precisely the kind of reading that Augustine champions in *Confessions*. Augustine's model of temperance, which he derives from Plato, connects his allegorical method of writing and reading as a related process of discernment, of recognizing truth in fiction and vice versa, which allegory is fundamentally *for*: teaching readers to be better interpreters. In the Castle of Alma as throughout *The Faerie Queene*, self-fashioning represents a process of edification that amounts to remembering both how and why stories shape history, within the self and in others.

The process of recollection in Eumnestes' chamber bears a paradoxical relationship to the histories read there by Arthur and Guyon. Arthur's hand chances upon "An auncient booke, hight *Briton moniments*, / That of this lands first conquest did deuize" (2.9.59), while Guyon happens upon "another booke, / That hight *Antiquitie* of *Faerie* lond," in which he discovers "Th'off-spring of Elues and Faeries" (60). Although "burning both with feruent fire, / Their countries auncestry to vnderstond" (60), they appear to discover two radically different Englands. These two histories are typically opposed to one another, as scholars debate whether Guyon's "faerie" history works to redeem Arthur's bleak narrative of England's ruin. Michael O'Connell argues that "Spenser intends us to use our consciousness of history as a foil for the specifically idealized terrains of his poetic world, to contrast our sense of the past to his created ideal . . . best illuminated by Sidney's familiar comparison of the poet's fiction to the historian's 'truth'": as he concludes, "Faeryland, as the poet's golden world, can present a moral vision in a way that history's brazen world cannot."[48] Yet these paired histories hint at crucial differences that never materialize. While *Briton moniments* narrates England's history as a repeated cycle of ruin and re-edification, it also indirectly highlights its structural similarities to *Antiquitie of Faerie*, where empire and power are also built upon the spoils of conquest. Both Arthur and Guyon read in history what they most "desire," yet readers observe what these desires conceal. Just as Arthur's history repeatedly exposes the fictions that ground English history, so Guyon's history similarly reveals the poetic fictions of power in Faerie Land. The similarity of their histories provides a central irony here: readers observe how stories become history and history becomes stories – even faerie tales. Like Mammon's Cave, Alma's Castle is an allegory that unveils itself. By providing Arthur and Guyon with only deceptively different versions of history, Spenser points to key similarities. Both books reveal how the "Poet historical's" fictions are incorporated into history, and both histories unmask the illusion of endless empire (so unabashedly narrated in Book 3) as well as the use of divine fictions to justify the end, and means, of empire-building.

Although Book 2's narrative of history ostensibly recounts England's Trojan origins, offering a digest of Geoffrey of Monmouth's *History of the Kings of Britain*, this idealized genealogy is repeatedly undermined. Arthur's history reveals not Britain's perpetual empire but rather its perpetual ruination and re-edification, the rise and fall of power that finds a mirror in repeated uses of Trojan stories of history. Instead of demonstrating how later Britons are linked genealogically to Brutus, in other words, Arthur's history exposes Trojan origins as a recurring political fiction. With its pun on the word "raysd," the very title *Briton moniments* suggests the role of ruin in England's ongoing construction and destruction: "The land, which warlike Britons now possesse, / And therein haue their mighte empire raysd," the story begins, "In antique times was saluage wildernesse, / Vnpeopled, vnmanurd, vnprou'd, vnpraysd" (2.10.5). Arthur's history, ostensibly "the middest" of England's tripartite narrative, begins with Brutus' "fatall" (rather than "fated") arrival on England's shores and his conquest of the giants – precisely where Paridell's narrative leaves off. Recall that Paridell also describes Aeneas' arrival in Italy as a "fatall error," suggesting neither is "fated." *Briton moniments* describes the inhabitants of this allegedly unpeopled land: "farre in land a saluage nation dwelt, / Of hideous Giants, and halfe beastly men ... / By hunting and by spoiling liued then" who "with their filthinesse / Polluted this same gentle soyle long time" (2.10.7, 9). This "salvage nation" complicates the notion that Britannia was a blank map, and the giants themselves are conflated with "half beastly men" who, ironically, lived by "spoiling" that "soyle" much as Brutus and his offspring will. When Brutus defeats the legendary giants, their overthrow results in Albion's foundational fiction of settlement:

All were they borne of her own natiue slime,
Vntill that *Brutus* anciently deriu'd
From royall stocke of old *Assaracs* line,

> Driuen by fatall error, here arriu'd,
> And them of their vniust possession depriu'd. (9)

If Brutus' possession and the giants' dispossession are initially presented as just, the weight of Arthur's history ultimately suggests otherwise. The same rationale for conquest, seizing "uniust possession," pervades *Briton moniments*.

Briton moniments depicts the growth of Brutus' family tree as grafted through violation. Like Guyon's Golden Age history of Mother Earth's rape and ruin, Arthur's history describes how "the second *Brute*" achieved "euerlasting fame" through despoliation:

> his victour sword first opened
> The bowels of wide Fraunce, a forlorne Dame,
> And taught her first how to be conquered;
> Since which, with sundrie spoils she hath been ransacked. (23)

The sudden end of Brutus' "sacred progenie" when "The noble braunch from th'antique stocke was torne" finds an ironic parallel in images of ruin, and demonstrates the political value of Trojan fictions:

> Thenceforth this Realme was into factions rent,
> Whilest each of *Brutus* boasted to be borne,
> That in the end was left no moniment
> Of *Brutus*, nor of Britons glory auncient. (36)

What remains of this Trojan genealogy becomes a "moniment," or admonishment, to a pervasive political fiction. The lack of "moniment" here implies that Brutus' Golden Age left no monuments but also that a lack of antiquarian evidence calls into question the truth of this narrative. What follows the rupture of Brutus' genealogy is a repeated cycle of despoliation, ruin, and re-edification. Readers learn that "*Lud* / Left of his life most famous memory, / And endlesse moniments of his great good," for "The ruin'd wals he did reædifye / Of *Troynouant*, gainst force of enimy, / And built that gate, which of his name is hight" (46). But the conquest of his sons – "*Cassibalane* . . . / Who on him tooke the royall Diademe, / And goodly well long time it gouerned, / Till the prowd *Romanes* him disquieted" – continues the cycle of ruination that pervades the narrative (47). Even the history's ostensibly triumphant moments, exemplified by Lud leaving his "endlesse moniments of great good" described by "The ruin'd walls he did reædify / Of *Troynouant*," turns into further examples of ruination. Because Lud's son "betrayd his countrey vnto forreine spoyle" (48), the newly "reædified" Troynovant falls to ruin again, an irony compounded by the arrival of Rome's "endless empire":

> And warlike *Caesar*, tempted with the name
> Of this sweet Island, neuer conquered,
> And enuying the Britons blazed fame,
> (O hideous hunger of dominion) hither came. (47)

There are no endless monuments in *Briton moniments*, only endless attempts to build them. Instead, the promise of re-edifying Troy's ruins in England's permanent Troynovant is always broken, while the retelling of Trojan tales is repeated throughout history in "the middest." Imperial theft – rulers who "tooke the royall Diademe" – occupies the better part of this history, and Spenser would seem to pose Augustine's question in *City of God*: what are kingdoms but great robberies? The absence of an "end" to *Briton moniments* is emphasized when Arthur's tale breaks off – ending in a fragment – with history's ruins mirrored in fiction:

> Succeding There abruptly it did end,
> Without full point, or other Cesure right,
> As if the rest some wicked hand did rend,
> Or th'Authour selfe could not at least attend
> To finish it: that so vntimely breach
> The Prince him selfe halfe seemeth to offend,
> Yet secret pleasure did offence empeach,
> And wonder of antiquitie long stopt his speach. (68)

This "untimely breach" might refer to England's prophetic history, as some have argued, as *Briton moniments* ends at precisely the point when Arthur would himself appear in the future. Yet this fragmentation also underscores how his history book depicts the ruins of imperial history. The pun on Arthur's name – "th'Authour selfe could not at least attend / To finish it" – draws attention to Spenser's authority. Since Arthur "authorizes" not only Tudor genealogy but also Spenser's fictional history, this wordplay can suggest how Spenser distances himself from the kinds of presumably legitimating fictions portrayed in *Briton moniments*.

Readers are invited to discriminate between Arthur's innocence and Spenser's heightened self-consciousness about matters of history. As Arthur finishes *Briton moniments*, he is "quite rauished with delight" and ironically declares the necessity of remembering England's history:

> Deare countrey, O how dearely deare
> Ought thy remembraunce, and perpetuall band
> Be to thy foster Childe, that from thy hand
> Did commun breath and nouriture receaue?
> How brutish is it not to vnderstand,
> How much to her we owe, that all vs gaue,
> That gaue vnto vs all, what euer good we haue. (69)

This ending speaks to some semi-veiled truths about his history. Arthur rapturously describes the pattern of *Briton moniments*; his "remembraunce" takes the shape of an ongoing cycle of ruination, a "perpetuall band." By calling himself a "foster Childe," Arthur also implies the fictiveness of his own British genealogy. "How brutish is it not to vnderstand," Arthur asks, and with this punning question Spenser suggests the necessity of recognizing Trojan tales as such.

Far from repairing the ruins of *Briton moniments*, Guyon's *Antiquitie of Faerie* offers a brief providential history of the Tudors' rise to power that provides, writ small, a mirror for Arthur's history. Spenser echoes Paridell in his partial recollection of this history:

> *Guyon* all this while his booke did read,
> Ne yet has ended: for it was a great
> And ample volume, that doth far excead
> My leasure, so long leaues here to repeat. (70)

As in Paridell's version of English history in Book 3, the mythic origins and ideal end of Faerie Land are recalled, omitting what happens in "the middest" of history and leaving readers to fill in the blank. The genealogy of Faerie Land begins with a theft – Prometheus stealing fire from the gods to animate his creation, "A man, of many partes from beasts deriued," named Elfe, "the first authour of all Elfin kind" (70, 71). Wandering in the "gardins of *Adonis*," Elfe encounters

> A goodly creature, whom he deemd in mind
> To be no earthly wight, but either Spright,
> Or Angell, th'authour of all woman kind;
> Therefore a *Fay* he her according hight. (71)

This allegory of "elf fashioning" reveals and conceals the method by which divine genealogies are made: the "linage right" from which "all *Faeryes* spring" (71). "The first author of all Elfin kind" is a fiction found, ironically, in the "gardins of *Adonis*," where "eterne" is found in "mutabilitie" rather than in permanence.[49]

The same pattern of ruination found in Arthur's history is transformed into faerie fiction:

> Of these a mighty people shortly grew,
> And puissaunt kings, which all the world warrayd,
> And to them selues all Nations did subdew:
> The first and eldest, which that scepter swayd,
> Was *Elfin*; him all *India* obayd,
> And all that now *America* men call:
> Next him was noble *Elfinan*, who layd
> *Cleopolis* foundation first of all:
> But *Elfiline* enclosd it with a golden wall. (72)

"Enclosd . . . with a golden wall," Cleopolis' very structure suggests that the desire for gold motivates history, even in this fiction. And as in Arthur's history, imperial houses are built by genealogical fictions. Crowns are spoils, and genealogies are produced to justify these thefts:

> His sonne was *Elfinell*, who ouercame
> The wicked *Gobbelines* in bloudy field:
> But *Elfant* was of most renowmed fame,
> Who all of Christall did *Panthea* build. (73)

Rather than recalling what happens in "the middest," just how "all their Ofspring, in their dew descents" accomplished similar feats, the story concludes with a Paridell-like gesture to the history he forgets:

That were too long their infinite contents
Here to record, ne much materiall:
Yet should they be most famous moniments
. . . both of martiall,
And ciuill rule to kings and states imperial. (74)

Like Paridell's recollection of Troy, Guyon's history elides what happens in the middle in favour of its end. Despite this truncation, the *Antiquitie of Faerie* conveys Spenser's point about the architecture of English history. "With rich spoiles and famous victorie," these elves "Did high aduance the crowne of *Faery*" (75). Cleopolis receives a shape, an order that Spenser's "methode" makes visible, showing how he fashions the matter of England's history.

The *Antiquitie of Faerie* seems to draw to a prophetic conclusion with the assertion, "yet remains his wide memoriall . . . / Long mayst thou *Glorian* liue, in glory and great powre" (76). Yet in a manner similar to Arthur's history, Guyon's account of Faerie Land breaks off in "the middest." "Beguild thus with delight of nouelties," Arthur and Guyon are so rapt by "those antiquities" that "how the time was fled, they quite forgate," and their host must interject herself to bring them to an abrupt close: "gentle Alma, seeing it so late, / Perforce their studies broke" (77). This narrative break would seem to defer endlessly the possibility of endless empire, highlighting the ongoing process of ruin and recollection. If reading "those antiquities" allows Arthur and Guyon to "forgate" the passing of time, this episode paradoxically allows readers to remember those same "antiquities." This fragmentation draws attention to Spenser's "methode[s]" as both "Poet historical" and "Historiographer," reminding readers of the ongoing ruins of time. The circularity of Faerie Land's history suggests less a progression between Arthur's and Guyon's varied versions of English history than their re-enactment.

Highlighting the similarities between Arthur's and Guyon's versions of history, exposing the fictions foundational to England's empire, Spenser reveals how he constructs Faerie Land as an allegory of English history, at once veiling and unveiling the despoliation that builds and destroys empires. Spenser's competing versions of history are found not between Arthur's and Guyon's histories but within both of them: he both offers England a Trojan tale of history and demonstrates that empire is built not upon the ruins of Troy but rather the ruins of conquest made in the name of Troy and its gods. Whereas Augustine makes his personal story into an allegory of Christian history, Spenser makes the art of memory into an allegory of England's history, indeed into an allegory of how stories of history are constructed. Spenser contrasts the "methodes" of the "Poet historical" and the "Historiographer" in order to highlight the inextricability of story from history in the midst of time, the place of "historical fictions" not only within historiography but also throughout history itself as it is recollected and re-enacted in both writing and the world.

The End of English History

Merlin's prophecy for Britomart marks the chronological end and narrative centre of England's three-part history. Spenser thus ends this history in "the middest" in Book 3, canto 3, leading readers in a circle that mirrors the pattern of history itself. Particularly in his proem here, Spenser suggests why he "orders" English history in this way. Calling love the source from "whence spring all noble deeds and neuer dying fame" (3.3.1), he explains:

> Well did Antiquitie a God thee deeme,
> That ouer mortall minds hast so great might,
> To order them, as best to thee doth seeme,
> And all their actions to direct aright. (2)

His emphasis on "order" can remind readers of the "Letter to Raleigh" and the difference between how the "Poet historical" and the "Historiographer" order their narratives. On the one hand, Spenser justifies "The fatall purpose of diuine foresight" as a source of inspiration:

> Thou doest effect in destined descents,
> Through deepe impression of thy secret might,
> And stirredst vp th'Heroes high intents,
> Which the late world admyres for wondrous moniments. (2)

Believing such fictions inspires those who "through the earth haue spred their liuing prayse, / That fame in trompe of gold eternally displayes" (3):

> Begin then, O my dearest sacred Dame,
> Daughter of *Phœbus* and of *Memorie*,

That doest ennoble with immortall name
The warlike Worthies, from antiquitie,
In thy great volume of Eternitie:
Begin, O *Clio*, and recount from hence
My glorious Soueraines goodly auncestrie,
Till that by dew degrees and long protense,
Though haue it lastly brought vnto her Excellence. (4)

Even as he invokes the muse "Clio" and the "great volume of Eternitie," Spenser announces the fiction of this history, analogous to the "God" that "Antiquitie" fashioned to inspire men to great deeds. But Spenser also implies that this "good auncestrie" is less a "long protense" than a pretence, a justification for exalting the Tudors' "immortall name." Indeed, he praises fictions of love in ways that echo Augustine's complaint about the use of such political fictions.

By portraying "Love" as an antique fiction and by investing it with the power to "order" earthly existence, Spenser suggests the role that desire plays in English history, essentially making Varro's argument (through Augustine) about why rulers fashion divine genealogies: because it inspires greatness. But Spenser slyly implies that such fictions have the opposite effect. When he refers to "the fatall purpose of diuine foresight" he suggests a double meaning, both fated and deadly. And when Spenser refers to Elizabeth's "effect in destined descents," he indicates both her long lineage and its inevitable decline. Genealogical fictions intended to "sirredst vp th'Heroes high intents," to be the impetus for building England's empire, instead produce what "the late world admyres for wondrous moniments." While Elizabeth's self-fashioned persona as the Virgin Queen means that she will likely reproduce Tudor genealogy only through fiction and myth, Spenser hints at a similar fate for Britomart's future offspring. In a sense, Elizabeth's and Britomart's identities merge to propagate England's genealogical and prophetic fictions. By beginning his proem with the fictional god of "Love" and ending with an invocation of the muse of historical fiction – "Begin, O *Clio*, and recount... / My glorious Soueraines goodly auncestrie" – Spenser underscores this mingling of fact and fiction.

Merlin's prophecies for the end of English history, Britomart's future progeny who will foster the growth of England's empire, seem to contrast sharply with "the middest" history of Book 2, which depicts England's many kingdoms as thefts and England's divine genealogy as theological fiction. Yet crucially, Merlin portrays England's empire as built upon gold: Britomart and Artegall will "rayse / Most famous fruits of matrimonial bowre," who "through the earth haue spred their liuing prayse, / That fame in trompe of gold eternally displayes" (3). As always, the word "gold" connotes Spenser's suspicion about England's formation into an "empire without end"; this empire's fame will be "rayse[d]" – as with the opening of *Briton moniments*, implying both construction and destruction – upon gold that represents, as the phrase "trompe of gold eternally displays" suggests, the triumphs or spoils of war. The relation between despoiling gold and history, particularly as represented in Mammon's Cave, finds an important parallel in Merlin's cave, "a deepe delue, farre from the vew of day" (7). Merlin's cave, like Mammon's, represents a fallen Golden Age where labour conquers all:

> And there such ghastly noise of yron chaines,
> And brasen Caudrons thou shalt rombling heare,
> Which thousand sprights with long enduring paines
> Doe tosse . . .
> When too huge toile and labour them constraines. (9)

His prophecies of history are described like the gold, the spoils, which Mammon hoards underground, "As if ought in this world in secret store / Were from him hidden, or vnknowne of yore" (15). And like Mammon, Merlin reveals a "fatall end" to history.

Merlin appears to illuminate what Britomart "cannot read aright": her future (16). "With that the Prophet still awhile did stay . . . Most noble Virgin, that by fatall lore / Hast learn'd to loue," Spenser writes (21). Calling Britomart's destiny "fatall lore" highlights the violence inscribed in Merlin's prophecy of a Trojan genealogy for England. In his "charmed looking glas" (24), Merlin sees a "famous Progenie" that "shall spring" from Britomart's womb and "out of the auncient *Troian* blood," which will repair the future: "decayed kingdoms shall amend: / The feeble Britons, broken with long warre, / They shall vpreare" (22–3). Asserting that it is "the streight course of heauenly destiny, / Led with eternall prouidence" that guides Britomart's fortune, Merlin commands her to "by all dew meanes thy destiny fulfill" (24). In one sense, his prophecy is clear – Britomart must marry Artegall – but in other ways it is deeply ambiguous:

> The man whom heauens haue ordaynd to bee
> The spouse of *Britomart*, is *Arthegall*:

He wonneth in the land of *Fayeree*,
Yet is no *Fary* borne, ne sib at all
To Elfes, but sprong of seed terrestriall,
And whilome by false *Faries* stolne away,
Whiles yet in infant cradle he did crall;
Ne other to himselfe is knowne this day,
But that he by an Elfe was gotten of a *Fay*. (26)

Spenser questions the basis of this union by raising questions about Artegall's origins. This changeling narrative repeats, significantly, the same one told to Redcross Knight: both Artegall and Redcross are of "sprong of seed terrestriall" who were "stolne away" and thus are (like Arthur) adopted sons of faeries. Merlin's prophecies undermine the very premise of Britomart's divine progeny, for her offspring with Arthegall will then share in this dubious origin. His lament for the violence that marks England's "royall seed, the antique *Troian* blood" (42) prompts Britomart to ask if this marks the end of England's memory: "But shall their name for euer be defast, / And quite from of the earth their memory be rast?" (43). Without saying so directly, Merlin predicts continued war, "Th'vsurped crowne . . . / the spoile of the countrey conquered" that forms England's cyclical pattern of ruin and repair, seemingly without end (47).

Merlin ultimately prophesies an equally ambiguous end for both Britomart and Britannia, for he describes a "sacred Peace" that is followed by war, military triumph that produces ruin:

So shall the Briton bloud their crowne againe reclame.

Thenceforth eternall vnion shall be made
Betweene the nations different afore,
And sacred Peace shall louingly perswade
The warlike minds, to learne her goodly lore,
And ciuile armes to exercise no more:
Then shall a royall virgin raine, which shall
Stretch her white rod ouer the *Belgicke* shore,
And the great Castle smite so sore with all,
That it shall make him shake, and shortly learne to fall. (48–9)

This "royall virgin" – Elizabeth as Britomart – triumphs over Roman Catholic Spain in Belgium, the "*Belgicke* shore," extending her protection to Protestant causes. Readers might interpret this image of "the great Castle" in ruins (or shortly thereafter, as it will "shortly learne to fall") as revelatory: as a religious crusade whose violence is directed toward a holy end. Yet the contradictions in Merlin's conclusions, the movement from peace to war rather than vice versa, cannot be ignored, as it charts a trajectory from repair in "eternal vnion" to ruination with a religious justification, the presence of the "Royall Virgin." This "eternall vnion" results not in "sacred Peace" but rather in England's continued ruin. Merlin's prophecy thus underscores the violence by which empire is achieved, serving as a reminder of the history in Alma's Castle. To "learn to fall" is the continuation of ruin in history, a story that Spenser continues in Book 5.

Merlin's final vision, a "ghastly spectacle," suggests that Gloriana's Cleopolis will follow this course of history until its final end (50). Yet Spenser also suggests that Britomart misinterprets Merlin's unspoken vision of England's future; instead, he concludes simply by stating, "yet the end is not" (50). The historical narrative ends with "faire" Britomart putting on her armour and preparing to do battle for England's destiny. Disguising herself as a man to fight for England's eternal glory, she dresses "with all the other ornaments" that enable warriors to achieve "endless moniments / Of . . . successe and gladfull victory"; "therein appareled / Well as she might" (59), Britomart follows the path to her kingdom, to the end that she desires:

> Ne rested they, till that to Faery lond
> They came, as *Merlin* them directed late:
> Where meeting with this *Redcrosse* knight, she fond
> Of diuerse things discourses to dilate,
> But most of *Arthegall*, and his estate.
> At last their wayes so fell, that they mote part:
> Then each to other well affectionate,
> Friendship professed with vnfained hart,
> The *Redcrosse* knight diuerst, but forth rode *Britomart*. (62)

In a chiasmus, Britomart and Redcross pass one another, never to meet again in Faerie Land. This final appearance of Redcross matters since, unlike Britomart, he has presumably learned the difference between the two cities, Cleopolis and the New Jerusalem. Britomart only knows what she believes to be her and Cleopolis' intertwined destinies, which she recalls later in Book 3.

The Faerie Queene ends England's history by pointing readers in a circle and thereby confirming history's circularity. Returning to the chronological beginning and narrative end 'of England's tripartite history in Book 3, readers can see Britomart and Paridell's parodic reproduction of Trojan tales as more than just harmless fiction. Despite their confident assertions of the "end" of England's history, a new Troynovant and all that it implies, Spenser reminds readers of the problem with their re-enactment. Book 3, in short, does not promise a clear providential end for England, as Spenser reminds readers who may have forgotten the history given in Book 2. Paridell apologizes to Britomart for having forgotten about Brutus' arrival in England, recalling that "aged *Mnemon*" has recorded this tale for posterity. "If I remember right," Paridell says, from "the antique *Troian* stocke, there grew / Another plant . . . that same *Brute*" (3.9.47–8), offering in the stanzas that follow a condensed version of Book 2's history. But like E.K. in *The Shepheardes Calender*, Paridell does not "remember right"; he forgets what happens in the "the middest" of England's history. Readers, however, may remember at this prompting. Paridell concludes by asserting that "His worke great *Troynouant*" is

> renowmed far away,
> That who from East to West will endlong seeke,
> Cannot two fairer Cities find this day,
> Except *Cleopolis*; so I heard say
> Old *Mnemon*. (51)

The history of Book 2 interjected thus serves as a reminder of history's ongoing ruin, pointing less to the end of history than to its circularity: the end they will "endlong seeke" until time's end. And it is the work of the "Historiographer," "old *Mnemon*" – using the "methode" of the "Poet historical" – to recollect the ruins of the past while helping readers remember what they might otherwise forget: that is, how history is fashioned.

Chapter Five

Golden Age Recollections: Prehistory as Present in Spenser's Later Work

In the midst of the two halves of *The Faerie Queene*, Spenser interrupts his presumably Virgilian career path by publishing the *Complaints* and *Colin Clouts Come Home Againe*. These so-called minor poems have been relatively ignored, for reasons that seem clear. Difficult to define generically, frustrating to understand aesthetically, and nearly impossible to comprehend politically (given their blunt, impolitic criticisms of Queen Elizabeth and her court), these works seem to take Spenser's poetry in a new direction. From another perspective, however, they remind readers of the very path that Spenser has followed all along. As I will argue in this chapter, Spenser returns to the art of memory in his later work in order to redefine his position both poetically and politically. He remembers his earlier uses of locational memory in the context of a new location, Ireland – or rather, a new duality of location: England *and* Ireland.

Colin Clouts Come Home Again, which recalls Spenser's journey with Walter Raleigh to England in order to present the first part of *The Faerie Queene* to Elizabeth, establishes this paradoxical change of place.[1] Appropriately for a poem about returning, *Colin Clout* begins with a reminder, as "The shepheards boy (best knowen by that name) / That after *Tityrus* first sung his lay," sings again for a grateful pastoral audience, "Who all the while with greedie listfull eares, / Did stand astonisht at his curious skill."[2] Readers seem to return here to the familiar world of *The Shepheardes Calender*. But clearly much has changed: the home to which Colin now returns is Ireland, not England. In addition to the question of *where* the poem takes place is the problem of *when*. The Colin Clout of the *Calender*, after all, has given up on poetry and love, refuses to sing for the shepherd community, and by the end of the poem he appears to be dying. Although *Colin Clout* has often been

understood as following upon the events of the *Calender*, it seems unlikely that the same Colin who bids adieu to Rosalind and the world
would later reappear as a happy-go-lucky poet, returned to "Laies of
sweet love" (3). Instead, Spenser paradoxically suggests that *this* Colin
is the earlier incarnation, the figure that the shepherds will later recall in the *Calender*.[3] In short, Colin presumably "first sung his lay" in
this new location. With this jarring change, Spenser indirectly reminds
readers of another time and place when the shepherds formed their collective memory of Colin's Golden Age of love and poetry.

Colin Clout thus both precedes *The Shepheardes Calender* and follows
upon it. The later poem might best be understood as a reconstruction of
the past in a new location – a location, readers learn, that lies in ruins.
As Colin recalls for the shepherds, the impetus for his journey was his
heartbreak over Rosalind, as the "shepheard of the Ocean" (Raleigh)
hears Colin's song about love gone wrong and invites him to sing for
Elizabeth (66). Yet Colin substitutes another story for that of Rosalind:
a tale of rivers centred on the tragic love of the river Mulla, daughter of
the mountain Mole. Punishing his daughter for her secret marriage to
the river Bregog, Mole "In great avenge did roll downe from his hill /
Huge mightie stones" to break the path of the river, now "scattred all
to nought, / And lost among those rocks into him rold, / Did lose his
name" (149–55). This story of love leading to metaphorical and literal
ruin displaces Rosalind's love and its associations of Roma and Amor
onto another landscape, one that holds strong personal connections for
Spenser. Colin describes how Mulla in her winding journey from Mole

> giveth name unto that auncient Cittie,
> Which *Kilnemullah* cleped is of old:
> Whose ragged ruines breede great ruth and pittie,
> To travailers, which it from far behold. (112–15)

The ruins of "Kilnemullah" or Buttevant point to Spenser's nearby ruined castle, Kilcolman – a private castle of the soul, as it were, or perhaps
an analogue to Verlame, pitied by "travailers." This bleak landscape
moves readers well away from pastoral conventions, and when Colin
describes his visit to Cynthia's court (with language recycled from the
June eclogue) readers can see that his home bears little resemblance to
the pleasant place of *The Shepheardes Calender*:

> For there all happie peace and plenteous store
> Conspire in one to make contented blisse:

No wayling there nor wretchednesse is heard,
No bloodie issues nor no leprosies,
No griesly famine, nor no raging sweard,
No nightly bodrags, nor no hue and cries;
The shepheards there abroad may safely lie,
On hills and downes, withouten dread or daunger:
No ravenous wolves the good mans hope destroy,
Nor outlawes fell affray the forest raunger. (310–19)

Readers learn about Colin's home only indirectly: the place of "wretch-edness," "bloodie issues," "griesly famine," and "ranging seard," where shepheards live in "dread" and "daunger" contrasts with Cynthia's realm, the ideal location for poetry that represents "home" in *The Shep-heardes Calender*.[4] If the *Calender* suggests that to write about "home" is to write about England, *Colin Clout* instead implies that "home" means to write about England *and* Ireland. With this transition, the *Calender*'s discussion of place becomes contradictory and problematic; and with "home" now double, Spenser's literary loyalties divide between these places.

With this crucial change of location, Spenser returns to the subject of locational memory. In this chapter, I explore how and why the art of memory persists as a principal concern and "methode" for Spenser, de-spite the dramatic changes in the overall tone and direction of his epic. I begin with this brief discussion of *Colin Clout* (to which I will return later) because the poem both recalls the first half of Spenser's epic and forms a preamble to the second half. In a sense, *Colin Clout* functions as another "Letter to Raleigh," restating and emending Spenser's in-tentions for *The Faerie Queene* and reframing his career. Specifically, it interrogates the myth of Colin's Golden Age of love and poetry in *The Shepheardes Calender*, as framed in *Aprill* and *June*. If the *Calender* sug-gests a teleological view of Colin's decline as a lover and a poet – a fall from an idealized time of love for Eliza and poetic potency to a ruinous love of Rosalind and poetic impotency, which only a return to this time and place could repair – *Colin Clout* suggests a far different trajectory. In this regard, Spenser follows the art of memory's path in the writing of Plato, Cicero, and Augustine. Although it might seem that the *locus amoenus*, the sweet spot, is the ideal place for recollection, this place is itself only recollected in retrospect from within a space of ruin, whether literal (as in Cicero's dialogue amid the ruins of Rome), or figurative (as in Plato's dialogues, all of which are framed by the death of Socrates), or theological (within time, the City of God must be recollected within the ruins of the City of Man). Like Plato remembering Socrates, or Cicero his interlocutors, Spenser recollects this early, significant moment in Colin's life and career after the "death of the author." At once posthumous and proleptic, *Colin Clout* returns to edification as a process of building and learning through an origin tale about Colin Clout's divided, doubled "home."

The impossible fact of Spenser's two homes figures as the central problematic in the second half of *The Faerie Queene*, where Spenser repositions Ireland as the symbolic edifice in which to recall both England and its empire. As this chapter will explore in detail, the second half of *The Faerie Queene* returns again and again to the myths that surround the Golden Age – most notably in Book 5's proem, a lament for the present state of the world and England.[5] "For from the golden age, that first was named, / It's now at earst become a stonie one," Spenser writes, asking that none "blame" him "if in discipline / Of Vertue and of ciuill vses lore, / I doe not forme them to the common line / Of present dayes."[6] But past is clearly present in Spenser's exploration of Golden Age tales and their uses in civil lore: specifically, Elizabeth's self-fashioned myth as Astraea, the virgin who returns a Golden Age to England. This focus on the myths of the Golden Age counterpoints the focus on the Trojan tales in the first half of *The Faerie Queene*, especially in terms of their political significance. The political links between Trojan tales and Golden Age myths largely derive from Virgil's *Fourth Eclogue* read in conjunction with the *Aeneid*; in this work, Virgil revises Hesiod's chronology, such that Italy becomes the once and future location of earthly perfection, the location where a paradise lost will be forever regained. Against this fantasy of eternal repair, Spenser recalls revisionary Golden Age stories associated with the art of memory, tales that locate ruin as the true point of historical origin and return. And in this tradition, Spenser's poetry explores the *topos* of the *locus amoenus* as an originary myth, treating it less as lost perfection than as a catalyst for new tales of edification from ruin – as a past recollected for the present not permanently but perpetually.

While the earlier chapters of this book were largely built around the intertexual influence of other authors, from Plato to Sidney, the principal intertexts in this chapter are mostly Spenser's own. The second half of *The Faerie Queene* proceeds through a mechanism of reminders, not only of stories and characters (resumed after a gap of six years) but also of thematic and philosophical structures. In particular, I will argue, the Castle of Alma remains the lynchpin for the poem as a whole, albeit in new terms, as Spenser continues his investigation of stories about history (including his own) in new contexts. The second half of *The Faerie Queene* is concerned with reassessing, and perhaps redressing, Spenser's career-long engagement with the art of memory. In this regard, Spenser's later writing is part of an attempt to reconcile his use of locational memory with the locational problems in which he found himself. Working with these issues, Spenser substantially reforms the apparatus of his writing – using, I argue, the dialogic structure that defines his method as both "Poet historical" and "Historiographer."

In keeping with Spenser's revisionary history of his own poetic persona after his death, this chapter begins with a discussion of two posthumously published works, the *Mutabilitie Cantos* and *A Viewe of the Present State of Ireland*, before turning to Books 5, 4, and 6 of *The Faerie Queene*. The *Viewe* and (to a lesser extent) the *Mutabilitie Cantos* have profoundly influenced Spenser's reception as both an English poet and a colonialist in Ireland. Both these works make explicit the Irish context in which they are staged, both are concerned (in different ways) with understanding Ireland as a place of ruin and recollection, and both works provide a necessary frame for Book 5's complex engagement with issues of justice. The dialogic structures clearly at work in these two pieces helps to show how these techniques manifest themselves in the second half of *The Faerie Queene*. Moreover, both works explore similar matters as well as methods: the fact of mutability, ruin, and recollection, within time and within stories of history. The chapter then turns to a second triad of texts: *Colin Clouts Come Home Again* and Books 4 and and 6 of *The Faerie Queene*. Just as Spenser presents England's history out of order in the first half of *The Faerie Queene*, I take these books out of order to highlight Spenser's method as both "Poet historical" and "Historiographer": the art of memory. Just as Book 2 operates as the crux of the 1590 *Faerie Queene*, representing the historiography that undermines the imperial fictions of Books 1 and 3, so the Golden Age fictions of Book 5 present particular problems that the adjoining Books 4 and 6 address in related ways. While the historiography in the first half of *The Faerie Queene* focuses on the Trojan legend, the historiography of the second half represents the beginning and the end of history through Golden Age tales. In a sense, Books 2 and 3 add up to Book 5, which reposition earlier Trojan tales, if only retrospectively, in "the middest" of time. However, Spenser refuses to locate a Golden Age origin or end, suggesting instead that this story finds continual reiteration: as in Books 2 and 3, where the re-enactment of Trojan stories throughout history undermines the fiction of "empire withoute end," so the Golden Age fictions of Book 5 repeat throughout history both in, and as, current events. Jove's war with the Titans and Giants, his seizure of power by force and use of force to put down rebels, is the prehistory continually re-enacted in the present tense. This pattern of ongoing ruin, as I argue, becomes Spenser's indirect way to "tell the truth" about fictions of power and divinity, the means by which he reveals how Golden Age fictions play a part in the ongoing story of English history.

Legends of the Fall in the *Mutabilitie Cantos*

The presumably unfinished *Faerie Queene* ends with a fragment, called the *Mutabilitie Cantos*. For a poet who finds "eterne in mutabilitie" (3.6.47), the incomplete and textually unstable Book 7 – ironically named the "Legend of Constancie" – appropriately encapsulates Spenser's career-long preoccupation with ruins recollected in (and as) both story and history. Indeed, what might appear a hasty addendum instead reflects the order of the poem as a whole, as outlined in the "Letter to Raleigh," and with similar misdirection.[7] Beginning in "the middest" with Canto 6, a reminder of Spenser's "methode" of organizing his historical fictions, the *Mutabilitie Cantos* end *The Faerie Queene* at the beginning, with a prehistory to Faerie Land that nevertheless speaks to the present state of England and Ireland. Here as before, a poetic representation of historiography emblematizes Spenser's art of recollecting the ruins of the past, used to tell certain truths about historical fictions, including his own. Like the histories in the Castle of Alma, Mutability's history unveils its own allegory, revealing the self-made gods of empire as thinly disguised humans who, while promising immortality, only perpetuate ruin. This case puts Jove and Elizabeth on trial, as sovereigns who rule under the "Legend of Constancie." Comparing Mutability to one of Elizabeth's personae, Cynthia, Spenser writes:

> So likewise did this *Titanesse* aspire,
> Rule and dominion to her selfe to gaine;
> That as a Goddesse, men might her admire,
> And heauenly honours yield, as to them twaine. (7.6.4)

This desire to be worshipped as a goddess finds a parallel in the heading description to Canto 6:

> Proud *Change* (not pleasd, in mortall things,
> beneath the Moone, to raigne)

Pretends, as well of Gods, as Men,
to be the Soueraine.

This can be read at least two ways: Mutability "pretends, as well" (also) to "be the Soueraine," or Mutability "pretends, as well" (as convincingly) as Gods and humans pretend to be "Soueraine."

Read either way, this potential conflation or confusion of "Gods, as Men" suggests the book's central point: Mutability's divinity is no more or less false than the so-called gods in this history. Mutability argues as much when she stakes a claim to the heavens by right of her birth: "My heritage, *Iove's* self cannot deny, / From my great Grandsire *Titan*, vnto mee, / Deriv'd by dew descent" (7.7.16). This genealogical claim can be read ironically: in immortal families, after all, there can be no "dew descent," only violent usurpation. Nevertheless, she asks Nature

> by what right
> These gods do claime the worlds whole souerainty;
> And that is onely dew vnto thy might
> Arrogate to themselues ambitiously:
> As for the gods own principality,
> Which *Ioue* vsurpes vniustly. (16)

As Mutability sees it, Jove arrogates power to himself by fashioning himself as a god. And in this regard Jove's empire closely resembles earthly empires, built upon conquest and perpetually threatened by ruin, though represented as eternal. Complaining about what "*Ioue*" and "his fellow gods . . . faine to be," Mutability argues that "heauen and earth I both alike do deeme" (15) – a charge of mutability that Jove's own defence of his power ironically would seem to support.

Although readers learn from the outset that Jove triumphantly preserves his "heavens Empire" from the mutinous Mutability, Spenser nevertheless implies that Mutability *de facto* reigns over earth. In so doing, he begins by denying the end of Trojan narratives: "empire without end" and, with it, the promise of a returned Golden Age of peace and justice. Crucially, Spenser has Mutability herself replace any overt mythology of a once or future Golden Age:

> For, she the face of earthly things so changed,
> That all which Nature had establisht first
> In good estate, and in meet order ranged,

She did pervert, and all their statutes burst:
And all the worlds faire frame (which none yet durst
Of Gods or men to alter or misguide)
She alter'd quite, and made them all accurst
That God had blest: and did at first prouide
In that still happy state for euer to abide. (7.6.5)

Through Mutability, Spenser tacitly rejects the Golden Age myths of both Virgil and Ovid.[8] Rather than attributing either the beginning or the end of the Golden Age to Jove's rebellion against his Father Time, Saturn, Spenser instead blames (or credits) Mutability for ruining an original order of things unrelated to these gods. In a related sense, he also undermines any Golden Age myth by making the pagan goddess Nature responsible for creating "that still happy state" that was "for euer to abide," while also implying that the "God" who "blest" this original perfection is not Jove but the "God of Sabbaoth" (7.8.2). This slippage from classical to Christian contexts points in two directions at once: toward fortifying Jove's authority allegorically, and toward a clear distinction between true and false divinity. With this condensed origin story, Spenser questions the truth of his own history, bringing the heavens down to earth.

Gordon Teskey, describing the violence implicit in Christian allegories of pagan gods, writes that "it is . . . memory that Mutability attempts to awaken in those whom she addresses," memory which "can subvert the anaesthetic contemplation of power."[9] Recognizing the "genealogical struggle" inscribed in these cantos means recognizing what Spenser conspicuously omits here, Teskey further argues: "The most important structural fact about *Mutabilitie* is the absence of that particular political myth," the "Trojan genealogy of the Tudors."[10] In a sense, though, Spenser reminds readers of this implicit subtext throughout the cantos by framing them as historiography, and in ways that return to the "methode" and matter found in Alma's Castle of the Soul. Reading Mutability's case as ancient history creates, in effect, competing verdicts: one that commemorates Tudor power, and one that challenges the fictions on which it is based.

This divided view relates to Spenser's dual role as both "Poet historical" and "Historiographer." He first condemns Mutability, asking

What man that sees the euer-whirling wheele
Of *Change*, the which all mortall things doth sway,

> But that therby doth find, and plainly feele,
> How *MVTABILITY* in them doth play
> Her cruell sports, to many mens decay? (7.6.1)

But then he turns to the facts of the case, in order that "all may better yet appear," offering a less biased view: "I will rehearse that whylome I heard say / How she at first her selfe began to reare, / Gainst all the Gods" (1). Spenser's phrasing echoes Paridell's partial memory of "that whilome I heard tell / From aged *Mnemon*" (3.9.47), reminding readers of what he only half-remembers of England's history. In Book 3's account of English settlement, Paridell describes how Brute and his company were driven

> Into an Island spatious and brode . . .
> Fruitfull of all thinges fit for liuing foode,
> But wholy wast, and void of peoples trode,
> Saue an huge nation of the Geaunts broode. (49)

Through "wearie wars and labours long," these monstrous giants "Were ouerthrowne, and layd on th'earth full cold / Which quaked vnder their so hideous masse," as Paridell concludes, gesturing to the history in the Castle of Alma: "A famous history to been enrold / In euerlasting moniments of brasse, / That all the antique Worthies merits far did passe" (50). Paridell's description of Eumnestes' archive, of course, is only partly correct but entirely suggestive: in place of a Golden Age history, readers find monuments of brass, "euerlasting" despite being written on decaying books and scrolls that are constantly falling to ruin and constantly being recollected. Spenser prefaces his account of Mutability's rebellion with a similarly ironized view of history:

> But first, here falleth fittest to vnfold
> Her antique race and linage ancient,
> As I have found it registred of old,
> In *Faery* Land mongst records permanent. (7.6.2)

These earthly "records" can be no more "permanent" than the history of mutability that they recount. By reminding readers of Eumnestes' chamber, Spenser again returns to the location where England's history is written and read, and to the place of ruin in his "methode" of recollecting stories about history. Here as in Alma's Castle, Spenser distinguishes between historians and poets only to suggest how their roles intertwine in matters of memory. These reminders also gesture to the fact that here, as in Alma's Castle, Spenser again remembers the larger history that Paridell forgets or omits: the wars with giants that make up a foundational fiction for Faerie Land and England.

Questions about the truth of history resound throughout the *Mutabilitie Cantos*. As a "Poet historical" Spenser conventionally calls upon Clio, the muse of history, asking,

> who but thou alone,
> That art yborne of heauen and heauenly Sire,
> Can tell things doen in heauen so long ygone;
> So farre past memory of man that may be knowne. (7.7.2)

In the context of Mutability's challenge to Jove, however, the guidance of the daughter of that "heauenly Sire" seems unlikely to be impartial. "Who . . . can tell thinges done in heauen so long ygone" might also be understood as: who can tell the truth about the origins of power? The case ostensibly concerns Mutability's rebellion, her failed forceful "attempt" to gain "the empire of the heauens hight," and her rightful conviction in Nature's court of law (7.6.7). But ultimately, Spenser implies that this case concerns authority, divine and human, and the right to write history. To the victors go the spoils, it seems, including the power to determine historical truth. Though the verdict against Mutability represents the official history of "Faery Land," Spenser intimates that this history serves to justify the rule of gods whose power derives from Jove's victorious war in the heavens with rebels such as Mutability. As this history reveals, Jove's usurpation of power was never complete or permanent, but it enabled him to rewrite history.

Even before Mutability takes the stand, her rule over the heavens (as well as earth) is established, as Jove recalls how history has repeated itself in the ongoing wars over the heavens:

> Ye may remember since th'Earths cursed seed
> Sought to assaile the heauens eternall towers,
> And to vs all exceeding feare did breed:
> But how we then defeated all their deed,
> Yee all doe knowe, and them destroied quite;
> Yet not so quite, but that there did succeed
> An off-spring of their bloud, which did alite
> Vpon the fruitfull earth, which doth vs yet despite. (7.6.20)

Jove's recollections evoke competing versions of history that challenge his own fiction. He remembers wars with rebellious giants but conveniently overlooks his own rebellion against the Titans.[11] Such wars repeat previous wars in a kind of infinite regress of origins. By conflating different stories or histories of power struggles in the heavens, Jove inadvertently acknowledges an instability that might well confirm Mutability's rule over the gods who she presumably must serve. In the broadest terms, Jove's recurring wars with giants might be understood as a mythological opposition between fictions of permanence and histories of ruin and re-edification. Past is prologue as the attempt to kill giants instead reproduces them, and this persistence epitomizes the reality of earthly history, the transience of all states and structures of power.

Spenser may not defend mutability per se, but like Mutability he challenges myths of immortality through reminders of the past. The better part of the cantos recounts Mutability's accusations against Jove: that his legend of constancy belies his own continual metamorphoses and mutability. Many of her attacks hit the mark – so much so that who and what is on trial shifts, placing Jovian permanence on the defensive. Mutability argues against the legitimacy of Jove's power, both its origin and its present state; he usurped the throne, she contends, by virtue of "might makes right," yet claimed it as the work of fate. In a dramatic moment in the trial, she dares Jove to reveal his genealogy, goading him to confess that he is no more than human:

> But you *Dan Ioue*, that only constant are,
> And King of all the rest . . .
> Where were ye borne? some say in *Crete* by name,
> Others in *Thebes*, and others other-where. (7.7.53)

Drawing attention to the competing tales of Jove's origin, Spenser demonstrates the unreliability of historiography. For Mutability, the differing accounts of Jove's birthplace point to a fictionalized origin that undermines his claim to being the only "constant" force in the heavens. "Then are ye mortall borne, and thrall to me," she infers, "Vnlesse the kingdome of the sky yee make / Immortall, and vnchangeable to bee" – an apt charge, considering that Jove promises "empire without end" (54).

Despite her undeniably forceful arguments, Mutability loses her case. Nature decides in favour of Jove and his favourites – but not for the reasons we might expect:

But time shall come that all shall changed bee,
And from thenceforth, none no more change shall see.
So was the *Titaness* put down and whist,
And *Ioue* confirm'd in his imperiall see. (7.7.59)

Spenser offers readers a divided view on this verdict. On the one hand, Jove is "confirm'd in his imperiall see" and Mutability put in her place; on the other hand, Nature's final judgment about time and change ultimately reflects less upon the god Jove than the "God of Sabbaoth." In effect, Spenser denies Mutability's absolute authority, recasting this pagan drama as a divine comedy, pointedly in *The Faerie Queene*'s last, "unperfite" Canto 8, the number symbolizing infinity:

Then gin I thinke on that which Nature sayd,
Of that same time when nor more *Change* shall be,
But stedfast rest of all things firmly stayd
Vpon the pillours of Eternity,
That is contrayr to *Mutabilitie*:
For, all that moveth, doth in *Change* delight:
But thence-forth all shall rest eternally
With Him that is the God of Sabbaoth hight:
O that great Sabbaoth God, graunt me that Sabaoths sight. (7.8.2)

As Spenser reflects on Nature's verdict, he affirms that Mutability indeed rules over earth rather than heaven. But he also suggests a clear distinction between Jove's endless empire and that of the "God of Sabbaoth," as well as between time and its end, when "all things [will be] firmly stayd, / Vpon the pillours of Eternity." More than an anodyne hope for apocalypse eventually, this reflects upon the perpetual prophecies of "empire without end" in Faerie Land and England.

The *Mutabilitie Cantos* ultimately appeals its own verdict, undermining the divinity of Jove and the myth of England's renewed Golden Age. Here as throughout his writing, Spenser locates "eterne in mutabilitie," for now, anyway (3.6.47). The *Mutabilitie Cantos* echo Ovid's sceptical response to Virgil's poetry by recalling the *Metamorphoses*, particularly its portrait of a fallen Golden Age; by representing a thoroughly suspect and destructive deity in Jove; by suggesting that empires rise and fall with cyclical regularity; and by intimating that literary immortality is only as durable as Rome's stones.[12] Readers might even conclude that Spenser has, all along, fashioned himself not as England's new Virgil but rather as England's new Ovid. Such a juxtaposition, however, would be too simple a formulation of Spenser's complex response to, and reception of, historical fictions. Just as Spenser imitates Virgil while refusing to represent his poetry as Christian allegory, so Spenser imitates Ovid while refusing his poetry the status of divine revelation. Spenser's ending to *The Faerie Queene* punctuates this point by viewing history – its beginning and end – not according to imperial gods (Jove or Elizabeth) but according to the "God of Sabbaoth." Such an assertion of alpha and omega paradoxically locates readers in the here and now: in "the middest" of time. Throughout this trial, readers have seen that Jove must defend himself and can barely do so, while Mutability seeks justice but cannot find it. This alone reveals the earthbound nature of Nature's court. Spenser suggests, in other words, that perfect justice cannot exist in the middle of time, but more importantly that what passes for justice represents the self-justifying fictions of imperial power, both Elizabeth's and Jove's. The effect of re-enacting such stories of history, or taking royal historiography as the "light of truth," ultimately matters in a more concrete sense.

Mutability's charges against Jove are also clearly directed against Tudor legitimacy. Among the gods she accuses of fraudulent divinity is Cynthia – the goddess of the moon, "*Ioues* dearest darling" – and one of Elizabeth's many avatars (3.7.50). As with Jove, Mutability brings Cynthia down to earth by questioning her place of origin – "she was bred and nurst / On *Cynthus* hill, whence she her name did take: / Then is she mortall borne" – and her legend of constancy:

> Besides, her face and countenance euery day
> We changed see, and sundry forms partake,
> Now hornd, now round, now bright and gray:
> So that *as changefull as the Moone* men vse to say. (50)

Attacking Cynthia's realm in Canto 6, Mutability attempts to displace her: "Thence, to the Circle of the Moone she clambe, / Where *Cynthia* raignes in euerlasting glory" (7.6.8). Coveting her "bright shining palace" – which, "vp-held / With thousand Crystall pillors of huge hight," strongly recalls Chaucer's palace of Fame – Mutability attempts to force Cynthia from her "souerainge seat / By highest *Jove* assign'd" (8, 10, 12). The apparent opposition between Mutability and Cynthia repeatedly and pointedly reflects upon Elizabeth as a mutable monarch.[13]

This case thus creates a double view of history. Jove's victory over Mutability can stand for Elizabeth's own triumph against time, but Mutability's charges against Jove as a self-made god who pretends to permanence are clearly levelled against the Tudors too. These cases are related by a profound questioning of authority: Jove and Elizabeth stand accused of illegitimate rule, of falsifying their own divinity, and with ruinous consequences. Yet neither Jovian permanence nor worldly Mutability will reign forever – the reason why recognizing fictions of permanence matter. Spenser draws readers' attention from prehistory to the present tense by locating Mutability's trial in a place close to home. As Spenser explains, Nature held her court at "the highest hights / Of *Arlo-hill* (Who knowes not *Arlo-hill?*)," at the top of "my old father *Mole*" (7.6.36), the mountain of which Colin Clout sings at the start of *Colin Clout* and the location of Spenser's ruined castle, Kilcolman. Ireland is thus made the place of these trials of empire, and the location for recollecting ruins of both the past and the present.

The interrogation of Elizabeth-as-Cynthia also takes place in the context of Ireland. Interrupting his narrative of Mutability, Spenser introduces a poetic digression – a Golden Age origin story that tells the history of how Arlo Hill "was made the most unpleasant, and most ill" (37) of Ireland's hills through the spite of Cynthia:

> Whylome, when *IRELAND* florished in fame
> Of wealths and goodnesse, far aboue the rest
> Of all that beare the *British* Islands name,
> The Gods then vs'd (for pleasure and for rest)
> Oft to resort there-to, when seem'd them best:
> But none of all there-in more pleasure found,
> Then *Cynthia*; that is soueraine Queene profest
> Of woods and forrests, which therein abound,
> Sprinkled with wholsom waters, more then most on ground. (38)

Cynthia – usually called Diana here – once loved Arlo Hill best, resorting there "with all her Nymphes enranged on a rowe" to bathe in the "sweet streames" of the river Molanna, "sister vnto *Mulla*" who "That Shepheard *Colin* dearely did condole" (39–42). The satyr Faunus persuades Molanna to reveal when he might find Diana bathing:

> There *Faunus* saw that pleased much his eye,
> And made his hart to tickle in his brest,
> That for great ioy of some-what he did spy,
> He could him not containe in silent rest;
> But breaking forth in laughter, loud profest
> His foolish thought. (46)

In anger at this violation, Diana re-enacts the tale of Actaeon, dressing Faunus in deerskin and hunting him with hounds. Greater torment is visited on Molanna, who like the river in *Colin Clout* is filled with stones. But Diana inflicts the greatest punishment on Ireland. She abandons her "delicious brooke" and on the "faire forrests about *Arlo*" lays a "curse":

> To weet, that Wolues, where she was wont to space,
> Should harbour'd be, and all those Woods deface,
> And Thieues should rob and spoile that Coast around.
> Since which, those Woods, and all that goodly Chase,
> Doth to this day with Wolues and Thieues abound:
> Which too-too true that lands in-dwellers since haue found. (54–5)

If the story of Mutability might be framed as myth told as history, this digression reads as history told as myth; Spenser acknowledges the shift by asking Calliope to take the place of Clio as his muse. And yet the relation between these two modes resists any simple division. In mythic terms – indeed, in terms of Elizabeth's own mythology as a goddess in various guises – Ireland's ruin appears as a Golden Age fall: Diana and the nymphs depart, giving the country over to wolves and thieves, and leaving the place disenchanted. Even as myth, however, this embedded episode clearly speaks to history: like Diana's revealed body, Spenser reveals Elizabeth's mythic body as merely human. Elizabeth's power depends upon her virgin divinity and inaccessibility, and thus the naked truth of her humanity undermines her divine, sovereign body. To see the truth of divinity, and to *laugh* at it, cuts to the heart of the virgin queen's myth.[14] The *Mutabilitie Cantos* explicitly challenge Jovian and Tudor divinity, not only in the mythic histories of a fallen Troy or Golden Age, but also in the lived histories of England and Ireland. The ruined landscape of Ireland, abandoned by something resembling a vindictive maker, forms the necessary location for Mutability's trial of empire and Spenser's recollection of it, here as in *A Viewe of the Present State of Ireland*.

"No certain truth": A Long View of *A Viewe of the Present State of Ireland*

In *A Viewe of the Present State of Ireland*, as in the Castle of Alma and the Faerie Land archives of the *Mutabilitie Cantos*, Spenser plays the part of historiographer in order to expose the fictions that make up history.

He returns to his "methode" as a poet, the art of memory, I will argue, in order to recollect the matter of Ireland and as an implicit challenge to Tudor myths of power and empire. I read the *Viewe* as a work that explores the boundaries between story and history in ways that run parallel to Spenser's fiction. Although the scholarship of the past few decades has revealed Ireland's central importance to Spenser's life and work, the *Viewe* has often been seen as history that reveals *the* truth about Spenser's fiction: as built upon the brutal subjugation, even ruin, of Ireland.[15] Along with scholars who have demonstrated that this divided dialogue speaks to Spenser's ambivalence about Tudor power, counterpointed in his poetry, I question the truths of the *Viewe* by exploring its own vexed representation of truth.[16] The *Viewe* is not simply a fiction, yet in common with *The Faerie Queene*'s historical fictions it offers an illusion of verisimilitude that paradoxically challenges its own authority and provokes questions about the truths it tells. The original title in the Stationer's Register, *A Viewe of the Present State of Ireland*, situates the text's focus on the "present" rather than the "past" – a claim that the work itself repeatedly undercuts. When Matthew Lownes first published the *Viewe* in 1634, he changed the title simply to "State," partly because it no longer represented the present state of Ireland but also to emphasize its historiographic tenor. I retain the "Present" tense partly to underscore its inherent irony: though framed by current events, this work examines the relation of story and history in ways that speak to Spenser's poetic historiography; and similarly, the *Viewe* creates a dialogue with more than one (or "a") view of Ireland. The dialogue's interlocutors, Irenius and Eudoxus, may ultimately agree, yet the *Viewe* offers other views that speak directly through neither interlocutor.

The *Viewe* reverses the itinerary of *Colin Clouts Come Home Again*: whereas Colin recalls his journey to England from (and in) Ireland, Irenius journeys to England where he recalls his experience in (and of) Ireland. The topic of Ireland's ruin introduces the dialogue between Irenius and Eudoxus, who opens the discussion by observing, "So have I heard it often wished . . . that all that land were a sea-poole; which kinde of speech, is the manner rather of desperate men farre driven, to wish the utter ruine of that which they cannot redress."[17] The desire to "redress" or repair the "ruine" of Ireland takes centre stage in the *Viewe*, as Irenius seeks nothing less than "eternall peace," and means to achieve this end by violently reforming Irish society and culture (133). As Irenius opines, "it is all in vain that they now strive and endeavour by faire meanes and peaceable plotts to redresse the same, without first remmoving all those inconveniences, and new framing (as it were) in the forge, all that is worne out of fashion: For all other meanes will be but as lost labour, by patching up one hole to make many" (91). Better, Irenius thinks, to rebuild Ireland from the ground up. Yet his echo of E.K.'s complaint about reforming the English language – his diatribe against poets who "patched up the holes with peces and rags of other languages" (*The Shepheardes Calender*, 16) – gestures to a crucial contradiction: as a document ostensibly dedicated to erasing Ireland's past, much of the *Viewe* is devoted to remembering Ireland. Against Irenius' desire to wipe the slate clean stands his and Eudoxus' fascination with Ireland's history and culture. Such recollection might be dismissed as the nostalgia of the colonialist for the culture that he ruins, yet the *Viewe* does more than remember what it would destroy: it also ruins many of the historical truths upon which Britain's empire was built.

Spenser constructs the *Viewe* as a dialogue that stages his ambivalence, self-consciously exploring the tensions between humanism and colonialism by reminding readers of his method as "Poet historical" and "Historiographer" in *The Faerie Queene* and throughout his career. This dialogue alternates between two opposed positions: one that seeks to impose a permanent peace upon Ireland through radical and violent means, and one that seeks to remember an Ireland whose ongoing ruin marks the mutability inherent in all political structures. However, this dialogue takes place less between its two interlocutors than within the space of Irenius' shifting and contradictory views, and ultimately between the text and its audience. To appreciate this double perspective entails seeing the *Viewe* in light of Spenser's literary engagement with stories about history, through which he explores the difficulty of "telling the truth," in every sense. One of Spenser's principal techniques, as critics have long observed, involves the creation of characters that articulate positions that are then critiqued by the larger dynamics of the work. Of course, the opinions expressed in the *Viewe* must correlate to Spenser's views in some regard. Given the context of the work, and what we know of the dominant opinions of the New English community he inhabited, we must assume that he shares at least some common ground with Irenius. Yet it would not be ridiculous to imagine some significant distance between Spenser and Irenius. If Irenius is not another E.K., created to get things wrong (or half right), he nevertheless expresses views to which Spenser appears only partially, intermittently committed.[18]

Scholars such as Andrew Hadfield have argued for the importance of Machiavelli's example in the *Viewe*, suggesting it might be read as a proto-republican document.[19] I will offer a somewhat different reading of Machiavelli here by focusing on his rhetorical use of opposing, even incommensurate arguments. As Victoria Kahn has demonstrated, the Raleigh school typically drew upon Machiavelli's writing in order to express contradictory, countervailing truths, to explore issues related to resisting royal power.[20] To call the *Viewe* "Machiavellian," then, is to draw attention not only to its views but also to its method, its complex dynamic of argumentation relating to discourses of power. In his conclusion, Irenius cites Machiavelli to support the increased power of local governors: "And this (I remember) is worthily observed by Machiavel in his discourses upon Livie, where he commendeth the manner of the Romans government, in giving absolute power to their Councellors and Governours, which if they abused, they should afterwards dearely answere" (160). This citation refers not to the text it appears to resemble, *The Prince*, but to the pro-republican *Discourses*, a longer and more complex commentary on Livy's Roman history. This work provides what could be a rebuttal to Irenius' desire for an "eternal peace," a permanent repair of Ireland: "as all human things are kept in a perpetual movement, and can never remain stable," Machiavelli writes, so "states naturally either rise or decline."[21] Such observations on the mutability of all political structures seem at odds with Irenius' plan to repair Ireland – but such contradictions are perhaps the point.

This Machiavellian moment may remind readers of what Irenius only half-remembers about the *Discourses*, especially as it relates to *The Prince*. Machiavelli speaks in two voices in these works, particularly when he reveals truths about truth. Writing in the *Discourses* about the dangers of advising, he weighs the problem of how "those who counsel princes and republics are placed between two dangers": on the one hand, "if they not advise what seems to them for the good of the republic or the prince, regardless of the consequences to themselves, then they fail of their duty"; on the other hand, "if they do advise it, then it is at the risk of their position and their lives; for all men are blind in this, that they judge of good and evil counsels only by the result" (514). This balanced – or, from another angle, duplicitous – approach to truth informs all of the *Discourses*. Machiavelli's views invariably appear as double, but perhaps less in order to deceive than in order to acknowledge the irreducible complexity of truth. Ruin forms a central *topos* here as in *The Prince*: because all states change state, Machiavelli's only absolute truth about power is mutability itself, visible in the rise and ruin of states, and he thus repeatedly draws vivid analogies between the "fall" of states and the "fall" of people. Characteristically, he gives two opposed examples of the perils of not changing with the times: Pietro Soderini "in all his actions governed by humanity and patience" but wrought "his own and his country's ruin" when new "circumstances arose," while Pope Julius II acted with "impetuosity and passion" fitting for his time and place, but "would unquestionably have been ruined" had times "changed so that different counsels would have been required" (442). Successful government depends upon decorum in the broadest sense: adapting to new times and places, to change itself.

But how can an advisor tell such multiple truths, given a ruler's desire for one truth? "In reflecting as to the means for avoiding this dilemma of either disgrace or danger," Machiavelli writes, "I see no other course than to take things moderately, and not to undertake to advocate any enterprise with too much zeal; but to give one's advice calmly and modestly" (514). He maintains this indirect method of speaking truth to power, even when times change. Although the *Discourses* reveals Machiavelli's preference for the greater freedom of republican rule, he only suggests this truth indirectly and ironically in *The Prince*: by advocating overzealously for Medici conquest, "so that Italy may at length find her liberator" (98). Remarking on "the love with which he would be received in all those provinces which have suffered under these foreign invasions," Machiavelli asks, "What doors would be closed against him? What people would refuse him obedience? What envy could oppose him? What Italian would withhold allegiance?" (98). Machiavelli's over-zealous argument for complete power takes the form of obvious flattery, a performance that he underscores by ending with a recollection of Petrarch:

> Valour against fell wrath
> Will take up arms; and be the combat quickly sped!
> For, sure, the ancient worth,
> That in Italians stirs the heart, is not yet dead. (98)

Petrarch's poetry, notoriously divided in its political views on Rome, can remind readers of the *Discourses* and Machiavelli's own divided views on the Medici conquest of Italy. Through such fictions, moreover, Machiavelli may gesture to the necessity of using "lies" to reveal "truths."

The irony of such a zealous cry for conquest may be lost on Irenius but probably not on Spenser: when ruin threatens a state, anything that salvages it – even political fictions – may be better than nothing.

The ambiguity and ambivalence of Machiavelli's works, so alive to the danger of speaking truths to power, provide Spenser the freedom to voice complex, contradictory truths in his divided *Viewe of . . . Ireland*. Although on one level the *Viewe* offers a specific answer to the problems of Ireland, on another level it stages a debate about problems for which Spenser provides no simple solutions. The dialogue's structure mostly functions in this dual way, presenting truths that the dialogue then undercuts; indeed, the dialogue ultimately suggests the absence of any certain truth about history or politics – except, perhaps, that of constant change. Irenius' identification with a clichéd idea of absolute Machiavellian power suggests a central irony in the *Viewe*: Machiavelli represents the truth of history as the fact of mutability, and through this Spenser tacitly counters fantasies of imperial permanence. At the same time, such *realpolitik* may point to Elizabeth as a feminine "Machiavelle": an endlessly mutable monarch whose vacillating support for the "Old" and "New" English in Ireland manifests a ruthless will to triangulate in the service of power, which Spenser suggests leaves both states unstable.

Spenser aligns his own method of telling truths slant with Machiavelli's. The *Viewe* begins with what appears to be an oblique reference to the "Letter to Raleigh," as Eudoxus exhorts Irenius to remember Ireland by expanding upon his topics: "Tell them then, I pray you, in the same order that you have now rehearsed them; for there can be no better method then this which the very matter itselfe offereth" (12). This phrasing, the emphasis on "method" and "order," recalls Spenser's distinction between the "methode" of the "Poet historical" and "Historiographer": while "an Historiographer discourseth of affayres orderly as they were donne, accounting as well the times as the actions," he explains, "a Poet thrusteth into the middest, euen where it most concerneth him, and there recoursing to the thinges forepaste, and diuining of thinges to come, maketh a pleasing Analysis of all."[22] In the *Viewe* as in *The Faerie Queene*, Spenser belies this distinction by linking the method and matter of both "Historiographer" and "Poet historical," and for a similar end: to reveal how stories pervade history. In a sense, Irenius plays both parts, recollecting Ireland's history out of order in a way that recalls *The Faerie Queene*'s three-part history of England: he begins in "the middest" by recollecting Ireland's medieval chronicles, particularly Gerald of Wales' twelfth-century propaganda-cum-history of Ireland. As another Eumnestes, Irenius offers a "remembrance" of Ireland; and Eudoxus, as another Anamnestes, in turn prompts Irenius' memory of matters, reminding him of their place in the discussion (84).

"As for the point where you left," Eudoxus typically promises, "I will not forget afterwards to call you back again thereunto" (26). These reminders, though intended to suggest a linear discourse on Ireland's reformation, instead create a circular narrative of ruin.

Matter finds a mirror in method, for ruin forms the principal matter of Irenius' initial and repeated historical digressions. Spurred by Eudoxus' surprise that parts of Ireland have never been fully conquered, Irenius turns from common law to a history of Ireland since the conquest by Henry II. Yet Irenius clearly forgets as much as he remembers. He mistakenly attributes Irish rebellion to the departure of English lords during the War of the Roses (it happened earlier), during which time the rebel "Oneale . . . gathering unto him all the reliques of the discontented Irish, eftsoones surprised the said castle of Clare, burnt, and spoyled all the English there dwelling . . . breaking downe all the holds and fortresses of the English, defacing and utterly subverting all corporate townes, that were not strongly walled" (24). "So in short space" they "cleane wyped out many great townes," including Buttevant (Spenser's home region) and "many others, whose names I cannot remember," Irenius says, "and of some of which there is now no memory nor signe remaining" (25) – a complaint that echoes Verlame in *The Ruines of Time*.[23] Irenius then suggests a still earlier origin of Ireland's ruin, when the Scottish "Edward le Bruce spoyled and burnt all the olde English Pale inhabitants, and sacked and rased all citties and corporate townes . . . Thus was all that goodly countrey utterly wasted" (26–7). This disorderly order suggests parallels and repetitions that Irenius may not intend: beginning and ending this brief history with "O'Neal" rebellions, he implies an historical pattern of ruin that would undercut both his ostensible present-day focus and his ambition to achieve a permanent state.

A particularly complex example of Irenius' historical illustrations opening up counter-arguments to his ostensible purposes occurs almost at the end of the discourse, in the context of Henry VIII. Hearing of the "ruines . . . in many places to be seene, and of some no signe at all remaining," Eudoxus asks why the corporate towns were never "reedified" (158). Irenius replies:

After their desolation, they were begged by gentlemen of the Kings, under colour to repaire them, and gather the poore reliques of the people againe together, of whom having obtained them, they were so farre from reedifying of them, as that by all means they have endeavoured to keepe them waste, least that, being repaired, their charters might be renewed, and

their Burgesses restored to their lands, which they had now in their possession; much like as in those old monuments of abbeyes, and religious
houses, we see them likewise use to doe: For which cause it is judged that
King Henry the Eight bestowed them upon them, conceiving that thereby
they should never bee able to rise again. (158)

With its multiple, contradictory implications, Irenius' comparison is
perfectly Machiavellian.[24] On one level, he praises Henry for prosecut-
ing his ambitions in such a brutally effective manner, applauding the
king for preventing the Catholic Church from ever reforming itself in
England. On another level, the passage suggests a deeply cynical and
disillusioning view of Tudor power, founded not on the symbolic ruins
of Troy but the ruins they created in England by dismantling the Roman
Catholic Church and redistributing its wealth. This also implies a critique of Tudor benevolence toward the Old English, who still (Irenius
suggests) use royal prerogative to keep Ireland in ruins. The passage
twists in upon itself: an apparently deliberate policy of ruin appears
"much like" inadvertent neglect, just as ruined English monasteries resemble decayed Irish charter towns. The charter cities serve as a key
topos of ruin throughout the *Viewe*, and these places appear Machiavellian in two ways: their re-edification could either increase or decrease
crown control of Ireland, and reveal either Spenser's monarchial or republican views. These ruined cities form locations for recollecting histories of England and Ireland that run parallel throughout this work. A
double reading of these towns, either as locations for increased English
power or freer forms of Irish government, speaks to the double perspective of the *Viewe*.

Irenius has far from total recall, despite his professed authority, and
a tension between remembering and forgetting, story and history, fact
and fiction, pervades the dialogue. Eudoxus repeatedly challenges Irenius' authority, albeit through delighted incredulity. Responding to
Irenius' history of Irish origins, he exclaims, "neither indeede would I
have thought, that any such antiquities could have been avouched for
the Irish, that maketh me the more to long to see some other of your
observations, which you have gathered out of that country, and have
earst promised to put forth" (53). Such paroxysms of enthusiasm tend
to paint Irenius as an unwitting "Poet historical" rather than a truth-
telling "Historiographer." "Surely Iren.," Eudoxus marvels, "I would
have thought had bin impossible to have bin spoken of times so remote,
and customes so ancient," though "delight whereof I was all that while

as it were intranced, and carried so farre from my selfe" trumps scepticism for him, if not for readers (64). The question of whether Irenius'
recollections should be interpreted as fact or fiction, story or history,
is one that the dialogue takes up slyly yet insistently. Irenius attacks
the Irish bards as "tending for the most part to the hurt of the English,
or maintenance of their owne lewde libertie"; and he draws a sharp
line between Irish bards and English poets, whose "writings doe labour
to better the manners of men" (76, 75). Eudoxus agrees with Irenius
about the lies of the bards but uses them to criticizes his historiographic
integrity: "You doe very boldly Iren. adventure upon the histories of
auncient times, and leane too confidently on those Irish Chronicles
which are most fabulous and forged, in that out of them you dare take
in hand to lay open the originall of such a nation so antique, as that no
monument remaines of her beginning and first inhabiting; especially
having been in those times without letters, but only bare traditions
of times and remembrances of Bardes, which use to forge and falsifie
every thing as they list, to please or displease any man" (46). Irenius
acknowledges the point, but argues for the appropriateness of his historical "method." Supplementing the "remembrances of Bardes" with
his own (dubious) research, effecting a "comparison of times, likewise
of manners and customes . . . and many other like circumstances," he
produces "a likelihood of truth" and "a probability of things, which I
leave to your judgement to believe or refuse" (46). The fictions of the
Irish bards thus find important if paradoxical use:[25]

> Besides, the Bardes and Irish Chroniclers themselves, though through
> desire of pleasing perhapes too much, and ignorances of arts, and purer
> learning, they have clauded the truth of those lines; yet there appeares
> among them some reliques of the true antiquitie, though disguised, which
> a well eyed man may happily discover . . . Those Bardes indeed, Caesar
> writeth, delivered no certaine truth of any thing, neither is there any cer-
> taine hold to be taken of any antiquity which is received by tradition, since
> all men be lyars, and many lye when they wil; yet for the antiquities of the
> written Chronicles of Ireland, give me leave to say something, not to justi-
> fie them, but to show that some of them might say truth. (46–7)

Irenius seems to speak as a sceptical historiographer or antiquarian
here, committed to an empirical idea of the truth of history, however
imperfectly it might be approached. Such a judicious and learned
investigator would be able to unearth "some reliques of the true

antiquitie" amid the chaff of myth and fiction. Nevertheless, this passage might well be read against the grain, pointing not only to the inevitable mingling of fact and fiction in history (explored in all of Spenser's work) but also the perpetuation of fictions of power both *within* and *as* history.

Irenius' invitation "to believe or refuse" his history may well be addressed to the "well eyed" reader as well as Eudoxus, who can discern the dialogue's competing views of history. As postcolonial critics have noted, stories of Irish origins underpin Irenius' political scaffolding. Linking the Irish to ancient and warlike Scythians, Irenius intends to demonstrate the ongoing savageness of the Irish, and the desperate need for the English to bring them into modern times – to "civilize" the Irish "other." All the same, readers may have good reasons to question the truth of his history. Indeed, Irenius never sounds more like E.K. in one of his wilder glosses than when he demonstrates Irish descent from Scythians through common cultural rites and ceremonies, including swearing by the sword, bewailing their dead, and, to clinch the matter, this: "Also the Scythians said, That they were once a yeare turned into wolves, and so it is written of the Irish: Though Master Camden in a better sense doth suppose it was a disease, called Lycanthropia, so named of the wolfe. And yet some of the Irish doe use to make the wolfe their gossip" (64). In asserting confraternity between the Irish and wolves, Irenius appears to be a long way from the rational "well eyed" man who can discern truth from fiction. Camden's greater scepticism (in *Britannia*, one of Spenser's principal sources) provides a useful counterpoint. "As for the story of some Irish (and those too, such as would be thought credable,) that certain men in these parts are every year converted into wolves," Camden argues here, " 'tis without question fabulous, unless perhaps through excess of melancholy, they may be affected with that distemper which the Physicians call [lycanthropia], which will make them fancy and imagine themselves thus transformed."[26] Nevertheless, Irenius cites Camden as a source that confirms this legend.

Without saying so, Irenius builds much of his history upon the medieval historian Gerald of Wales, whose history of Ireland, dedicated to Henry II, provides rationales for Irish conquest. In its imitation of Gerald and the repetition of his cultural fictions of the Irish, the *Viewe* thereby evinces a fascinating double structure: Irenius discusses the problems that the historiographer faces in his search for the truth, but himself demonstrates these difficulties in his narrative. At one point,

Irenius mocks Richard Stanihurst, an Old English historian, for not being able to "see the light of the truth" in his repetition of fanciful tales of Irish origins (60), and yet (as the Variorum editors note with some bewilderment) this work is principally a redaction of Gerald's history. In *Britannia*, Camden recalls the crux of Gerald's Irish history, albeit with dry scepticism: "I shall neither meddle with the truth nor falsity of these relations; antiquity must be allowed some liberty in such things" (966). Nevertheless, Camden also works from Gerald as a key historical source for cataloguing the so-called barbarous customs of the Irish, and for a similar end: to support English monarchial rule over Ireland. Thus, even as Irenius mocks older Irish histories, he participates in the reiteration of their myths throughout history and historiography.[27] Irenius' inconsistencies suggest how the *Viewe* can be seen in a productive tension with *The Faerie Queene*. Irenius rejects the tale of Brutus, drawn from Geoffrey of Monmouth, as an improbable fiction, along with the stories of battles against giants similar to those that populate *The Faerie Queene* (45). However, he happily accepts the accuracy of Geoffrey's history when they support England's claims to Ireland: "Finally it appeareth by good record yet extant, that King Arthur, and before him Gurgunt, had all that iland under their allegiance and subjection" (52). Given Spenser's sceptical treatment of Arthur in the "Letter to Raleigh," Irenius' acceptance undercuts his claims to objectivity, suggesting the arbitrariness of his truths.[28]

The extent to which Irenius speaks for Spenser, or represents the "truth" of his views, needs to be understood in the context of the *Viewe*'s divided perspective: on the one hand, a plan to "repair" Ireland through violent reformation, and, on the other hand, a history of "ruin" that undermines this plot. Through Irenius, in short, Spenser both promotes England's complete subjugation of Ireland and exposes the ideological illegitimacy, indeed the impossibility, of this same endeavour. Both perspectives represent Spenser's views but neither, finally, tells *the* truth about Spenser – except, perhaps, as irreconcilable parts of a whole. Like a holographic image, the *Viewe* shifts positions depending on how readers see it. Certainly, though, this dialogue represents not one view but rather competing views, resulting in opposed stories of history: an official narrative of imperial repair and a counter-narrative of continued ruin. Spenser uses the same method to reveal a counter-intuitive truth, that story and history, poetry and politics, meet in ruin as a place for recollection and continued dialogue. Exploring the relation between the ideal and the real, the past and the present, Spenser's *Viewe* suggests that poetry speaks to politics not from the twin towers of immortality and empire but within the inevitable ruin and re-edification of both, and as stories that shape our view of history: memory, both individual and collective. With the *Viewe*, Spenser lays bare for all to see his own dividedness between poetry and politics, his double role as participant in and witness of history, his place in Ireland's ruin and recollection. Palinode and propaganda sit side by side in this painful, extraordinary work.

Memory could be said to be the enemy of Irenius' plans, based on an idea of a blank slate – or a blank state, one might say – and scholars such as Stephen Greenblatt have argued that Irenius wants to erase such memorial persistence in order to fashion the Irish as model subjects: his cultural inventory doubles as a death list. Yet counter-narratives can also be heard. Irenius depends on the storehouse of cultural memory in his investigations of Irish history, and adjoining his view of Ireland as a place of perpetual ruination is a view of Ireland as a place of enduring memory. Moving the conversation from laws to customs, Eudoxus observes that Irenius has, within this topic, "a faire champian layde open unto you, in which you may at large stretch out your discourse into many sweete remembrances of antiquities, from whence it seemeth that the customes of that nation proceeded" (43). Irenius insists that such "sweet remembrances" do not suit the present discourse. "Heere onely it shall suffise to touch such customes of the Irish as seeme offensive and repugnant to the good government of the realme," suggesting they might find a more appropriate time and place in which to recall Irish antiquities (43). "I shall the better content my selfe to forbeare my desire now," Eudoxus agrees, "in hope that you will, as you say, some other time more aboundantly satisfie it" (43–4). Yet the dialogue concludes with yet another reminder of this same promise: "I thanke you, Irenaeus, for this your gentle paines; withall not forgetting, now in the shutting up, to put you in minde of that which you have formerly halfe promised, that hereafter when wee shall meete againe, upon the like good occasion, you will declare unto us those your observations, which you have gathered of the antiquities of Ireland" (161). Perhaps Spenser intended to write another pamphlet of Ireland, one that would focus exclusively on recalling its rich history. Yet the presence of these reminders repeatedly signals that the entire story of Ireland is not being presented to us – and this other, unspoken dialogue stands as the tacit counter-argument to the positions put forward by Irenius. In short, what the *Viewe* does not say matters as much as what it does say. From yet another perspective, we might conclude that Spenser *does* embed this counter-narrative of recollection within the *Viewe* itself, the very "remembrances" that form the unstated subtext of the work: the obverse of Irenius' attempts to erase Irish culture could be viewed as Spenser's attempt to recollect them. We might view the closing promise of further discussion of "the antiquities of Ireland" as analogous to Du Bellay's closing exhortation to the *Ruines of Rome*: "Cease not to sound these olde antiquities."[29] As I have suggested, Spenser treats the *Viewe of the Present State of Ireland* as an art of memory, remembering Ireland from within the space of ruin. "Gathering antiquities," whether of people or stones, textual or material artefacts, story or history, marks an important process in the *Viewe*. If despair at the "utter ruine and desolation of that poore realme" (159) and the desire to remember Ireland in the context of Tudor power represents only one facet of this infinitely deceptive work, nevertheless Spenser invites readers to continue remembering Ireland's ruin, and he fashions the *Viewe* as a location where such a conversation can take place.

Legends of Justice: Falling Golden Ages in Book 5

The central conceit of Book 5 of *The Faerie Queene* is that the "Legend of Justice" concerns *then* and not *now*. Spenser's proem positions his subject as ancient history alone, suggesting he recalls Faerie Land's glorious past rather than Britannia's sad present state. "So oft as I with state of present time, / The image of the antique world compare," he laments, "Me seemes the world is runne quite out of square, / From the first point of his appointed sourse, / And being once amisse growest daily wourse and wourse" (5.Proem.1). Considering current events, Spenser complains that "from the golden age, that first was named, / It's now at earst become a stonie one"; and even the supposedly constant heavens have changed, the constellations shifted

> out of their proper places . . .
> And all this world with them amisse doe moue,
> And all his creatures from their course astray,
> Till they arriue at their last ruinous decay. (2, 6)

Spenser claims that his story of "vertue and of ciuill vses lore" will not follow "the common line / Of present days," but will instead conform "to the antique vse, which was of yore," a time "When Iustice was not for most need outhyred, / But simple Truth did rayne, and was of all admyred" (3). Yet Spenser gives readers more than a few reasons to question the "simple Truth" of this claim. Book 5 instead explores "ci-uill vses lore" – political uses of Golden Age myths – then *as* now.[30] By declaring the Golden Age passed, Spenser indirectly denies that Elizabethan England represents a new Golden Age. Still more ironically, Spenser explores the fall of the Golden Age as a story of history that finds continual re-enactment in Britannia's present state.

Equating prehistory with present-day politics, Book 5 examines Elizabeth's self-fashioned myth as Astraea, the virgin who returns the Golden Age to England. Spenser questions "ciuill vses lore" from the very start, alluding to Astraea (as yet unnamed) as the embodiment of ideal justice during the Golden Age, when "Peace vniversall rayn'd mongst men and beasts," and "Iustice sate high ador'd with solemne feasts, / And to all people did diuide her dred beheasts" (9). Yet the context for justice undergoes an important shift as Spenser turns from the past to the present, from Astraea to Queen Elizabeth, who "doest highest sit / In seate of iudgement, in th'Almighties stead" and "Doest to thy people righteous doome a read, / That furthest Nations filles with awfull dread" (11). The movement suggests the difference between Elizabeth as a mythical goddess of justice and Elizabeth as a ruler with human responsibilities. The former speaks to an idea of justice within a fictional framework of the past, while the latter speaks to the imperfect truth of the present, a justice that borrows from "God" but is only, ultimately, on loan. The proem thus gestures ironically to the problem of reading the present through the lens of historical fiction. This opening bears fruit in the rest of Book 5, which challenges Astraea-cum-Elizabeth's right to judge in "place" of God: that is, to "read" the "righteous doome" of the "furthest Nations" that she "filles with awfull dread." Ultimately, this question of reading concerns both Elizabeth's and the reader's ability to "a read" or judge justly, a judgment focusing on "the instrument" of justice in Book 5: Artegall, a flawed hero of justice.

The *Mutabilitie Cantos* and *Viewe of the Present State of Ireland* put into sharp relief the central issue of "The Legend of Justice": how Golden Age tales of empire relate to Tudor power in England, Ireland, and beyond. In a complementary manner to Book 3, where the repetition of Trojan stories throughout history offers a rebuttal to fantasies of endless empire, in Book 5 repeated wars with rebel giants, writ small in the *Mutabilitie Cantos*, tacitly refute the existence of any Golden Age, once or future. Here as there, Jove's wars with the Titans and Giants form a mythic prehistory continually retold in present politics, where the defeat of giants serves as the foundational fiction of empire. *A Viewe of the Present State of Ireland* also clearly speaks to the uneasy fit in Book 5 between the fiction of the Golden Age and the reality of politics, manifested in the repetitive episodes with the giant representations of Europe, particularly Artegall's attempt to save "Irena." Ireland is the crucial location for observing the deleterious place of Golden Age fictions in history and, as in the *Viewe*, Spenser places the present state of Ireland in the larger context of history, with all of its uncertainties, contradictions, and outright fictions.[31] Presenting Elizabeth in "mirrours more than one" (3.Proem.5) – as Astraea, Britomart, Mercilla – Book 5 reflects upon the matter of Tudor justice at home and abroad, and the place of poetry in politics.

Trojan tales and Golden Age fictions conjoin in the Temple of Isis, where Britomart receives another prophecy of her future conjugal union with Artegall, supplementing Merlin's prophecy in Book 3 and implicitly extending the story of England's history to current events. When Britomart falls asleep in the temple at the altar of Isis, she dreams of a crocodile attacking and impregnating her, then giving birth to a lion, and then becoming a ruler like Isis. The dream portends Britomart's future imperial triumph, a priest explains: Britomart-as-Isis will subdue Artegall-as-Osiris, and together they will produce a king of beasts, a lion, symbolic of their future reproduction of a royal Trojan line. This dream closely parallels an episode in Geoffrey of Monmouth's *History of the Kings of Britain*, in which Jove's prophecy of endless empire for Rome is repeated for Britannia. As Brutus dreams in the Temple of Diana, the goddess tells him that "beyond the setting of the sun, past the realms of Gaul, there lies an island in the sea, once occupied by giants. Now it is empty and ready for your folk. Down the years this will prove an abode suited to you and to your people; and for your descendants it will be a second Troy."[32] But as they discover, the giants never left and Brutus must wrest the land from them in bloody battle. Recall that Arthur's history in Book 2, *Briton moniments*, also narrates how Brutus arrives in a land where "a saluage nation dwelt / Of hideous Giants, and halfe beastly men," and "them of their vniust possession depriu'd" (2.10.7, 9). In England's fictions of settlement, as in Jove's own, power depends upon defeating giants.[33]

Yet this episode also challenges such fictions of settlement and the role of giants therein. Spenser indirectly contradicts the priest's interpretation, which inverts that of its primary source, Plutarch's *Isis and Osiris*.

Plutarch reads the crocodile as Typhoeus, the monster created in order to contest Jove's usurpation of the heavens.[34] Jove's wars with the gigantic offspring of Earth finds a crisis point in the battle with Typhoeus, who terrifies the Olympian gods; by defeating Typhoeus, Jove finally consolidates his power, according to Hesiod, forcing the remaining Titans to accept his rule.[35] However, this victory remains incomplete, as Typhoeus has many offspring. Indeed, a number of the giants and monsters of *The Faerie Queene* have genealogies tracing back to Typhoeus: this includes Argante in Book 3; Geryon, the father of Geryoneo, whom Arthur fights in Book 5; and, most notably, the Blatant Beast. Spenser casts further doubts on the priest's interpretation by revealing his belief that wine "is blood, / Euen the bloud of Gyants, which were slaine / By thundring Ioue in the Phelgrean plaine" (5.7.10). Such references to "the bloud of Gyants" connect to Hesiod's *Theogony* and to Ovid's recasting of the Golden Age myth; in *Metamorphoses*, the blood of giants (who attack Jove and Olympus after "Justice, virgin divine, / The last of the immortals, fled away" from earth) begets humans, which then results in further rebellion.[36] In the Temple of Isis, wine alludes to an analogous pattern of repetition:

> The fruitfull vine, whose liquor blouddy red
> Hauing the mindes of men with fury fraught,
> Mote in them stirre vp old rebellious thought,
> To make new warre against the Gods againe. (5.7.11)

The reference to "the Phlegrean plaine" echoes Spenser's introduction to the history read in the Castle of Alma in Book 2, when he wishes for an argument

> worthy of great *Phœbus* rote,
> Whereon the ruines of great *Ossa* hill,
> And triumphes of *Phlegrææan Ioue* he wrote,
> That all the Gods admird his loftie note. (2.10.3)

As these allusions to rebellion suggest, epic tales are built upon the symbolic ruins of Giants, both in writing and in history. The giants represent the "ruines of great *Ossa* hill," both their giant rock pile and the giants' broken bodies, and the foundation for fashioning empires in myth and history. Crucially, the priests' aversion to wine illustrates in compact form the continued threat of the giants; their ruins, ever arising again, never form a stable foundation for empire.

Like the Castle of Alma, the Temple of Isis represents a memorial edifice, and a place in which to recollect the place of stories within history. In this location as well, Spenser indirectly challenges the divinities of Justice, Jove and Astraea, through a comparison with Egyptian myth. Spenser begins by affirming Jove's power to mete out justice, distinguishing what might be understood as Christian allegory from pagan idols of justice. "Nought is on earth more sacred or diuine, / That Gods and men doe equally adore, / Then this same vertue, that doth right define," he asserts, adding that "mortal men" are "rul'd by righteous lore" that comes from

> highest Ioue, who doth true iustice deale
> To his inferiour Gods, and euermore
> Therewith containes his heauenly Common-weale:
> The skill whereof to Princes hearts he doth reueale. (5.7.1)

Yet this "righteous lore," with its dual implications of divinity or merely useful fictions of power, finds an ironic parallel in what follows:

> Well therefore did the antique world invent,
> That Iustice was a God of soueraine grace,
> And altars vnto him, and temples lent,
> And heavenly honours in the highest place;
> Calling him great *Osyris*, of the race
> Of th'old Ægyptian Kings, that whylome were;
> With fayned colours shading a true case:
> For that *Osyris*, whilest he lived here,
> The iustest man alive, and truest did appeare. (2)

The distinction between *then* and *now* collapses from the start of the episode. The "antique world did inuent" gods of justice in Isis and Osiris, and though presumably the modern world has no such need of idols of justice, Spenser's reflections on history speak in the present tense: the survival of pagan gods still depends upon Jove revealing divine truth to his "Princes." Even though Spenser presumably distinguishes Jove from these other "fayned" gods, the episode suggests that they may represent England's own "righteous lore," its own self-fashioned gods whose ministry of justice stands on trial.

Elizabeth-as-Mercilla, as another allegorical figure of justice, finds similarly sceptical treatment. "Some Clarkes doe doubt in their deuicefull art" that mercy is divine, Spenser begins, but affirms that she "first was bred, and borne of heauenly race; / From thence pour'd down on men, by influence of grace" (5.10.1). Yet as the context shifts from heaven to earth, his assertion becomes a question:

> Who then can thee, *Mercilla*, throughly prayse,
> That herein doest all earthly Princes pas?
> What heauenly Muse shall thy great honour rayse
> Vp to the skies, whence first deriu'd it was,
> And now on earth it selfe enlarged has,
> From th'vtmost brinke of the *Armericke* shore,
> Vnto the margent of the *Molucas*?
> Those Nations farre thy iustice doe adore:
> But thine owne people do thy mercy prayse much more. (3)

As with the shift from Astraea to Elizabeth in the proem to Book 5, the change from "heauenly" Mercy to "earthly" Mercilla draws attention to the problem of idolatry in terms of power and justice. Spenser's apostrophe to Mercilla clearly addresses Elizabeth specifically, whose empire has been "enlarged . . . From th'vtmost brinke of the *Armericke* shore, / Vnto the margent of the *Molucas*." Different forms of allegory figure here, moving from allegorical abstraction (Divine Mercy), to allegorical personification in a fictional queen (within the world of the poem Mercilla is an actual ruler), to a real monarch both flattered and flattened by her representation.

Spenser interrogates the issue of idolatry most directly at the trial of Duessa in Mercilla's court, where Spenser effectively places "Mercilla" on trial even as he defends her divine imperative. The spectacle of poetic injustice that greets Artegall and Talus as they enter Mercy's court amply illustrates the episode's duality, and the political imperatives under which Spenser's poetry must operate. Nailed to a post by his tongue is a poet who did "foule blaspheme that Queene for forged guyle, / Both with bold speaches . . . / And with lewd poems"; above his head, his former name of "Bon Font" has been altered by the law: "*bon* that once had written bin, / Was raced out, and *Mal* was now put in. / So now *Malfont* was plainely to be red" (5.9.25–6). This might represent a case of judging between appropriate and inappropriate uses of poetry, but it may also represent arbitrary judgment, witnessed by the palimpsest of the poet himself: "Malfont" written across "Bon Font" recalls the capriciousness in Chaucer's *House of Fame*, where Fame and Slander can defame just as arbitrarily as they can confer the name of fame. Disciplined not unlike Faunus in the Diana episode in the *Muta-bilitie Cantos*, perhaps for similarly blasphemous expression, the poet's execution and display acts as a sort of theatre for worldlings: a warning against any who might dare to speak against, or laugh at, the gods of state. From this perspective, the silenced poet suggests what Spenser cannot or will not say.

This episode may also speak to a change in Spenser's allegorical method, a form of self-censorship visible in Duessa's transformation from a complex figure of multiple truths in Book 1 to a singular, transparent truth whose meaning serves particular political ends in Book 5. Duessa undeniably appears reduced in Mercilla's court – strangely "Una-fied" in meaning. Though sometimes regarded as a marker of Spenser's artistic decline, this representation reflects upon issues of allegory outside poetry's realm: specifically, the "ciuill vses lore" used to fashion political fictions, producing one-to-one allegorical correspondences that belie, even conceal, complex truths of art and life (5.Proem.3). On one level, the Duessa of Book 1 represents an allegory of the Roman Catholic Church whose destruction would signal the final ruin of history and the rise of the City of God; to destroy this Duessa, it would seem, would be to destroy the threat of Roman Catholicism and its false idols. Yet Spenser counters this view by suggesting that scripture, especially the book of Revelation, has been fashioned as present day-allegory (and justification for holy wars) throughout history. In the midst of time, Duessa could just as easily stand for Roman Catholic crusades against the Islamic threat as she could the later Roman Catholic threat to the English Protestant Church. The Duessa of Book 5 shows little of this expansive sense of duplicity: as though bound by a different historical allegory, she represents only Mary, Queen of Scots. Doubleness has been reduced to a single meaning, one that directly applies to current events. Yet Spenser also intimates how this reading does not do justice to the character, suggesting his own use of "allegory" as an unjust possession – as a fiction of authority.

Spenser's flattened allegory of Duessa corresponds with his representation of Malfont. The will to reduce double meaning to a unitary truth deemed acceptable by the monarch-judge results in both the death of Duessa and the public punishment of the poet. Like Malfont's sentence, Duessa's trial is portrayed as political theatre, especially once Ate appears to bear witness against her: "She, glad of spoyle and ruinous decay, / Did her appeach, and to her more disgrace, / The plot of all her practise did display" (5.9.47). Ate's presence – as a figure of deception and duplicity, one "glad of spoyle and ruinous decay" – speaks to a profound hypocrisy at play in this show of mercy: after all, what is Ate but another Duessa? Yet, ironically, Ate bears witness to the impossibility of truly killing Duessa, even allegorically. In one regard, we might see the death of Duessa as spoken by Irenius, as it were: the voice that would banish ambiguity, that would read poetry only for the historical truths that it can truly deliver, that positions the conquest of Ireland in terms of the larger battle between Protestant and Catholic Europe. However, another perspective insinuates itself through this discourse. If the constrained allegory of Duessa (and the European giants that immediately follow this episode in the narrative) allows England to read its history and contemporary events in terms of divine revelation, the story itself operates as a kind of political fiction. The problem of how to "tell the truth" dominates this episode, and ultimately turns on the problem of idolatry. Spenser suggests in Duessa's trial, as he does throughout Book 5, that fashioning political fictions of divinity never ends in justice or peace. Rather, self-justifying stories of history perpetuate wars with giants, and ultimately continue the cycle of ruination that forms the foundation of empire.

Not only metaphorically, Spenser associates ruination with edification – specifically, with Astraea's education of Artegall in "the rules of iustice."[37] Artegall's tutelage begins with his seduction and abduction by Astraea, who "did allure with gifts and speaches milde" the "gentle childe" she happens upon (5.1.6). Teaching him to "weigh both right and wrong / In equal ballance with due recompence," she has him "make experience / Vpon wyld beasts" that "with wrong-full powre" were "oppressing others of their kind" (7). Although this "experience" of killing animals would seem to defeat the ideal of his moderating human or humane justice, it nevertheless accords with the book's allegorical representations of people as other-than-human. The beasts who "feare his awfull sight" prefigure the giants that Artegall will face, conquering them with the same "steely brand" Jove used to defeat generations of giants: "*Chrysaor* that all other swords excelled, / Well prou'd in that same day, when *Ioue* those Gyants quelled" (8–9). Described as "Tempred . . . and garnisht all with gold" (10), the golden sword stands in for a familiar trope: the replacement of the Golden Age with the violent desire for gold. Ironically, the goddess of justice steals this instrument of justice from the king of the gods; it was "gotten by her slight / And earnest search, where it was kept in store / In *Ioues* enternall house" (9). The theft of this sword suggests both Jove's usurpation of power and a certain castration anxiety: his "instrument" should emblematize authority, as a phallic symbol of his victory over his father. Astraea's parting gift to Artegall – her "groome" and axe man, the "yron man" Talus – presents the most serious challenge to this representation of ideal justice. Astraea may have "willed" Talus to "doe what euer thing he did intend," but the vague "he" (referring to either Artegall or Talus) implies a lack of control over this "instrument" (12). Throughout the battles of Book 5, Talus acts violently of his own accord and Artegall can barely restrain him. In place of justice, the iron man uses violence to maintain a Golden Age ideal of Faerie Land. Finally, as with Diana in the *Mutabilitie Cantos*, Astraea abandons Faerie Land, and with similarly disastrous consequences.[38]

The problem of re-enacting Golden Age fictions takes centre stage in the debate between Artegall and the Equality Giant, which parallels debates about change and permanence found in the *Viewe*, in the *Mutabilitie Cantos*, and indeed throughout Spenser's work. The Giant's arguments rehearse Mutability's view of the world – "The sea it selfe doest thou not plainely see / Encroch vppon the land there vnder thee; / And th'earth itself how daily its increast, / By all that dying to it turned be?" (5.2.37) – though he arrives at a radically different conclusion, wanting to return the world to what he imagines was its former pristine state. Artegall, in turn, speaks in terms reminiscent of Eudoxus' response to Irenius' plans for radical reformation. Affirming that all things "created were / In goodly measure, by their Makers might" (35), Artegall looks to the heavenly constellations to prove the point that nothing ever really changes:

> Such heauenly iustice doth among them raine,
> That euery one doe know their certaine bound,
> In which they doe these many yeares remain,
> And mongst them al no change hath yet beene found. (36)

Artegall's emphatic insistence on this point contradicts Spenser's proem to Book 5, which claims that the constellations have shifted "out of their proper places . . . / And all this world with them amisse doe moue" (5.Proem.6). Further, this argument about divine order would seem to fly in the face of Artegall's own experience. After all, why would Astraea abandon earth if "no change hath yet been found" in the world – in fact, why would she need Artegall at all? Artegall's desire to preserve his Golden Age ideal prevents him from noticing that things have changed in Faerie Land. Much like Guyon and Mammon's dialogue about history in Book 2, his debate with the giant proves to be a false one. Although the giant and Artegall represent opposed views – the giant arguing for radical change, Artegall arguing for the status quo – they base their arguments on the same premise. Ironically, it seems, both long for different versions of the Golden Age.[39]

In Artegall's battles with less abstract giants, current events similarly come into contact with ancient myths, repeated and re-enacted. In keeping with the trial of Duessa, these giants – seemingly Duessa's offspring – represent transparent allegories of Roman Catholic foes in the ongoing story of English history. Moreover, these wars appropriately continue where Merlin leaves off in Book 3, with the prophecy that ends the three-part story of English history. The final three cantos re-enact Jove putting down the rebellion of multiple giants – Geryon, Geryoneo, and Grantorto – tales that represent recent wars in Protestant Christendom. As in the *Mutabilitie Cantos*, Ireland becomes a testing ground for fictions of justice and empire. When Artegall vanquishes Grantorto, "the people" respond with unbridled happiness:

> Which when the people round about him saw,
> They shouted all for ioy of his successe,
> Glad to be quit from that proud Tyrants awe,
> Which with strong powre did them long time oppresse. (5.12.24)

Yet this straightforward victory then transposes into the complexities of rule and of truly enacting justice:

> During which time, that he did there remaine,
> His studie was true Iustice how to deale,
> And day and night employ'd his busie paine
> How to reforme that ragged common-weale;
> And that same yron man which could reueale
> All hidden crimes, through all that realme he sent,
> To search out those, that vsd to rob and steale,
> Or did rebell gainst lawfull gouernment:
> On whom he did inflict most grieuous punishment. (26)

In a sense, Artegall only questions Astraea's brand of justice at the end of Book 5, when he tries to discover what "true Iustice" might look like in Ireland, something his education did not prepare him for. This experiment cannot last: "ere he could reforme it thoroughly, / He through occasion called was away, / To Faerie Court" (27). Recalled to stand trial on charges of brutality (likely an allegory of Lord Grey), Artegall's efforts break off like Arthur's history, making a related point. In the context of Ireland, the ideal of Arthur's heroic defeat of Geryoneo and rescue of the Netherlands read like pyrrhic victories. Ireland presents problems that will not easily be solved through battles with giants or indeed through the violent "redresse" offered by Talus (27).

En route to trial, Artegall meets two "Hags," Envy and Detraction, as well as the Blatant Beast, all allegorical symbols (in part, at least) of Grey's defamation at court. In Book 6, the Blatant Beast relates to both Virgil's and Ovid's different representations of Fame – as the monster who tells truth and lies, fact and fiction, story and history, who sees and hears all; who symbolizes the transmission of information, the creation and destruction of reputation.[40] Here, Spenser presents the Blatant Beast as *only* telling lies, "bitter wordes . . . / Most shamefull, most vnrighteous, most vntrew" (42). And yet its accusations against Artegall – that he who "the sword of Iustice lent" is guilty of "reprochfull crueltie, / In guiltlesse blood of many an innocent" (40) – function as part of the counter-narrative of Book 5, speaking against the dominant voices of the narrative. This is not to say that Spenser seeks to undermine Grey specifically; rather it speaks to the double voice and double vision that provides the larger context of justice in Book 5 and in relation to Ireland. Deriving from Typhoeus, born of Jove's wars in heaven, the beast's appearance after the defeat of Grantorto suggests the continuation of history's ruinous cycles.

The *Mutabilitie Cantos* and the *Viewe of the Present State of Ireland* would seem to supply different answers to Artegall's unresolved attempt to reform Ireland. However, both posthumous works are linked by a profound investigation of the archives of history, England's and Faerie Land's, and the place of justice therein. If Irenius would suspend the rule of law in Ireland in the service of political efficacy, and if Mutability's case is dismissed through an argument that proves her point about the fraudulent divinity of Jove, then how are readers to understand the operations of "the sword of justice" in Book 5? Spenser stages an ambivalent reply through Artegall and the allegory of Ireland. The problem of telling the truth, and what constitutes justice, finds expression in the Blatant Beast, who may represent the symbolic return of Duessa-like allegory; with this creation, Spenser affirms duality and duplicity over the dream of singular truth. Duessa's trial, a prelude to the wars with European giants, suggests again how past is prologue: these trials of justice are repeat performances. Despite the execution of Duessa, the punishment of Malfont, the destruction of the giants, the Golden Age continues to fall – in England as in Faerie Land – revealing both the pattern of history and the stories that underlie it. Turning now to Book 4 and Book 6, as well as *Colin Clouts Come Home Againe*, this chapter continues investigating Spenser's articulation of doubleness. Yet it also returns more strongly to the pressing question of how the ongoing ruin of the world should be redressed, as well as how – and *where* – the past might be recollected. As I will suggest, the poetics and politics of pastoral form the location for both ruin and recollection.

Allegories of Love in *Colin Clouts Come Home Againe*

In the Proem to Book 4 of *The Faerie Queene*, Spenser famously criticizes those who "cannot loue, / Ne in their frosen hearts feele kindly flame" (4.Proem.2). But what does love have to do with "kingdomes causes, and affaires of state," and how can "vaine poems" instruct readers "in vertues" (1)? Spenser answers this question with a history lesson:

> who so list looke backe to former ages,
> And call to count the things that then were donne,
> Shall find, that all the workes of those wise sages,
> And braue exploits which great Heroes wonne,
> In loue were either ended or begunne:
> Witnesse the father of Philosophie,
> Which to his *Critias*, shaded oft from sunne,
> Of loue full manie lessons did apply,
> The which these Stoicke censours cannot well deny. (3)

That Spenser misremembers the name of the *Phaedrus*, the only dialogue in which "the father of Philosophie" finds himself atypically *a topos* (outside of Athens, and therefore out of place), serves as an ironic reminder of the common place that Phaedrus and Socrates construct within and as the sweet spot of philosophy. The philosophical sweet spot, "shaded oft from sunne," where "of loue full manie lessons did apply," stands as a place for recollection: a space in writing for remembering stories of history, particularly Golden Age origin myths. Spenser's hope that Elizabeth "may hearke to loue, and reade this lesson often" points to the power of "loue" as his "sacred Saint" and "souer-aigne Queene" (5,4). Such allegories of love double as origin stories of history. The question remains, *which* tales of love and history will instruct his sovereign?

As this language reminiscent of *The Ruines of Time* implies, the sweet spot is both a place of recollection and itself recollected in the place of ruin. Just as Socrates tells a new tale of love that recalls a lost Golden Age as transparently fictional, and relocates recollection in the fallen and forgetful soul, so Spenser suggests that this Golden Age common place is only ever temporarily reconstructed. This point is made more explicitly in Canto 4, after Arthur and Amoret spend the night in Sclaunder's hovel, where Spenser again defends his treatment of love:

> Here well I weene, when as these rimes be red
> With misregard, that some rash witted wight,
> Whose looser thought will lightly be misled,
> These gentle Ladies will misdeeme too light. (4.8.29)

But Spenser's characters are of another time: "But antique age yet in the infancie / Of time, did liue then like an innocent, / In simple truth and blamelesse chastitie" (30). This is a rhetorical manoeuvre Spenser makes at a number of crucial points. In the Cave of Mammon in Book 2, Guyon declares that "the antique world, in his first flowring youth, / Found no defect in his Creatours grace . . . / But later ages pride, like corn-fed steed, / Abusd her plenty" (2.7.16). And of course, as discussed above, it is the comparison between "the image of the antique world" and the "state of present time" that allegedly animates Book 5. The first half of this chapter focused on the obvious untruth in Spenser claiming that he presents things not "to the common line / Of present dayes," but "to the antique vse" (5.Proem.3), arguing that the purpose of this tactic was to comment on the contemporary political uses of Golden Age mythology. In the context of stories of love, Spenser's desire to recollect a Golden Age of "simple truth" and chaste love appears less nostalgic than ironic, even Platonic. The pleasant place of love is recalled from and within the ruins of time; to remember it is to understand it as always ironized, improvised, and contingent.

The contingency of the sweet spot is highlighted throughout *Colin Clouts Come Home Again*, which provides a paradoxical origin point for Colin's own Golden Age in the ruins of Ireland while demystifying Cynthia's English court as an ideal location of poetry.[41] The journey to visit Cynthia represents a voyage of redemption for Colin and his fellow exiled shepherd: through her love they can be recalled from ruinous banishment, and allowed to reside in Cynthia's court, where "learned arts do florish in great honor, / And Poets wits are had in peerlesse price" (320–1). It would seem that Cynthia's court answers the question posed in the *October* eclogue of *The Shepheardes Calender*: "O pierlesse Poesye, where is then thy place," if not "in Princes pallace"?[42] Yet "peerlesse price" might imply either ample patronage or whorish flattery, a reading that accords with Colin's ensuing complaints about "gracelesse men [who] greatly do abuse" their power, the underside of this seemingly ideal court (327). As it builds, the story that Colin recollects suggests less a voyage from ruin to repair than a lesson in edification, one that mirrors Chaucer's similarly edifying journey in *The House of Fame*. Cynthia's court is neither a truly ideal place nor the appropriate place for Colin's poetry. "Why didst thou ever leave that happie place," a shepherd asks, "In which such wealth might unto thee accrew? / And back returnedst to this barrein soyle, / Where cold and care and penury do dwell" (654–7). Colin's answer is simple: he returns home because Cynthia's court houses the wrong kind of love. In place of true love for the god of love, idolatry reigns supreme and her courtiers only worship the god of love blasphemously: "Vaine votaries of laesie love . . . / Whose service high so basely they ensew, / That *Cupid* selfe of them ashamed is" (766–8).

Colin's description of Cynthia is reminiscent of Chaucer's *House of Fame*, both in his glorification of Cynthia and his refusal to idolize her. Although Colin would "lyken" Cynthia to "faire *Phebes* garlond shining new, / In which all pure perfection one may see" (337, 342–3), he significantly qualifies this praise: "But vaine it is to thinke by paragone / Of earthly things, to judge of things divine," for "Her power, her mercy, and her wisedome, none / Can deeme, but who the Godhead can define" (344–7). Denying his ability to define "Godhead," he then asks, "Why then do I base shepheard bold and blind, / Presume the things so sacred to prophane?" (348–9). Colin concludes with a more appropriate way to praise Cynthia, as human rather than divine: "More fit it is t'adore with humble mind, / The image of the heavens in shape humane" (350–1). He thus expresses a poetic and Platonic love for Cynthia, implicitly returning to Socrates' critique of idolatry: namely, that humans make idols of their loves, and such love gods are only human. However, Colin never blames Cynthia-cum-Elizabeth for fashioning herself as an idol; instead, he accuses her courtiers of indulging in the false love of flattery for the sake of wealth and preferment. The complaint remains the same, however: the language of love poetry, whether on the page or the political stage, offers only a thin disguise for fictions of power.

Just as Chaucer's persona visits the Palace of Fame only to reject the idolatry he sees there, ultimately finding the place for his poetry in the ever-changing labyrinthine structure where the matter of memory resides, so Spenser creates a contrast between Cynthia's court as a palace of fame and the pastoral world as an edifice of texts, stories, voices, and ongoing recollection. When Cuddie accuses the "base shepheard" of having overweening ambitions, Colin declares his true love, promising to build Cynthia a house of fame in his pastoral home: "Her name in every tree I will endosse, / That as the trees do grow, her name may grow" (632–3). The emphasis on texts as trees or twigs can remind us of Chaucer's other labyrinthine house of fame, the swirling unstable edifice of *textus* where he hears new tales of love. Crucially, too, the language Colin uses to describe the slow growth of fame in collective memory echoes his Chaucerian ideal of authorship in *June*:

> And long while after I am dead and rotten:
> Amongst the shepheards daughters dancing rownd,
> My layes made of her shall not be forgotten,
> But sung by them with flowry gyrlonds crownd.
> And ye, who so ye be, that shall survive:
> When as ye heare her memory renewed,
> Be witnesse of her bountie here alive,
> Which she to *Colin* her poore shepheard shewed. (640–7)

Colin Clout thus remembers the art of memory in the *Calender*, recalling its earlier history of locational memory from Plato to Chaucer as both a method of fiction-making (whether in poetry's pastoral places or in other fields) and as a matter of memory – a story about history. Spenser imagines Colin's and Cynthia's shared house of fame not as an immortal monument but rather as an edifice that changes, grows, stays alive in the Platonic sense, through recollection. In a sense, *Colin Clout* might be regarded as a reminder that *anamnesis* means "to be reminded," for Colin's new tale of love, and new story about history, reminds readers of Spenser's past poetry. This poem incorporates a number of origin tales that illustrate recollecting the past from ruin: Colin's personal history; Colin's own recollection of Cynthia's court and the history of the world; and a recollection of the art of memory at the origin of Spenser's poetry.

Yet *Colin Clout* is more than a reminder of the *Calender*; it also revises the earlier work retrospectively. Colin's journey to Cynthia's court marks a return to the central dynamic of *The Shepheardes Calender*, the journey through the "common Labyrinth of Love," as E.K. puts it (19). As in the *Calender*, the travails of love lead inevitably back to the *Phaedrus*, but here they also lead directly to the *Symposium*. *Colin Clout* offers a eulogy to the god of love and an origin story of history, one that recalls the varied eulogies of the *Symposium*, especially Socrates' own eulogy toward the dialogue's end. Like Socrates' Hesiodic narrative, drawn from the Golden Age myth of *Theogony*, Colin's eulogy also "speaks other": allegorically. Explaining to the shepherds why they must worship the god of love, Colin first describes him as Cupid, in a manner reminiscent of Socrates' account in the *Phaedrus*:

> For him the greatest of the Gods we deeme,
> Borne without Syre or couples of one kynd . . .
> So pure and spotlesse *Cupid* forth she [Venus] brought,
> And in the gardens of *Adonis* nurst. (799–804)

Colin then provides a contradictory explanation, celebrating love as older than the world itself:

> For long before the world he was y'bore
> And bred above in *Venus* bosome deare:
> For by his powre the world was made of yore,
> And all that therein wondrous doth appeare. (839–42)

Love is portrayed as the creative force that forged concord from an original state of discord:

> For how should else things so far from attone
> And so great enemies as of them bee,
> Be ever drawne together into one,
> And taught in such accordance to agree? (843–6)

Love's power to bring together disparate elements, Colin relates, serves to explain why

> cold began to covet heat,
> And water fire . . .
> So being former foes, they wexed friends,
> And gan by litle learne to love each other. (847–52)

Through this origin tale, Spenser evokes both the *Symposium* and its complex relationship to the *Phaedrus*. Just as Plato obscures the temporal order of these two dialogues, so Spenser creates a similar ambiguity between the *Calender* and *Colin Clout*, precisely in order to highlight the problem of origin tales themselves. The *Symposium*'s frame – multiple levels of recollection in which a reconstructed banquet hall and its disinterred members find parallel lives apropos to the tale of Simonides – is similarly reflected in *Colin Clout*'s frame, in which Colin remembers Cynthia's court from within a place of ruin: the shepherd land that doubles as Ireland.

The paradoxical relation between the two poems, and their complementary associations with the two Platonic dialogues, is shown clearly in *Colin Clout*'s examinations of divinity and idolatry, especially in relation to Rosalind. Toward the end of the poem, a shepherd warns those who would criticize Rosalind for rejecting Colin, saying

> it is foolhardie thing,
> Rashly to wyten creatures so divine,
> For demigods they be and first did spring
> From heaven, though graft in frailnesse feminine. (915–18)

To prove these dangers, Colin recalls the tale of Stesichorus:

> And well I wote, that oft I heard it spoken,
> How one that fairest *Helene* did revile:
> Through judgement of the Gods to been ywroken
> Lost both his eyes and so remaynd long while,
> Till he recanted had his wicked rimes,
> And made amends to her with treble praise. (919–24)

This serves as a reminder of E.K.'s argument in the *Calender*, which used Stesichorus' palinode to support the divinity of Elisa, ignoring the implications of Socrates' recollection – his performance or invention – of Stesichorus' poetry. Calling love objects "demigods" also recalls Socrates' edification in the *Symposium*, when Diotima teaches him to see love as neither god nor human but as something in between. Socrates' tacit refutation of his own palinode in the *Phaedrus* suggests how an author's various dialogues can speak to one another.[43] Similarly, *Colin Clout* answers the central debate of the *Calender*, explaining why Colin refuses to give up Rosalind's seemingly deleterious "amor" for Elisa's edifying love. In the *Calender*, both Hobbinol and E.K. argue that human love ideally leads to divine love, and thus Colin's love of Rosalind *should* lead to love of Elisa. That the *Calender*'s Colin rejects this path points to Elizabeth's humanity and Spenser's refusal to deify either her or the Tudors. In *Colin Clout*, he rejects the court in favour of his far from ideal pastoral home, eulogizing not Cynthia but rather Rosalind, whose praise forms the culmination of the poem. Describing Rosalind as a "thing celestiall which ye never saw" (930), Colin's earlier reluctance to idolize seems to fall away:

> For she is not like as the other crew
> Of shepheards daughters which emongst you bee,
> But of divine regard and heavenly hew,
> Excelling all that ever ye did see. (931–4)

The poem ends with Colin asserting his real love for Rosalind, not Cynthia. Reversing the ideal trajectory of love at this "earlier" time provides a rationale for Colin's "later" refusal to turn his attention in the so-called right direction. In *The Shepheardes Calender*, Colin's love for Rosalind is framed as a reluctance to move forward to Elisa; here, however, Cynthia-cum-Elisa is clearly superseded by Rosalind. This revisionist history explains what before seemed inexplicable: Colin rejects a place at Elizabeth's court if it means worshipping her as a goddess rather than human.

Colin's idolatrous love of Rosalind in *Colin Clout* finds its fullest context, and most complex range of meanings, in his eulogy to love. By recalling Plato's two dialogues together, Spenser acknowledges idolatry as the supremely human impulse to fashion love objects as gods, while at the same time carefully questioning the belief in fictions of divinity whether those of poets or politicians. Unlike animals, who love by mere instinct, "man that had the sparke of reasons might, / More then the rest to rule his passion: / Chose for his love the fairest in his sight" (867–9). As in the *Phaedrus*, reason leads us to beauty, "the bayt which with delight / Doth man allure, for to enlarge his kynd" (871–2), and beauty leads to the temperate love of wisdom itself:

So love is Lord of all the world by right,
And rules the creatures by his powrfull saw:
All being made the vassals of his might,
Through secret sence which therto doth them draw. (883–6)

The "secret sence" that draws us to worship love recalls Socrates' observation in the *Phaedrus* that "the mind has a kind of divining power," an ability both to find and fashion divinity internally rather than externally.[44] For the other shepherds, Colin has provided something that resembles divine revelation: "*Colin*, thou now fully deeply has divynd: / Of love and beautie and with wondrous skill, / Hast *Cupid* selfe depainted in his kynd" (896–8). This qualified language refers to the human ability to recollect in every sense – to imagine, reason, remember – and every tense: past, present, future. The subtext of the shepherds' praise relates not to Colin's divine knowledge but his talent for divining certain human truths. Colin admits as much, when he confesses that his tale may be fiction, but an edifying one all the same:

Of loves perfection perfectly to speake,
Or of his nature rightly to define,
Indeed (said *Colin*) passeth reasons reach,
And needs his priest t'expresse his powre divine. (835–8)

What "passeth reasons reach," Colin as love poet instead imagines, a confession which applies to this history lesson: the prior knowledge that he recalls through his mind's "divining" power.

Spenser emphasizes the difference between idolizing the court of a fictional divinity and idolizing Cynthia's court. Those who reject love's rule are outlaws, Colin explains, and "Ne mongst true lovers they shall place inherit, / But as Exuls out of his court be thrust" (893–4). Asserting that only true love can find a "place" in Cupid's "court" implicitly provides a rationale for Colin's absence from Cynthia's court, which is inhabited by false lovers. Colin's affirmation of true divine love thus functions ironically, for Spenser draws attention to its fictional status and in so doing distances himself from Cynthia's other lovers. Through Colin's eulogy, in other words, Spenser qualifies how he serves the Faerie Queene. His love for Elizabeth is Platonic because it manifests only a fiction, a story of history, a tale of ruin and recollection by which Spenser builds Cynthia-cum-Elizabeth's house of fame and, within it, his own too.

With *Colin Clout*, Spenser reframes Colin's idolatrous love for Rosalind as a reminder of the art of memory: a new tale of love-as-recollection to which he contrasts old stories of history by which poets and political figures fashion themselves as divine. Idolatry acquires new significance in the context of England's relationship to Ireland. Choosing Rosalind over Cynthia amounts to choosing Ireland over England – choosing the reality of ruin in history over the fiction of endless empire. Recalling Colin's less-than-golden past, this poem again dismantles fictions of an Elizabethan Golden Age. Within this place of ruin, Colin's and Elizabeth's Golden Age myths are recollected and revealed as myths: Colin's revisionary Golden Age history takes place in an Ireland that is always already in ruins, tacitly refuting the myth of Cynthia's English court as the ideal place for poetry or recollection. The poem's return to the art of memory creates a circularity in Colin's life story that affirms the circle of poetry as part of the circle of life. Just as the *Calender*'s shepherds remember Colin's ruined lovelife and lyrics, unconsciously building his house of fame, so the dialogue of *Colin Clout* recalls this house's foundation. *The Shepheardes Calender* picks up where *Colin Clouts Come Home Againe* (as both prehistory and prologue) leaves off, pointing to the circularity of history here as throughout *The Faerie Queene*. Further, that shepherds in both poems misremember the past belies a more important truth. Colin's new tale indirectly refutes any notion of a static Golden Age, for it credits Love as a spirit with creating concord out of a state of discord, now as then. That Love's creation repairs and unites disparate elements, bringing them together however provisionally in harmony, tacitly denies any original state of perfection ruined by gods or men. By relocating the pastoral in *Colin Clout*, Spenser ironizes the truth of the *locus amoenus* in the *Calender*, suggesting that this sweet spot only ever existed in memory.

Friends Have All Things in Common:
Houses of Memory in Book 4

Book 4 provides a series of powerful reminders about the art of memory in Spenser's writing, from *The Shepheardes Calender* to *Colin Clouts Come Home Againe*. Such reminders gesture toward the larger operations of *The Faerie Queene* as memorial edifice, spurring readers to recollect both the past (writ large and small) and Spenser's poetic method of edification. Book 4 explores allegories of love as stories about history, contrasting and interweaving "old" Golden Age tales of ruin with "new" tales of recollection from Plato to Chaucer and beyond. These culminate in the House of Proteus, where the marriage of the Thames and Medway reminds us of a paradoxical truth: story and history have always been married, in matters of memory as well as matters of state.[45] Both the inevitability of mutability and fictions of permanence are facts of history, here as elsewhere in Book 4. Given this mingling of truth and fiction, in art as in life, telling the truth about the past – and telling the truth to power – finds recourse in ironic, indirect discourse, a point which Spenser underscores through a focus on allegorical figures of language.

One such figure is Ate, the legendary figure of discord who plays a central part in the prehistory to the Trojan War, and who introduces the parodic Golden Age fictions that pervade Book 4. Ate's house explicitly recalls Mammon's Cave, as another allegorical underworld where readers bear witness to the ruins of history: "Great cities ransackt, and strong castles rast, / Nations capitued, and huge armies slaine: / Of all which ruines there some relicks did remaine" (4.1.21). The sign of "sad Ilion" hangs among the "ragged monuments of times forepast" that decorate Ate's walls: "For memorie of which on high there hong / The golden Apple, cause of all their wrong, / For which the three faire Goddesses did striue" (21–2). As an uninvited guest, Ate famously destroys the peace at the marriage of Peleus and Thetis with a proleptic Trojan horse: a golden apple addressed "to the fairest," which leads to the questionably fair judgment of Paris, the rape of Helen, and the Trojan War. If playfully, Spenser blames language – and, presumably, stories – as the "cause of all . . . wrong" in history. But despite calling Ate the "mother of debate, / And all dissention, which doth dayly grow" (22, 19), Spenser paints her divisive language as duplicity in a more exact sense:

> Her lying tongue was in two parts diuided,
> And both the parts did speake, and both contended;
> And as her tongue, so was her hart discided,
> That neuer thoght one thing, but doubly stil was guided. (27)

As a poet himself, Spenser speaks "doubly" about Ate: as a representation of language, she stands for both the distortion of truth and its necessary duality. On the one hand, Spenser asserts that only poetry can defeat the divisive power of discord, citing Orpheus and David, "that celestiall Psalmist," as examples (4.2.2). On the other hand, despite this desire to make poetry into an expression of unity – a desire that we might say reaches an apex in Book 5, with the silencing of Malfont – Spenser's views on poetry and language are undeniably more divided. Ate's Duessa-like capacity for poetic ambiguity, he suggests, depends less on the intrinsic nature of words than on their interpretation, especially by those "led with euery light report," who transmit the "false rumors and seditious trouble, / Bred in assemblies of the vulgar sort" (4.1.28). Ate here resembles the negative view of "Fama" drawn by Virgil and Ovid, similarly demonstrating the inextricable mingling of truth and lies. In this regard, she acts as a vehicle for articulating profound if paradoxical truths about poetry and its perpetuation. A necessary evil, so to speak, Ate's destructive language can also represent the transmission and reception of stories over time and space, within and as history, and in the form of ruins. The tales of ruin in Book 4 disseminate and reproduce in this fashion: just as the fall of Troy (and seduction, if not rape, of Helen) is re-enacted in Book 3, so in Book 4 the Golden Apple contest is re-enacted with the Golden Girdle contest – thus repeating the prehistory of Troy's fall, not as tragedy but as farce.

Spenser's interweaving of Trojan and counter-Trojan tales of love achieves a climax of sorts in the Temple of Venus, where he represents poetry as an art of recollecting ruin. A vivid reminder and reimagining of Chaucer's Temple of Venus in *The House of Fame*, the Temple of Venus stands as a house of memory on multiple levels: as an edifice strongly connected to the architectural mnemonic, and as a place for recollecting tales of love.[46] Spenser describes this dazzling architectural edifice as both a "temple faire and auncient, / Which of great mother *Venus* bare the name, / And farre renowmed through exceeding fame," as well as an incomparably sweet spot: "The onely pleasant and delightfull place" is a seemingly Edenic garden, one filled with "Delightfull bowres" and "False Labyrinths, fond runners eyes to daze; / All which by nature made did nature selfe amaze" (4.10.5, 214). This doubling of memory places points to the dual locations for recollection from Plato to Chaucer, fame's palace and philosopher's *locus amoenus*. As discussed in chapter 2, the Temple of Venus in Chaucer's *House of Fame* represents a place for recollecting old Trojan tales – a place that Geffrey must pass through en route to finding new tales of love in the constantly changing house that supplies him with the matter of memory, the shifting labyrinth that belies the shining palace.[47] Spenser's Temple of Venus reforms this structure and recalls the pattern of Chaucer's poetry, a pattern that he demonstrates in part by ruining and recollecting his own earlier poetry. The origin story told here in Book 4, the genesis of Amoret and Scudamor's relationship, rewrites his previous ending in Book 3. In the 1590 *Faerie Queene*, he reunites Scudamour and Amoret in a state of hermaphroditic bliss, in which they complete one another, bringing to its conclusion what was then the final book of *The Faerie Queene*; in the 1596 edition, Spenser divides what love formerly had wrought, delaying the reunion of these lovers. However, this represents more than a romance device, despite the characteristic deferral of satisfaction. Spenser provides competing versions of this story, a double vision of sorts: Book 4's retrospective histories, Scudamour's and Spenser's, radically alter the view of Book 3. By eliding any sense of completion, Spenser places the Temple of Venus within the art of memory tradition traced in Book 4, emphasizing perpetual recollection over permanent repair, and underscoring the ever-altering process of reception.

In one sense, the tale of the temple would seem to confirm the moral of Trojan tales, that love leads to ruin. As Scudamour recalls a supposedly romantic history with Amoret, what promises to be a happy ending instead recounts a brutish beginning: Scudamour rapes Amoret in an echo of the rape of Helen, and despite his efforts to frame this as a heroic narrative, numerous ironies emerge.[48] Although admitting that "sacrilege me seem'd the Church to rob" (4.10.53), Scudamour does just that, despoiling the temple by taking Amoret against her will (albeit with what he imagines is Venus' consent). Despite the "sharpe rebuke" of Amoret, who protests that "it was to Knight vnseemely shame / Vpon a recluse Virgin to lay hold," and despite her subsequent prayers, tears, and complaints, Scudamour finally ignores her, "for no intreatie would foregoe so glorious spoyle" (54–5). From the start, moreover, he reveals his selective memory:

> Long were to tell the trauell and long toile,
> Through which this shield of loue I late haue wonne,
> And purchased this peerlesse beauties spoile,
> That harder may be ended, then begonne. (3)

Told out of order, the story's happy ending in fact begins a tale with no conclusion as of yet. Scudamour ends his story at the beginning, repeating the circular pattern by which Spenser tells England's story of history in Books 2 and 3. When Scudamour celebrates having regained Amoret, "this peerelesse beauties spoile," he unwittingly points up the episode's history lesson: love stories double as histories and, in the end, this marriage reads like an allegory of conquest.[49]

In another sense, the Temple of Venus is also a location for edifying stories of love. The temple's association with Platonic memory, as the sweet spot where "friends have all things in common," emerges in Scudamour's passing account of "another sort / Of louers lincked in true harts consent"; far from bowers of sporting lovers, famous friends tied "In bands of friendship, there did liue for euer, / Whose liues although decayed, yet loues decayed neuer" (26–7). Yet faced with this vision, Scudamour ironically can only "enuye" their lack of "gealosye" and bemoan the "paines and perlous ieopardie" of his pursuit of love; turning away from this kind of love, he declares "Much dearer be the things, which come through hard distresse" (28). As Scudamour recounts a lover's prayer to Venus, another Platonic memorial emerges. One of the lovers around the statue of Venus "could not containe" his torment, breaking forth in a plea to "Great *Venus*, Queene of beautie and of grace" (43–4) that ends with a Golden Age origin story:

So all the world by thee at first was made,
And dayly yet thou does the same repayre:
Ne ought on earth that merry is and glad,
Ne ought on earth that louely is and fayre,
But thou the same for pleasure didst prepayre.
Thou art the root of all that ioyous is,
Great God of men and women, queene of th'ayre,
Mother of laughter, and welspring of blisse,
O graunt that of my love at last I may not misse. (47)

This story of love's creation of the world resembles the eulogies to love performed in the *Symposium* and recalled in *Colin Clout*, both of which reiterate Hesiodic origin tales as the creation of concord out of discord, repair out of ruin. Here too, this allegory of love ultimately undermines the Golden Age origin stories it seems to represent. Yet as an ironic reminder of Colin's palinode to the Stesichorus' blasphemy, the prayer speaks to the problem of idolatry.

In the Temple of Venus, Spenser both renovates Chaucer's temple and emulates his method of edification, building Chaucerian irony into the recollection of the ruins of poetry. Elsewhere in Book 4, Spenser similarly rewrites ancient history as a continuation of Chaucer's unfinished *Canterbury Tale*, "The Squire's Tale." Describing Chaucer as "On

Fames eternall beadroll worthie to be fyled," Spenser nevertheless laments that "wicked Time that all good thoughts doth waste, / ... That famous moniment hath quite defaste" (4.2.32–3). He then promises to repair this ruin:

> That I thy labours may thus reuiue,
> ... through infusion sweete
> Of thine owne spirit, which doth in me surviue,
> I follow here the footing of thy feete,
> That with thy meaning so I may the rather meete. (34)

With echoes of *The Shepheardes Calender* and *The Ruines of Time*, Spenser evokes the immortality of poetry *topos* only to invert it. Like Sidney in *The Ruines of Time*, Chaucer may be "worthie" of "Fames eternall beadroll" but his memory, "that famous moniment," has been ruined; these ruins of history and poetry join in a house of fame that Spenser recalls to build anew. Such ruin represents not the failure of poetry but the place of continued recollection; remembering Chaucer's poetry becomes another reminder of the art of memory, a counter to the story of the Trojan legend. Spenser's treatment of Chaucer's poetry reframes the subject of friendship in figurative terms in order to encompass the relationship between the living and the dead.

Yet Spenser's completion of Chaucer's ruined poetry asks to be understood ironically. Despite promising to follow Chaucer's "footing," little in "The Squire's Tale" warrants Spenser's inventions; he picks up from the final line of Chaucer's tale and ignores many of the details of the tale itself. Furthermore, scholars generally agree that "The Squire's Tale" was never meant to be complete: the Franklin's interjection, which brings it to an abrupt end, comically interrupts a story that promised to go on much too long. Spenser's "misreading" of Chaucer can thus suggest what the art of memory means: he ruins Chaucer's writing in order to remember it anew. Spenser punctuates this irony by concluding the tale with a contrived device for forgetting the past.[50] Cambell and Triamond's friendship becomes possible only after a journey to the underworld procures them "Nepenthe," the gods' own nectar, which they drink to forget their past discord. Spenser explains that nepenthe is normally reserved for those humans whom Jove "will haue aduanced to the skie, / And there made gods, though borne of mortall berth"; before they may enter heaven they must drink so that "all cares forepast / Are washt away quite from their memorie" (4.3.44). Spenser's specific source for nepenthe is the *Odyssey*, where Helen serves the drink to Telemachus and Menelaus as a way to ease their melancholy about Troy. Yet Homer's characters drink not to forget tales of Troy but to remember them – or at least to recall the memories associated with an idealized heroism. Spenser's recasting of nepenthe as the elixir of the newly divine thus both rejects the romance of Troy and introduces the same criticism levelled in the trial of Mutability: the gods drink to forget their inconvenient human origins.[51] And what better way to remember Chaucer than by emulating his complaint about epic fictions of divine self-fashioning in *The House of Fame*? Chaucer's portrait of Fame's many mansions casts a jaundiced eye on epic underworlds and heavens (especially Dante's), a perspective that Spenser remembers here in multiple senses. Thus woven into a tale of Troy, Cambell and Triamond's competition for the Golden Girdle, is a new tale of love (friendship) that alters Chaucer's poetry while paying fitting tribute to him. On the level of plot, true friendship comes as a result of forgetting, but on a more important level it comes from remembering Chaucer and extending his method of recollection. Writing forms the common place for Spenser's recollection of Chaucer, his ruined poetry the material for Spenser's new literary edifice.

Book 4's marriage of story and history emerges most clearly in its culminating marriage of rivers, the Thames and the Medway, which appropriately enough takes place in the House of Proteus. Within this house of change, Spenser illustrates the place of Trojan fictions over time, repeated *in* and re-enacted *as* history, and provides a counter-narrative of ruin and recollection. As the Temple of Venus resembles both Chaucer's Temple of Venus and his Palace of Fame, so the House of Proteus corresponds to Chaucer's Labyrinth, a similarly mutable location where Spenser receives "new" tales of love. Like Chaucer's house of fame, Spenser's House of Proteus demonstrates that truth and lies, fact and fiction, story and history have always been married. This house of change paradoxically represents a place for memory: a location for remembering certain truths about history and, I will suggest, for remembering Spenser's personal history.

Framed as historiography, this episode returns to the art of memory as both edifice and method of edification. Even with "an hundred tongues to tell . . . / And endlesse memorie," Spenser confesses, he could not fully remember the gods who "repayr'd" to Proteus' house to attend this marriage (9). Acknowledging the limits of human memory, he appeals to Clio, the muse of history and "noursling of Dame *Memorie*," who holds "those rolles, layd vp in heauen aboue, / And records of antiquitie . . . / To which no wit of man comen neare" (10). Such an invocation contrasts sharply with the historiography found in the Castle of Alma; the heavenly rolls and records held by Clio remain inaccessible to the chamber where Eumnestes resides amid the ruins of memory. This paradoxical truth (only the "gods" know the truth of history) serves as an indirect reminder of Spenser's "methode" as "Historiographer" and "Poet historical." Spenser associates his "endlesse" task with Eumnestes' and Anamnestes' endless recollection of "records of antiquity," recalling the genealogy and legacy of this marriage "in order" and in order to build a house of memory. A pun on edification, all "the Gods" have "repayr'd" to *Proteus* house" (9), suggests Spenser's dual ambition: to repair history's ruins and to reveal the impermanence of this endeavour.

The marriage of the rivers intertwines history and myth, which in the broadest sense are associated with the Thames and Medway respectively. The entry of the Thames "with all his goodly traine" and "His auncient parents" (24) initiates a dominantly historiographic inventory of English rivers and history, drawn from sources such as Camden's *Britannia*, while the entry of the Medway, "Clad in a vesture of vnknowen geare" (45), follows with a genealogy drawn in large part from Hesiod's *Theogony*. Yet history and myth interpenetrate throughout, suggesting the rivers' more complex story. The Medway runs near Penshurst, the Sidney estate, and thus represents not only poetry but also the location of shared memory and history in Spenser's literary relationship with that family. As a counterpoint, descriptions of the Thames' mythic associations pervade the flow of history. The jewel at the centre of Thamis' coronet is "the famous Troynouant, / In which her kingdomes throne is chiefly resiant," likened to the "Diademe embattild wide / With hundred turrets, like a Turribant" worn by "Old Cybele, arayd with pompous pride" (28). In the *Aeneid*, Anchises identifies Cybele as the mother of the gods, most notably "Caesar Augustus, son of the deified, / Who shall bring once again an Age of Gold / To Latium, to the land where Saturn reigned / In early times."[52] Rather than recounting a Golden Age history, however, Spenser instead recalls Nereus' prophecy that the "famous prise" won by Paris would "finally destroy / Proud *Priams* towne" (19), and includes among the famous rivers of the world the "Diuine Scamander, purpled yet with blood / Of Greekes and Troians" (20).

Throughout the episode, Spenser draws attention to the violence inherent in fashioning England as a Troynovant. The marriage of the Thames and the Medway shares with many of the so-called love stories of Book 4 (especially that of Scudamour's marriage to Amoret) an origin in rape, culminating in Spenser's disturbing exhortation to conquer "virgin land" in search of gold:

> Ioy on those warlike women, which so long
> Can from all men so rich a kingdome hold;
> And shame on you, O men, which boast your strong
> And valiant hearts, in thoughts lesse hard and bold,
> Yet quaile in conquest of that land of gold.
> But this to you, O Britons, most pertaines,
> To whom the right hereof it selfe hath sold;
> The which for sparing litle cost or paines,
> Loose so immortall glory, and so endlesse gaines. (22)

On one level, Spenser makes an apparently straightforward plea for English imperial conquest – a popular position and one closely connected with Spenser's friend and patron, Walter Raleigh, who once famously complained to Elizabeth that the lovely Guiana "hath yet her maidenhead." At the same time, another voice echoes the Cave of Mammon, where gold represents a desire that defines the pursuit of empire; in this tarnished Golden Age, Spenser intimates here, Britain's empire is built upon despoiling for gold, "the right hereof it selfe hath sold." From yet another perspective, this can be read as an attack on Elizabeth's mythology as a "Virgin Queen," whose cost can be registered in the absence of an heir to England's "endlesse gaines." The multiplicity of voices here speaks, as much as anything, to Spenser's own Ate-like persona.

Indeed, the ambiguous, ambivalent history of the House of Proteus may represent Spenser's own: a story of the marriage of poetry and power throughout his life, and a tale of his divided homes. Spenser takes readers on a tour of his most important memorial sites, English and Irish, introducing his education as "My mother Cambridge, whom as with a Crowne / He doth adorne, and is adorn'd of it / With many a gentle Muse, and many a learned wit" (34). Spenser also recalls, if only partially, the history lessons represented by the rivers of Ireland:

> Ne thence the Irishe Riuers absent were,
> Sith no lesse famous then the rest they bee,
> And ioyne in neighbourhood of kingdome nere . . .
> Though I them all according their degree,

Cannot recount, nor tell their hidden race,
Nor read the saluage cuntreis, thorough which they pace. (40)

Despite demurring that he "cannot recount" the tales of the Irish rivers, Spenser recalls the fact that he has already done so, reminding readers of this story of love thwarted by power, a riparian tale with a parallel in Raleigh's secret marriage and subsequent banishment from the royal court: "There was the Liffy rolling downe the lea, / . . . Strong Allo tombling from Slewlogher steep, / And Mulla mine, whose waves I whilom taught to weep" (40–1). This serves as a reminder of Spenser's other chorographical poem, *Colin Clouts Come Home Againe*, and the tale of rivers whose doomed love offers an etiological myth for the ruin of Spenser's home in Ireland, Kilcolman.[53] As in *Colin Clout*, where allusions to the *Symposium* allow Colin to tell a new story of history about his love for Rosalind, so in the House of Proteus another tale of rivers in love and in marriage interrupts the official story – the marriage of the Thames and the Medway – and, it seems, the official history of a greater Britain. Implying that such tragic love stories would be out of place in an epithalamion, Spenser says he cannot "tell their hidden race" but he does nevertheless. Despite gesturing to a kind of river of Lethe in his house of memory, Spenser recalls the bloodletting involved in Ireland's subjugation, the violence of empire-building, the history embedded in the myth.[54] The last Irish river Spenser names is the "balefull Oure, late staind with English blood" (44), suggesting a straightforward view that is complicated by the suggestion that he cannot tell the whole truth about Ireland's past: "With many more, whose names no tongue can tell. / All which that day *in order* seemly good / Did on the Thamis attend" (44, my emphasis). As the last to appear in the Thames' retinue, the Irish rivers lead directly to the Medway and mythology, indicating the impossibility of adequately recounting Ireland's relationship to England. Yet by virtue of telling this history "in order," the same way he describes historiography in the "Letter to Raleigh," Spenser points to partial truths that, as in Alma's Castle, require recollection. That he cannot "tell" Ireland's history fully thereby signifies doubly – as not knowing or speaking fully – and might also suggest that Spenser leaves this task to readers: that is, to tell the whole truth.

"What an endlesse worke haue I in hand," Spenser says in conclusion, "To count the seas abundant progeny" (4.12.1). Casting his mind over the sheer plenitude of the rivers and oceans, "So huge their numbers, and so numberlesse their nation," he then praises the usefulness of fiction: "Therefore the antique wisards well inuented, / That *Venus* of the fomy sea was bred; / For that the seas by her are most augmented" (1, 2). Stories of history serve the same end: they offer a point of origin, even if only a mythical one. This allusion to "antique wisards" fashioning gods of gold, here Venus, reminds readers of the Temple of Isis in Book 5, where Spenser writes of Osiris, "Well therefore did the antique world inuent, / That Iustice was a God of soueraine grace" (5.7.2). In both instances, so-called ancient history reflects upon the present, as the self-made gods of England share in these genealogies. Spenser praises the fiction of Venus borne of the sea, always fertile and ever growing. Yet this underscores the inextricable relationship of love stories and history: they reflect mutual desires – indeed, are married – in imperial conquest. Spenser admits that Venus represents a well-invented fiction of "the antique wisards" because this fiction reproduces itself endlessly in new, indeed "numberlesse" nations; Venus serves to explain the origin of love (as in the *Phaedrus*) as a tale that can be endlessly reinterpreted. The intertwining of story and history in the House of Proteus ironizes Ate as a figure of duplicity; and as with Mammon's Cave and Alma's Castle, the House of Proteus finds clear parallels with the House of Ate, the ruinous underworld of history and house of memory where Book 4 begins. As in Alma's Castle, the House of Proteus continues to be built, and the broken endings of these memory places make a virtue of necessity: incompletion becomes a space for renovation.

This chapter emphasizes the ways in which Spenser "speaks double": staging his ambivalence in these later works, presenting two perspectives that cannot be reconciled. In this regard, it seems wholly appropriate that the second half of *The Faerie Queene* begins with a figure of doubleness such as Ate, which Spenser describes in a negative manner that seemingly contradicts his earlier discussions of fame. Yet the presence of Ate in Book 4 might be understood as an announcement of method for the rest of Spenser's epic. And, appropriately, what Ate represents lead in two directions, toward two incommensurable locations. The first, as already discussed, is the trial of Duessa in Book 5, which, on one level, seeks to render truth and poetry unified through the application of political force. The second, to which I will turn next, is associated with the Blatant Beast – especially as portrayed in Book 6, where duplicity cannot be contained, even symbolically. In the context of Book 6, only duplicity survives the ruin of the pastoral world, and this survival expresses unspeakable truths.

Book 6: Pastoral Ruin and "Wisemens threasure"

O peerless poesy, where is then thy place? Book 6 returns to the central question of *The Shepheardes Calender* and to the art of memory. The speaker begins by recalling "The waies, through which my weary steps I guyde, / In this delightfull land of Faery" (6.Proem.1). Through the "exceeding spacious and wyde" landscape of Faerie Land, "sprinck-led with such sweet variety," he may "forget" his "tedious trauell" by being "ravished with rare thoughts delight" (1):

> Ye sacred imps, that on *Parnasso* dwell,
> And there the keeping haue of learnings threasures,
> Which doe all worldly riches farre excell . . .
> . . . Guyde ye my footing, and conduct me well
> In these strange waies. (2)

Poetry is both a means of forgetting the tedium of life's travails and a way to remember experience, in every sense. Faerie Land, as scholars at least since Coleridge have observed, represents the mind's own place – a space of imagination, judgment, and memory – but also a place where writing inevitably intersects with the world. Shaped through the experience of traversing Faerie Land, readers fashion themselves in ways that speak to the mind's own "divining power," as Plato puts it in the *Phaedrus*: the power to remember the past and divine the future, to make both present through a continued process of ruining and recollecting the truth.[55]

Book 6, the "Legend of Covrtesie," challenges Golden Age myths in the intersecting places of court and country and the intersecting realms of pastoral and politics. This book ostensibly recalls a Golden Age of courtliness, a prehistory that contrasts with the present state of things. Though courtesy in the "present age doe plentous seeme," Spenser writes, "Yet being matcht with plaine Antiquitie, / Ye will them all but fayned showes esteeme" (4). After declaring in the proem that nowadays courtesy appears to be "nought but forgerie," he turns to Elizabeth and her court as a "patterne" of courtesy that serves as his model of antiquity: "Then pardon me, most dreaded Soueraine, / That from your selfe I doe this vertue bring, / And to your selfe doe it returne againe" (5–7). The proem subtly undercuts the ideal of Elizabethan England as a renewed Golden Age. Book 6's portrait of courtesy represents a point of departure against which to judge the present state of things: "Its now so farre from that, which then it was, / That it indeed is nought but forgerie, / Fashion'd to please the eies," and such deception can "blynd / The wisest sight, to thinke gold that is bras" (5). The inverse may be true too: some might mistake this brazen age for an Elizabethan Golden Age. Where might such Golden Age virtue be found? In the place of "vertues seat . . . deepe within the mynd" (5). This search for an ideal of Golden Age courtesy, "so faire a patterne" (6), also recalls *The Shepheardes Calender*, the earlier quest for both the "perfecte paterne of a Poete" and a "paterne of a perfect Oratour."[56] To this prehistory of courtesy, Spenser adds another frame, one that belies its antique appearance: the legend of Colin Clout. Spenser offers a revisionist history of Colin, re-enacting the scene recollected by Hobbinol in *Aprill*, the Golden Age eclogue, in a radically new way. Once again, Spenser skews the chronology of his persona's history by telling his tale out of order, ending with what appears to be the beginning: an origin tale of how Colin's land and love, pastoral place and poetry, fell to ruin. As in *Colin Clouts Come Home Againe*, this return to origins reveals that Golden Age histories have always been retrospective stories remembered within the space of ruin. While E.K.'s reading of Colin's poem in *Aprill* suggests that authorship can permanently repair a fallen Golden Age, Book 6 confirms that such perfection never existed in the first place. In a sense, Book 6 fulfils the order described in the "Letter to Raleigh": *The Faerie Queene* ends at the beginning, with Colin Clout's (and poetry's) origin in ruin.[57]

In this supremely self-reflexive book, Spenser reintroduces Colin by asking, "who knowes not *Colin Clout*?" (6.10.16), a rhetorical question that parallels a similar question in the *Mutabilitie Cantos*: "Who knowes not *Arlo-hill*?" (7.6.36), the location of Mutability's trial and Spenser's Irish home. As in Book 7, the question leads the reader outside the frame of the episode, to the larger world of poetry and place that informs Faerie Land. As well, this question might be understood as more than simply rhetorical, both for readers (asked to recollect Colin and his complex presence in Spenser's poetry) and for Spenser himself, as a question of self-knowledge and self-critique. Nor does Colin represent Spenser's only ambiguous double identity in Book 6. Although the hero of Book 6, the knight Calidore who pursues the Blatant Beast, has often been interpreted as a portrait of Sidney, this figure can represent Spenser as well – a dual characterization supported by *The Ruines of Time*, which describes Spenser and Sidney's relationship through the twin Gemini, Castor and Pollux. Spenser thus brings together his two homes, England and Ireland, and two of his personae: courtly in Calidore and poetic in Colin. Through Calidore, Spenser also figures his own youthful ambition to "followe flying fame," despite Colin's disclaimer in the *June* eclogue of the *Calender* (75). Dividing himself in Book 6, Spenser dramatizes his ambivalence with two poetic personae: Colin and Calidore meet on the plain of memory, where friends hold all things in common – even, or especially, in Arcadia.[58]

In keeping with an image of idealized antiquity, Calidore represents an ideal knight who "loathd leasing, and base flattery, / And loued simple truth and stedfast honesty" (6.1.3). But though Calidore may "loath" dishonesty and "love" honesty, the "simple truth" remains as elusive, as difficult to capture or maintain, as the duplicitous monster that he ardently pursues. What seems an ennobling quest to contain lies appears, from another perspective, as an attempt to force a certain truth: to secure the Blatant Beast is to secure a place in Faerie Land's court. From yet another view, Calidore's heroism charts a fruitless quest for fame – a name and reputation – and his chase for the Blatant Beast resembles, not coincidentally, Virgil's related monster, Fama:

> Him first from court he to the citties coursed,
> And from the citties to the townes him prest,
> And from the townes into the countrie forsed,
> And from the country back to priuate farmes he scorsed. (6.9.3)

The beast's restless movement mirrors Fama's frantic motion from place to place in the *Aeneid*, but a movement that may also suggest a journey back in time: from civilized courts to country pleasures. Calidore's pursuit of "flying fame," his willingness "To tread an endless trace, withouten guyde," is central to the many places where fame can be found in Book 6 (6.1.6). Like the pursuit of the fame, such courtliness has its costs, and they register together.

Courtliness and its double occupy multiple places in the Faerie Land of Book 6. As Spenser brings the court to the country and vice versa, he makes the difference between truth and lies, civility and savagery, fame and defamation increasingly difficult to tell – an ever-shifting mark produced through continual double-voicing. Particularly in the "Salvage Nation" episode, Spenser challenges the so-called civilizing effect of poetry by examining its use by the courtiers who reside there. "In these wylde deserts . . . / There dwelt a saluage nation" of men, who do no work but survive by living off "stealth and spoile" and the "labours of poore men" (6.8.35) – cannibals who "eate the flesh of men" with "monstrous cruelty" (36). These savages represent a parody of courtiers who compose self-consuming artefacts of poetry. When Serena stumbles into this "saluage nation," the courtier-like savages "view [her] with "lustfull fantasyes" and "of her dainty flesh they did deuize / To make a common feast, and feed with gurmandize" (41, 38), which results in a sonnet, a blazon mingling sexual and martial conquest:

> Her yuorie necke, her alablaster brest,
> Her paps, which like white silken pillowes were,
> For loue in soft delight thereon to rest;
> Her tender sides, her bellie white and clere,
> Which like an Altar did it selfe vprere,
> To offer sacrifice diuine thereon;
> Her goodly thighes, whose glorie did appeare
> Like a triumphall Arch, and thereupon
> The spoiles of Princes hang'd, which were in battel won. (42)

This episode punctures the fantasy that poetry's ideal place lies at court, depicting courtly poets as savages whose idolatrous love poetry cannot disguise their desire for imperial conquest. This view of poetry as a pleasing gloss on violent victory may implicate Spenser as well. Is this "Salvage Nation" England or Ireland? Spenser suggests both: concentric circles where courtly love poetry doubles as a vocabulary for imperial conquest. As either place, or as a palimpsest of the two, this reads as a savage critique of both the English court and the poetics of empire.

Here as elsewhere, Spenser refuses to idealize poetry's pastoral place. The central episode of Book 6 offers a prehistory of Colin Clout, representing the apex of his Golden Age, singing among the Graces – the time that the shepherds of the *Calender* will nostalgically recollect in *Aprill*. Calidore happens upon the place where four figures dance to the pipings of "Poore *Colin Clout* (who knowes not *Colin Clout?*)" (6.10.16). Enraptured by this vision yet unsure "Whether it were the traine of beauties Queene, / Or Nymphes, or Faeries, or enchaunted show," Calidore's curiosity drives him forward, symbolically, toward Colin's house of fame (17):

> But soone as he appeared to their vew,
> They vanisht all away out of his sight,

And cleane were gone, which way he neuer knew;
All save the shepheard, who for fell despight
Of that displeasure broke his bag-pipe quight,
And made great mone for that vnhappy turne. (18)

This moment returns to the apotheosis of Colin's poetic prowess, and yet at the same time it re-enacts the very moment when Colin breaks his pan pipe and symbolically gives up on poetry. This episode reveals that his past was never the ideal world that E.K. and the shepherds longed for; it was always ruined and remembered as it was in the present tense of the *Calender*. Spenser deflates the shepherds' nostalgia once again, providing readers with a larger view of history (Colin's and England's) than these characters can either know or understand. The art of memory functions here in ways similar to the *Calender*, as readers bear witness to a crucial moment in Colin's history when his *locus amoenus* falls to ruin; yet this ruin (of both poetry and the place of pastoral) later becomes the location for recollection – the memory that builds Colin's house of fame. This can only be known in retrospect, however, and unhappy Colin ironically complains that the mysterious figures Calidore chased away "by no meanes thou canst recall againe, / For being gone, none can them bring in place, / But whom they of them selues list so to grace" (20). The word "recall" indicates how Colin's response can be both true and false. A moment gone can never be retrieved or returned; nevertheless, this exact moment will be recalled – indeed, has already been recalled multiple times, both in the shepherd world and in Spenser's poetry.[59]

Recollection, as this study has continually emphasized, always adapts what it recalls: E.K.'s interpretation of Hobinnol's remembrance of Colin's poem about his encounter with the Graces stands at a great distance from Spenser's opinions on love, idolatry, heroic authorship, and the recollection of the past. The episode in Book 6 thus revisits and revises the *Calender*'s central dialogue about poetry and power. Colin depicts the Graces, handmaidens of Venus, as the embodiment of courtesy, in ways that draw upon Tudor mythology: "They are the daughters of sky-ruling Ioue," he tells Calidore, who teach "all the complements of curtesie," the "skill men call Ciuility" (22–3). These reminders clarify the place of the exceptional fourth maid whom the Graces made an honorary Grace: "graced her so much to be another Grace" (26). Spenser reminds readers that in the *Aprill* eclogue of the *Calender*, Elizabeth stands for the fourth Grace, but in Book 6 she instead stands as a point of contrast. "Another Grace she well de-serues to be," Colin explains, for in her "so many Graces gathered are" that produce a "Diuine resemblaunce, beauty soueraine rare, / Firme Chastity . . . / All which she with such courtesie doth grace" such that "when she is in place" no other can "compare" (27). At first, this ap-pears to refer to the queen (given the pun on "grace" and "her grace" or majesty), to deify her, and thus to reinforce E.K.'s interpretation of this event in the *Aprill* eclogue as following a Golden Age pattern of Virgilian poetry. Crucially, however, Spenser here replaces Elizabeth with Rosalind, "that iolly Shepheards lasse," as the fourth Grace (16). Stepping outside the frame of the poem to apologize for this substitution – "Great *Gloriana*, greatest Maiesty, / Pardon thy poor shepheard" – Spenser pleads for Rosalind to share in the house of fame that is *The Faerie Queene*: "That when thy glory shall be farre displayd / To future age of her this mention may be made" (28). This apology for poetry serves as a point of return to another key Golden Age fiction: the tale of Stesichorus' palinode, which here as in the *Calender* and *Colin Clout* rep-resents a Platonic love poem about political fictions of divinity.[60] In de-nying Elizabeth as the fourth Grace, Spenser recalls an origin of the art of memory: Socrates' poetic story of history in the *Phaedrus*, his vision of love that leads not to Troy's ruin but the soul's recollection within, and as, the commonplace and pleasant place of discourse. By dwelling on the place of the fourth Grace, Spenser's defence of Rosalind (and implicitly of poetry) rewrites this palinode and the art of recollection therein. His qualified praise of Elizabeth underscores the subtext of the *Aprill* eclogue, reminding readers that Spenser's love poetry never ex-tends beyond the realm of myth.

Spenser complicates such reminders of locational memory through a duality of locations. The impossible intersection of England and Ireland in his earlier two pastoral poems, where Colin led parallel lives in alter-nate universes, returns in Book 6. As in the "Salvage Nation" episode, readers can see double, the place of Colin's vision as England *and* Ire-land. Spenser locates the scene of Colin's triumphant playing on Mount Acidale, the place of the Graces; in another sense, this location would seem to represent both England and Ireland, as well as a counterpoint to his insertion of Arlo Hill into the classical framework of Mutability's trial. This mountain stands for the *locus amoenus* of both poetry and philosophy, a place of fiction-making:

> For all that euer was by natures skill
> Deuized to worke delight, was gathered there,

And there by her were poured forth at fill,
As if this to adorne, she all the rest did pill. (6.10.5)

The language of pillage recalls the *Ruines of Rome*, where travellers to Rome "doo somewhat pill: / As they which gleane, the reliques use to gather," making Mount Acidale less a location of ideal permanence than one for gathering together Nature's spoils.[61] Rather than viewing poetry's and philosophy's sweet spots as divided, readers can also see what they hold in common as locations for recollection.

To further trouble this paradise Spenser describes it through language reminiscent of the Diana episode in the *Mutabilitie Cantos*, recalling the origin myth of Ireland's fall from Golden Age perfection to ruin:

They say that *Venus*, when she did dispose
Her selfe to pleasaunce, vsed to resort
Vnto this place . . .
. . . with the Graces there to play and sport. (6.10.9)

Venus abandons Acidale much as Astraea abandons earth and Diana abandons Ireland:

That euen her owne Cytheron, though in it
She vsed most to keepe her royall court,
And in her soueraine Maiesty to sit,
She in regard hereof refusde and thought vnfit. (9)

The result is ruin that cannot be separated from stories of history and divinity. Colin's disillusionment with and abandonment of poetry coincide with attacks on the pastoral world:

A lawlesse people, *Brigants* hight of yore . . .
. . . The dwelling of these shepheards did inuade,
And spoyld their houses, and them selues did murder;
And droue away their flocks, with other much disorder. (6.10.39)

The seemingly ideal pastoral world of Book 6 falls victim to conquest and greed, plundered of "spoile and booty" (39). Like a page ripped out of Arthur's history book and England's collective book of memory, this episode reveals the ongoing place of despoliation, of ruin, within English history. Life and freedom are exchanged for wealth in this brutal economy. The shepherds not killed are captured, including Meliboe and Pastorella, to be sold into slavery: "For slaues to sell them, for no small reward, / To merchants, which them kept in bondage hard, / Or sold againe" (43). Taken allegorically, selling people and poetry for power reads as the history of gold.

Spenser would seem to implicate himself in the ruin of this place and people, pastoral and Pastorella, implying that this allegory tells a story about his own history. Any accusations of "Spenser For Hire" must begin at home: with his own accusations of selling himself and his poetry, by serving at the court and pleasure of *The Faerie Queen*. The sale of Pastorella and the murder of Meliboe, a figure familiar from Virgil's pastoral poetry, at least partly registers the price of Spenser's own desire for preferment.[62] This episode, an allegory of a fallen Golden Age, ends in slaughter and terror: "Old *Meliboe* is slaine, and him beside / His aged wife, with many others wide," and Pastorella is buried alive underneath a pile of corpses (6.11.18). The death of Meliboe and others reckons the cost of gold and all that it represents in human terms. When Meliboe reflects upon his former life at court, "Where I did sell my selfe for yearely hire," this also reflects upon Spenser's own courtly and colonial ambitions; so, too, does Meliboe's palinodic rejection of a savage court and its all-consuming desire for gold (6.9.24). Spenser-as-Calidore appears to hold himself partly responsible for this ruin: "following flying fame" leads him to a place that he disturbs irretrievably – as though driving grace from the land, and which fractures his once innocent desire to be like Colin Clout: to inhabit a pastoral world of poetry.

Some scholars have argued that the Brigants who destroy this place represent the Irish, especially given the rebellions in Ireland that Spenser experienced personally and his portrait of the Irish in the *Viewe*. Yet the name "Brigants" confuses the question of identity. Camden's discussion of the "Brigantes" in *Britannia* emphasizes their English origins and their likely spread to Ireland, but also their uncertain identification. Although Spenser relates the Brigants to the "saluage nation," that savage portrayal of courtiers further complicates issues of place and identity. Moreover, the "sort of merchants, which were wount / To skim those coastes, for bondmen there to buy," would suggest English colonialists rather than Irish renegades (6.11.9). Spenser offers more than one perspective on ruin, showing multiple forces at work both in the present states of Ireland and England, which symbolize the ongoing life of Mammon's offspring. "What are kingdoms but great robberies?" Augustine asks, the question to which Spenser implicitly returns, in a place where England and Ireland can hardly be discerned from one another.[63] These two truths become one with the revelation of Pastorella's royal lineage: the discovery of her birthmark, a (likely Tudor) Rose on her breast described as the "speaking markes of passed monuments," which represents an admonishment to Tudor power as well (6.12.20). As Pastorella finds her true home at court, Elizabeth views herself in yet another mirror. But whether this signifies the triumph of time remains dubious. Since country and court, pastoral and power, finally occupy the same place, only the fiction of their division makes possible their romantic reunion. Returning to court reveals that the Tudors bear some relation to the merchants and brigands who threaten Pastorella and pastoral. Self *is* Other, in other words.

The Blatant Beast returns at this moment, as if to underscore the duality of truth itself. Though drawn partly from Virgil's and Ovid's descriptions of duplicitous Fama, Spenser represents his creation in absolute and unitary terms: as a monster who only lies and destroys. But Spenser ultimately presents a more complex truth through this creature that speaks to language and its reception: poetry lies in order to tell truths – not *a* truth but truths as restless and changing as the beast and readers alike. "Telling the truth" amounts to "double talk" and a double vision, for Spenser and his audience. The final monster of *The Faerie Queene* embodies this duality, partly through its relationship to other rebellious giants: born of Echnida, a "Monster direfull dred, / Whom Gods doe hate, and heauens abhor to see" and "Cruell *Typhaon*, whose tempestuous rage / Make th'heauens tremble oft, and him with vowes asswage" (6.6.10–11). Genealogically, the Blatant Beast relates to all the monstrous forces against Jovian supremacy that mark the continuing fall of the Golden Age into mutability and metamorphosis. Spenser's monster can stand for divided truths in the court of history, for he represents an overt challenge to the authority of self-fashioned gods, much as Typhoeus did. When the Beast rages and ranges through the religious houses of Faerie Land, sacking and spoiling them, he takes on the role of Henry VIII in dismantling the Catholic Church, or what might be read as a parody of Protestant iconoclastic fervour such as that shown by Guyon. In these ways, the Blatant Beast becomes a vehicle for ironized revelation: the destruction of the Church leads neither to the final ruin of time or a re-edified Jerusalem (implied in Book 1) but merely to the Tudors' rise. Duessa cannot be killed, except as a fiction of providential history and divine revelation. Calidore follows the trace of "outragious spoile" at the end of Book 6, as the Beast creates "such spoile, such hauocke, and such theft" with his religious desecrations that "thence all goodnesse he bereft, / That endlesse were to tell" (6.12.22–3). Catching up to the monster as he despoils a monastery, "Regarding nought religion, nor their holy heast" (24) Calidore witnesses its pillaging:

> From thence into the sacred Church he broke,
> And robd the Chancell, and the deskes downe threw,
> And Altars fouled, and blasphemy spoke,
> And th'Images for all their goodly hew,
> Did cast to ground, whilest none was them to rew;
> So all confounded and disordered there. (25)

But this is an open secret. As Irenius wryly notes in the *Viewe* – and as Jan Van der Noot awkwardly celebrates in *A Theatre for Worldlings* – the wealth of the ruined monasteries financed Tudor rule. Associated with the slander and lies of the Blatant Beast, these spoils indirectly tell the truth: the English state built itself not upon Troy's ruins but, in the name of "empire without end," upon the ruins of the Roman Catholic Church.[64] As the beneficiary of such spoils, Spenser may implicate himself in this ruin as well. His celebration of Tudor power ends ironically at the beginning, locating the Tudors' origin in the work of a lying monster. By destroying these edifices, the beast also destroys the places of memory of pre-Tudor England. By writing about medieval England – beginning in "the middest" – Spenser suggests that he has recollected Faerie Land from ruin.

The Blatant Beast is blamed for ruining Golden Age simplicity and truth, but the monster itself, with its long literary legacy, embodies a deeper truth: fiction speaks the truth to power through indirection, underneath the veils of poetry, as fiction which reveals itself as such. In other words, the Blatant Beast's "lies" allow Spenser to tell certain "truths" about Tudor history, their role in the ruin of Ireland and England, and truths that run counter to Trojan myths of power. The Blatant Beast is also a vehicle by which Spenser achieves a negative capability about his own poetry and posterity. What critics have called the darkening vision of the 1596 *Faerie Queene* offers a perspective on fame that reminds readers of Chaucer's *House of Fame* and thus Spenser's earlier work. Just as Chaucer provides a double vision of fame in two places – as monster-cum-monarch in Fame's palace, and as cacophonous crowd in the labyrinthine house that lies beneath it – so Spenser offers a double vision of fame through one image, that of the Beast.[65] And just as Chaucer celebrates the duality of fame – as stories that inextricably mingle truth and lies, history and fiction, making telling the truth difficult if not impossible – so this idea of fame survives until the end of Spenser's poetry. As the Blatant Beast roams wild and free over place and time, the ruins of time become the matter of story and history, and the place for the recollection that is fame. These ruins can stand for the matter of all textual edifices as well as a method of edification: an art of recollection that finally represents Spenserian self-fashioning.

In this conclusion, Spenser suggests how stories and history travel together: the ruins of power are also the ruins of poetry, and the cycle of ruin and recollection unites them. As Kenneth Gross has argued, "for all that the Beast represents a threat to the poet, the story of its destructive career reads . . . ultimately as a closing gesture of resistance, a way of cheating death – the poet possessing for himself and for his poem an image of the equivocal energies that exist both inside and outside that poem, that both drive and thwart the poem, which include the generosities and poisons of the poetic word."[66] As a figure of Fama, the Blatant Beast also represents the process of cultural transmission, the reception of poetry that continues after the death of the author. "So now he raungeth through the world againe, / . . . Ne any is, that may him now restraine" – accosting everyone, whether "worthy blame, or cleare of crime," in the arbitrary fashion of Fama:

> Ne spareth he most learned wits to rate,
> Ne spareth he the gentle Poets rime,
> But rends without regard of person or of time.
>
> Ne may this homely verse, of many meanest,
> Hope to escape his venemous despite,
> More then my former writs, all were they clearest
> From blamefull blot, and free from all that wite,
> With which some wicked tongues did it backebite,
> And bring into a mighty Peres displeasure,
> That neuer so deserued to endite.
> Therefore do you my rimes keep better measure,
> And seeke to please, that now is counted wisemens threasure (6.12.40–1)

Spenser describes his own poetry as ruined by the Blatant Beast but also recollected from its ruin; as the matter of memory at once caused and conveyed by the forces of history; as "wisemens threasure." Such treasure is the symbolic wealth to be plundered within the space of Faerie Land, and Spenser exhorts once and future readers to despoil this gold for new edifices. As Spenser reminds us, readers alone (and collectively) fashion history's spoils into the foundation for edification, not by reconstructing the past but by reforming it, renovating it for new uses, times, and places. Through the Blatant Beast, Spenser releases his poetry into the world, as in his first work: "Go lyttle Calender, thou hast a free passporte" (*The Shepheardes Calender*, "Epilogue," 7). In this paradoxical fashion, Spenser's poetry survives as the ruins of the Blatant Beast – the origin, end, and continued life of memory.

Conclusion: Misprision and Freedom: Ruining and Recollecting the Bower of Bliss

In *Areopagitica*, John Milton calls "our sage and serious poet Spenser" a "better teacher than Scotus or Aquinas," damning both the medieval theologians and the Renaissance poet with faint praise.[1] Milton was right, of course: Spenser *is* a great teacher. But was Milton his worst student? When Milton acknowledges Spenser's fame, he makes an equally infamous error by forgetting Spenser in the very act of remembering him. "Describing true temperance under the person of Guyon," he writes, Spenser "brings him in with his palmer through the cave of Mammon and the bower of earthly bliss, that he might see and know, and yet abstain" (729). Milton remembers, or rather misremembers, two important places in Book 2 of *The Faerie Queene*: the underworld Cave of Mammon, where Guyon endures all kinds of worldly and other-worldly temptations; and the Bower of Bliss, the "earthly" and seductive false Eden that Guyon (with the help of his Palmer) thoroughly destroys, as though to eradicate temptation forever from Faerie Land. Milton was wrong, of course, on one count – or partially right: Guyon *is* separated from the Palmer and consequently journeys through the Cave of Mammon without a Christian guide, reuniting with him only after his famous faint and en route to fulfill his quest to destroy the Bower of Bliss.

This notorious instance of misreading is foundational to Harold Bloom's discussion of the anxiety of influence, a theory of imitation that continues to exert a profound (if now somewhat occluded) influence on literary studies. In Bloom's model, feelings of belatedness, scarcity, and the oppressive weight of the literary past leads to misremembering and "misprision" on the part of authors who unconsciously seek to make space for themselves in an already crowded house of fame.

"Milton's is no ordinary error, no mere lapse in memory," Bloom argues, "but is itself a powerful misinterpretation of Spenser, and [thus] a strong defense against him."[2] This Freudian model suggests that the literary son's desire to slay his forefathers is veiled even from himself, contradicting his conscious desire for continuity, and thus expresses itself only in unconscious gaffes or gaps in memory: that is, through forgetting. Witness Milton misremembering Spenser. Throughout this book I have argued that Spenser analyses the anxiety of influence, *consciously* exploring the *unconscious* elements of literary reception, and illustrating the paradoxical truth that to read is ultimately to misread. This is vividly demonstrated in his first complete work, *The Shepheardes Calender*, where the character-cum-critic E.K. "ruins" the text through his desire for rebirth, unintentionally creating the space for its continued life in new times and places. In this way, Spenser searches the souls of readers and critics alike as the continued architects of memory. In paying homage to Spenser in *Areopagitica*, I will suggest here, Milton fashions himself as a momentarily forgetful reader – an every-Guyon, so to speak – in an intentional act of misreading. He thereby indirectly reminds readers of Spenser's "methode" as a "Poet historical," the art of memory, demonstrating how reading (like writing) entails both "ruining" and "recollecting" previous works.[3] By way of a conclusion, I argue that Milton's misprision in fact remembers Spenser fittingly, revealing as much about our own psyches as those of early modern writers, for Milton's tract on censorship speaks to the judgments of readers from ancient Greece to Renaissance England and beyond.

Why would Milton *intentionally* misremember Spenser's work? Milton's sense of irony provides one answer. His Spenser appears to be not only "sage and serious" but also witty and irreverent, and Milton remembers Spenser here in the most appropriate way possible: by imitating his method of recollection. In so doing, Milton emulates the rich tradition of "Poets historical" populating this book – Sidney, to be sure, but also Plato, Cicero, and even Augustine, as well as Spenser-cum-E.K., might be added to the list of authors who write "non-fictional" prose that nevertheless employs the strategies of fiction writers, or the "methode" of the poets: the art of memory.[4] To "forget" at key moments, to ask the reader to remember (indeed, to learn) what the hero fails to, represents the crux of the Spenserian education. The interplay between reading and misreading (as well as remembering and forgetting) so central to Spenser's edifying poetry is precisely the education that Milton (as reader of Spenser) ironically demonstrates through misprision.[5] Not coincidentally, I argue, Milton omits what takes place in "the middest" of these episodes, en route from the Cave of Mammon to the Bower of Bliss: Guyon's visit to the Castle of Alma. This absent place paradoxically returns readers to the space where Spenser portrays locational memory – the "wel-head of the History" in *The Faerie Queene* (738). As the key memory locus in Spenser's corpus, the Castle of Alma represents a model of edification within *Areopagitica*. By indirectly reminding readers of this place, Milton remembers Spenser's speaking picture of the psyche as an allegorical lesson in writing, reading, and judgment.

Although Milton asserts that Guyon learns to distinguish virtue from vice in the Cave of Mammon with the help of his Palmer, this mistake ironically reminds readers that Spenser suggests just the opposite. Without the Palmer, without a guide through the underworld of history, Guyon is lost – not literally, for Mammon serves as his trusty Virgil, but spiritually, for Guyon can remember neither divinity nor history without the Palmer's prophylactic doctrine. What might be viewed as Guyon abstaining from sin, as I argue above, points to a problem of historical amnesia revealed in Mammon's Cave and other places: the Castle of Alma and especially the Bower of Bliss, where Guyon's resistance to seductive structures manifests, in part, a wilful ignorance. Although he seems to resist all of the temptations that Mammon's gold can purchase, including the seduction of endless empire embodied by Philotime, he does so for all the wrong reasons. Guyon rejects the god of gold and his imperial offspring not because they are idols – self-fashioned gods – but because they are not *his* idol: the Faerie Queene, and perhaps by analogy Queen Elizabeth. Guyon's inability to "read" Mammon's "riches" ironically leads him unwittingly to re-enact the fall of humanity in himself (2.7.12). Indeed, Mammon's initial reading of Guyon – "I read thee rash, and heedlesse of thy selfe" – proves correct in the end (7). Wandering through a kind of fallen Eden, the Garden of Proserpina, Guyon meets Tantalus and Pilate; however, when both figures confess their idolatry, their mistaking of divinity and subsequent punishment, Guyon *still* cannot "read" the situation, instead simply viewing each as an "Ensample . . . of mind intemperate" (60). Guyon famously faints at the end of the episode, yet he never falls into history. Instead, Guyon's naive virtue remains intact: untested, untried, unsurprised by sin. He "abstains," as Milton puts it, but only by virtue of his profound obliviousness. Guyon never partakes of the apple of knowledge that Mammon offers him, ironically refusing that which might save him: that is, an unsentimental education about the relation of idolatry to imperium, or poetry to power. In this allegory of reading, Guyon never learns to recognize the stories that make up history.

Ruining the Bower of Bliss thus represents a logical conclusion to Guyon's miseducation. At the end of Book 2, Guyon finally gets the adventure he has been longing for: by "Palmers governaunce," as the heading to Canto 12 notes, he leaves on an epic journey to destroy the Bower of Bliss, but not without first "passing . . . perils great" (2.12). Unlike in the Cave of Mammon, the Palmer guides Guyon through temptations, offering him an education along the way about the perils of these places where "Pleasure dwelles in sensuall delights / Mongst thousand dangers, and then thousand magick mights" (2.12.1). Passing through the "Gulfe of Greedinesse" and the "Rocke of vile Reproch," they witness forces that "ruinate" heroes like Guyon (3, 7–8). The Palmer teaches Guyon how to "read" these figures: that is, as sinful. "Behold th'ensamples in our sights, / Of lustfull luxurie and thriftlesse wast," he tells Guyon, "shame and sad reproch, here to be red, / By these rent reliques," concluding "hereby be counselled" (9). Yet these examples speak doubly, suggesting other interpretations of the temptations that Guyon meets with, especially his second encounter with "the wanton Phaedria, which late / Did ferry him ouer the Idle lake" (17). This "Phaedria" might obliquely remind readers of Plato's Phaedrus and the discussion of love therein, where the temptations of love ideally lead to recollection rather than ruin, in which true love can offer a safe haven of sorts. But Guyon and the Palmer see only perils rather than possibilities in this "Labyrinth" of love, as confirmation of the commonplace notion that beauty represents the devil's snare (20). Passing "A seemely Maiden, sitting by the shore . . . / with great sorrow and sad agony," the Palmer warns Guyon to show no "foolish pitty," for "then her guilefull bayt / She will enbosome deeper in your mind, / And for your ruine at the last away" (27, 29). The mind's own place is a fortress under attack from such seductions, the Palmer instructs Guyon, never realizing that the real enemy might lie within.

Yet Spenser offers other ways to read these places, particularly the Bower of Bliss. After narrowly escaping other "hellish Harpies" (36) they finally arrive at Acrasia's island paradise:

Thence passing forth, they shortly do arriue,
Whereas the Bowre of Blisse was situate;

A place pickt out by choyce of best aliue,
That natures worke by art can imitate. (42)

Here as elsewhere in Faerie Land, readers can see double: a deceptive
facade intended to seduce and destroy, on the one hand, and a mirror in
which to see ourselves, on the other. To be sure, this pleasant place has
poetry's ruinous love stories written all over it; on the entryway gates
"all the famous history / Of *Iason* and *Medea* was ywritt" (44). Against
such figurative warnings, though, stands a "comely personage" (46) as
an ironic reminder about more temperate loves:

They in that place him *Genius* did call:
Not that celestiall powre, to whom the care
Of life, and generation of all
That liues, pertaines in charge particulare,
Who wondrous things concerning our welfare,
And straunge phantomes doth let vs oft forsee,
And ofte of secret ill bids vs beware:
That is our Selfe, whom though we do not see,
Yet each doth in him selfe it well perceiue to bee. (47)

The "place" of reading merges with the space of the self and the mind's
own "kind of divining power," as Socrates calls it.[6] "Therefore a God
him sage Antiquity / Did wisely make, and good *Agdistes* call" (48),
Spenser writes, punctuating this powerful reminder of the spirit of love
in *The Symposium*, if ironically, as its twin, double, opposite. "But this
same was to that quite contrary," Spenser writes of the Genius, describing him as "The foe of life, that good enuyes to all, / That secretly doth
vs procure to fall / Through guilefull semblaunts" (48). This contrast
indirectly reminds readers of the genius within all humans, the self that
acts as our guide through "secret ill," the self that cannot be seen but
which can be nevertheless can be recognized. This spirit – the "genius"
or daemon of love that plays such an important role in Socrates' edification, the origin story of his history – represents divinity in a particular sense: as the best part of humanity. Plato portrays such love of
wisdom as an art of recollection, a process which he demonstrates by
rewriting the tale of Simonides in the *Phaedrus* and the *Symposium*, recollecting from ruin the house that Socrates built both as (and through)
dialogue with writing.

By representing this Genius as Plato's evil twin, Spenser also reminds readers that the Bower of Bliss finds its own twin in the Garden of Adonis, which also recalls the *Phaedrus* as an originary common place for philosophy and poetry. In the Garden of Adonis, readers discover the Porter, "Old *Genius*, the which a double nature has" (3.6.31). Spenser portrays "eterne in mutabilitie" (47) through a rewriting of Socrates' story of the soul's journey in the *Phaedrus*, with the Porter playing the role of Minos in the underworld, the figure whose judgment determines the "eternall fate" of all souls after death (32). Yet this allegory of rebirth is firmly planted on the earth, especially given that the "Great enimy" here is "wicked *Time*" and its terrible "scyth" (39). The Garden of Adonis represents the cycle of life and death as a Platonic and poetic myth, as a *locus amoenus* where the "substance" of life "is not chaunged, nor altered, / But th'only forme and outward fashion" (38). By framing such matter in terms of memory, Spenser reminds readers of what the Garden of Adonis signifies in Plato's *Phaedrus*: the place of writing. To make a case for dialogue over writing, Socrates argues that nobody "with serious intent" to teach "writes [his thoughts] in water or the black fluid we call ink," just as no farmer "with serious intent" would "plant [his seeds] during the summer in a garden of Adonis," where the fruit would just as quickly die as it would bloom (522, 521). When no more serious work is to be done, Socrates acknowledges, such a person "will sow his seed in literary gardens . . . and write when he does write by way of pastime, collecting a store of refreshment both for his own memory against the day 'when age oblivious comes,' and for all such as tread in his footsteps, and he will take pleasure in watching the tender plants grow up."[7] That Plato refers to himself as a philosopher poet here seems clear; Socrates does the same when he ironically remarks, "Then we may regard our literary pastime as having reached a satisfactory conclusion" (524). Writing itself is no "matter of reproach" but rather a matter of perspective, dangerously deceptive only if one "regards it as containing important truth of permanent validity" – which speaks as much to philosophy as to poetry (523).

In *The Faerie Queene* as in the *Phaedrus*, the Garden of Adonis represents a common place for fiction writers in a variety of fields, and a place where the transience of writing is in fact the basis of immortality, at least within time and history. For writing to achieve "eterne in mutabilitie," it must continue a cycle of life and death, ruin and recollection; such changes in the "forme and outward fashion" of writing mirrors the process by which readers are "fashiond . . . within their inmost part," and vice versa (3.6.38, 44). To underscore that this garden's allegory of life and love also represents an allegory of poetry, Spenser links this place with another location for memory: Chaucer's labyrinth of love in *The House of Fame*. The Garden of Adonis is similarly composed of texts, a swirling tree house of motion in which the other poets' writing becomes the matter of memory to be fashioned anew:

> There was a pleasaunt arbour, not by art,
> But of the trees owne inclination made,
> Which knitting their rancke braunches part to part,
> With wanton yuie twyne entrayld athwart . . .
> Fashiond aboue within their innmost part. (44)

The Garden of Adonis also recalls the myth of Cupid and Psyche, implied in Socrates' allegory of the soul in the *Phaedrus*, in ways that return to Spenser's allegory of Psyche in Alma's Castle:

> And his true loue faire *Psyche* with him playes,
> Fayre *Psyche* to him lately reconcyld,
> After long troubles and vnmeet vpbrayese,
> With which his mother *Venus* her reuyld,
> And eke himselfe her cruelly exyld. (50)

With Love and the Soul reunited here, they give birth to a daughter, "Pleasure" – symbolically, that which Guyon and the Palmer attempt to destroy as though the true "enimy" of Faerie Land.

As an allegory of love, the Garden of Adonis represents a place made of writing, a place fashioned by poets and readers alike, who participate in the continued life of stories throughout time. This space implicitly counters Guyon's ruin of the Bower of Bliss by suggesting that poetry survives in ruins, indeed, that it finds "eterne in mutabilitie." Readers can thus see what Guyon and the Palmer cannot, though their blindness produces our insight. The Bower itself, "A large and spacious plaine" (2.7.50), resembles more than one sweet spot: "*Ida*, where the Gods lou'd to repaire," the site of the judgment of Paris, "When euer they their heauenly bowres forlore; / Or sweet *Parnasse*, the haunt of Muses faire; / Or *Eden* selfe, if ought with *Eden* mought compaire" – a space that evokes Milton's own paradise lost and found (52). Like the twin of Socrates' temperate lover, Guyon attempts to steer his soul's chariot of desire, "Bridling his will, and maistering his might" until he meets his greatest temptation, Acrasia herself (53). Approaching the bower, Guyon sees "No gate, but like one, being goodly dight / With boughes and braunches, which did broad dilate / Their clasping armes, in wanton wreathings intricate" (53). Like Chaucer's labyrinthine house of fame, this entryway consists of *textus* – trees, twigs, branches, which also represent writing itself: a bower made from the matter of other texts. When Guyon and the Palmer finally discover Acrasia in the midst of practicing her "sorceree / And witchcraft" with "a new Louer" (72), they hear one "chaunt this louely lay": "Ah see the Virgin Rose . . . / Gather therefore the Rose, whilest yet is prime, / For soone comes age, that will her pride deflowre" (74–5). The enemy thus appears in the form of a *carpe diem* poem, an ironic play upon the seductive wiles of fiction. Indeed, Acrasia's witchcraft is her beauty – the bait that makes heroes fall from arms to the woman, from actions to words, as evidenced by the "braue shield" of her victim: "full of old moniments, / Was fowly ra'st, that none the signes might see" (80).

In this parodic portrait of puritanical perspectives on poetry, Spenser humorously laments, "O horrible enchantment, that him so did blend" (80). But Guyon takes these dangers seriously, releasing Acrasia's victims, then supplying "counsell sage in steed thereof to him applyde" (82). After briefly reiterating the Palmer's teachings, Guyon obliterates the Bower:

> But all those pleasaunt bowres and Pallace braue,
> *Guyon* broke downe, with rigour pittilesse;
> Ne ought their goodly workmanship might saue
> Them from the tempest of his wrathfulnesse,
> But that their blisse he turn'd to balefulnese:
> Their groues he feld, their gardins did deface,
> Their arbers spoyle, their Cabinets suppresse,
> Their banket houses burne, their buldings race,
> And of the fairest late, now made the fowlest place. (83)

Guyon ruins the Bower as though the place itself, rather than his response to it, posed a threat to humanity. He transforms "those pleasant bowres and Pallace braue," symbolic locations for memory (philosopher's field and prince's palace), into "the fowlest place" imaginable by ruining and defacing, burning and erasing all that dangerous beauty. As an allegory of reading, Guyon attempts to destroy writing itself. With the "place" of poetry obliterated, albeit temporarily, they liberate those whom Acrasia had "charm'd" into "those wild-beasts" (84). As the Palmer explains,

These seeming beasts are men indeed,
Whom this Enchauntresse hath transformed thus,
Whylome her louers, which her lusts did feed,
Now turned into figures hideous,
According to their mindes like monstruous.
Sad end (quoth he) of life intemperate. (85)

Observing Grill, a victim who is unhappy to be returned from swine to humanity, Guyon provides the concluding moral of the story, repeating the Palmer's lessons about temperance:

See the mind of beastly man,
That hath so soone forgot the excellence
Of his creation, when he life began,
That now he chooseth, with vile difference,
To be a beast, and lack intelligence. (87)

Such beasts cannot be saved, the Palmer replies, as if taking the high road: "Let *Grill* be *Grill*, and haue his hoggish minde; / But let vs hence depart, whilest wether serues and wind" (87).

Guyon defeats a Circe-like figure and, like Odysseus, sails on, unable to see himself in this place, which like the Cave of Mammon holds up a mirror to his desires. Yet Spenser thoroughly ironizes Guyon's pious homily about the importance of memory – remembering yourself and humanity. After all, what have readers witnessed prior to this episode if not Guyon forgetting "the excellence / Of his creation," especially in the Cave of Mammon? Spenser suggests that Guyon himself acts like a pig without knowing it. Blind to his "self," Guyon cannot see that he worships his own Acrasia, in a sense affirming what the Cave of Mammon merely implies: that Guyon already serves Mammon by serving the Faerie Queene. The desire for fame, power, immortality is the same "gold" with which Mammon tempts Guyon. Such desires motivate Guyon's actions, even though he wraps them in a narrative of epic heroism and chivalric knighthood. Unconsciously re-enacting stories of history dooms Guyon to repeat what he cannot remember, as he ruins poetry's places in the name of love and with the Palmer's blessing. In a sense, they embody the danger of taking fiction as truth;

symbolically destroying the space of their own allegory, they dehuman-
ize themselves. Readers again can see what eludes Guyon: the vision of
history in Mammon's Cave. Here as there, readers observe that empire
is built upon the ruins of conquest, a desire for gold only thinly veiled
by self-fashioning fictions.

As an allegory of reading, the Bower of Bliss has elicited a range of
responses from readers. In *Renaissance Self-Fashioning*, Stephen Greenblatt contrasts the Cave of Mammon and the Bower of Bliss, while (like
Milton) omitting or forgetting the place in between them: Alma's Castle. "The Bower's dangerous attractiveness is in sharp contrast to the
Cave of Mammon," Greenblatt reflects, "where Guyon's experience,
and ours, is remarkable for the complete absence of sympathetic response to the temptation"; whereas Guyon merely faints at the exit of
Mammon's Cave, "In the Bower of Bliss, Guyon . . . does not merely
depart from the place of temptation but reduces it to ruins."[8] "To help
us understand more fully why he must do so in order to play his part
in Spenser's fashioning of a gentlemen," Greenblatt invokes Freud's
Civilization and its Discontents, apt for its portrait of the psyche as layers of Rome's ruins. Greenblatt reads the Bower's ruin partly through
Freudian lens – with the crucial difference that he attributes to Spenser
a *conscious* rather than an *unconscious* will to ruin. "Spenser, who participates with Freud in a venerable and profoundly significant intertwining of sexual and colonial discourse, accepts sexual colonialism only
with a near-tragic sense of the cost," he argues:

> The Bower of Bliss must be destroyed not because its gratifications are un-
> real but because they threaten "civility" – civilization – which for Spenser
> is achieved only through renunciation and the constant exercise of
> power . . . The violence directed against Acrasia's sensual paradise is both
> in itself an equivalent of erotic excess and a pledge of loving service to the
> royal mistress. Even when he most bitterly criticizes its abuses or records
> its brutality, Spenser loves power and attempts to link his own art ever
> more closely with its symbolic and literal embodiment. *The Faerie Queene*
> is, as he insists again and again, wholly wedded to the autocratic ruler of
> the English state.[9]

The same ideology that impels Guyon to destroy the Bower, Greenblatt
suggests, can be seen elsewhere throughout early modernity, in "the
European response to the native cultures in the New World, the English
colonial struggle in Ireland, and the Reformation attack on images."[10]

Greenblatt thus attempts to remember the ruins of history that Spenser and readers may have repressed or forgotten. Rather than benighted, he views self-fashioning as a self-conscious response to social constraints placed on freedom, imagining the self as built upon the ruin of others – an identity often made in deals with the devil, so to speak. Turning to *A Viewe of the Present State of Ireland*, Greenblatt specifically equates Guyon's destruction of the Bower of Bliss with Spenser's role in Ireland's reconquest. Greenblatt thereby reminds readers that the matter of Ireland matters not only in Book 5 but throughout *The Faerie Queene*, arguing that this seminal work bears significantly on how readers judge Spenser:

> If it is true that we are highly sensitive to those aspects of the Renaissance that mark the early, tentative, conflict-ridden fashioning of modern consciousness, then *The Faerie Queene* is of quite exceptional significance, for Spenser's stated intention is precisely "to fashion a gentleman or noble person in vertuous and gentle discipline." This mirroring – the conscious purpose of the work seeming to enact the larger cultural movement – may help to account for the reader's sense of encountering in Spenser's poem the process of self-fashioning itself. In the Bower of Bliss that process is depicted as involving a painful sexual renunciation: in Guyon's destructive act we are invited to experience the ontogeny of our culture's violent resistance to a sensuous release for which it nevertheless yearns with a new intensity. The resistance is necessary for Spenser because what is threatened is "our Selfe, whom though we do not see, / Yet each doth in him selfe it well perceive to bee" (2.12.47). We can secure that self only through a restraint that involves the destruction of something intensely beautiful; to succumb to that beauty is to lose the shape of manhood and be transformed into a beast.[11]

For Greenblatt, Spenser's self-fashioning builds upon the ruin of Ireland, "the destruction of something intensely beautiful." Playing "a game that reflects the simultaneous perception of a tragic choice and the determination to 'forget' that perception in an illusory resolution," he argues that Spenser's "identity is achieved" only "through . . . service" to the "ideal values embodied in a female ruler."[12] Greenblatt thereby identifies Guyon with Spenser: both serve the Faerie Queene, destroying and forgetting, ruining and repressing whatever threatens their sense of self. In no uncertain terms, he paints a Spenser for hire, selling himself to power at whatever cost.

Yet we are all Guyons, Greenblatt further argues, grounding our collective identity upon repression: that is, forgetting the past. "The experience I have just described is . . . common to us all," he writes, "embedded in each of our personal histories, though a protective cultural amnesia may have led us to forget it until we reexperience it in art," adding that "we need, at this level, to bring nothing to the text but ourselves."[13] Against such forgetfulness, he asserts the importance of remembering history: "Fuller understanding, however, requires that we confront not only personal history but the history of peoples. We must . . . incorporate the work of art into the texture of a particular pattern of life, a collective experience that transcends it and completes its meaning. If Spenser told readers a story, they listened, and listened with pleasure, because they themselves, in the shared life of their culture, were telling versions of that story again and again, recording the texts on themselves and on the world around them."[14] Using language that evokes the Castle of Alma and the Trojan tales read there, as well as the process of "recording" stories told "again and again" that form our "collective experience," Greenblatt suggests that readers should not forget history in order to idolize art, or believe that the "pursuit of the divine in man" justifies inhumanity, even if Spenser's poetry makes "exquisite ethical discriminations." He argues, in short, that readers should not see poetry and politics, story and history, ideas and ideology, or for that matter self and other, as inhabiting separate realms. At the same time, he identifies the space for such collective memory with Spenser's modern readers. To make this argument, however, Greenblatt must forget about the Castle of Alma, which I would suggest allows him to position Spenser as the proverbial "other" to ourselves. Greenblatt implies that readers must judge Spenser as such: "The rich complexities of Spenser's art are not achieved in spite of what is for us a repellent political ideology – the passionate worship of imperialism – but are inseparably linked to that ideology."[15] The key word here is "us": if we find imperialism "repellent," how can we not find Spenser's poetry, bound to bad faith politics, repellent as well?

Although far from new, Greenblatt's insights nevertheless retain their power, in part because they illuminate Spenser's work in profound and profoundly ironic ways. If we say that Greenblatt misreads the Bower of Bliss, we need to ask how and why this matters. He appears to confuse author with character, attributing Guyon's actions and motivations to Spenser, judging his life and work through the eyes of our modern perspective. He also finds Spenser guilty of malicious intent, of telling the same story of history "again and again," as though a Circe-like figure seducing readers into a state of "collective amnesia," causing them to forget themselves and the truth of history. Yet much of what Greenblatt attributes to Spenser, Spenser ironically attributes to Guyon: the "worship of power," a blindness to his own idolatry, a re-enactment of imperial fictions in the name of love for God and country, a legacy of destruction. In my view, as I have argued throughout this study, it is a mistake to believe that "Spenser told readers *a* story" – one unifying truth – or that he imagined culture as built upon the repression of history's ruins. His characters may forget the past but Spenser does just the opposite, continually reminding readers about devastating truths, including the ones that he lived. Such reminders continually find ironic expression in the form of his characters' forgetfulness, which in turn prompts the remembrance of his readers. This art of recollection *is* Spenserian self-fashioning. Moreover, and still more ironically, Spenser's poetry speaks to the very cultural poetics that defines Greenblatt's attempts to shape a newer historicism, for it continually reminds readers of how art intersects with life, and poetry with power, how stories intertwine with history in the making, how ideological fictions are re-enacted in the past and in the present state – such truths that ironically are expressed perhaps most clearly, in *A Viewe of the Present State of Ireland*. In many ways, Greenblatt and Spenser would seem to agree about poetry's place in culture.

Nevertheless, we might recognize a certain anxiety of influence at play in Greenblatt's view of Spenser, a conscious identification with Guyon that leads to an unconscious performance of his own thesis: "we can secure that self only through . . . the destruction of something intensely beautiful."[16] Greenblatt appears to fashion or "secure" his "self" by destroying idealized images of Spenser, a dynamic that can especially be recognized, ironically enough, in his arguments about iconoclasm. Comparing Guyon's destruction of the Bower of Bliss to Protestant reformers' destruction of images associated with the Roman Catholic Church, Greenblatt observes that "the art destroyed by Guyon does not pretend to image holy things" because of Spenser's fear that art itself may be idolatrous: "it is precisely this possibility that is suggested by Guyon's iconoclasm, for Acrasia's realm is lavishly described in just those terms which the defenders of poetry in the Renaissance reserved for imagination's noblest achievements."[17] In Greenblatt's view, Spenser "deeply distrusts" the Renaissance aesthetic of *ars celare artem*, and this distrust stems from a fear of idolatry, that "images may make a blasphemous claim to reality" that will compel worship: "Spenser, in the face of deep anxiety about the impure claims of art, save[s] art for himself and his readers by making its createdness explicit."[18] In contrast to the "achievement of great drama . . . and supremely of Shakespeare, whose constant allusions to the fictionality of his creations only serve paradoxically to question the status of everything outside themselves," he asserts that "Spenser's profoundly *undramatic* art, in the same movement by which it wards off idolatry, wards off this radical questioning of everything that exists."[19] Greenblatt concludes: "It is art whose status is questioned in Spenser, not ideology; indeed, art is questioned precisely to spare ideology that internal distantiation it undergoes in the work of Shakespeare or Marlowe. For Spenser this is the final colonialism, the colonialism of language, yoked to the service of a reality forever outside itself, dedicated to 'the most High, Mightie, and Magnificent Empresse . . . Elizabeth by the Grace of God Queene of England Fraunce and Ireland and of Virginia Defendour of the Faith.'"[20] Yet Greenblatt clearly engages in some idol-smashing of his own: in effect, he "ruins" Spenser, doing violence to the text (ironically, in the context of an episode about doing violence to texts) in order to fashion the "other" to what would become a newer historicism's defining sense of "self." By dethroning the "Prince of Poets," Greenblatt makes a new space in the field, displacing Spenser for Shakespeare, poetry for drama, the history of ideas for popular culture, ruin for monumental fantasies of rebirth. He achieves this in *ad hominem* fashion, drawing Spenser as a failed social climber, a power-hungry Machiavel, and the plague of Ireland: a nobody who tried to become somebody by any means necessary. Spenser, who calls his own persona "Immeritô," might have been the first to agree with him. As I have suggested here, Spenser may be his own worst critic, and his writing insistently examines the contradictions that define him as both a humanist *and* a colonialist, as a creator *and* a recollector of ruin. Indeed, Spenser himself may suggest that Guyon represents a part of himself – but only in part.

What I take to be Greenblatt's "misreading" of Spenser nevertheless reveals profound truths about all acts of reading. To a degree, all literary critics (myself included) have a bit of E.K. in them, boldly asserting the hidden truth of a text, in the process taking it apart and then remaking the dismantled text in his or her own image. We might call this process of reception, of ruining and recollecting, an "art of dialectic," as Socrates does in the *Phaedrus* when he confesses to being a lover of divisions and collections: seeing the part in relation to the whole, ruining structures in order to rebuild and reform edification itself (522). These are the ruins that readers make, consciously and unconsciously, in the act of reading, and yet these ruins become places in which to recollect the past anew. In this way, the Blatant Beast roams free, for his destruction creates the space for new constructions. If Greenblatt's writing destroyed an idealized Spenser, it also gave birth to another Spenser with a greater touch of the real, generating a continued dialogue. This act of reading demonstrates the life cycle of creativity: the ongoing process of ruin and recollection, the conscious and unconscious refashioning of the past.

This may be Milton's central point in *Areopagitica*, where he reads the Bower of Bliss in a manner not unlike Greenblatt. Milton also forgets what happens in "the middest" of Guyon's journey, though for different reasons. Yet Milton also defends Guyon, so to speak, from Greenblatt's accusations and Spenser's implied self-accusations, by judging this fiction in light of history. What falls in between the Cave of Mammon and the Bower of Bliss – between these spaces of epic remembering and forgetting, poetry's hell and heaven, underworld and Edenic sweet spot – is Spenser's allegory of the soul and psyche: Alma's Castle. In this place, as I have argued, Spenser illustrates saving the soul and mending the psyche as an art of recollecting the past, individually and collectively. This memory theatre dramatizes self-fashioning as an art of memory, as Guyon along with a once and future King Arthur traverses the allegorical edifice of the human body before arriving in the mind's own place: the room where Eumnestes and Anamnestes gather together the matter of England's collective memory. Spenser represents the art of memory as both an edifice and a process of edification, an allegorical story of history about the endless task of recollecting the ruins of the past. I have further suggested that this dovetails closely with the origin myth of the art of memory: the tale of the poet Simonides who "discovers" the importance of location to memory when he memorially reconstructs a fallen edifice, recalling the dead by virtue of their places – their "heads" as *topoi* – within this space. Alma's Castle stands as a mnemonic space in which buildings and books double as locations for locational memory, as parallel structures continually falling to and being recollected from ruin. This episode thus emblematizes how the processes of writing and reading share a related method.

The Castle of Alma also suggests that the problem of reading idolatrously relates to both poetry and politics, as well as, more broadly, the issue of how to tell that truth – how to discern it by virtue of (rather than in spite of) its double. Arthur and Guyon each read one of Eumnestes' history books, histories which seem to tell very different stories and yet ultimately reveal a similar paradoxical truth: the inextricability of story and history, in writing as in the world. Arthur's history exposes the ongoing re-enactment of the tales of Troy, the reiteration of ruin and re-edification in ever-newer Troynovants. Guyon's history book, though a fanciful Faerie Land history, reveals a similar view: these faerie tales also re-enact a similar pattern of ruin and re-edification. To underscore this similarity, Spenser locates the origin of "all Elfin kind" – punning on its "first authour" – in "the gardins of *Adonis*" (2.10.71). Unveiling his own allegory with this allusion, revealing how and why such fictions need to be "read" as such in writing and in the world, Spenser lies in order to tell certain truths about how stories are used in living history to fashion gods of gold, Mammon's offspring, and to conceal ruin with fictions of "endless empire." Such idols of power can also play God in another equally important sense: as judges of good and bad, right and wrong, truth and lies, as the arbiters of justice in the related realms of politics and poetry. From Virgil's monstrous Fama, to Chaucer's Dame Fame, to Spenser's monarchial Mercilla, such figures have populated this study. Yet the ability to judge writing as worthy of fame or shame, as Spenser intimates and Milton argues explicitly, is a power that resides not only in princes but also in ordinary people.

The ability to *judge* writing, to do justice to a text or a person (unlike in the Areopagate court of power), lies at the heart of the Spenserian education. As Milton implies in *Areopagitica*, poetry is not dangerous except insofar as readers judge it so, a case he makes by remembering Guyon's bad example. Guyon's hypocrisy and blindness, and Spenser's method of revealing this, provide Milton with an unstated moral to his misreading of *The Faerie Queene*: Guyon's response mirrors those who would censor writing. Milton argues in *Areopagitica* that poetry should remain in the Republic precisely because it teaches readers to tell the truth – a truth that he tells indirectly by fashioning himself as a fiction. Guyon's ruin of the Bower of Bliss, and his fall into forgetfulness rather than history, serves as one way that Milton defends the virtue of freedom of expression: that is, ironically. He asserts that Guyon needs a guide in order to read the temptations of Mammon's Cave and Acrasia's Bower correctly, to "see and know, and yet abstain." By forgetting, Milton indirectly reminds readers that in both the absence *and* the presence of his Palmer, Guyon plays the part of an everyman, re-enacting the Fall by deifying humans and demonizing knowledge.

Yet Guyon's misprision allows Milton to make a case for the place of ruin in edification. To judge "good" from "evil" means to see double and yet to discern: "Good and evil we know in the field of this world grow up together almost inseparably," Milton explains, "and the knowledge of good is so involved and interwoven with the knowledge of evil, and in so many cunning resemblances hardly to be discerned that those confused seeds which were imposed on Psyche as an incessant labor to cull out and sort asunder, were not more intermixed . . . perhaps this is that doom which Adam fell into of knowing good and evil, that is to say, of knowing good by evil" (728). This allusion to "Psyche" recalls a range of narratives about the soul – from Spenser's Castle to Plato's Chariot – in which allegories of love represent stories about history, most explicitly the myth of Cupid and Psyche, a subtext in the *Phaedrus* as in *The Faerie Queene*. Unable to see her divine lover Cupid, who appears only under cover of the night, Psyche must endure a number of tests so that she might come to know her love fully. Milton presents this tale of darkness made visible as a way to explain the task of Psyche in history: the search for an invisible god. Just as Psyche laboured to "discern" virtue and vice, so the human psyche comes to know truth – Una – by virtue of its double – Duessa – and even then, such duality itself reflects in mirrors more than one. Guyon exemplifies this endeavour, paradoxically but not tragically; after all, Milton suggests, how can the fall into knowledge not be judged a happy one? "Since therefore, the knowledge and survey of vice is in this world so necessary to the constituting of human virtue, and the scanning of error to the confirmation of truth," he asks rhetorically, then "how can we more safely and with less danger scout into the regions of sin and falsity than by reading all manner of tractates and hearing all manner of reason?" (729). "This is the benefit," he concludes, "which may be had of books promiscuously read" (729). The point of Milton's irony, his forgetfulness, thus becomes clear: Guyon's ruin of the Edenic Bower of Bliss can be part of the reader's edification – the "other" who helps fashion "self" knowledge. Guyon's self-deceptive abstinence ultimately reveals the importance of reading "promiscuously," an activity which finds a parallel in Augustine's insistence upon charitable reading: readers are exhorted to remember rather than to forget, to find truth in unlikely regions of "sin" by finding themselves in that same place. Indeed, Milton puts himself in that very position, repeating Guyon's mistake so that readers might also make this discovery themselves.

By playing Guyon's part, it seems, Milton fashions *Areopagitica* as an art of memory. Reminding us of Guyon's failed education in the Cave of Mammon and the Bower of Bliss, Milton returns to the central locus of Spenserian edification, his Castle of Psyche, where readers can find truth *as* its double. This place fashions readers as their own best guides – indeed, as the only guides worth having. In effect, Milton reforms this edifice, remembering Alma's Castle from within poetry's ruins, perhaps most poignantly by telling a new (and old) story of history: reading as misreading. Delivering *Areopagitica* like an oration, Milton dramatizes his art of memory as a method of recollecting the past. Yet the story itself matters – remembering it consciously rather than unconsciously re-enacting it. This history of reading, as Milton recalls to readers' minds, doubles as the history of censorship. Writing that challenges the orthodoxies of gods or states has always been judged deceptive, blasphemous, dangerous, immoral, and corrupting – a threat to the good of all. Then again, Milton indirectly asks, who can tell *the* truth, either its prosecutors or defenders? This unspoken question lies at the heart of Milton's history, his charge against those who would judge writing yet never themselves. Wilful innocence that refuses knowledge bears false witness, he implies, with a history of misjudgment that spans from ancient Greece to early modern England. Milton begins with Protagoras – whose "books . . . were by the judges of Areopagus commanded to be burnt, and himself banished the territory for a discourse begun with his confessing not to know whether there were gods, or whether not" – and builds to the Inquisition during the Reformation, when "any subject that was not to their palate they either condemned in a prohibition . . . or had it straight into the new purgatory of an Index" (721, 724). What history damns as heresy is an ever-shifting mark, he suggests, so readers must trust their own authority over any who claim to reveal *the* truth, whether heads of church or state.

After all, as Milton argues, truth itself now lies in ruins – if it ever took any other shape:

> Truth indeed came once into the world with her divine Master, and was a perfect shape most glorious to look on. But when he ascended, and his apostles after him were laid asleep, then straight arose a wicked race of deceivers, who, as that story goes of the Egyptian Typhon with his conspirators, how they dealt with the good Osiris, took the virgin Truth, hewed her lovely form into a thousand pieces, and scattered them to the four winds. From that time ever since, the sad friends of Truth, such as durst appear, imitating the careful search that Isis made for the mangled body of Osiris, went up and down gathering up limb by limb still as they could find them. (741–2)

Milton's Golden Age origin tale of truth ironically invites readers' sceptical responses, particularly as it recalls Spenser's duplicitous Typhonic
narratives. What begins as Christian history metamorphizes into Pagan
myth, suggesting Milton's underlying point: the knowledge of truth,
like the knowledge of past, can only ever be partial, a fact that speaks
indirectly to the need for imagination as well as memory, for stories as
well as histories, for reserving judgments as well as making them. All
of Psyche's faculties together produce recollection, a process that leads
to fair judgment, and which Milton figures in symbolic terms as the
re-membering of Osiris' scattered limbs. By example, Milton demonstrates not only the mingling of story and history but also the impossibility of ever recovering the truth of origins. Readers strive to revive,
to reunite "those dissevered pieces which are yet wanting to the body
of Truth" even as they know this task is impossible – at least within
time (742). Milton portrays this paradox as the ongoing reformation of
a ruined edifice: even "when every stone is laid artfully together," he
writes, "it cannot be united into a continuity, it can but be contiguous
in this world; neither can every piece of the building be of one form;
nay rather the perfection consists in this, that out of many moderate
varieties and brotherly dissimilitudes that are not vastly dispropor-
tional, arises the goodly and the graceful symmetry that commends the
whole pile and structure" (744). Even as Milton rejects the fantasy of
reconstructing the past, and metaphorically that of rebirth, he nevertheless clarifies that each "piece" matters in itself, that "perfection consists
in this" same state of ruin. As Milton concludes, "Let us, therefore, be
more considerate builders, more wise in spiritual architecture, when
great reformation is expected" (744). Through this architectural mnemonic, he reminds readers that the art of salvation is an art of memory.
Milton thus explores the freedom of misprision. The right to read, the
right to be wrong, indeed the necessity of falling into error in order to
find a path to virtue, is at the heart of Milton's writing. By mistaking
story for history, truth for fiction, Milton represents himself not as a
perfect guide but rather as human, fallible – free to stand and free to
fall. Freedom to choose represents Milton's justification.

Though hardly the first to respond to Greenblatt's analysis of Spenser –
scholars have been replying for the past few decades – I may be the
first to have Milton reply to Greenblatt. Their shared desire to speak
with the dead, to reflect upon writing after the death of the author, suggests different ways of remembering Spenser from older and newer
historical perspectives. A written oration on the "liberty" of print,

Areopagitica identifies readers with Guyon, including Milton himself as he consciously re-enacts an unconscious act: reading as misreading (717). Hence the irony of his exhortation to read "promiscuously," to fall into knowledge, because the greater danger lies in unconsciously censoring the knowledge of ourselves. In *Renaissance Self-Fashioning*, Greenblatt similarly dismantles certain fictions of freedom, refusing to worship Spenser idolatrously (and thus, in a very real sense, falsely) by identifying readers with Guyon. Ironically, given its context, this reading has led to a certain censoring of Spenser's writing; moreover, Greenblatt's unveiling of the illusions of self-fashioning might just as well apply to Milton in the context of Ireland. Milton also wrote an infamous tract on Irish subjugation, and Ireland's brutal conquest accelerated under Cromwell's rule, during England's revolutionary (if temporary) liberation from monarchy. In other words, freedom for some never means freedom for all. But this may relate to Milton's point about "liberty" in *Areopagitica*: freedom in writing and in the world may finally mean refraining from absolute judgment, and instead recognizing the partial, provisional, Duessa-like nature of truth, seen from the vantage of our own place and time in history. What we as readers judge to be "repellent" depends upon how we define the word "liberty," particularly since the freedom to tell the truth, and act on it, has always been circumscribed by power – witnessed by the necessity of irony, from Socrates on – and because truth itself changes. This matters here, finally, in terms of how we judge Spenser and his writing. Spenser has been both idolized and demonized, yet neither view shows the whole truth. With this study, I have attempted to paint to a fuller picture of an infinitely complex writer.

In *Of Education*, Milton writes that the "end then of learning is to repair the ruins of our first parents by regaining to know God aright, and out of that knowledge to love him, to imitate him, to be like him, as we may the nearest by possessing our souls of true virtue" (631). To be *like* God, of course, is not to *be* God, an argument that applies to poets and princes alike. Yet with just a touch of idolatry, Milton names Spenser his "original," perhaps suggesting what it means "to repair the ruins" of the past: to recollect an edifice under construction indefinitely.

Notes

1. Spenser's Complaints: The Fall of Troy, the Ruin of Rome, and the Art of Recollection

1 Cicero, *On the Orator*, trans. and ed. Watson 186 (my emphasis). Text references are to this edition.
2 On the earliest known reference to Simonides as the inventor of the art of memory, the Parian Marble, see *Lyra Graeca*, ed. and trans. Edmonds, v. 2.
3 Patrick Hutton explores history as an art of memory, but whereas he argues that in "the eighteenth century . . . a new science of history was in the making, and it was in this context that the art of memory was to be reconceived," I suggest such connections much earlier (*History as an Art of Memory*, 33).
4 Yates, *The Art of Memory*, 46, 48. The main sources for the art of memory are Cicero's *On the Orator*, the anonymous *Ad Herrenium*, and Quintillian's *Institutio Oratorio*; Aristotle's *De anima, On Memory and Recollection*, is also central. On the art of memory, see Donald Beecher and Grant Williams, *Ars Reminiscendi*; Lina Bolzoni, *The Gallery of Memory*; Mary Carruthers, *Book of Memory* and *The Craft of Thought*; Susanne Küchler and Walter Melion, *Images of Memory*; Paolo Rossi, *Logic and the Art of Memory*; and Janet Coleman, *Ancient and Medieval Memories*.
5 Although my study does not deal with hermetic uses of the art of memory, Neoplatonic influences can be felt throughout Spenser's poetry, particularly in the *Complaints* in which his "memory theatres" in the ruins and visions poems clearly flirt with these Neoplatonic memory. On hermetic uses of the art of memory, see Yates, *Art of Memory* and *Giordano Bruno*.
6 Carruthers, *Book of Memory*, 20. On the relation of "orality" and "literacy" in the memory arts, cf. Walter Ong, *Orality and Literacy*.

7 Carruthers, *The Craft of Thought*, 12.

8 See Havelock, *Preface to Plato*, passim. Havelock explores the "living memory" of the "poetised tradition" and Plato's complex response to it (42–3).

9 Engel, "Mnemonic Criticism and Renaissance Literature," 19. He "contend[s] that Renaissance metaphorics was essentially mnemonic and emblematic, and that it took as its grounding the relation of the body and soul within time," that "emblematic designs are indexes to . . . Renaissance metaphoric processes and related methods of conveying, transporting, or translating thought images into graphic, discursive, and linguistic practices" (*Mapping Mortality*, 3).

10 As Thomas Greene writes, "Petrarch found it natural to use the term *ruinae* for the lost or fragmentary literary remains of antiquity, and he himself would be praised by later humanists for having brought the Latin language back to the light of day from among the ruins with which it had been entombed" (*The Light in Troy*, 92).

11 Maley, "Spenser's Languages," 175; Summit, *Memory's Library*, 106. Maley further describes Spenser as "a poet of exile and empire" who "writing in the ruins, among the relics and remains of an earlier English civilization . . . salvages something from sediments and secretions." "Spenser's Languages," 170. On Spenser's ruins, see Judith Anderson, *Reading the Allegorical Intertext*, passim; Engel, *Chiastic Designs*; Anne Janowitz, *England's Ruins*; J.M. Kennedy and J.A. Reither, *A Theatre for Spenserians*; Annabel Patterson, *Roman Images*; Philip Schwyzer, *Archaeologies of English Renaissance Literature*.

12 As M.J. Doherty explains, "Renaissance humanists applied the architectural analogy in rhetoric to the organization of speculative, practical, and linguistic arts and sciences and to the mechanical crafts. In this manner they recorded a cultural response to perceived changes in epistemology, especially in the structure of knowledge received from Platonic and Aristotelian traditions and transformed by medieval Augustinianism" (*The Mistress-Knowledge*, xiii).

13 Spenser, *The Faerie Queene*, ed. Hamilton, 3.9.47. Text references are to book, canto, and stanza of this edition.

14 Coleman, *Ancient and Medieval Memories*, 12.

15 As David Scott Wilson-Okamura succinctly puts it, "The allegorical tradition about Homer is older even than Socrates" (*Virgil in the Renaissance*, 148). On the allegorical tradition of reading epic as the soul's journey from history to eternity (sometimes analogous to a world-soul and epitomized by the hero's journey through the underworld), see, for example, Don Cameron Allen, *Mysteriously Meant*; Christopher Baswell, *Virgil in Medieval*

England; Robert Lamberton, *Homer the Theologian*; Michael Murrin, *The Allegorical Epic*; and Jon A. Quitslund, *Spenser's Supreme Fiction*.

16 *Aristotle on Memory*, trans. Richard Sorabji, 54. On Aristotle and memory, see Carruthers, *Book of Memory* and *Craft of Thought*; and Coleman, *Ancient and Medieval Memories*.

17 In the context of Aristotle, Peter Warnek treats Platonic *anamnesis* as "completely contrived.": "The actual point being made here is that one comes to know only what one in some sense already knows . . . Thus according to Gadamer Aristotle is to be read accordingly as the more developed (conceptual) formulation of what Plato already said (mythically and metaphorically). In Aristotle's thought, what Plato intended is transferred to the cautious and tentative language of philosophical concepts" (*Descent of Socrates*, 178, 114–15).

18 Sorabji, *Aristotle on Memory*, 35.

19 Yates, *Astraea*, 69. I am bringing this seminal work into contact with Yates' *Art of Memory*.

20 Yates, *Astraea*, 33.

21 Yates, *Astraea*, 50.

22 Virgil, *Aeneid*, trans. Fairclough, 1.229–300. Text references are to this edition.

23 Virgil, *Eclogues*, trans. Fairclough, 4.4–7. Yates argues in *Astraea*: "Through such associations, it was possible to use pagan imperial rhetoric concerning periodic renovations of the Empire, or returns of the golden age, of medieval Christian emperors, thus retaining something of the cyclic view of history which such expressions imply, though in a Christianized form. A *renovatio* of the Empire will imply spiritual renovation, for in a restored world, in a new golden age of peace and justice, Christ can reign" (4). Of course, this was not universally accepted or unproblematic. As Yates observes, "it is precisely as a phantom that Charles's empire was of importance, because it raised again the imperial idea and spread it through Europe in the symbolism of its propaganda, and at a time when the more advanced political thinking was discrediting it" (1). On Trojan stories of history, see David Armitage, *Theories of Empire, 1450–1800*; Ernst Breisach, *Historiography*; Arthur B. Ferguson, *Clio Unbound*; T.D. Kendrick, *British Antiquity*; F.J. Levy, *Tudor Historical Thought*; Marie Tanner, *The Last Descendant of Aeneas*; J.S.P. Tatlock, *The Legendary History of Britain*; and Yates, *Astraea*.

24 Protestant uses of *translatio imperii* maintained Rome's place in God's plan even if inverting its significance. See Katherine Firth, *The Apocalyptic Tradition*; and C.A. Patrides and Joseph Wittreich, *The Apocalypse in English Renaissance Thought and Literature*.

25 Manley, "Spenser and the City," 208.

26 Manley, "Spenser and the City," 203.

27 Greenblatt, *Renaissance Self-Fashioning*, 174, 192.

28 Greenblatt, *Renaissance Self-Fashioning*, 174.

29 Greenblatt, *Renaissance Self-Fashioning*, 2.

30 Greenblatt, *Renaissance Self-Fashioning*, 2.

31 Greenblatt, *Renaissance Self-Fashioning*, 175.

32 Greenblatt, *Renaissance Self-Fashioning*, 162, 175. Engaging with the *topos* of ruin in suggestive ways, Greenblatt writes that "Burckhardt's crucial perception was that the political upheavals in Italy in the later Middle Ages . . . fostered a radical change in consciousness," but that Burckhardt's notion that "in the process, these men emerged at last as free individuals must be sharply qualified"; Greenblatt argues, "While not only in Italy, but in France and England as well, the old feudal models gradually crumbled and fell into ruins, men created new models, precisely as a way of containing and channeling the energies which had been released" (161–2).

33 Greenblatt, *Renaissance Self-Fashioning*, 162.

34 There has also been an increasing frustration with the dominance of the *Viewe* in Spenser studies. In *Temperate Conquests*, David Read argues that critics "create a generalized version of 'imperial' Spenser functioning almost independently of his poetic output . . . citations of one or two significant episodes of *The Faerie Queene* [are often] enough to confirm Spenser's place as the great apologist for an Elizabethan dream of transoceanic monarchy" (12). For a similarly vociferous complaint about Spenser's reception, see Maley, *Salvaging Spenser*.

35 Greene, *Light in Troy*, 231.

36 Greene, *Light in Troy*, 92.

37 Greene, *Light in Troy*, 36.

38 McGowan, *The Vision of Rome in Late Renaissance France*, 187. On ruin and Renaissance, see Leonard Barkan, *Unearthing the Past*; Laurence Goldstein, *Ruins and Empire*; Anthony Grafton, *Rome Reborn*; Greene, *Light in Troy*; Janowitz, *England's Ruins*; Ann Kuttner, Alina Payne, and Rebekah Smick, *Antiquity and its Interpreters*; P.A. Ramsay, *Rome in the Renaissance: The City and the Myth*; and Annabel Patterson, *Roman Images*.

39 McGowan, *The Vision of Rome in Late Renaissance France*, 217.

40 Writing about issues of imitation, Anne Lake Prescott asks, "Why and how might a culture imitate or adapt not a text, genre, or conceit but a tangle of words and metaphors expressing less a particular philosophy or theory than a set of feelings or concerns?" "Du Bellay in Renaissance England," 126. On issues of literary imitation, especially as it relates to rhetoric, see

William Kennedy, *Rhetorical Norms in Renaissance Literature*; James Murphy, *Renaissance Eloquence*; Patricia Parker, *Literary Fat Ladies*; and Wayne Rebhorn, *The Emperor of Men's Mind*.

41 Greenblatt, *Renaissance Self-Fashioning*, 2.

42 Greenblatt, *Renaissance Self-Fashioning*, 167.

43 As Richard Rambuss has observed, Spenser's *Complaints* volume – which appears in between the two halves of *The Faerie Queene* – seems intentionally designed to subvert his clear imitation of Virgil, both by virtue of the interruption and because of the kinds of complaints about ruin and imitation that Spenser makes here. See his *Spenser's Secret Career*.

44 Yates, *Art of Memory*, 157–8; Carl J. Rasmussen, "Quietnesse of Minde," 7–8.

45 Jan Van der Noot, *A Theatre for Voluptuous Worldlings*, sig. F2v. Text citations are to this edition.

46 Bath, *Speaking Pictures*, 34. See also Rosemary Freeman, *English Emblem Books*; Jean H. Hagstrum, *The Sister Arts*; Thomas Hyde, "Vision, Poetry, and Authority in Spenser"; Malcolm Quainton, "Morte Peinture and Vivante Peinture"; and W. Lee Rensselaer, *Ut Pictura Poesis*.

47 Plutarch, "Whether Military or Intellectual Exploits Have Brought Athens More Fame," *Plutarch*, 157.

48 Ironically, Van der Noot soon after returns to the Roman Catholic fold.

49 On the Renaissance dialogue, see Virginia Cox, *The Renaissance Dialogue*; and James Murphy, *Renaissance Eloquence*.

50 Greene, *Light in Troy*, 41.

51 Carruthers, *Craft of Thought*, 27.

52 Carruthers, *Craft of Thought*, 27–8.

53 See, for example, Yates, *The Art of Memory*; and Ronald R. MacDonald, *Burial Places of Memory*.

54 *The Odyssey of Homer*, trans. Lattimore, 11.299–304.

55 *Odyssey*, 11.363–359.

56 See Havelock, *Preface to Plato*, 9 and passim.

57 "It was Plato who bridged the gap between poetry and philosophy," Erich Auerbach argues: "in his work, appearance . . . became a reflected image of perfection. He set poets the task of writing philosophically . . . He himself understood the art of mimesis more profoundly and practised it more consummately than any other Greek of his time, and apart from Homer he had greater influence as a poet than any other poet of antiquity" (*Dante*, 5). On Plato as poet, see Ronna Burger, *Plato's Phaedrus*; Jill Gordon, *Turning Toward Philosophy*; and Mary Nichols, *Socrates on Friendship and Community*.

58 See Lamberton, *Homer the Theologian*; and Murrin, *The Allegorical Epic*.

59 Plato, *Phaedrus*, in *The Collected Dialogues*, ed. and trans. Hamilton and Cairns, 476, 525. Text citations to the *Phaedrus* and other works by Plato are to this edition.

60 For Yates' discussion of the tale of Thoth (or Theuth) as an origin story for hermetic interpretations of the art of memory's history, see *Art of Memory*, esp. 38, 220, 268–9.

61 As Carruthers argues, "reading a book extends the process whereby one memory engages another in a continuing dialogue that approaches Plato's ideal expressed in the *Phaedrus* of two living minds engaged in learning" (*Book of Memory*, 169). Carruthers further argues that, "to Socrates, 'living discourse' is best" when "two living minds can engage one another, whereas in the solitary reading of a written text the mind encounters, he implies, only itself. But Socrates allows value to writing as a way of storing experience for oneself and posterity" (30). On writing as a reminder in this context, see Burger, *Plato's Phaedrus*.

62 On Stesichorus' role in the *Phaedrus*, see Patricia Berrahou Phillipy, *Love's Remedies*.

63 On the underworld as a mnemonic space, see MacDonald, *The Burial Places of Memory*; and Yates, *The Art of Memory*.

64 Socrates recalls the charges against him:"I must read their affidavit, so to speak, as though they were my legal accusers: Socrates is guilty of criminal meddling, in that he inquires into things below the earth and in the sky, and makes the weaker argument defeat the stronger, and teaches others to follow his example. It runs something like that. You have seen it for yourselves in the play by Aristophanes, where Socrates goes whirling round, proclaiming that he is walking on air, and uttering a great deal of other nonsense about things of which I know nothing whatsoever" (*Phaedo*, 5).

65 Murrin, *The Veil of Allegory*, 91.

66 Scholars disagree about the order in which Plato wrote these two dialogues, but the *Symposium* seems to expand upon the main topic of the *Phaedrus*. In the *Symposium*, Phaedrus praises love as that good "without which neither cities nor citizens are capable of any great or noble work," appearing to have learned the central lesson of the *Phaedrus* about true love (533).

67 Beginning in mid-conversation, the speaker Apollodorus corrects the other anonymous speaker about when this symposium took place: this party "was given . . . when you and I were in the nursery, the day after Agathon's celebrations with the players when he'd won the prize with his first tragedy" (*Symposium*, 527). Though not exactly ancient history, this story is represented as old news that nevertheless continues to live in the collective memory of Athens.

68 For example, "When Pausanius had paused – you see the kind of tricks
we catch from our philologists, with their punning derivations – the next
speaker, so Aristodemus went on to tell me, should have been Aristophanes," whose "hiccups" remind him of the speakers' order (539).

69 See Thucydides' *History of the Peloponnesian War*, 536 and passim.

70 Aristotle, *Metaphysics*, trans. Lawson-Tancred, 405. Text citations are to this
edition.

71 On Ciceronian memory, see Carruthers, *Book of Memory*; Yates, *Art of Memory*; Rossi, *Logic and the Art of Memory*; and Penny Small, *Wax Tablets of the
Mind*.

72 As does Cicero in his narrative of the "Dream of Scipio" in *On the
Commonwealth*.

73 Virgil, *Aeneid*, trans. Fitzgerald, 6.1005–8. Text citations are to this edition.

74 Plato, *Republic*, 841.

75 The *Confessions* is the *locus classicus* for considerations of Augustine and
the art of memory; see Yates, *Art of Memory*, 48 and passim; and Carruthers, *Book of Memory*, 193 and passim. On Augustine and memory more
broadly, see Carruthers, *Book of Memory*; Phillip Cary, *Augustine's Invention of the Inner Self*; Coleman, *Ancient and Medieval Memories*; Sandra Lee
Dixon, *Augustine: The Scattered and Gathered Self*; J.G. Kristo, *Looking for God
in Time and Memory*; Gareth B. Matthews, *The Augustinian Tradition*; John
A. Mourant, *Saint Augustine on Memory*; Rossi, *Logic and the Art of Memory*;
Brian Stock, *After Augustine*; Eleonore Stump and Norman Kretzmann, *The
Cambridge Companion to Augustine*; and Yates, *Art of Memory*.

76 Yates, *Art of Memory*, 47–8. Yates further argues that Augustine does not
find God through the art of memory but rather through Platonic memory –
anamnesis – in Christianized form.

77 Carruthers, *Book of Memory*, 199. Carruthers argues that Augustine's use of
the art of memory is rhetorical and fundamentally atemporal: "Augustine
journeys through his memory not to find his past but to find God, his present and his future . . . it is clear that Augustine assumed that the way to
God lay only through the re-presenting of his past in memory; he has no
interest in his past except as it provides him with a way and ground for
understanding his present" (193).

78 John Mourant writes that "memory is not to be considered as a 'part' or
a 'faculty' of the mind, although sometimes it is difficult to avoid the use
of such terms in translating Saint Augustine," that "memoria is not a faculty of the soul, but the whole soul, as conscious of itself and its contents"
(*Saint Augustine on Memory*, 12).

79 Augustine, *Confessions*, trans. Warner, 24. Text citations are to this edition.

80 Augustine, *City of God*, trans. Bettenson, 6. Text citations are to this edition.

81 In *City of God*, for example, Augustine interleaves discussions of secular historiography with scriptural history. Describing how "That *Aeneas* came into Italy when Abdon the judge ruled over the Hebrews," Augustine presents Trojan history as fact while also taking issue with related Trojan fictions. "After the capture and destruction of Troy, Aeneas with twenty ships laden with the Trojan relics, came into Italy, when Latinus reigned there," he writes, but adds: "Now the Latins made Aeneas one of their gods because at his death he was nowhere to be found" (626).

82 As Ernst Breisach explains, "Augustine's denial of the identity between the City of God and any earthly institution convinced few," such that "even Orosius, a confidante of Augustine's, deserted him with his *Seven Books of Histories against the Pagans*," and "despite Augustine's vigorous dissent, Orosius's most important legacy was the concept of a Christian Roman Empire: somehow Rome was essential to the continuity of the sacred story" (*Historiography*, 86–8). On Augustine's rejection of "a sacral conception of the Empire," see R.A. Markus, *Saeculum*, 157.

83 Discussed more fully in chapter 4.

84 Augustine, *On Christian Doctrine*, trans. Robertson, 13. Text citations are to this edition. "The originality of the *De doctrina christiana* lay in translating rhetorical theory into literary theory, or hermeneutics," as Rita Copeland argues ("The Ciceronian Rhetorical Tradition," 248).

85 Augustine, *Confessions*, 154. He argues much the same in *On Christian Doctrine*: "Did not the famous bishop, when he had considered the history of the pagans and found that Plato had traveled in Egypt during the time of Jeremias, show that Plato had probably been introduced to our literature by Jeremias so that he was able to teach or to write doctrines that are justly commended? . . . Thus from a consideration of times it becomes more credible that the Platonists took from our literature whatever they said that is good and truthful" (64).

86 Yates argues that Augustine must pass "deeper within to find God in the memory, but not as an image and in no place" (*Art of Memory*, 47). By contrast, Carruthers argues that Augustine must use places and images of memory to find God, even as he attempts to transcend them.

87 As Robert Edwards argues, "In the *Convivio* (1.2.14), Dante explains how the *Confessions* served him as literary model," (*Flight From Desire*, 69).

88 I pursue an ongoing connection between epic underworlds and the art of memory, which relate to Ronald R. Macdonald's important observations. "Some such act of re-membrance is what the epic poet aims at," Macdonald writes: "For true remembering, as opposed to compulsive repetition, is the only way the past can be experienced as masterable. Simonides of

Ceos, we are told in the *De oratore* of Cicero (2.86), invented the technique that would come to be known as the art of memory . . . Epic underworlds may be related to this venerable mnemonic technique, they may in fact contain the reminiscence of a technique of reminiscing. And yet the 'places' of memory (the technical term for both Cicero and the anonymous author of the rhetorical treatise called *Ad Herrenium* is *loci*) become the burial-places of memory only with the supervention of the idea of repression, an active forgetting, so to speak, as opposed to the merely passive decay of the memory trace." *The Burial-Places of Memory*, 9–10. See also Raymond Clark, *Catabasis: Vergil and the Wisdom Tradition*.

89 Dante Aligheri, *The Divine Comedy*, trans. Mandelbaum, canto 33, 85–90. Text citations are to this edition. Yates suggests that "Dante's *Inferno* could be regarded as a kind of memory system for memorising Hell and its punishments with striking images on orders of places," and that the "*Divine Comedy*" may offer "the supreme example" of this art in poetry (*Art of Memory*, 95–6). On Dante and memory, see also MacDonald, *Burial-Places of Memory*.

90 On Petrarch, see, for example, William Kennedy, *Authorizing Petrarch*; Giuseppe Mazzotta, *The Worlds of Petrarch*; and Thomas Roche Jr, *Petrarch and the English Sonnet Sequence*.

91 *Petrarch's Secret, or The Soul's Conflict with Passion*, 155.

92 Petrarch's partial epic *Africa* takes up the matter of republican Rome.

93 Toward the end of the *Metamorphoses*, Ovid offers what may be a witty memorial to Plato as the teachings of Pythagoras. In a parody of Virgil's prophecy for Rome's "empire without end" in the *Aeneid*, Ovid remembers Rome's past and reveals its future through a philosopher who, because of the transmigration of his soul, claims to remember the fall of Troy. What follows amounts to a parodic version of Virgil's underworld and the prophecy for Rome therein, which turns into a history lesson about the transience of all empires. Ovid's irreverent take on immortality – the soul's and Rome's – is reflected in his own qualified praise of poetic immortality: "Wherever through the lands beneath her sway / The might of Rome extends, my words shall be / Upon the lips of men. If truth at all / Is stablished in poetic prophecy, / My fame shall live to all eternity" (379). Ovid's "fame" and Rome's "eternity" are thus linked to mutability and metamorphosis – after all, if the soul is immortal, then perhaps Ovid's poetry can be too. On Ovid and Spenser, see Patrick Cheney, *Marlowe's Counterfeit Profession*; Syrithe Pugh, *Spenser and Ovid*; and M.L. Stapleton, *Spenser's Ovidian Poetics*.

94 *Petrarch's Lyric Poems*, #1, 365.

95 See John Freccero, "The Fig Tree and the Laurel," 31.

96 Van der Noot included only the ruins poetry appended to Du Bellay's sonnet sequence.

97 Throughout this discussion I will refer to Du Bellay's *Antiquitez de Rome* as Spenser's translation of it, *Ruines of Rome*. On Du Bellay's place in the *Complaints*, see Richard Danson Brown, "*The New Poet*"; Hassan Melehy, *Poetics of Literary Transfer*; Prescott, *French Poets and the English Renaissance* and "Spenser (Re)Reading du Bellay"; W.L. Renwick, in Spenser, *Complaints*; Alfred W. Satterthwaite, *Spenser, Ronsard, and Du Bellay*; Harold Stein, *Studies in Spenser's* Complaints; and George Tucker, *The Poet's Odyssey*.

98 *Ruines of Rome, The Yale Edition of the Shorter Poems of Edmund Spenser,* 1.1–2. Text citations are to this edition.

99 *Ruines of Rome*, 5.63–4..As Margaret Ferguson writes, "Du Bellay portrays the ancient city as an unattainable object of desire, an 'imperial mistress' endowed . . . with all the qualities Petrarch ascribed to Laura 'in morte'" ("The Afflatus of Ruin," 29). On Rome as long-lost lover, and Du Bellay as Petrarchan poet, see also Rebhorn, "Du Bellay's Imperial Mistress."

100 On Du Bellay's ambivalence, see Margaret Ferguson, *Trials of Desire*; Thomas Greene, *Light in Troy*; and George Pigman III, "Du Bellay's Ambivalence."

101 *Ruines of Rome*, 8.112. On the theology of Du Bellay's sequence, see Andrew Fichter, "Spenser's Ruines of Rome"; and Rebhorn, "Du Bellay's Imperial Mistress."

102 Joachim Du Bellay, *The Defense and Illustration of the French Language*, 54–5. On Du Bellay's *Defense*, see Ferguson, *Trials of Desire*.

103 On *The Courtier*, see Harry Berger Jr, *Absence of Grace*; Peter Burke, *The Fortunes of the Courtier*; and Rebhorn, *Courtly Performances*.

104 Baldassare Castiglione, *The Book of the Courtier*, ed. Cox, trans. Hoby, 22. Text citations are to this edition.

2. The Death of the "New Poete": Ruin and Recollection in *The Shepheardes Calender*

1 *Yale Edition of the Shorter Poems of Edmund Spenser*, ed. Oram et al., 13. Text citations are to this edition. Prose is cited by page, poetry by line number. Throughout this chapter, I refer to E.K.'s introductory epistle as his "Letter to Harvey."

2 "*The Shepheardes Calender* as Document and Monument," 5. McCanles also argued that "E.K. is treated as just another editor and critic," and

"consequently editors have felt little trepidation in either printing E.K.'s glosses among their own; or selecting judiciously some glosses and omitting others; or leaving them out altogether. In parallel fashion, critics quote E.K. when it suits them and ignore him when it doesn't, and in either case treat his glosses just as one would treat those of any other critic of the same text" (6). If critics once treated E.K.'s identity as a riddle to be solved, they now concur that he is part of the *Calender*'s fiction; see Roland Greene, "*The Shepheardes Calender,* Dialogue, and Periphrasis," 3–4. On the role of E.K.'s marginalia, see Sherri Geller, "You Can't Tell a Book by Its Contents"; Richard Halpern, *The Poetics of Primitive Accumulation*; Robert Lane, *Shepheardes Devises*, 71; Frances M. Malpezzi, "Readers, Auditors, and Interpretation"; Richard McCabe, "Annotating Anonymity"; Penny McCarthy, "E.K. was Only the Postman"; David L. Miller, "Authorship, Anonymity, and *The Shepheardes Calender*"; and Annabel Patterson, *Pastoral and Ideology*, 129.

3 What it means for Spenser to be a new Virgil has also changed. David Miller argues that Spenser "assumed a role not yet fully created, or instituted within their culture," and that "this general dilemma was intensified for Spenser inasmuch as he meant to be a specific kind of poet, a Vergilian apologist for the English *translatio imperii*"; as he concludes, "Spenser's [*Shepheardes Calender*], therefore, has in many ways to create the space it seeks to occupy as the 'classic' of a new golden age" ("Authorship, Anonymity, and *The Shepheardes Calender*," 220–1). On Virgil in the *Calender*, see Patrick Cheney, *Spenser's Famous Flight*; Richard Helgerson, *Self-Crowned Laureates*; Nancy Jo Hoffman, *Spenser's Pastorals*; Nancy Lindheim, "The Virgilian Design of *The Shepheardes Calender*"; Patterson, *Pastoral and Ideology*; Rambuss, *Spenser's Secret Career*; and John Watkins, *The Specter of Dido*.

4 Watkins, *The Specter of Dido*, 89. On Chaucer's relationship to Spenser, see Anderson, *Reading the Allegorical Intertext*; Theresa Krier, *Refiguring Chaucer in the Renaissance*; and Lindheim, "The Virgilian Design of *The Shepheardes Calender*".

5 Greene, *The Light in Troy*, 233, 193. On Greene's work, see Huw Griffiths, "Translated Geographies"; Lindheim, "Spenser's Virgilian Pastoral"; Manley, *Literature and Culture in Early Modern London*; McGowan, *Vision of Rome*; and Patterson, *Pastoral and Ideology*.

6 Greene, *Light in Troy*, 235.

7 Greene, *Light in Troy*, 236.

8 Helgerson, *Self-Crowned Laureates*, 26. Yet "without the great example of Virgil," he adds, "Spenser's laureate self-creation is unthinkable" (62–3).

I am suggesting that Spenser's "opposition to a set of contemporary expectations" leads him to more radical conclusions.

9 Helgerson, *Self-Crowned Laureates*, 26.

10 Harvey's fascination with Cicero and Castiglione, as well as with Ramism, must have influenced Spenser's uses of the art of memory. On Harvey's *Ciceronianus* and copious annotations of Castiglione's *Courtier*, see Jennifer Richards, *Rhetoric and Courtliness in Early Modern Literature*; and Virginia Stern, *Gabriel Harvey: His Life, Marginalia, and Library*. On the potential influence of Harvey's Ramism on Spenser, see Edward Armstrong, *Ciceronian Sunburn*, 194 and passim. On Spenser's and Harvey's letters, see Quitslund, "Questionable Evidence in the *Letters* of 1580 between Gabriel Harvey and Edmund Spenser," in *Spenser's Life and the Subject of Biography*.

11 Harvey, *The Works of Edmund Spenser*, vol. 9, 441–2, 471.

12 *The Book of The Courtier*, ed. Cox, trans. Hoby, 17. Text citations are to this edition.

13 E.K.'s letter at once conflates and confuses the three introductory epistles to Castiglione's work: by its English translator, Thomas Hoby; by his friend and fellow translator and editor, John Cheke; and finally, by Castiglione himself. In addition to sounding like Hoby, E.K. also echoes Cheke, who takes issue with Hoby's use of "unknowen words" derived from other languages, announcing that English "shold be written cleane and pure, unmixt and unmangled with borrowing of other tunges" (10). "To fascion a woord of our own," Cheke argues, poets and translators must use "old denisoned wordes" from English rather than foreign languages or resorting to neologisms – "unknowen wordes" (10). In contrast to both Hoby's deference to translation and Cheke's insistence on pure English, Castiglione defends his style as a mixture of old and new, ancient and modern, native and foreign – a mixture which he justifies by virtue of necessity: translation that results per force from *translatio* in the form of war. "Bicause the practising emonge sundrye Nations, hath alwayes bene of force to transport from one to an other (in a maner) as merchaundise," Castiglione reasons, "so also new woordes, which afterward remaine or decaye . . . are admitted by custome or refused," asking why he should then "burye alive such as have lasted nowe many yeeres, and have ben defended from the malice of time with the shield of use, and have preserved their estimation and dignity, when in the warres and turmoiles of Italy, alterations were brought up both of the tunge, buildings, garmentes, and maners" (15–16). Castiglione's defence of style as the recollection of ruin for new textual and cultural edifices recalls Cicero's dialogue, specifically in its treatment of

linguistic decorum and in its central framing device: that is, a rewriting of the tale of Simonides.

14 E.K. rarely distinguishes between reality and fiction – making Spenser equivalent to "Immeritô," the author of the *Calender*, to Colin, the *Calender*'s doomed hero, and both to Virgil. On Spenser's relationship to his various personae, see Leslie Whipp, "Weep for Dido"; Patrick Cullen, *Spenser, Marvell, and Renaissance Pastoral*, esp. 79; and Helgerson, *Self-Crowned Laureates*.

15 On unconscious (and conscious) imitation, see Pigman, "Versions of Imitation in the Renaissance."

16 For a related reading of Cicero, albeit in the context of Ramism, see Armstrong, *A Ciceronian Sunburn*; cf. Helfer, "The Death of the " 'New Poet.' "

17 Cicero, *On the Orator*, trans. and ed. Watson, 98. Text citations are to this edition.

18 See Trimpi, "Horace's *Ut Pictura Poesis*," 29 and passim.

19 On "decorum" in *On the Orator*, see 3.97–100.

20 Cicero writes to his brother that *On the Orator* is not a pedagogical manual designed to transmit teachings: "nor do I aim at instructing you [by] means of rhetorical treatises" (85). Rather, he writes, "let us [exhort] our children . . . not to trust that they can reach the height at which they aim, by the aid of the precepts, masters, and exercises, that they are all now following, but to understand that they must adopt others of a different character" (10–11).

21 Carruthers, *Book of Memory*, 25. Writing about the centrality of Ciceronian decorum to both rhetoric and poetry, Kathy Eden argues that "rhetoric itself is first and foremost the art of accommodation" (*Hermeneutics and the Ancient Rhetorical Tradition*, 14). See also William J. Kennedy, *Rhetorical Norms in Renaissance Literature*; and Rebhorn, *Renaissance Debates on Rhetoric*.

22 Other Ciceronian moments in E.K.'s commentary suggest that Cicero's influence in the *Calender* is not limited to the introduction but rather forms an important counter-narrative throughout; see especially E.K.'s glosses on Cicero in *Maye, June,* and *October*.

23 Chaucer, *Troilus and Creseyde*, in *The Riverside Chaucer*, ed. Benson, 306–7. Here as well, Chaucer fittingly observes that "Not all who find their way to Rome will trace / The self-same path" (46).

24 Eden, *Hermeneutics*, 4. See also Donald Cheney's "Colin Clout's Homecoming," where he describes the intertwining of "knowledge and memory" (146).

25 See Penelope Reed Doob, *The Idea of the Labyrinth*, on literary labyrinths.

26 For the earlier discussion of Stesichorus in Castiglione's *Courtier*, see chapter 1.

27 On *Januarye* as an example of Spenser's Virgilianism, see Ruth Samson Luborsky, "Illustrations to *The Shepheardes Calender*," 24–9.

28 Montrose, " 'The perfecte paterne of a poete': The Poetics of Courtship in *The Shepheardes Calender*," 35. Richard Mallette argues, Colin's "problem is that he is a poor lover and therefore cannot be a better poet" ("Spenser's Portrait of the Artist," 29). But with a broken pipe, who could be good at either?

29 On Petrarch's Roma and Amor, see William Kennedy, *Authorizing Petrarch*, 88.

30 On the *Phaedrus'* place in the *Calender*, see Elizabeth Bieman, *Plato Baptized*; Jonathan Goldberg, *Voice, Terminal, Echo*; and Phillippy, *Love's Remedies*.

31 Although *Aprill* was once where critics usually found proof of Spenser's Virgilianism, this has been increasingly problematized; see especially Miller, "Authorship."

32 Socrates introduces his tale of Stesichorus, "Now you must understand, fair boy, that whereas the preceding discourse was by Phaedrus, son of Pythocles, of Myrrhinus, that which I shall now pronounce is by Stesichorus, son of Ephemus of Himera" (*Phaedrus*, 491).

33 See chapter 1.

34 "*June* establishes Colin's love for Rosalind as a threat both to his own existence and to the existence of the pastoral world he inhabits," David Shore argues (*Spenser and the Poetics of Pastoral*, 77).

35 Beryl Rowland, "The Art of Memory and the Art of Poetry in the *House of Fame*," 163. On *The House of Fame*, see, for example, J.A.W. Bennett, *Chaucer's Book of Fame*; Sheila Delany, *Chaucer's House of Fame*; Doob, *The Idea of the Labyrinth*.

36 Mary Carruthers explores Dante's and Chaucer's arts of memory by exploring their "shared interest is the art of memory described in the *Rhetorica ad Herennium*" ("The Poet as Master Builder," 179). See also Carol A.N. Martin, "Authority and the Defense of Fiction"; and Karla Taylor, *Chaucer Reads "The Divine Comedy."*

37 Chaucer, *Dream Visions and Other Poems*, ed. Lynch, 120, 125–6. Text citations are to this edition.

38 Generally speaking, scholars believe *The House of Fame* antedates *Troilus and Criseyde*; still, the treatment given here to the amorous matter of Troy suggests the possibility of an ironic glance at Chaucer's own prior work. Indeed, perhaps it's no accident that Chaucer ends up in this place, for it

indicates his progress as a poet. Chaucer implies that he has been worshipping at the Temple of Venus in his earlier poetry. His fixation with these
"old tales" of love connects to *Troilus and Creseyde*, where he gives the Trojan legend a sceptical treatment.

39 Virgil connects his Fama with Hesiod's originary monster in *Theogony* –
"Monstrous, deformed, titanic. Pinioned, with / One eye beneath
for every body feather, / And, strange to say, as many tongues and
buzzing / Mouths as eyes, as many pricked-up eares" – described as a
force in constant motion: "Rumor goes / Thrives on motion, stronger
for the running . . . / harping on lies / And slander evenhandedly with
truth" (*Aeneid*, trans. Fitzgerald, 6.236–58). By contrast, Ovid locates
Fama in a house of fame, humanizing fame by associating it with power
as well as ordinary people: "At the world's centre lies a place . . . Whence
all things everywhere, however far, / Are scanned and watched, and
every voice and word / Reaches its listening ears. Here Rumour dwells, /
Her chosen home set on the highest peak, / Constructed with a thousand
apertures / And countless entrances and never a door. / . . . and rumours
everywhere, / Thousands, false mixed with true, roam to and fro" (*Metamorphoses*, trans. Melville, 275). What both versions of Fama have in common is the intertwining of truth and lies, which Chaucer's *House of Fame*
emphasizes.

40 Doob, *The Idea of the Labyrinth*, 328–30.

41 Patterson, *Chaucer and the Subject of History*, 59.

42 "The Wife of Bath's Tale," 857–66, *The Riverside Chaucer*. The point of the
Wife of Bath's Tale, that women want governance, is a moral that would
surely please Queen Elizabeth, as Spenser might have known as he em-
barked upon his own "faerie tale" in her honour.

43 As Cuddie proclaims in *August*, for example, "But tell me shepherds,
should it not yshend / Your roundels fresh, to hear a doolefull verse / Of
Rosalend (who knowes not Rosalend?) / That Colin made, ylke can I you
rehearse" (139–42).

44 Greene, "*The Shepheardes Calender* Dialogue, and Periphrasis," 27.

45 Louis Montrose argues, "In his creation of the *November* elegy, Colin
enacts "the perfecte paterne of a Poete" that Piers had advanced in
October . . . Colin now sings in a visionary, prophetic mode that leaves the
courtships of Rosalind and Eliza behind" ("Poetics of Courtship in *The
Shepheardes Calender*," 47–8.) See also Ronald Horton, "Spenser's Farewell
to Dido."

46 *Confessions*, 33.

47 Whipp, "Weep for Dido," 22.

3. *The Ruines of Time* and the Art of Recollection

1 *The Shepheardes Calender,* in *The Yale Edition of the Shorter Poems of Edmund Spenser,* ed. Oram et al., 20. Text citations are to this edition. Prose is cited by page, poetry by line number.

2 See A. Leigh DeNeef, "The Ruines of Time: Spenser's Defense of Poetry." On Sidney and Spenser, see Doherty, *Mistress-Knowledge*; David Galbraith, *Architectonics of Imitation*; S.K. Heninger Jr, *Sidney and Spenser*; and Kenneth Pask, *The Emergence of the English Author.*

3 MacLure, "Spenser and *The Ruines of Time,*" 7.

4 On the *Complaints,* see Brown, *"The New Poet"*; Patrick Cheney, "Spenser's Pastorals" and *Spenser's Famous Flight*; Prescott, "Spenser's Shorter Poems"; Rambuss, *Spenser's Secret Career*; and Stein, *Studies in Spenser's Complaints.*

5 As "the lineage of poets – from Roman to Du Bellay to Spenser – is established," Anne Janowitz writes, "so the fame of empire is also preserved," and "thus the immortality of the nation is ensured by the *topos* of the immortality of poetry" (*England's Ruines,* 24).

6 Melehy, "Antiquities of Britain: Spenser's *Ruines of Time,*" 159. See also Melehy, *The Poetics of Literary Transfer in Early Modern France and England,* passim.

7 See chapter 1 for the earlier discussion of Du Bellay and *Ruines of Rome.*

8 Richard Danson Brown writes that "this shifting exploration of parallel ideas and images underlies the sequence which Du Bellay uses to structure his central perception of Rome as inherently paradoxical, [and] this idea is never very far from the surface of the text" (*"The New Poet",* 73). See also Richard Cooper, "Poetry in Ruins."

9 *Ruines of Rome,* in *The Yale Edition of the Shorter Poems of Edmund Spenser,* 32.439–42. Text citations are to this edition

10 Coldiron, "How Spenser Excavates Du Bellay's *Antiquitez,*" 43. See also Prescott, "Du Bellay in Renaissance England," 121–8.

11 *The Ruines of Time,* in *The Yale Edition of the Shorter Poems of Edmund Spenser,* 1–7. Text citations are to this edition and are cited by line number.

12 Janowitz, *England's Ruins,* 21. Janowitz further argues: "In his discussion of Du Bellay's *Antiquitez,* Thomas Greene suggests that the sequence exemplifies the anxiety of influence . . . But while this may be true when Du Bellay responds to the classical model of poetic heritage, Spenser's version of continuity points his own nation and its poetry in the direction of futurity. His Protestantism moves him closer to domestic, national intentions and

delivers a strength equal to the burden of the past" (*England's Ruins*, 27).
On Du Bellay and Rome's ruins, see Margaret Ferguson, *Trials of Desire*,
and Fichter, "And nought of *Rome* in *Rome*."

13 M.L. Stapleton writes that if "Du Bellay uses the *exegi monumentum* convention to question the immortality of poetry," by contrast "Spenser's
aesthetics will not permit him to leave it at that . . . [and so] his *addendeum*
stresses the immutability of art" ("Spenser, the *Antiquitez de Rome*, and the
Development of the English Sonnet Form," 269). See also Goldstein, "Immortal Longings," 337.

14 In the *Complaints*, a Verlame-like figure appears in sonnet #10 of *The Visions
of Bellay*; in Van der Noot's *Theatre for Worldlings*, she appears in sonnet # 8.

15 See Rasmussen, "Spenser's *Ruines of Time*," 161.

16 See DeNeef, *Spenser and the Motives of Metaphor*, 30.

17 DeNeef also suggests that "a metaphoric line much like Britomart's conception of Troy-Rome-Troynovant corrects Verlame's notion that her city
is simply and literally destroyed. In each case, the poem posits metaphoric
correspondences that Verlame is unable to see, and it thereby instructs us
that the Idea toward which the poet is directing us must be broader than
any one of his subjects. Her failures of perception thus serve to dramatize
what Spenser successfully sees and we are invited to see" (*Spenser and the
Motives of Metaphor*, 35).

18 Hammill, "Republicanism and *The Ruines of Time*," 174.

19 *The Ruines of Time*, 134–9. The river trope indicates the cessation of cultural
transmission to Verlame's shores. As W.H. Herendeen explains, "if the rivers of antiquity flowed with the waters of religious rivalry, they reached
the Renaissance through the more capacious channels of Roman humanism [and] the result is that more clearly than ever, the river is symbolic of
the quest for knowledge rather than of the knowledge itself" ("The Rhetoric of Rivers," 111).

20 DeNeef, "The Ruines of Time," 267. Millar MacLure suggestively connects Spenser's art of memory with Camden's antiquarianism: "Spenser's
memory is the librarian of the Society of Antiquarians . . . [and] in his way
[Camden] is an eternizer, as the poet is. For the antiquary, as for the poet,
the distinction between myth and history dissolves in the relevance of all
that has been experienced or imagined of the human condition" ("Spenser
and *The Ruines of Time*," 9).

21 Philip Sidney, *An Apology for Poetry*, ed. Robinson, 89. Text citations are to
this edition.

22 Castiglione, *The Courtier*, ed. Cox, trans. Hoby, 18.

23 On the two tales of Simonides, see chapter 1.

24 As Alan Hager observes, Sidney "adopts the voice of the serious jester bent on leading the reader into entertaining like-like contradictions" (*Dazzling Images*, 40). See also William Craft, *Labyrinth of Desire*; Peter Herman, *Squitter-Wits and Muse-Haters*; Lisa Klein, *The Exemplary Sidney*; and Forrest G. Robinson, *The Shape of Things Known*.

25 As David Galbraith argues, "the terms of Sidney's defence concede that the divisions he has put in place between poetry and its neighbours are more flexible than he has admitted . . . Sidney's most forceful demarcation of poetry from its two rivals is achieved through a strategy of visualization and fiction-making . . . In his metaphorical architectonics, poetry is poised between philosophy and history, between precept and example" (*Architectonics of Imitation*, 11).

26 *Phaedrus*, in *The Collected Dialogues*, ed. and trans. Hamilton and Cairns, 525.

27 Sidney, *Apology for Poetry*, 11–12. On the Sidney's translations of the Psalms and the place of ruin therein, see Prescott, "The Countess of Pembroke's *Ruins of Rome*."

28 Ferguson, *Trials of Desire*, 137–8. Ferguson illuminates the relation between "apology" and fiction in this same work: "The example of Socrates, which was extremely important for Renaissance authors, reminds us that the word *apology* derives from a Greek word that means 'a speech in defense' (from *apo*, 'away', and *logia*, 'speaking') . . . though starting in the late sixteenth century it is also used, albeit often ambiguously, to denote a regretful acknowledgment of a fault. Even when Renaissance authors clearly employ the term in its older, 'Greek' sense, however, they implicitly acknowledge the necessity of admitting, if not error, then at least the possibility of being misunderstood . . . This concern underlies their frequent use of a type of story known, significantly, as the apologue. From the Greek *apologos*, meaning 'story' or 'fable,' the term came to be generally used in the Renaissance for didactic allegories like those of Aesop's fables. But for Renaissance defenders of poetry, there was a special conceptual link between the Greek terms *apologos* and *apologia*, a link suggested not only by the fact that both terms were sometimes translated as 'apologie' in sixteenth-century English, but also by a Platonic text that was crucial to Renaissance justifications of poetry. In Book 10 of the *Republic*, Plato uses *apologia* three times and *apologos* once; he deliberately exploits the verbal similarity between the two terms to illuminate the philosopher's role – or roles – in a complex scene of trial" (2–3). Ferguson also writes that "Renaissance authors, as we shall see, frequently follow Plato's lead in resorting to apologues [the myth of Er] as tools of defense" (4).

29 Hager argues that "Sidney's rhetor closes his *Defense of Poetry* with a complex jest" that shows "both his immersion in Platonism and his resistance to it" (*Dazzling Images*, 127–9). As suggested, this jest also recalls Castiglione's *Courtier* as, in part, a memento mori.

30 In the account in *The Odyssey*, Castor and Pollux exchange places endlessly: "both buried now in the life-giving earth though still alive. Even under the earth Zeus grants them that distinction: one day alive, the next day dead, each twin by turns, / they both hold honors equal to the gods" (*The Odyssey*, 11.344–7).

31 Verlame can sound as much like a virtuous pagan as an ardent Christian when she laments this "vaine world" and "sinfull earth" (43–4), warning against the "trustless state of miserable men, / That builde your blis on hope of earthly thing, / And vainly thinke your selves halfe happie then" (197–9). Richard Danson Brown argues that Verlame's mingling of sacred and profane ideas of immortality relates to Spenser's desire to accommodate the two ("*The New Poet*," 127). But their mingling can also point to his complaint about treating fiction as if divine truth.

32 These visions evoke the Neoplatonic art of memory. For memory theatres in relation to hermetic uses of the art of memory, see Yates, *Theatre of the World*.

33 M.J. Doherty's argument about Sidney also applies to Spenser: "In the proximate reality of one's historical moment, the Christian who strives to build up an earthly city according to his knowledge of Christian principles must remember that the true and lasting City he imitates is neither a republic of law and order nor a republic like Rome, but God's own temple (*CG*, 10.3). For this reason, as well as the historical one, the cities, republics, and societies of many renaissance poems compatible with Sidney's Augustinian aesthetics are imagined as ruins or works-in-progress or both" (*Mistress-Knowledge*, 108–9).

4. "The Methode of a Poet Historical [and] . . . an Historiographer": Recollecting the Past in the 1590 *Faerie Queene*

1 Sidney, *Apology for Poetry*, ed. Robinson, 24. Text citations are to this edition.
2 Spenser, *The Faerie Queene*, ed. Hamilton, 737. Text citations are to this edition. Prose is cited by page, poetry by book, canto, and stanza numbers.
3 Instead, Spenser describes *The Faerie Queene* as "coloured with an historicall fiction" – "the historye of king Arthure" – which he subtly discredits as being "furthest from the daunger of enuy, and suspition of present time"(737). Of course, nothing could be further from the truth, as Arthur

was a crucial legitimating figure for the Tudors. See Andrew King, *Spenser's Arthur*.

4 "Methode" here may also allude to Ramism, an educational "method" associated with the art of memory, which Frances Yates describes: "The French dialectician . . . [Peter] Ramus abolished memory as a part of rhetoric, and with it he abolished the artificial memory" (*Art of Memory*, 232). As Yates explains, "This was not because Ramus was not interested in memorising; on the contrary, one of the chief aims of the Ramist movement for the reform and simplification of education was to provide a new and better way of memorising all subjects. This was to be done by a new method whereby every subject was to be arranged in 'dialectical order' . . . as [Walter] Ong has said [in *Ramus: Method and the Decay of Dialogue*], the real reason why Ramus could dispense with memory as a part of rhetoric 'is that his whole scheme of the arts based on a topically conceived logic, is a system of local memory . . . Thus Ramus thinks of his dialectical method for memorising as the true classical art of memory'" (*Art of Memory*, 232). See also Paolo Rossi, *Logic and the Art of Memory*.

5 Murrin, *The Veil of Allegory*, 77. Mary Carruthers suggestively writes, "It may well be that much of what we suppose to be "allegory," and thus to have a specifically iconographic meaning (if only we knew what it was) is simply a mnemonic heuristic" (*Book of Memory*, 142).

6 Murrin, *Veil of Allegory*, 91.

7 David Galbraith argues that "Elizabeth's England is the typological fulfillment of Augustus's Rome" and "*The Faerie Queene* of the *Aeneid*" (*Architectonics of Imitation*, 74). This chapter builds upon Galbraith's argument that Spenser uses Trojan tales to reconsider the relation between poetry and history but with a significant difference: not in order to rewrite Virgil as a Protestant allegory but rather to explore and criticize the reception of Virgil's poetry as an allegory of history.

8 O'Connell, *Mirror and Veil*, 37.

9 Fichter, *Poets Historical*, 3. Fichter further argues, "the apparent distinction between romance and epic parts within the Renaissance narrative poem begins to fade once it is understood that both parts are components of what has been conceived as a new entity, the Christian epic" (17). On genre and *The Faerie Queene*, see Colin Burrow, *Epic Romance*; Andrew King, *The Matter of Just Memory*; David Quint, *Epic and Empire*; and Patricia A. Parker, *Inescapable Romance*.

10 Watkins, *The Specter of Dido*, 36–7. On Virgilian allegories, see also Baswell, *Virgil in Medieval England*.

11 Patrick Cheney, *Spenser's Famous Flight*, 23. Critics tend to see Spenser as rewriting Virgilian epic as Augustinian allegory. As Andrew Fichter writes, "Augustine is not blind to the greatness of the *Aeneid* or to its usefulness to Christian readers . . . [and] like the commentators and like the epic poets of the Renaissance, seeks finally to reserve a place of honor for the *Aeneid* in world literature" (*Poets Historical*, 21). Or as John Watkins argues, an allegorized Virgil solves the problem of Christianizing Virgilian *translatio*: "Augustine subsumes [Virgil's imperial model of history] in·the Christian view of historical experience fulfilling God's eternal decrees" (*The Specter of Dido*, 34). See also Thomas Greene, *The Descent From Heaven*.

12 Gross, *Spenserian Poetics*, 69.

13 See Cheney, *Spenser's Famous Flight*, 8–9. Dante's epistle to Can Grande describing *The Divine Comedy* as an allegory seems to be a clear subtext for Spenser's "Letter to Raleigh." As Peter Hawkins writes, "Dante asks the reader to see him as the earthly partner in a sacred collaboration. He is God's scribe. These claims are also reinforced by the Epistle to Can Grande, which suggests that the *Commedia* should be read according to the fourfold interpretation reserved for Scripture alone. Indeed, the text used to explicate the multiplicity of the poem's 'senses' or levels of meaning is none other than Psalm 113, 'In Exitu Israel de Aegypto,' the same stock example often chosen by masters of the 'sacred page' – such as Augustine – 'to demonstrate the principles of biblical exegesis'" ("Dante and the Bible," 133). From another perspective, though, Augustine appropriates the method of poets: allegory. On the "Dante controversy," see John Guillory, *Poetic Authority*, 4–5 and passim.

14 On epic as an allegory of the soul, see chapter 1.

15 Galbraith, *Architectonics of Imitation*, 23.

16 In critical discussions of allegory, one important debate concerns whether or not "ironic" forms of expression are considered allegorical. This debate centres on Northrop Frye's distinction between "allegory" and what he called ironic "anti-allegory" in *The Anatomy of Criticism*. My own view lines up most closely with that of Angus Fletcher, who labels ironies "collapsed allegories", or perhaps, "condensed allegories" (*Allegory: The Theory of a Symbolic Mode*, 229–30). Still more significantly, for my purposes, Fletcher examines Plato's response to the earliest examples of allegory – that is, allegorical interpretations of Homeric epic: "The ironic mode of the Platonic dialogues appears to follow from Plato's epistemology. With him things are an allegorical imitation of ideas, or, in another formulation, appearances are the allegorical equivalent of a higher reality . . . [Plato's use of] Mythos furthermore reminds us that the true assertion is always a

question, the true statement always an enigma" (231–3). Plato uses allegorical myths precisely to critique allegorical interpretations of myth that claim to reveal divine – historical, theological, political, etc. – truths, and that this brand of allegory exercises a profound influence on Spenser's allegory. Catherine Gimelli Martin describes the role of allegory in Milton's *Paradise Lost* in terms that, I think, speak equally well to Spenser's *Faerie Queene*: "*Paradise Lost* not only 'ruins' but 'gathers up' in order to mourn the hieratic remnants of its own fragmentation . . . *Paradise Lost* [exhibits] a highly self-reflexive or meta-allegorical form" (*The Ruines of Allegory*, 4–5). Kenneth Borris makes a similarly suggestive observation: "if allegory is ruinous in [Benjamin's] *Trauerspiel*, it can be much more concerned with reconstructive edification in different generic and cultural contexts" (*Allegory and Epic*, 2). See also Maureen Quilligan, *The Language of Allegory*; Gordon Teskey, *Allegory and Violence*; M.A. Treip, *Allegorical Poetics and the Epic*; and Rosemond Tuve, *Allegorical Imagery*.

17 On the problems with accommodating pagan myth and Christian allegory, see Teskey, *Allegory and Violence*, 88 and passim.

18 McCabe, *The Pillars of Eternity*, 185. See also Galbraith, *Architectonics of Imitation*, 55; and Parker, *Inescapable Romance*, 22.

19 See the discussion of Augustine in chapter 1. On Augustine and memory, see Carruthers, *Book of Memory*; Janet Coleman, *Ancient and Medieval Memories*; Mourant, *Saint Augustine on Memory*; and Yates, *Art of Memory*.

20 R.A. Markus argues, "The distinction between the two cities lies in the dimension of men's wills, in their inner response to their world and their experience . . . There can be no outward separation, no historically distinguishable careers discernible before the end" (*Saeculum*, 63). See also Jaroslav Pelikan, *The Mystery of Continuity*, 42–3.

21 Augustine, *City of God*, trans. Bettenson, 344. Text citations are to this edition.

22 Critics often argue that Augustine aligns epic and scripture. Fichter writes, "Augustine does not call for the rejection of classical epic but instead urges its completion in the light of Christian revelation," which "attests to his belief in the inclusiveness and continuity of the Providential plan" (*Poets Historical*, 64). See also Watkins, *Specter of Dido*, 31 and passim.

23 "Outside dissenting or schismatic circles, Augustine was the only thinker of any stature who was deeply disturbed by the developments of the fourth century towards a sacral conception of the Empire," Markus argues: "He rejected the identification of the Church's destiny with that of the Empire" (*Saeculum*, 157). See also Breisach, *Historiography*, 86–8.

24 In *City of God*, Augustine similarly interprets Revelation in allegorical terms, remarking, "prophetic diction delights in mingling figurative and real language, and thus in some sort of veiling the sense" (735).

25 Discussing this seeming paradox, O'Connell writes, "On the one hand, history must be 'read' as Scripture is read if one is to understand the patterns and discover meaning . . . On the other hand, history depends upon the actions of individuals" (*Mirror and Veil*, 67–8).

26 Spenser begins in "the middest" not only by beginning his narrative *in medias res* (both in *The Faerie Queene* as a whole and in the story of English history), but also by locating his poem in a medieval setting. This temporal location has a theological implication: the poem is set in the middle of time, between the First and Second Coming. As Parker explains, "The time between First and Second Coming is itself a respite or 'dilation' . . . the deferral of the promised end," but "as the threshold before the final separation of good and evil, this period is also a problematic middle" (*Inescapable Romance*, 19). In the "middest" of time, as Spenser's description of "clowdily enwrapt" allegory suggests, truth and fiction mingle. But if reading allegorically is a matter of necessity, how is a matter of debate.

27 Maureen Quilligan describes the place of remembering and forgetting for readers: "Readers of allegory . . . gain in sophistication only as they follow the narrative; they may in fact turn into allegorical critics at the end of the work when they *misremember* what it was like to read, but the experience of reading allegory always operates by a gradual revelation to a reader who, acknowledging that he does not already know the answers, discovers them, usually by a process of relearning them" (*Language of Allegory*, 227).

28 On the relation of Cleopolis to the New Jerusalem, see Anthea Hume, *Edmund Spenser: Protestant Poet*; and Darryl J. Gless, *Interpretation and Theology in Spenser.*

29 Castiglione, *The Courtier*, ed. Cox, trans. Hoby, 309. Text citations are to this edition.

30 See chapter 1 for this discussion of *The Courtier.*

31 In *On Christian Doctrine*, Augustine describes allegorical interpretation as temperate love: "Some things are to be enjoyed, others to be used, and there are others which are to be enjoyed and used . . . If we who enjoy and use things, being placed in the midst of things of both kinds, wish to enjoy those things which should be used, our course will be impeded and sometimes deflected, so that we are retarded in obtaining those things which are to be enjoyed, or even prevented altogether, shackled by an inferior love" (9). The peril of interpretation amounts to idolatry, mistaking signs

for signifiers: "If it is a carnal slavery to adhere to a usefully instituted sign instead of to the thing it was designed to signify, how much is it a worse slavery to embrace signs instituted for spiritually useless things instead of the things themselves?" (86).

32 In Dante's *Purgatory*, the poet Statius recalls the curse against the "hunger for gold" in Virgil's *Aeneid* (*Purgatory*, 22.40–1, and *Aeneid*, 3.56–7). Statius implicitly contrasts this lust for gold with his conversion to Christianity because of reading Virgil's Golden Age *Fourth Eclogue*, and the canto ends with praise of Rome's early empire as a harbinger of a renewed Christian Golden Age. Suggestively, when Statius describes the place of Christian poets in Purgatory, he locates Simonides among the relatively happy few.

33 "Guyon refuses to serve Mammon not in the name of God," Paul Alpers argues, "but in the name of knighthood and human mortal distinctions" (*Poetry of The Faerie Queene*, 248). For Alpers, this does not mark "a personal shortcoming of Guyon's" but a larger "difficulty that is inherent in human heroism as it is presented in Book II" (254). On the debate about the nature of Guyon's heroism, see also Anderson, *The Growth of Personal Voice*, 51 and passim; Berger Jr, *The Allegorical Temper*, 29 and passim; Quilligan, *The Language of Allegory*.

34 Augustine, *On Christian Doctrine*, 62. For the earlier discussion, see chapter 1.

35 *Faerie Queene*, 2.7.62. On Tantalus and Pilate, see Prescott, "Tantalus, Pilate," in *Spenser Encyclopedia*, ed. Hamilton, 676–7.

36 On the relation of Mammon's Cave to Alma's Castle, see James Nohrnberg, *The Analogy of* The Faerie Queene.

37 See chapter 1 for a discussion of Dante's *Divine Comedy*.

38 Judith Anderson explores the paradoxical immortality of these ruined texts, writing that "these physically decrepit records are explicitly contrasted with the disembodied purity and seeming transcendence of the content of memory, which derives from them" ("Myn auctor," 21).

39 In this episode, Andrew King observes, "Matter can designate either a physical substance or the very subject or sense of the text; Spenser combines both senses, the physical and the textual, in a very medieval view of the creation of work as an almost physical thrusting together or regurgitation of different volumes. Crucially, the matter of the books which Arthur and Guyon read, or which *The Faerie Queene* itself remembers, relates to native literary and historical traditions" (*The Matter of Just Memory*, 183). See also Berger, *Revisionary Play*, on how "Spenser places traditional material in historical perspective by revision and quotation" while "transform[ing]

it into something new" (38). On memory in Alma's castle, see Anderson, *Reading the Allegorical Intertext*; Elizabeth J. Bellamy, *Translations of Power*; Engel, *Chiastic Designs*; Andrew Escobedo, *Nationalism and Historical Loss*; Alan Stewart and Sullivan, "Worme-eaten, and full of canker holes"; Summit, "Monuments and Ruins" and *Memory's Library*; and Williams, "Phantastes Flies."

40 Relatedly, Jennifer Summit argues that "Spenser's allegory of Protestant nationhood" in Alma's Castle "meditates on the post-Reformation transformation of the library" following the dissolution of the monasteries. "Extending the aims of the post-Reformation book collectors who sought to recover England's own origins from bibliographic ruin, Spenser makes the library into the center of Protestant memory," Summit writes, and that "as Spenser's book 2 reveals, the post-Reformation library was dedicated to reshaping cultural memory from remnants salvaged from the ruined monastic past" (*Memory's Library*, 106 and passim).

41 Murrin, *The Veil of Allegory*, 79.

42 Murrin, *The Veil of Allegory*, 91.

43 *Aristotle on Memory*, trans. Richard Sorabji, 54.

44 Augustine, *Confessions*, 24. For the earlier discussion of Augustine, see chapter 1.

45 *Confessions*, 208. In *On Christian Doctrine*, Augustine describes the pleasurable uses of fiction: "No one doubts that things are perceived more readily through similitudes and that what is sought with difficulty is discovered more with pleasure" (37).

46 Apropos of the Castle of Alma as an allegory of the mind and body, Augustine writes that "we repair the daily wastage of our bodies by eating and drinking," though he warns readers not to "follow the counsel of appetite" (234, 236): "For in addition to our bodily appetites, which make us long to gratify all our senses and our pleasures and lead to our ruin if we stay away from you [God] by becoming their slaves, the mind is also subject to a certain propensity to use the sense of the body, not for self-indulgence of a physical kind, but for the satisfaction of its own inquisitiveness . . . and since it derives from our thirst for knowledge and sight is the principal sense by which knowledge is acquired, in the Scriptures it is called gratification of the eye" (241). As critics have observed, "gratification of the eye" is the temptation (at least in part) that leads Guyon into Mammon's Cave. See Berger, *The Allegorical Temper*.

47 Etienne Gilson argues, "In Augustinism . . . thinking, learning and remembering are all one to the soul . . . [But] this sense excludes any sort of

Platonic pre-existence, as we have seen already, but it also excludes the notion that God has deposited in us, once and for all, ideas ready-made, and that we have but to look for them there in order to find them" (*The Christian Philosophy of Saint Augustine*, 74–5).

48 O'Connell, "History and the Poet's Golden World," 246, 253. See also McCabe, *Pillars of Eternity*, 104; and Roche, *The Kindly Flame*, 46.

49 *FQ*, 2.10.71. See the discussion of the Garden of Adonis in the Conclusion.

5. Golden Age Recollections: Prehistory as Present in Spenser's Later Work

1 A quasi-autobiographical poem published in between the two instalments of *The Faerie Queene*, *Colin Clout* recalls Spenser's journey from Ireland to England (and back again) to present Queen Elizabeth with his poem. This shorter poem thus recounts a particularly important moment in Spenser's career, and though it looks back to the 1590 *Faerie Queene* it is published immediately before the 1596 edition. If I were taking Spenser's works in order, the *Complaints* would fall here too, as another work that frames the 1596 *Faerie Queene* in significant ways.

2 *Colin Clouts Come Home Againe*, in *The Yale Edition of the Shorter Poems of Edmund Spenser*, ed. Oram et al. (1–2, 7–8). Text citations are to this edition.

3 Spenser suggests Colin's rebirth through Hobbinol's excitement at his return: "*Colin* my liefe, my life, . . . / That us late dead, hast made againe alive" (16–31). Colin's responses also seem pregnant with fantasies of rebirth, as when he promises "in remembrance of . . . / My lifes sole blisse, my hearts eternall threasure" to "Wake . . . my sleepie *Muse*" (46–8).

4 Cf. *June*, where Hobbinol describes their "place" as the "pleasaunt syte" of poetry (*The Shepheardes Calender*, in *Shorter Poems*, 1). Text citations are to this edition. Prose is cited by page, poetry by line number.

5 On the Golden Age, see Donald Cheney, *Spenser's Image of Nature*; Arthur B. Ferguson, *Utter Antiquity*; A.C. Hamilton, *The Structure of Allegory in* The Faerie Queene; Harry Levin, *The Myth of the Golden Age in the Renaissance*; and O'Connell, *Mirror and Veil*.

6 Spenser, *The Faerie Queene*, ed. Hamilton, 5.Proem.2–3. Text citations are to this edition. Prose is cited by page, poetry by book, canto, and stanza numbers.

7 For considerations of the legitimacy of the *Mutabilitie Cantos*, given their belated posthumous publication, see J.B. Lethbridge, "Spenser's Last Days," in *Edmund Spenser: New and Renewed Directions*, 302–6; and *Celebrating Mutabilitie*, ed. Grogan. If only as a thought experiment, what would it

mean to approach these cantos as another author's (or authors') memorial to Spenser that emulates both his method and matter as a poet? And what would it mean to have the Blatant Beast mark the poem's end?

8 In the *Aeneid*, Virgil changes Hesiod's tale so that Jove's rebellion begins the Golden Age; in *Metamorphoses*, Ovid alters the tale again so that Jove ends rather than begins the Golden Age.

9 Teskey, *Allegory and Violence*, 181.

10 Teskey, *Allegory and Violence*, 184.

11 This description tacitly evokes not only Jove's usurpation of Saturn's throne but also Saturn's usurpation of his father's power. In Hesiod's *Theogony*, Saturn's usurpation of power from Uranus results in a castration, the blood of which becomes the seed of a new race of giants. In Ovid's retelling of this Golden Age tale in *Metamorphoses*, Jove's wars with giants gives birth to humans, as their fallen blood impregnates Mother Nature. The question of Mutability's status, whether she represents a god or a titan (or a monster), is also a central point of tension, given that she is referred to both as a "Giant" and a "Titan." On giants, see Jane Aptekar, *Icons of Justice*; Walter Stephens, *Giants in Those Days*; and Susanne Wofford, "Spenser's Giants."

12 Mutability's case is drawn in large part from the ironized "Doctrines of Pythagoras" at the end of Ovid's *Metamorphoses*; Pythagoras' cyclical vision of history undercuts the Jovian prophecy of "empire without end," which, coyly, Ovid never delivers. The transmigration of Pythagoras' soul over time, as I earlier suggested, can be read as a playful memorial to Plato.

13 "Cynthia is not just exposed by Mutability," Richard McCabe has argued, "she is exposed as Mutability," adding that "Nowhere was Cynthia's vacillation more evident to Spenser than in her Irish policy" (*Spenser's Monstrous Regiment*, 259).

14 On this naked truth, see Krier, *Gazing on Secret Sights*.

15 "Ireland" has been central to Spenser studies since Stephen Greenblatt's *Renaissance Self-Fashioning*, itself building upon Edward Said's seminal work of postcolonial criticism, *Culture and Imperialism*. On the subject of Spenser and Ireland, see, for example, Brendan Bradshaw, Andrew Hadfield, and Willy Maley, eds., *Representing Ireland*; Patricia Coughlan, *Spenser and Ireland*; David J. Baker, *Between Nations*; Hadfield, *Edmund Spenser's Irish Experience*; Maley, *Salvaging Spenser*; McCabe, *Spenser's Monstrous Regiment*; and Annabel Patterson, *Reading Between the Lines*. On the *Viewe* in the context of memory and forgetting, see Christopher Ivic, "Spenser and Interpellative Memory."

16 As Maley argues, "Spenser's purpose in the *View*, according to David Baker, is 'to tell the intolerable truth of Ireland.' I prefer to say truths rather than truth, and myths rather than truths" (*Salvaging Spenser*, 147). Maley further argues that "Spenser has long functioned as a 'take-the-blame,' a scapegoat, onto whom all of the anxieties and tensions around the representation of Ireland and the Irish have been projected . . . [and] literary historians have been only too eager to connect Spenser's Irish vocation with his poetic career, and in ways that are often hackneyed, stereotyped or dogmatic" (*Salvaging Spenser*, 2).

17 Spenser, *A View of the State of Ireland*, ed. Hadfield and Maley, 12. Text citations are to this edition.

18 As Judith Anderson argues, "If we think that the poet of Faerie wrote the *Viewe* (and there is considerable verbal evidence that he did), we really should not be surprised that his twin – his duplicitous – personae Irenius and Eudoxus should manage between them to utter a 'saying self' that lands us in cultural quicksand, even though this possibly bottomless mirroring directly implicates the special nature of sovereignty, the danger of regicide, and more exactly the threats, including that of the imagination, to Spenser's Queen" (*Reading the Allegorical Intertext*, 177). Similarly, David Summers argues that "Irenius certainly provided a public guise under which Spenser may express with certainty attitudes and opinions about a variety of things which the writer may have either held at some distance or was deeply divided about" (*Spenser's Arthur*, 179). On the *Viewe* as dialogue, see also Coughlan, "Ireland and Incivility in Spenser."

19 Specifically, Hadfield suggests that "If *A View* would seem to validate an absolutist politics, it also comes dangerously close to supplanting the authority of the queen's title to Ireland in favour of her loyal English subjects in residence there . . . On the one hand, Machiavelli would seem to function like the other authorities (Classical and contemporary) cited in the *A View* and this can be passed over as another piece of supporting detail to help Irenius' argument that power needs to be devolved to the magistrates and governors . . . [on the other hand,] the deliberate reference possibly signals an awareness of, if not involvement in, the development of a series of alternative political ideas in Irish intellectual society, ones which openly criticized the Queen and defended the rights of subjects" (*Spenser's Irish Experience*, 77–8); see also "Was Spenser a Republican?" On England and republicanism, see John F. McDiarmid, *The Monarchial Republic of Early Modern England*; Markku Peltonen, *Classical Humanism and Republicanism in English Political Thought*; and J.G.A. Pocock's classic study, *The Machiavellian Moment*.

20 As Kahn explains, "Machiavelli's criticism of the humanist version of prag-
matism follows from his recognition of the intrinsic irony of politics, or of
action within the contingent realm of human affairs: 'If you look at matters
carefully, you will see that something resembling virtue, if you follow it,
may be your ruin, while something resembling vice will lead, if you follow
it, to your security and well-being' (45, 66). But this formulation also allows us to see that Machiavelli wants to control this irony, or rather that he
conceives of the man of *virtu* as someone who can *use* the ironies of political action to achieve political stability . . . This recognition of the irony of
politics leads in turn to a revision of humanist argument in *utramque partem*
(on both sides of the question)" (*Machiavelli and the Discourse of Literature*,
199–200).

21 Niccolo Machiavelli, *The Prince and the Discourses*, ed. Lerner, 129. Machiavelli also argues that a republic offers no guarantee of permanence. "It is
equally difficult," he blithely notes, "to save a monarchy as to save a republic" (406). Text citations are to this edition.

22 Spenser, *The Faerie Queene*, ed. Hamilton, 738. Text citations are to this edition. Prose is cited by page, poetry by book, canto, and stanza numbers.

23 Spenser's speaker begins *The Ruines of Time* with this complaint-cum-
recollection of his education under Verlame's sentimental tutelage: "Nigh
where the goodly *Verlame* stood of yore, / Of which there now remaines no
memorie, / Nor anie little moniment to see" (3–5).

24 Irenius' plan is openly "Machiavellian" in ways that don't seem to accord
with Spenser-qua-radical Protestant. For example, Irenius confesses "For
religion little have I to say, my selfe being (as I said) not professed therein,"
yet he acknowledges it as an opiate of the people: "Next care in religion is
to build up and repayre all the ruined churches," adding "I would wishe
that there were order taken to have them built in some better forme, according to the churches of England; for the outward shew (assure your
selfe) doth greatly drawe the rude people to the reverencing and frequent-
ing thereof. What ever some of our late too nice fooles say, there is nothing
in the seemely forme, and comely order of the Church" (153–5).

25 Irenius' charges ironically recall Sidney's defence of Welsh bards in the
Apology, praised for their resistance to invaders who "did seek to ruin all
memory of learning from among them" (10).

26 William Camden, *Britannia*, 986. Text citations are to this edition.

27 Christopher Highly argues that "exploring such evidence as Gerald's
troubled ambivalence about Anglo-Norman designs in Ireland . . . reveals
what most past criticism has either ignored or denied, that even the most
apparently reactionary and essentialist representations of Ireland and the

Irish could create counter-meanings and even inspire radical insights" (*Shakespeare, Spenser, and the Crisis in Ireland*, 12). I would suggest that this ambivalence can be seen in both Gerald's and Geoffrey's histories. Gerald's concluding remarks in praise of Henry II and dispraise of the accuracy of his account are reminiscent of Geoffrey's miraculous discovery of "a certain very ancient book written in the British language . . . attractively composed to form a consecutive and orderly narrative, [in which is] set out all the deeds of these men, from Brutus, the first King of the Britons to the once and the future King of Britain, Arthur" (51), which he then translates into Latin. This book might be read as Geoffrey's winking admission that the history represents a hoax, or perhaps a rhetorical exercise, but it also expresses a profound truth in jest: history inevitably builds upon stories, borrowing "methods" both fictional and rhetorical. This point relates to Spenser's "method" of remembering both Gerald and Geoffrey: as in the Castle of Alma, where remembering Geoffrey's history anew figures so prominently, so in the *Viewe* Spenser rewrites Gerald's history, in part at least, as a means of revealing the stories repeated throughout history, tales that, more often than not, are taken as truth – if only in retrospect.

28 In his "Letter to Raleigh," Spenser implies that he chose Arthur as a subject because he is the stuff of legend, presumably about the past rather than the present. "To fashion a gentleman or noble person in vertuous and gentle discipline," Spenser "coloured [*The Faerie Queene*] with an historicall fiction"; as he explains, "I chose the historye of king Arthure, as most fitte for the excellency of his person, being made famous by many mens former workes, and also furthest from the daunger of enuy, and suspition of present time," adding that he has "followed all the antique Poets historicall" in his "labour to pourtraict . . . Arthure, before he was king" (737). One clear irony lies with Arthur's importance to the "present time" and to the Tudor myth: an Arthurian genealogy legitimates Tudor rule over England and Ireland. If Spenser tacitly disavows the Arthurian legend, Irenius, by contrast, simply takes Arthur as truth and one that speaks to the "present" state of Ireland as well as England. Given his sceptical treatments of Arthur throughout his work, it seems unlikely that Spenser would share Irenius' view. That E.K. ironically dismisses the truth of Arthur in no uncertain terms in the key *Aprill* eclogue of *The Shepheardes Calender* – disparaging "certain fine fablers and lowd lyers, such as were the Authors of King Arthure" – may well support this view. (*The Shepheardes Calender*, 82). On the subject of Arthur, see Summers, *Spenser's Arthur*.

29 *Ruines of Rome*, in *Shorter Poems*, 32.444.

30 On Book 5 as an allegory of the present state of England and its foreign policy, see Bart Van Es, *Spenser's Forms of History*, 154–6.

31 On Ireland in Book 5, see for example Hadfield, *Spenser's Irish Experience*; Maley, *Salvaging Spenser*, and Read, *Temperate Conquests*.

32 Monmouth, *History of the Kings of Britain*, 64.

33 To borrow Lawrence Manley's term of art in *Literature and Culture in Early Modern London*.

34 See Clifford Davidson, "Isis Church," on Plutarch's story.

35 In Hesiod's *Theogony*, the giants are born of Saturn's usurpation of power from his father, Heaven – Saturn castrates Heaven and the blood catalyzes the Earth's conception of giants – but Typhoeus results from Jove's rebellion (8, 27). Typhoeus appears to be related to Virgil's and Ovid's descriptions of Fama as a monstrous force born of the earth and related to giants; see chapter 2.

36 *Metamorphoses*, 5. The point in *Metamorphoses* as in *The Faerie Queene* is the multiplication of rebels that issue from Jove's usurpation of power. Ovid reiterates this tale to make explicit the connection between monsters and humans: the same humans whom Jove attempts (and fails) to destroy, and who later claim a divine genealogy from Jove.

37 5.1.5. On this education, see Jeff Dolven, *Scenes of Instruction*, 209–37.

38 Like Diana's abandonment of Ireland, Astraea's departure coincides with earthly degeneration: "Now when the world with sinne gan to abound, / *Astræa* loathing lenger here to space / Mongst wicked men, in whom no truth she found, / Return'd to heauen, whence she deriu'd her race" (11). Astraea apparently finds "an euerlasting place, / Mongst those twelue signs" as the "*Virgin*" symbol of justice holding "her righteous balance"; yet the mutability of the heavens, the constellations shifting from their "proper place," also contradict her "constancy."

39 Writing about the Equality Giant, Annabel Patterson argues: "there are equally clear narrative and iconic indications that the confrontation between Knight and Giant is not simply a case of right versus wrong. Indeed, one of the central points of the debate is to establish how difficult it is to distinguish *between* right and wrong" (*Reading Between the Lines*, 93–5).

40 See Leo Braudy, *The Frenzy of Renown*.

41 On *Colin Clouts Come Home Againe*, see Patrick Cheney, *Spenser's Famous Flight*; Hoffman, *Spenser's Pastorals*; and Shore, *Spenser and the Poetics of Pastoral*.

42 *Shepheardes Calender*, 79–80. See also the discussion of *June* in chapter 2.

43 On palinode in Spenser's poetry, see Phillippy, *Love's Remedies*.

44 *Phaedrus*, 489.

45 On the marriage of the rivers, see "Two Spenserian Retrospectives"; Goldberg, *Endlesse Worke*; Guillory, *Poetic Authority*; Herendeen, "The Rhetoric

of Rivers"; Nohrnberg, *Analogy of* The Faerie Queene; Quint, *Origin and Originality in Renaissance Literature*; and Roche, *Kindly Flame*.

46 As Judith Anderson writes, "Whenever the poet of *The Faerie Queene* thought about love, any kind of love, he evidently thought about Chaucer; the very presence of a Temple of Venus in Book IV would appear in itself an invocation of Chaucer, who memorably depicted three such temples" (*Reading the Allegorical Intertext*, 143). On Chaucer here, see also Goldberg, *Endlesse Worke*, 35–51; A. Kent Hieatt, "Chaucer and *The Faerie Queene*," 147–64; and Lauren Silberman, *Transforming Desire*, 87–98.

47 See chapter 2 for this discussion of Chaucer's *House of Fame*.

48 Describing this narrative circularity as erasure, Jonathan Goldberg writes: "Looking back, he tells the beginning of his story, and it turns out to be the end as well," he argues, describing how both "the narrator is effaced" along with "Spenser's narrator" (*EW*, 63).

49 *Faerie Queene*, 4.10.3. See Silberman, *Transforming Desire*, on the subject of love and marriage in Book 4, 71–86 and passim, 109–23.

50 On forgetfulness in Faerie Land, see Bellamy, *Translations of Power*; and Elizabeth D. Harvey, "Displacements of Generation in *The Faerie Queene*," in Ivic and Williams, *Forgetting in Early Modern English Literature and Culture*, 53–64.

51 In recasting nepenthe as the elixir of the newly divine Spenser also reminds readers of the epic tradition of heroes drinking from the river of forgetfulness, Lethe, before entering the underworld. Significantly, in completing Chaucer's tale Spenser inserts a journey to an underworld, a *catabasis*, in which the legitimacy of the gods is challenged, especially Jove's. This fully accords with Chaucer's light-hearted but thoroughly sceptical treatment of classical epic and its representations of divinity and history in *The House of Fame*. Agape – charity, love – takes her boys into the underworld to find out their fate (a story that also echoes an episode in Virgil's *Aeneid* 8.564–7). Here, the Fates are shown to be greater than Jove: "Downe in the bottome of the deepe *Abysse*," Agape discovers that "what the Fates do once decree, / Not all the gods can chaunge, no *Ioue* him self can free" (*The Faerie Queene*, 4.2.47, 51). Rather than affirming Jove's power in history, this symbolic journey into history instead undermines it.

52 *The Aeneid*, trans. Fairclough, 6.1046–67. Text citations are to this edition.

53 "Much more than a way of putting local myth and history in perspective," Bart Van Es writes, "chorography provided Spenser with a tool for exploring his nation's geographical and historical integrity" (*Spenser's Forms of History*, 64).

54 See David Miller on the relation of such violence to mnemonics: "a connection between violence as a physical and historical event, violence as a subject of representation, and violence as part of the dynamics of representation" (*The Poem's Two Bodies*, 22–3).

55 *Phaedrus*, 489.

56 See chapter 2.

57 On the return to pastoral, see John D. Bernard, *Ceremonies of* Innocence; Hoffman, *Spenser's Pastorals*; Mallette, *Spenser, Milton, and Renaissance Pastoral*; Shore, *Spenser and the Poetics of Pastoral*.

58 On Book 6 as a supremely self-reflexive book, see Berger, *Revisionary Play*, 215–42; Isabel MacCaffrey, *Spenser's Allegory*, 343–422; Parker, *Inescapable Romance*, 101–13; Shore, *Spenser and the Poetics of Pastoral*, 132–69; and Humphrey Tonkin, *Spenser's Courteous Pastoral*.

59 On forgetting and remembering in Book 6, see Elizabeth Mazzola, "Legends of Oblivion."

60 On the return of Stesichorus, see Phillippy, *Love's Remedies*.

61 *Ruines of Rome*, 30.418–19.

62 As Judith Anderson argues, this may also allude to Chaucer's Melibee; see *Reading the Allegorical Intertext*, 91–105.

63 *City of God*, 112.

64 Philip Schwyzer observes: "For Spenser, the ruined monastery is both symbol and repository of the kind of ambiguity that will not let itself be tidied away, the ambiguity that lies, arguably, at the heart of poetic freedom. Later generations would find peace and pleasure in the shattered remnants of the religious houses. The Elizabethans, by contrast, discovered ugliness, anguish, shame – and, in some cases, liberation" (*Archaeologies of English Renaissance Literature*, 97–8). On the dissolution of monasteries, see Gross, *Spenserian Poetics*; John King, *Spenser's Poetry and the Reformation Tradition*; Mary Claire Moroney, "Spenser's Dissolution"; Summit, *Memory's Library*.

65 For the earlier discussion of Chaucer and fame, see chapter 2.

66 Gross, "Reflections on the Blatant Beast," 111. Describing how "the Beast is represented as the agent, the allegorical memory of Henry VIII's programmatic dissolution of the English monasteries," Gross further argues: "The monster's ravages here become a deeply troubled figure for (or translation of) the complex program of judicial investigation, institutional dismantling, economic appropriation and redistribution, as well as organized and disorganized physical violence, that helped found the dynasty of Gloriana ... The image of that violence here takes a form that the upholders of the settlement would presumably repudiate as a slander; but it is an image

that Spenser nonetheless internalizes, or appropriates, in order to shape one of his strangest, most dream-like images of the movement of questing" (111–14). On the Beast, see also Thomas Herron, *Spenser's Irish Work*, 185–224; and Nohrnberg, *Analogy of* The Faerie Queene, 688–96.

Conclusion: Misprision and Freedom: Ruining and Recollecting the Bower of Bliss

1 Milton, *Areopagitica*, in *Complete Poems and Major Prose*, ed. Hughes, 728–9. Text citations are to this edition.
2 Bloom, *A Map of Misreading*, 127. In a work that continues that of *The Anxiety of Influence*, Bloom writes that Milton "too had his starting point: Spenser: 'Milton has acknowledged to me, that Spenser was his original,' Dryden testified, but the paternity required no acknowledgement. A darker acknowledgement can be read in Milton's astonishing mistake about Spenser in *Areopagitica*, written more than twenty years before *Paradise Lost* was completed . . . Milton's is no ordinary error, no mere lapse in memory, but is itself a powerful misinterpretation of Spenser, and a strong defense against him. For Guyon is not so much Adam's precursor as he is Milton's own, the giant model imitated by the Abdiel of *Paradise Lost*. Milton re-writes Spenser so as to *increase the distance* between the poetic father and himself. St. Augustine identified memory with the father, and we may surmise that lapse in a memory as preternatural as Milton's is a movement against the father" (*Map of Misreading,* 127–8). Though I disagree with Bloom, especially on Augustine's influence, I agree with his reading of Spenser's (less anxious) influence on Milton's poetry. As Bloom argues, "Spenser's cave of Mammon is Milton's Hell; far more than the descents to the underworld of Homer and Virgil, more even than Dante's vision, the prefigurement of Books I and II of *Paradise Lost* reverberates in Book II of *The Faerie Queene*" (128). I would further suggest, in keeping with this conclusion, that Milton's epic rebuilds the Cave of Mammon as an art of recollecting Spenser's ruins. With this study, I hope to have allayed Bloom's own anxiety about ruin, his "prophecy" that "the first true break with literary continuity will be brought about in generations to come, if the burgeoning religion of Liberated Woman spreads from its clusters of enthusiasts to dominate the West," when "Homer will cease to be the inevitable precursor, and the rhetoric and forms of our literature then may break at last from tradition" (33). And yet the end is not – not yet, anyway. On the anxiety of Bloom's relationship with Greenblatt, see Larissa MacFarquhar, "The Prophet of Decline."

3 Spenser, "Letter to Raleigh," *The Faerie Queene*, 738. See chapter 4.

4 The discussion in this conclusion encapsulates material from chapter 4.

5 See Quilligan, *Milton's Spenser: The Politics of Reading*.

6 Plato, *Phaedrus*, in *The Collected Dialogues*, trans. and ed. Hamilton and Cairns, 489. Text citations are to this edition.

7 Plato, *Phaedrus*, 522. Socrates continues, "And when other men resort to other pastimes, regaling themselves with drinking parties and suchlike, he will doutless prefer to indulge in the recreation I refer to," seemingly an allusion to Plato's literary drinking party, the *Symposium*.

8 Greenblatt, *Renaissance Self-Fashioning*, 172, 173.

9 Greenblatt, *Renaissance Self-Fashioning*, 173–4.

10 Greenblatt, *Renaissance Self-Fashioning*, 179.

11 Greenblatt, *Renaissance Self-Fashioning*, 175.

12 Greenblatt, *Renaissance Self-Fashioning*, 178.

13 Greenblatt, *Renaissance Self-Fashioning*, 179.

14 Greenblatt, *Renaissance Self-Fashioning*, 179.

15 Greenblatt, *Renaissance Self-Fashioning*, 173–4.

16 Greenblatt, *Renaissance Self-Fashioning*, 175.

17 Greenblatt, *Renaissance Self-Fashioning*, 189.

18 Greenblatt, *Renaissance Self-Fashioning*, 190.

19 Greenblatt, *Renaissance Self-Fashioning*, 192.

20 Greenblatt, *Renaissance Self-Fashioning*, 192.

Bibliography

Adams, A., and A. Harper, eds. *The Emblem in Renaissance and Baroque Europe.* New York: E.J. Brill, 1992.

Allen, Don Cameron. *Mysteriously Meant: The Rediscovery of Pagan Symbolism and Allegorical Interpretation in the Renaissance.* Baltimore: Johns Hopkins University Press, 1970.

Alpers, Paul J. "Community and Convention in Vergilian Pastoral." In *Vergil at 2000: Commemorative Essays on the Poet and his Influence*, edited by John D. Bernard. New York: AMS Press, 1986.

– "Pastoral and the Domain of Lyric in Spenser's *Shepheardes Calender.*" *Representations* 12 (Fall 1995): 83–100.

– *The Poetry of* The Faerie Queene. Princeton, NJ: Princeton University Press, 1967.

– *The Singer of the* Eclogues: *A Study of Virgilian Pastoral.* Berkeley: University of California Press, 1979.

Anderson, Judith H. *The Growth of Personal Voice:* Piers Plowman *and* The Faerie Queene. New Haven, CT: Yale University Press, 1976.

– "'Myn auctour': Spenser's Enabling Fiction and Eumnestes' 'Immortal Scrine.'" In *Unfolded Tales: Essays on Renaissance Romance*, edited by George M. Logan and Gordon Teskey. Ithaca, NY: Cornell University Press, 1989.

– *Reading the Allegorical Intertext: Chaucer, Spenser, Shakespeare, Milton.* New York: Fordham University Press, 2008.

Anonymous. *Rhetorica ad Herennium.* Translated by Harry Caplan. Cambridge, MA: Harvard University Press; Loeb Classical Library, 1954.

Aptekar, Jane. *Icons of Justice: Iconography and Thematic Imagery in Book V of* The Faerie Queene. New York: Columbia University Press, 1969.

Aristotle. *Aristotle on Memory.* Translated by Richard Sorabji. Chicago: University of Chicago Press, 1972.

– *Metaphysics*. Translated by Hugh Lawson-Tancred. London: Penguin, 2004.

Armitage, David, ed. *Theories of Empire, 1450–1800*. Aldershot, UK: Ashgate, 1998.

Armstrong, Edward. *A Ciceronian Sunburn: A Tudor Dialogue on Humanistic Rhetoric and Civic Poetics*. Columbia: University of South Carolina Press, 2006.

Ascoli, Albert Russell, and Victoria Kahn, eds. *Machiavelli and the Discourse of Literature*. Ithaca, NY: Cornell University Press, 1993.

Atchity, Kenneth John, ed. *Eterne in Mutability: The Unity of* The Faerie Queene. Hamden, CT: Archon, 1972.

Auerbach, Erich. *Dante: Poet of the Secular World*. Translated by Ralph Manheim. Chicago: University of Chicago Press, 1929.

Augustine. *City of God*. Translated by Henry Bettenson. New York: Penguin, 1984.

– *The Confessions of Saint Augustine*. Translated by Rex Warner. New York: Penguin, 1981.

– *On Christian Doctrine*. Translated by D.W. Robertson Jr. Saddle River, NJ: Prentice Hall, 1958.

Baker, David J. *Between Nations: Shakespeare, Spenser, Marvell, and the Question of Britain*. Stanford, CA: Stanford University Press, 1997.

Barkan, Leonard. *The Gods Made Flesh: Metamorphosis and the Pursuit of Paganism*. New Haven, CT: Yale University Press, 1986.

– "Ruins and Visions." In *Edmund Spenser: Essays on Culture and Allegory*, edited by Jennifer Klein Morrison and Matthew Greenfield. Aldershot, UK: Ashgate, 2000.

– *Unearthing the Past: Archaeology and Aesthetics in the Making of Renaissance Culture*. New Haven, CT: Yale University Press, 1999.

Baswell, Christopher. *Virgil in Medieval England: Figuring the* Aeneid *from the Twelth Century to Chaucer*. Cambridge: Cambridge University Press, 1995.

Bath, Michael. *Speaking Pictures: English Emblem Books and Renaissance Culture*. New York: Longman, 1994.

Bellamy, Elizabeth J. *Translations of Power: Narcissism and the Unconscious in Epic History*. Ithaca, NY: Cornell University Press, 1992.

Baucom, Ian. *Out of Place: Englishness, Empire, and the Locations of Identity*. Princeton, NJ: Princeton University Press, 1999.

Beecher, Donald, and Grant Williams, eds. *Ars Reminiscendi: Mind and Memory in Renaissance Culture*. Toronto: University of Toronto Press, 2009.

Beer, Jeanette, and Kenneth Lloyd-Jones, eds. *Translation and the Transmission of Culture Between 1300 and 1600*. Kalamazoo, MI: Medieval Institute Press, 1992.

Beiman, Elizabeth. *Plato Baptized: Towards the Interpretation of Spenser's Mimetic Fictions*. Toronto: University of Toronto Press, 1988.

Bender, John. *Spenser and Literary Pictorialism*. Princeton, NJ: Princeton University Press, 1972.

Benjamin, Walter. *The Origins of German Tragic Drama*. Translated by John Osborne. London: Lowe & Brydone Printers Ltd, 1977.

Bennett, J.A. W. *Chaucer's Book of Fame: An Exposition of the "House of Fame."* Oxford: Clarendon Press, 1968.

Berger, Harry, Jr. *The Absence of Grace: Sprezzatura and Suspicion in Two Renaissance Courtesy Books*. Stanford, CA: Stanford University Press, 2000.

– *The Allegorical Temper: Vision and Reality in Book II of Spenser's* Faerie Queene. London: Oxford University Press, 1957.

– *Revisionary Play: Studies in the Spenserian Dynamics*. Berkeley: University of California Press, 1988.

Bernard, John D. *Ceremonies of Innocence: Pastoralism in the Poetry of Edmund Spenser*. Cambridge: Cambridge University Press, 1989.

Bieman, Elizabeth. *Plato Baptized: Towards the Interpretation of Spenser's Mimetic Fictions*. Toronto: University of Toronto Press, 1988.

Bloom, Harold. *The Anxiety of Influence: A Theory of Poetry*. Oxford: Oxford University Press, 1973.

– *A Map of Misreading*. Oxford: Oxford University Press, 1975.

Blumenfeld-Kosinsky, Renate, Luise Von Flotow, and Daniel Russel, eds. *The Politics of Translation in the Middle Ages and the Renaissance*. Ottawa: Medieval and Renaissance Texts and Studies, 2001.

Bolzoni, Lina. *The Gallery of Memory: Literary and Iconographic Models in the Age of the Printing Press*. Translated by Jeremy Parzen. Toronto: University of Toronto Press, 1995.

Borris, Kenneth. *Allegory and Epic in English Renaissance Literature: Heroic Form in Sidney, Spenser, and Milton*. Cambridge: Cambridge University Press, 2000.

Bradshaw, Brendan, Andrew Hadfield, and Willy Maley, eds. *Representing Ireland: Literature and the Origins of Conflict, 1534–1660*. Cambridge: Cambridge University Press, 1993.

Braudy, Leo. *The Frenzy of Renown: Fame and its History*. Oxford: Oxford University Press, 1986.

Breisach, Ernst. *Historiography: Ancient, Medieval, and Modern*. Chicago: University of Chicago Press, 1994.

Brown, Richard Danson. *"The New Poet": Novelty and Tradition in Spenser's Complaints*. Liverpool: Liverpool University Press, 1999.

Bubacz, Bruce. *St. Augustine's Theory of Knowledge*. New York: E. Mellen Press, 1981.

Budick, Sanford, and Wolfgang Iser, eds. *The Translatability of Cultures.* Stanford, CA: Stanford University Press, 1996.

Burger, Ronna. *Plato's* Phaedrus: *A Defense of a Philosophic Art of Writing.* Tuscaloosa: University of Alabama Press, 1980.

Burke, Peter. *The Fortunes of the Courtier: The European Reception of Castiglione's* Cortegiano. University Park: Pennsylvania State University Press, 1995.

Burrow, Colin. *Epic Romance: Homer to Milton.* Oxford: Clarendon Press, 1993.

Camden, William. *Britannia.* London: F. Collins, 1695.

Carruthers, Mary. *The Book of Memory: A Study of Memory in Medieval Culture.* Cambridge: Cambridge University Press, 1990.

– *The Craft of Thought: Meditation, Rhetoric, and the Making of Images, 400–1200.* Cambridge: Cambridge University Press, 1998.

– "Italy, *Ars memorativa*, and Fame's House." *Studies in the Age of Chaucer* 2 (1987): 179–88.

– "The Poet as Master Builder: Composition and Locational Memory in the Middle Ages." *New Literary History* 24, no. 4 (Autumn 1993): 881–904.

Cary, Phillip. *Augustine's Invention of the Inner Self: The Legacy of a Christian Platonist.* Oxford: Oxford University Press, 2000.

Castiglione, Baldassare. *The Book of the Courtier.* Edited by Virginia Cox. Translated by Thomas Hoby. London: Everyman, 1994.

Chaucer, Geoffrey. *Dream Visions and Other Poems.* Edited by Kathryn L. Lynch. New York: W.W. Norton & Company, 2007.

– *The Riverside Chaucer.* Edited by Larry D. Benson. Boston: Houghton Mifflin Company, 1987.

– *Troilus and Criseyde.* Translated by Nevill Coghill. London: Penguin, 1971.

Cheney, Donald. "The Circular Argument of *The Shepheardes Calender*." In *Unfolded Tales: Essays on Renaissance Romance*, edited by George M. Logan and Gordon Teskey. Ithaca, NY: Cornell University Press, 1989.

– "Colin Clout's Homecoming: The Imaginative Travels of Edmund Spenser." *Connotations* 72 (1997–8): 146–58.

– *Spenser's Image of Nature: Wild Man and Shepherd in* The Faerie Queene. New Haven, CT: Yale University Press, 1966.

Cheney, Patrick. *Marlowe's Counterfeit Profession: Ovid, Spenser, Counter-Nationhood.* Toronto: University of Toronto Press, 1997.

– *Spenser's Famous Flight: A Renaissance Idea of a Literary Career.* Toronto: University of Toronto Press, 1993.

– "Spenser's Pastorals: *The Shepheardes Calender* and *Colin Clouts Come Home Againe*." In *The Cambridge Companion to Spenser*, ed. Andrew Hadfield. Cambridge: Cambridge University Press, 2001.

Cicero. *De oratore; or, On the Character of the Orator*. In *Cicero on Oratory and Orators*. Translated and edited by J.S. Watson. Carbondale: Southern Illinois University Press, 1970.

Clark, Raymond. *Catabasis: Vergil and the Wisdom Tradition*. Amsterdam: Gruner, 1979.

Clements, Roger J. *Picta Poesis: Literary and Humanistic Theory in Renaissance Emblem Books*. Rome: Edizioni di Storia e Letteratura, 1960.

Coldiron, A.E.B. "How Spenser Excavates Du Bellay's *Antiquitez*; or, the Role of the Poet, Lyric Historiography, and the English Sonnet." *Journal of English and Germanic Philology* (2002): 41–67.

Coleman, Janet. *Ancient and Medieval Memories: Studies in the Reconstruction of the Past*. Cambridge: Cambridge University Press, 1992.

Conte, Gian Biagio. *The Rhetoric of Imitation: Genre and Poetic Memory in Virgil and Other Latin Poets*. Translated and edited by Charles Segal. Ithaca, NY: Cornell University Press, 1986.

Cooper, Richard. "Poetry in Ruins: The Literary Context of du Bellay's Cycles on Rome." *Renaissance Studies* 3, no. 2 (1989): 156–65.

Copeland, Rita. "The Ciceronian Rhetorical Tradition and Medieval Literary Theory." In *The Rhetoric of Cicero in Its Medieval and Early Renaissance Commentary Tradition*, edited by Virginia Cox and John O. Ward. Leiden: Brill, 2006.

Coughlan, Patricia. " 'Some secret scourge which shall by her come unto England': Ireland and Incivility in Spenser." In *Spenser and Ireland: An Interdisciplinary Perspective*, edited by Patricia Coughlan. Cork: Cork University Press, 1989.

Cox, Virginia. *The Renaissance Dialogue: Literary Dialogue in its Social and Political Contexts, Castiglione to Galileo*. Cambridge: Cambridge University Press, 1992.

Craft, William. *Labyrinth of Desire: Invention and Culture in the Work of Sir Philip Sidney*. Newark: University of Delaware Press, 1994.

Cullen, Patrick. *Spenser, Marvell, and Renaissance Pastoral*. Cambridge, MA: Harvard University Press, 1970.

Daly, Peter M. *Literature in the Light of the Emblem: Structural Parallels between the Emblem and the Literature in the Sixteenth and Seventeenth Centuries*. Toronto: University of Toronto Press, 1979.

Dante Aligheri. *The Divine Comedy*. Translated by Allen Mandelbaum. Everyman's Library Edition. New York: Alfred A. Knopf, 1995.

Davidson, Clifford. "Isis Church." In *The Spenser Encyclopedia*, edited by A.C. Hamilton. Toronto: University of Toronto Press, 1997.

Delany, Sheila. *Chaucer's House of Fame: The Poetics of Skeptical Fideism.* Chicago: University of Chicago Press, 1972.

DeNeef, A. Leigh. "'The Ruines of Time': Spenser's Apology for Poetry." *Studies in Philology* 76 (1979): 262–71.

– *Spenser and the Motives of Metaphor.* Durham, NC: Duke University Press, 1982.

Dixon, Sandra Lee. *Augustine: The Scattered and Gathered Self.* St Lous, MO: Chalice Press, 1999.

Doherty, M.J. *The Mistress-Knowledge: Sir Philip Sidney's* Defense of Poesie *and Literary Architectonics in the English Renaissance.* Nashville, TN: Vanderbilt University Press, 1991.

Dolven, Jeff. *Scenes of Instruction in Renaissance Romance.* Chicago: University of Chicago Press, 2007.

Doob, Penelope Reed. *The Idea of the Labyrinth From Classical Antiquity Through the Middle Ages.* Ithaca, NY: Cornell University Press, 1990.

Du Bellay, Joachim. *The Defense and Illustration of the French Language.* Translated by Gladys Turquet. London: J.M. Dent & Sons, 1939.

Dunseath, T.K. *Spenser's Allegory of Justice in Book Five of* The Faerie Queene. Princeton, NJ: Princeton University Press, 1968.

Eden, Kathy. *Hermeneutics and the Ancient Rhetorical Tradition.* New Haven, CT: Yale University Press, 1997.

Edwards, Robert. *The Flight From Desire.* Basingstoke, UK: Palgrave Macmillan, 2006.

Engel, William E. *Chiastic Designs in English Literature from Sidney to Shakespeare.* Aldershot, UK: Ashgate Press, 2009.

– *Mapping Mortality: The Persistence of Memory and Melancholy in Early Modern England.* Amherst: University of Massachusetts Press, 1995.

– "Mnemonic Criticism and Renaissance Literature: A Manifesto." *Connotations* 1, no. 1 (March 1991): 12–33.

Erskine, Andrew. *Troy Between Greece and Rome: Local Tradition and Imperial Power.* Oxford: Oxford University Press, 2001.

Escobedo, Andrew. *Nationalism and Historical Loss in Renaissance England.* Ithaca, NY: Cornell University Press, 2004.

Ferguson, Arthur B. *Clio Unbound: Perception of the Social and Cultural Past in Renaissance England.* Durham, NC: Duke University Press, 1979.

– *Utter Antiquity: Perceptions of Prehistory in Renaissance England.* Durham, UK: Duke University Press, 1993.

Ferguson, Margaret W. "'The Afflatus of Ruin': Meditations on Rome by Du Bellay, Spenser, and Stevens." In *Roman Images*, edited by Annabel Patterson. Baltimore: Johns Hopkins University Press, 1982.

– *Trials of Desire: Renaissance Defenses of Poetry*. New Haven, CT: Yale University Press, 1983.

Fichter, Andrew. "'And nought of *Rome* in *Rome* perceiv'st at all': Spenser's *Ruines of Rome*." *Spenser Studies* 2 (1981): 183–92.

– *Poets Historical: Dynastic Epic in the Renaissance*. New Haven, CT: Yale University Press, 1982.

Firth, Katherine. *The Apocalyptic Tradition in Reformation Britain, 1530–1645*. Oxford: Oxford University Press, 1979.

Fitzpatrick, Joan. *Irish Demons: English Writings on Ireland, the Irish, and Gender by Spenser and his Contemporaries*. Lanham, MD: University Press of America, 2000.

Fletcher, Angus. *Allegory: The Theory of a Symbolic Mode*. Ithaca, NY: Cornell University Press, 1964.

– *The Prophetic Moment: An Essay on Spenser*. Chicago: University of Chicago Press, 1971.

Fox, Susan C. "Eterne in Mutability: Spenser's Darkening Vision." In *Eterne in Mutability: The Unity of* The Faerie Queene, edited by Kenneth John Atchity. Hamden, CT: Archon, 1972.

Freccero, John. "The Fig Tree and the Laurel: Petrarch's Poetics." In *Literary Theory/Renaissance Texts*, edited by Patricia Parker and David Quint. Baltimore: Johns Hopkins University Press, 1986.

Freeman, Rosemary. *English Emblem Books*. London: Chatto & Windus, 1970.

Freud, Sigmund. *Civilization and its Discontents*. Translated by John Riviere. New York: Doubleday, 1958.

Frye, Northrop. *The Anatomy of Criticism: Four Essays*. New York: Atheneum, 1967.

Gadamer, Hans-Georg. *The Idea of the Good in Platonic-Aristotelian Philosophy*. Translated by P. Christopher Smith. New Haven, CT: Yale University Press, 1986.

Galbraith, David. *Architectonics of Imitation in Spenser, Daniel, and Drayton*. Toronto: University of Toronto Press, 2000.

Geller, Sherri. "You Can't Tell a Book by Its Contents: (Mis)Interpretation in/of Spenser's *The Shepheardes Calender*." *Spenser Studies* 13 (1999): 23–64.

Geoffrey of Monmouth. *The History of the Kings of Britain*. Translated by Lewis Thorpe. London: Penguin, 1966.

Gerald of Wales. *The History and Topography of Ireland*. Translated by John J. O'Meara. London: Penguin, 1982.

Gilson, Etienne. *The Christian Philosophy of Saint Augustine*. Translated by L.E M. Lynch. New York: Random House, 1960.

Gless, Darryl J. *Interpretation and Theology in Spenser*. Cambridge: Cambridge University Press, 1994.

Goldberg, Jonathan. *Endlesse Worke: Spenser and the Structures of Discourse*. Baltimore: Johns Hopkins University Press, 1981.

– *Voice, Terminal, Echo*. New York: Methuen, 1986.

Goldstein, Laurence. "Immortal Longings and 'The Ruines of Time.'" *Journal of English and German Philology* 75 (1976): 337–51.

– *Ruins and Empire: The Evolution of a Theme in Augustan and Romantic Literature*. Pittsburgh: University of Pittsburgh Press, 1977.

Gordon, Jill. *Turning Toward Philosophy: Literary Device and Dramatic Structure in Plato's Dialogues*. University Park: Pennsylvania State University Press, 1999.

Grafton, Anthony, ed. *Rome Reborn: The Vatican Library and Renaissance Culture*. New Haven, CT: Yale University Press, 1993.

Greenblatt, Stephen. *Hamlet in Purgatory*. Princeton, NJ: Princeton University Press, 2001.

– *Renaissance Self-Fashioning: From More to Shakespeare*. Chicago: University of Chicago Press, 1980.

Greene, Roland. "*The Shepheardes Calender*, Dialogue, and Periphrasis." *Spenser Studies* 8 (1987): 1–33.

Greene, Thomas. *The Descent from Heaven: A Study in Epic Continuity*. Baltimore: Johns Hopkins University Press, 1971.

– *The Light in Troy: Imitation and Discovery in Renaissance Poetry*. New Haven, CT: Yale University Press, 1982.

Greenfield, Matthew, and Jennifer Klein Morrison, eds. *Edmund Spenser: Essays on Culture and Allegory*. Aldershot, UK: Ashgate, 2000.

Gregerson, Linda. "Colonials Write the Nation: Spenser, Milton, and England on the Margins." In *Edmund Spenser: Essays on Culture and Allegory*, edited by Jennifer Klein Morrison and Matthew Greenfield. Aldershot, UK: Ashgate, 2000.

Griffiths, Huw. "Translated Geographies: Edmund Spenser's 'The Ruines of Time.'" *Early Modern Literary Studies* (September 1988): 1–16.

Grogan, Jane, ed. *Celebrating Mutabilitie: Essays on Edmund Spenser's* Mutabilitie Cantos. New York: Palgrave Macmillan, 2010.

Gross, Kenneth. *Spenserian Poetics: Idolatry, Iconoclasm, and Magic*. Ithaca, NY: Cornell University Press, 1985.

– "Reflections on the Blatant Beast." *Spenser Studies* 18 (1999): 101–23.

Guillory, John. *Poetic Authority: Spenser, Milton, and Literary History*. New York: Columbia University Press, 1983.

Hadfield, Andrew. *Edmund Spenser's Irish Experience: Wilde Fruit and Salvage Soyl*. Oxford: Clarendon Press, 1997.

– *Literature, Politics, and National Identity: Reformation to Renaissance*. Cambridge: Cambridge University Press, 1994.

– "Was Spenser a Republican?" *English: The Journal of the English Association* 47 (1998): 169–82.

Hadfield, Andrew, and Willy Maley. "A View of the Present State of Spenser Studies: Dialogue-Wise." In *Edmund Spenser: Essays on Culture and Allegory*, edited by Jennifer Klein Morrison and Matthew Greenfield. Aldershot, England: Ashgate, 2000.

Hager, Alan. *Dazzling Images: The Masks of Sir Philip Sidney*. Newark: University of Delaware Press, 1991.

Hagstrum, Jean H. *The Sister Arts: The Tradition of Literary Pictorialism and English Poetry from Dryden to Gray*. Chicago: University of Chicago Press, 1958.

Halpern, Richard. *The Poetics of Primitive Accumulation: English Renaissance Culture and the Genealogy of Capital*. Ithaca, NY: Cornell University Press, 1991.

Hamilton, A.C. *The Structure of Allegory in "The Faerie Queene."* Oxford: Clarendon Press, 1961.

Hammill, Graham. " 'The thing / Which never was': Republicanism and *The Ruines of Time*." *Spenser Studies* 18 (2003): 165–83.

Hankins, John. *Source and Meaning in Spenser's Allegory*. Oxford: Clarendon Press, 1971.

Harvey, Elizabeth D. "Displacements of Generation in *The Faerie Queene*," in *Forgetting in Early Modern English Literature and Culture*, edited by Christopher Ivic and Grant Williams, 53–64.

Havelock, Eric A. *Preface to Plato*. New York: Grosset & Dunlap, 1963.

Hawkins, Peter. "Dante and the Bible." In *The Cambridge Companion to Dante*, edited by Rachel Jacoff. Cambridge: Cambridge University Press, 1993.

Helfer, Rebeca. "Arts of Memory and Cultural Transmission." In *Translatio, or the Transmission of Culture*, edited by Laura H. Hollengreen. ACMRS 13. Turnhout, Belgium: Brepolis, 2008.

– "The Death of the 'New Poet': Virgilian Ruin and Ciceronian Recollection in *The Shepheardes Calender*." *Renaissance Quarterly* 56 (2003): 723–56.

– "Falling Into History: Trials of Empire in *The Faerie Queene*." In *Fantasies of Troy in the Renaissance Social Imaginary*, edited by Alan Shepherd. Toronto: University of Toronto Press, 2004.

– "Remembering Sidney, Remembering Spenser: The Art of Memory and *The Ruines of Time*." *Spenser Studies* 22 (2007): 127–51.

Helgerson, Richard. *Forms of Nationhood: The Elizabethan Writing of England.* Chicago: University of Chicago Press, 1992.

– *Self-Crowned Laureates: Spenser, Jonson, Milton and the Literary System.* Berkeley: University of California Press, 1983.

Heninger, S.K., Jr. *Sidney and Spenser: The Poet as Maker.* University Park: Pennsylvania State University Press, 1989.

Herendeen, Wyman H. "The Rhetoric of Rivers: The River and the Pursuit of Knowledge." *Studies in Philology* 78, no. 2 (Spring 1981): 107–27.

Herman, Peter C. *Squitter-Wits and Muse-Haters: Sidney, Spenser, Milton and Renaissance Antipoetic Sentiment.* Detroit: Wayne State University, 1996.

Herodotus. *The Histories.* Translated by Aubrey de Sélincourt. London: Penguin, 1954, 1972.

Herron, Thomas. *Spenser's Irish Work: Poetry, Plantation, and Colonial Reformation.* Aldershot, UK: Ashgate, 2007.

Hesiod. *Theogony.* Translated by M.L. West. Oxford: Oxford University Press, 1988.

Hieatt, A. Kent. *Chaucer, Spenser, Milton: Mythopoeic Continuities and Transformations.* Montreal: McGill-Queen's University Press, 1975.

Hieatt, A. Kent, and Anne Lake Prescott. "Contemporizing Antiquity: the *Hypnerotomachia* and its Afterlife in France." *Word and Image* 8, no. 4 (October–December 1992): 291–321.

Highly, Christopher. *Shakespeare, Spenser, and the Crisis in Ireland.* Cambridge: Cambridge University Press, 1997.

Hoffman, Nancy Jo. *Spenser's Pastorals:* The Shepheardes Calender *and "Colin Clout."* Baltimore: Johns Hopkins University Press, 1977.

Homer. *The Iliad of Homer.* Translated by Richmond Lattimore. Chicago: University of Chicago Press, 1951.

– *The Odyssey of Homer.* Translated by Richard Lattimore. New York: Harper Collins, 1967.

Horton, Ronald. "Spenser's Farewell to Dido: The Public Turn." In *Classical, Renaissance, and Postmodernist Acts of Imagination*, edited by Arthur F. Kinney. Newark: University of Delaware Press, 1996.

Hume, Anthea. *Edmund Spenser: Protestant Poet.* Cambridge: Cambridge University Press, 1984.

Hutton, Patrick. *History as an Art of Memory.* Hanover: University of Vermont Press, 1993.

Hyde, Thomas. "Vision, Poetry, and Authority in Spenser." *English Literary Renaissance* 13, no. 2 (Spring 1983): 127–45.

Ivic, Christopher. "Spenser and Interpellative Memory." In *Ars Reminiscendi: Mind and Memory in Renaissance Culture.* Edited by Donald Beecher and

Grant Williams. Toronto: Centre for Reformation and Renaissance Studies, 2009.

Ivic, Christopher, and Grant Williams, eds. *Forgetting in Early Modern English Literature and Culture: Lethe's Legacies*. New York: Routledge, 2004.

Jacoff, Rachel, ed. *The Cambridge Companion to Dante*. Cambridge: Cambridge University Press, 1993.

Janowitz, Anne. *England's Ruins: Poetic Purpose and National Landscape*. Oxford: Basil Blackwell, 1990.

Johnson, W.R. *Darkness Visible: A Study of Vergil's Aeneid*. Berkeley: University of California Press, 1976.

Kahn, Victoria. *Machiavellian Rhetoric: From the Counter-Reformation to Milton*. Princeton, NJ: Princeton University Press, 1994.

Kendrick, T.D. *British Antiquity*. London: Methuen, 1970.

Kennedy, J.M., and J.A. Reither, eds. *A Theatre for Spenserians*. Toronto: University of Toronto Press, 1973.

Kennedy, William J. *Authorizing Petrarch*. Ithaca, NY: Cornell University Press, 1994.

– "Petrarchan Audiences and Print Technology." *Journal of Medieval and Renaissance Studies* 14, no. 1 (Spring 1984): 1–20.

– *Rhetorical Norms in Renaissance Literature*. New Haven, CT: Yale University Press, 1978.

King, Andrew. The Faerie Queene *and Middle English Romance: The Matter of Just Memory*. Oxford: Clarendon Press, 2000.

King, John. *Spenser and the Reformation Tradition*. Princeton, NJ: Princeton University Press, 1999.

Klein, Lisa M. *The Exemplary Sidney and the Elizabethan Sonneteer*. Delaware: University of Delaware Press, 1998.

Krier, Theresa M. *Gazing on Secret Sights: Spenser, Classical Imitation, and the Decorums of Vision*. Ithaca, NY: Cornell University Press, 1990.

– *Refiguring Chaucer in the Renaissance*. Gainesville: University Press of Florida, 1998.

Kristo, J.G. *Looking for God in Time and Memory: Psychology, Theology, and Sprituality in Augustine's* Confessions. Lanham, MD: University Press of America, 1991.

Küchler, Susanne, and Walter Melion, eds. *Images of Memory: On Remembering and Representation*. Washington, DC: Smithsonian Institution Press, 1991.

Kucich, Greg. "The Duality of Romantic Spenserianism." *Spenser Studies* 8 (1987): 287–307.

Kuttner, Ann, Alina Payne, and Rebekah Smick, eds. *Antiquity and Its Interpreters*. Cambridge: Cambridge University Press, 2000.

Lamberton, Robert. *Homer the Theologian: Neoplatonist Allegorical Reading and the Growth of Epic Tradition*. Berkeley: University of California Press, 1986.

Lane, Robert. *The Shepheardes Devises: Edmund Spenser's* The Shepheardes Calender *and the Institutions of Elizabethan Society*. Athens: University of Georgia Press, 1983.

Lethbridge, J.B., ed. *Edmund Spenser: New and Renewed Directions*. Madison, NJ: Fairleigh Dickenson University Press, 2006.

Levin, Harry. *The Myth of the Golden Age in the Renaissance*. Bloomington: Indiana University Press, 1969.

Levy, F.J. *Tudor Historical Thought*. San Marino, CA: Huntington Library, 1967.

Lim, Walter S.H. *The Arts of Empire: The Poetics of Colonialism from Raleigh to Milton*. Newark: University of Delaware Press, 1998.

Lindheim, Nancy. "Spenser's Virgilian Pastoral: The Case for *September*." *Spenser Studies* 11 (1990): 1–16.

– "The Virgilian Design of *The Shepheardes Calender*." *Spenser Studies* 13 (1999): 1–21.

Luborsky, Ruth Samson. "Illustrations to *The Shepheardes Calender*." *Spenser Studies* 2 (1981): 3–53.

Lyne, Raphael. *Ovid's Changing Worlds: English Metamorphoses, 1567–1632*. Oxford: Oxford University Press, 2001.

Lyra Graeca. Edited and translated by J.M. Edmonds. Cambridge:, MA: Library, 1924.

MacCaffrey, Isabel. *Spenser's Allegory: The Anatomy of Imagination*. Princeton, NJ: Princeton University Press, 1976.

Macaulay, Rose. *Pleasure of Ruins*. Toronto: McClelland and Stewart, 1953.

MacFarquhar, Larissa. "The Prophet of Decline." In *The New Yorker*, 30 September 2002: 86–97.

MacCormack, Sabine. *The Shadows of Poetry: Virgil in the Mind of Augustine*. Berkeley: University of California Press, 1998.

MacDonald, Ronald. *The Burial-Places of Memory: Epic Underworlds in Vergil, Dante, and Milton*. Amherst, MA: University of Massachusetts Press, 1987.

Machiavelli, Niccolo. *The Prince and the Discourses*. Edited by Max Lerner. New York: Random House, 1950.

Maclean, Hugh. *Edmund Spenser's Poetry*. 2nd ed. New York: Norton, 1982.

MacLure, Millar. "Spenser and *The Ruines of Time*." In *A Theatre for Spenserians*, edited by Kennedy and Reither. Toronto: University of Toronto Press, 1973.

Maley, Willy. *Salvaging Spenser: Colonialism, Culture, and Identity*. New York: St Martin's Press, 1997.

– "Spenser's Languages: Writing in the Ruins of English," In *The Cambridge Companion to Spenser*, edited by Andrew Hadfield. Cambridge: Cambridge University Press, 2001.

Mallette, Richard. *Spenser, Milton, and Renaissance Pastoral.* Lewisburg, PA: Bucknell University Press, 1981.

– "Spenser's Portrait of the Artist in *The Shepheardes Calender* and *Colin Clout Comes Home Again.*" *SEL* 19, no. 1 (1979): 19–41.

Malpezzi, Frances M. "Readers, Auditors, and Interpretation." *Connotations* 7, no. 1 (1997–8): 80–6.

Manley, Lawrence. *Literature and Culture in Early Modern London.* Cambridge: Cambridge University Press, 1995.

– "Spenser and the City: The Minor Poems." *MLQ* 43 (1982): 203–30.

Markus, R.A. *Saeculum: History and Society in the Theology of St. Augustine.* Cambridge: Cambridge University Press, 1970.

Martin, Carol A.N. "Authority and the Defense of Fiction: Renaissance Poetics and Chaucer's *House of Fame.*" In *Refiguring Chaucer in the Renaissance,* edited by Theresa M. Krier. Gainesville, FL: University Press of Florida, 1998.

Martin, Catherine Gimelli. *The Ruines of Allegory: Paradise Lost and the Metamorphosis of Epic.* Durham, NC: Duke University Press, 1998.

Matthews, Gareth B., ed. *The Augustinian Tradition.* Berkeley, CA: University of California Press, 1999.

Mazzola, Elizabeth. "Legends of Oblivion: Enchantment and Enslavement in Book 6 of Spenser's *Faerie Queene.*" In *Forgetting in Early Modern English Literature and Culture: Lethe's Legacies,* edited by Christopher Ivic and Grant Williams, 122–34.

Mazzotta, Giuseppe. *The Worlds of Petrarch.* Durham, NC: Duke University Press, 1993.

McCabe, Richard A. "Annotating Anonymity, or Putting a Gloss on *The Shepheardes Calender.*" In *Ma(r)king the Text: The Presentation of Meaning on the Literary Page,* edited by Miriam Handley. Aldershot, UK: Ashgate, 2000.

– *The Pillars of Eternity: Time and Providence in* The Faerie Queene. Dublin: Irish Academic Press, 1989.

– *Spenser's Monstrous Regiment: Elizabethan Ireland and the Poetics of Difference.* Oxford: Oxford University Press, 2002.

McCanles, Michael. "*The Shepheardes Calender* as Document and Monument." *SEL* 22, no. 2 (Spring 1982): 5–19.

McCarthy, Penny. "E.K. was Only the Postman." *Notes and Queries* 47, no. 1 (March 2000): 28–31.

McDiarmid, John F., ed. *The Monarchial Republic of Early Modern England.* Aldershot, UK: Ashgate Press, 2007.

McEachern, Claire. *The Poetics of English Nationhood, 1590–1612.* Cambridge: Cambridge University Press, 1992.

McGowan, Margaret. *The Vision of Rome in Late Renaissance France*. New Haven, CT: Yale University Press, 2000.

Melehy, Hassan. "Antiquities of Britain: Spenser's *Ruines of Time*." *Studies in Philology* 102, no. 2 (Spring 2005): 159–83.

– *The Poetics of Literary Transfer in Early Modern France and England*. Burlington, VT: Ashgate, 2010.

Miller, David Lee. "Authorship, Anonymity, and *The Shepheardes Calender*." *MLQ* (September 1979): 219–36.

– *The Poem's Two Bodies: The Poetics of the 1590* Faerie Queene. Princeton, NJ: Princeton University Press, 1988.

Milton, John. *Complete Poems and Major Prose*. Edited by Merritt Y. Hughes. Indiana: Bobbs-Merrill, 1957.

Montrose, Louis Adrian. "Interpreting Spenser's February Eclogue: Some Contexts and Implications." *Spenser Studies* 2 (1981): 67–74.

– "The perfecte paterne of a poete": the Poetics of Courtship in *The Shepheardes Calender*." In *edmund Spenser*, edited by Andrew Hadfield. New York: Longman, 1996.

Moroney, Mary Claire. "Spenser's Dissolution: Monasticism and Ruins in *The Faerie Queene* and *The View of the Present State of Ireland*." *Spenser Studies* 12 (1998): 105–32.

Mourant, John A. *Saint Augustine on Memory*. Villanova, PA: Villanova University Press, 1980.

Munro, Ian. *The Figure of the Crowd in Early Modern London: The City and Its Double*. New York: Palgrave Macmillan, 2005.

Murphy, James, ed. *Renaissance Eloquence*. Berkeley: University of California Press, 1983.

Murrin, Michael. *The Allegorical Epic: Essays in its Rise and Decline*. Chicago: University of Chicago Press, 1980.

– *The Veil of Allegory*. Chicago: University of Chicago Press, 1969.

Nelson, William. *The Poetry of Edmund Spenser*. New York: Columbia University Press, 1963.

Nichols, Mary P. *Socrates on Friendship and Community: Reflections on Plato's* Symposium, Phaedrus, *and* Lysias. Cambridge: Cambridge University Press, 2009.

Nohrnberg, James. *The Analogy of* The Faerie Queene. Princeton, NJ: Princeton University Press, 1976.

Norbrook, David. *Poetry and Politics in the English Renaissance*. Oxford: Oxford University Press, 2002.

O'Connell, Michael. "History and the Poet's Golden World: The Epic Catalogues in *The Faerie Queene*." *ELR* 4 (1974): 241–67.

– *Mirror and Veil: The Historical Dimension of Spenser's* Faerie Queene. Chapel Hill: University of North Carolina Press, 1977.

Ong, Walter. *Orality and Literacy: The Technologizing of the Word*. New York: Routledge, 1982.

Ovid. *Metamorphoses*. Translated by A.D. Melville. Oxford: Oxford Worlds Classics, 1986.

Parker, Patricia A. *Inescapable Romance: Studies in the Poetics of a Mode*. Princeton, NJ: Princeton University Press, 1979.

– *Literary Fat Ladies: Rhetoric, Gender, and Property*. New York: Methuen, 1987.

Pask, Kevin. *The Emergence of the English Author: Scripting the Life of the Poet in Early Modern England*. Cambridge: Cambridge University Press, 1996.

Patrides, C.A., and Joseph Witt, eds. *The Apocalypse in English Renaissance Thought and Literature: Patterns, Antecedents, and Repercussions*. Ithaca, NY: Cornell University Press, 1984.

Patterson, Annabel. *Pastoral and Ideology: Virgil to Valéry*. Berkeley: University of California Press, 1987.

– *Reading Between the Lines*. Madison: University of Wisconsin Press, 1993.

Patterson, Annabel, ed. *Roman Images*. Baltimore: Johns Hopkins University Press, 1982.

– "Vergil's *Eclogues*: Images of Change." In *Roman Images*, edited by Annabel Patterson. Baltimore: Johns Hopkins University Press, 1982.

Patterson, Lee. *Chaucer and the Subject of History*. Madison: University of Wisconsin Press, 1991.

Pelikan, Jaroslav. *The Mystery of Continuity: Time and History, Memory and Eternity in the Thought of Saint Augustine*. Charlottesville: University Press of Virginia, 1986.

Peltonen, Markku. *Classical Humanism and Republicanism in English Political Thought*. Cambridge: Cambridge University Press, 1995.

Perry, Kathleen. *Another Reality: Metaphor and Imagination in Ovid, Petrarch, and Ronsard*. New York: P. Lang, 1990.

Petrarch, Francisco. *Petrarch's Secret, or The Soul's Conflict with Passion*. Translated by William H. Draper. Westport, CT: Hyperion Press, 1978.

– *Petrarch's Lyric Poems: The Rime Sparse and Other Lyrics*. Translated and edited by Robert M. Durling. Cambridge, MA: Harvard University Press, 1976.

Phillippy, Patricia Berrahou. *Love's Remedies: Recantation and Renaissance Lyric Poetry*. London: Associated University Presses, 1995.

Pigman, G.W., III. "Du Bellay's Ambivalence Towards Rome in the *Antiquitez*." In *Rome in the Renaissance: The City and the Myth*, edited by P.A. Ramsay. Binghamton, NY: Medieval and Renaissance Texts and Studies, 1982.

– "Versions of Imitation in the Renaissance." *Renaissance Quarterly* 33, no. 1 (1980): 1–32.

Plato. *The Collected Dialogues of Plato.* Translated and edited by Edith Hamilton and Huntington Cairns. Princeton, NJ: Princeton University Press, 1961.

Plutarch. *Essays.* Translated by Robin Waterfield. New York: Penguin, 1992.

Pocock, J.G.A. *The Machiavellian Moment: Florentine Political Thought and the Atlantic Republican Tradition.* Princeton, NJ: Princeton University Press, 1975.

Posch, Viktor. *The Art of Vergil.* Translated by Gerda Seligson. Ann Arbor: University of Michigan Press, 1962.

Praz, Mario. *Mnemosyne: The Parallel Between Literature and the Visual Arts.* Princeton, NJ: Princeton University Press, 1967.

– *Studies in Seventeenth-Century Imagery.* Rome: Edizioni di Storia E Letteratura, 1964.

Prescott, Anne Lake. "The Countess of Pembroke's *Ruines of Rome.*" In *Ashgate Critical Essays on Women Writers in England, 1550–1700, Volume 2: Mary Sidney, Countess of Pembroke,* edited by Margaret P. Hannay. New York: Ashgate Press, 2009.

– "Du Bellay in Renaissance England: Recent Work on Translation and Response." *Euvres et Critiques* 20, no. 1 (1995): 121–8.

– *French Poets and the English Renaissance: Studies in Fame and Transformation.* New Haven, CT: Yale University Press, 1978.

– "Spenser (Re)Reading du Bellay: Chronology and Literary Response." In *Spenser's Life and the Subject of Biography,* edited by Judith Anderson, Donald Cheney, and David Richardson. Amherst: University of Massachusetts Press, 1996.

– "Spenser's Shorter Poems." In *The Cambridge Companion to Spenser,* edited by Andrew Hadfield. Cambridge: Cambridge University Press, 2001.

– "Tantalus," "Pilate." In *The Spenser Encyclopedia,* edited by A.C. Hamilton. Toronto: University of Toronto Press, 1997.

Pugh, Syrithe. *Spenser and Ovid.* Aldershot, UK: Ashgate Press, 2005.

Putnam, Michael. *Virgil's Aeneid: Interpretation and Influence.* Chapel Hill, NC: University of North Carolina Press, 1995.

Quainton, Malcolm. "Morte Peinture and Vivante Peinture in *Les Antiquitez de Rome* and *Les Regrets.*" *Renaissance Studies* 3, no. 2 (1989): 167–77.

Quilligan, Maureen. *The Language of Allegory: Defining the Genre.* Ithaca, NY: Cornell University Press, 1979.

– *Milton's Spenser: The Politics of Reading.* Ithaca, NY: Cornell University Press, 1983.

Quint, David. *Epic and Empire: Politics and Generic Form from Virgil to Milton.* Princeton, NJ: Princeton University Press, 1993.

– *Origin and Originality in Renaissance Literature: Versions of the Source*. New Haven, CT: Yale University Press, 1983.

Quintillian. *Institutio oratoriae*. Translated by H. E. Butler. Cambridge, MA: Loeb Classical Library, 1922.

Quitslund, Jon A. "Questionable Evidence in the *Letters* of 1580 between Gabriel Harvey and Edmund Spenser." In *Spenser's Life and the Subject of Biography*, edited by Judith Anderson, Donald Cheney, and David Richardson. Amherst: University of Massachusetts Press, 1996.

– *Spenser's Supreme Fiction: Platonic Natural Philosophy and* The Faerie Queene. Toronto: University of Toronto Press, 2001.

Rambuss, Richard. "Ireland: Policy, Poetics, and Parody." In *The Cambridge Companion to Spenser*, edited by Andrew Hadfield. Cambridge: Cambridge University Press, 2001.

– *Spenser's Secret Career*. Cambridge: Cambridge University Press, 1993.

Ramsay, P.A., ed. *Rome in the Renaissance: The City and the Myth*. Binghamton, NY: Medieval and Renaissance Texts and Studies, 1982.

Rasmussen, Carl J. " 'How Weak Be the Passions of Woefulness': Spenser's *Ruines of Time*." *Spenser Studies* 2 (1981) 159–81.

– "Quietnesse of Minde: *A Theatre for Worldlings* as a Protestant Poetics." *Spenser Studies* 1 (1980): 3–27.

Read, David. *Temperate Conquests: Spenser and the Spanish New World*. Detroit: Wayne State University Press, 2000.

Rebhorn, Wayne. *Courtly Performances: Masking and Festivity in Castiglione's Book of the Courtier*. Detroit: Wayne State University Press, 1978.

– "Du Bellay's Imperial Mistress: *Les Antiquitez de Rome* as Petrarchist Sonnet Sequence." *Renaissance Quarterly* 33, no. 4 (Winter 1980): 609–22.

– *The Emperor of Men's Minds: Literature and Renaissance Discourses of Rhetoric*. Ithaca, NY: Cornell University Press, 1995.

– *Renaissance Debates on Rhetoric*. Ithaca, NY: Cornell University Press, 2000.

Rensselaer, W. Lee. *Ut Pictura Poesis: The Humanistic Theory of Painting*. New York: W.W. Norton, 1967.

Richards, Jennifer. *Rhetoric and Courtliness in Early Modern Literature*. Cambridge: Cambridge University Press, 2003.

Robinson, Forrest G. *The Shape of Things Known: Sidney's Apology in its Philosophical Tradition*. Cambridge, MA: Harvard University Press, 1972.

Roche, Thomas P., Jr. *The Kindly Flame: A Study of the Third and Fourth Books of Spenser's Faerie Queene*. Princeton, NJ: Princeton University Press, 1964.

– *Petrarch and the English Sonnet Sequence*. New York: AMS Press, 1989.

Rossi, Paolo. *Logic and the Art of Memory: The Quest for a Universal Language*. Translated and introduced by Stephen Clucas. Chicago: University of Chicago Press, 2000.

Rowland, Beryl. "The Art of Memory and the Art of Poetry in the *House of Fame.*" *University of Ottawa Quarterly* 51 (1981): 162–71.

Said, Edward W. *Culture and Imperialism.* New York: Vintage, 1994.

Satterthwaite, Alfred W. *Spenser, Ronsard, and Du Bellay: a Renaissance Comparison.* Princeton, NJ: Princeton University Press, 1960.

Schwyzer, Philip. *Archaeologies of English Renaissance Literature.* Oxford: Oxford University Press, 2007.

Shore, David R. *Spenser and the Poetics of Pastoral: A Study of the World of Colin Clout.* Montreal: McGill-Queen's University Press, 1985.

Sidney, Philip. *An Apology for Poetry.* Edited by Forrest G. Robinson. New York: Macmillan, 1970.

Silberman, Lauren. *Transforming Desire: Erotic Knowledge in Books III and IV of* The Faerie Queene. Berkeley: University of California Press, 1995.

Small, Jocelyn Penny. *Wax Tablets of the Mind: Cognitive Studies of Memory and Literacy in Classical Antiquity.* London: Routledge, 1997.

Smith, Bruce R. "On Reading *The Shepheardes Calender.*" *Spenser Studies* 1 (1980): 69–93.

Spenser, Edmund. *Complaints.* Edited by W.L. Renwick. London: The Scholaris Press, 1928.

– *The Faerie Queene.* Edited by A.C. Hamilton. New York: Longman, 1977.

– *The Yale Edition of the Shorter Poems of Edmund Spenser.* Edited by William A. Oram et al. New Haven, CT: Yale University Press, 1989.

– *A View of the State of Ireland.* Edited by Andrew Hadfield and Willy Maley. Malden, MA: Blackwell Publishers, 1997.

– *Works of Edmund Spenser.* Edited by E. Greenlaw et al. Baltimore: Johns Hopkins Press, 1949.

Stapleton, M.L. "Spenser, the *Antiquitez de Rome,* and the Development of the English Sonnet Form." *Comparative Literature Studies* 27, no. 4 (1990): 259–74.

– *Spenser's Ovidian Poetics.* Newark: University of Delaware Press, 2009.

Stein, Harold. *Studies in Spenser's* Complaints. New York: Oxford University Press, 1934.

Stephens, Walter. *Giants in Those Days: Folklore, Ancient History, and Nationalism.* Lincoln: University of Nebraska Press, 1989.

Stern, Virginia F. *Gabriel Harvey: His Life, Marginalia and Library.* Oxford: Clarendon Press, 1979.

Stewart, Alan, and Garrett A. Sullivan. "'Worme-eaten, and full of canker holes': Materializing Memory in *The Faerie Queene* and *Lingua.*" *Spenser Studies* 17 (2003): 215–38.

Stock, Brian. *After Augustine: The Meditative Reader and the Text*. Philadelphia: University of Pennsylvania Press, 2001.

Strong, Roy. *The Cult of Elizabeth: Elizabethan Portraiture and Pageantry*. London: Thames and Hudson, 1977.

Stump, Eleonore, and Norman Kretzmann, eds. *The Cambridge Companion to Augustine*. Cambridge: Cambridge University Press, 2001.

Sullivan, Garrett A., Jr. *Memory and Forgetting in English Renaissance Drama: Shakespeare, Marlowe, Webster*. Cambridge: Cambridge University Press, 2005.

Summers, David. *Spenser's Arthur: The British Tradition and The Faerie Queene*. New York: University Press of America, 1997.

Summit, Jennifer. *Memory's Library: Medieval Books in Early Modern England*. Chicago: University of Chicago Press, 2008.

– "Monuments and Ruins: Spenser and the Problem of the English Library." *ELH* 70, no. 1 (2003): 1–34.

– "Reading Reformed: Spenser and the Problem of the English Library." In *Forgetting in Early Modern English Literature and Culture: Lethe's Legacy*, edited by Christopher Ivic and Grant Williams. London: Routledge, 2004: 165–78.

Syed, Yasmin. *Vergil's Aeneid and the Roman Self*. Ann Arbor: University of Michigan Press, 2005.

Tanner, Marie. *The Last Descendant of Aeneas: The Hapsburgs and the Mythic Image of the Emperor*. New Haven, CT: Yale University Press, 1993.

Tatlock, J.S.P. *The Legendary History of Britain*. Berkeley: University of California Press, 1950.

Tayler, Edward W. *Nature and Art in Renaissance Literature*. New York: Columbia University Press, 1964.

Taylor, Karla. *Chaucer Reads "The Divine Comedy."* Stanford, CA: Stanford University Press, 1989.

Teskey, Gordon. *Allegory and Violence*. Ithaca, NY: Cornell University Press, 1996.

Thomas, Richard, *Reading Virgil and His Texts*. Ann Arbor: University of Michigan, 1999.

Thucydides. *The History of the Peloponnesian War*. Translated Rex Warner. Baltimore, MD: Penguin, 1954, 1968.

Tonkin, Humphrey. *Spenser's Courteous Pastoral: Book Six of* The Faerie Queene. Oxford: Clarendon Press, 1972.

Treip, M. A. *Allegorical Poetics and the Epic: The Renaissance Tradition to Paradise Lost*. Lexington: University Press of Kentucky, 1994.

Trimpi, Wesley. "Horace's *Ut Pictura Poesis*: The Argument for Stylistic Decorum." *The Journal of Warburg and Courtauld Institutes* 36 (1973): 29–73.

Tucker, George Hugo. *The Poet's Odyssey: Joachim Du Bellay and the Antiquitez de Rome*. Oxford: Clarendon Press, 1990.

Tuve, Rosemond. *Allegorical Imagery: Some Mediaeval Books and Their Posterity*. Princeton, NJ: Princeton University Press, 1966.

Van der Noot, Jan. *A Theatre for Voluptuous Worldlings*, 1569. New York: Scholars' Facsimilies and Reprints, 1936.

Van Es, Bart. *Spenser's Forms of History*. Oxford: Oxford University Press, 2002.

Vasaly, Ann. *Representations: Images of the World in Ciceronian Oratory*. Berkeley, University of California Press, 1993.

Virgil. *The Aeneid*. Translated by H. Rushton Fairclough. Cambridge, MA: Loeb Classical Library, 1967.

– *The Aeneid*. Translated by Robert Fitzgerald. New York: Vintage, 1990.

– *Eclogues*. Translated by H. Rushton Fairclough. Cambridge, MA: Loeb Classical Library, 1967.

– *Georgics*. Translated by L.P. Wilkinson. New York: Penguin, 1982.

Wanamaker, Melissa C. *Discordia Concors: The Wit of Metaphysical Poetry*. New York: National University Publications, 1975.

Warnek, Peter. *Descent of Socrates: Self-Knowledge and Cryptic Nature in the Platonic Dialogues*. Bloomington: Indiana University Press, 2005.

Waswo, Richard. *The Founding Legend of Western Civilization: From Virgil to Vietnam*. Hanover, CT: Wesleyan University Press, 1997.

Watkins, John. *The Specter of Dido: Spenser and Virgilian Epic*. New Haven, CT: Yale University Press, 1995.

Weinrich, Harald. *Lethe: The Art and Critique of Forgetting*. Translated by Steven Rendall. Ithaca, NY: Cornell University Press, 2004.

Whipp, Leslie. "Weep for Dido: Spenser's November Eclogue." *Spenser Studies* 11 (1990): 17–31.

Williams, Grant. "Phantastes's Flies: The Trauma of Amnesic Enjoyment in Spenser's Memory Palace." *Spenser Studies* 18 (2003): 231–52.

Williams, Kathleen. *Spenser's World of Glass: A Reading of* The Faerie Queene. Berkeley: University of California Press, 1966.

Wilson-Okamura, David Scott. *Virgil in the Renaissance*. Cambridge: Cambridge University Press, 2010.

Wofford, Susanne. "The Enfolding Dragon: Arthur and the Moral Economy of *The Faerie Queene*." In *Edmund Spenser: Essays on Culture and Allegory*, edited by Jennifer Klein Morrison and Matthew Greenfield. Aldershot, UK: Ashgate, 2000.

– "Spenser's Giants." In *Critical Essays on Edmund Spenser*, edited by Mihoko Suzuki. New York: Macmillan, 1996.

Yates, Frances A. *The Art of Memory*. Chicago: University of Chicago Press, 1966.

– *Astraea: The Imperial Theme in the Sixteenth Century*. London: Routledge & Kegan Paul, 1975.

– *Giordano Bruno and the Hermetic Tradition*. Chicago: University of Chicago Press, 1964.

– *Theatre of the World*. London: Routledge & Kegan Paul, 1969.

Index